The Mac OS 8 Book

The Ultimate Macintosh User's Guide

VENTANA

The Mac OS 8 Book

The Ultimate Macintosh User's Guide

Craig Danuloff
Mark R. Bell

The Mac OS 8 Book

Library of Congress Cataloging-in-Publication Data

Danuloff, Craig, 1963-
The Mac OS 8 Book/ Craig Danuloff.
p. cm.
Includes index.
ISBN 1-56604-688-2
1. Mac OS 2. Operating systems (Computers) 3.Macintosh (Computer) I. Bell, Mark R. II. Title
QA76.76.063D347 1997
005.4'469—DC21 97-20919
CIP

Fourth Edition 9 8 7 6 5

Printed in the United States of America

Ventana Communications Group
P.O. Box 13964
Research Triangle Park, NC 27709-3964
919.544.9404
FAX 919.544.9472
http://www.vmedia.com

Ventana Communications Group is a division of International Thomson Publishing.

President
Michael E. Moran

Vice President of Content Development
Karen A. Bluestein

Director of Acquisitions and Development
Robert Kern

Editorial Operations Manager
Kerry L. B. Foster

Production Manager
John Cotterman

Art Director
Marcia Webb

Brand Manager
Jamie Jaeger Fiocco

Creative Services Manager
Diane Lennox

Acquisitions Editor
JJ Hohn

Project Editor
Paul Cory

Development Editor
Martin V. Minner

Copy Editor
Judy Flynn

CD-ROM Specialist
Ginny Phelps

Technical Reviewer
Rob Terrell

Desktop Publisher
Scott Hosa

Proofreader
Tom Collins

Indexer
Lynn Brown

Cover Illustrator
Lisa Gill

About the Authors

Craig Danuloff is a writer, consultant, and lecturer on computer topics. The author of *Up & Running With PageMaker on the Macintosh*, he is co-author of *Encyclopedia Macintosh*, *The PageMaker Companion*, and *Desktop Publishing Type & Graphics*.

Mark R. Bell is the Webmaster and Macintosh Specialist for the Duke University Office of Information Technology. A prolific author, he coauthored Ventana's *The Mac Web Server Book* as well as many books and software manuals for Netscape Press, Ventana Press, Maxum Development Corporation, Bare Bones Software, and others. Mark holds degrees in English, history, political science, and theology, and is married to Virginia D. Smith, a writer and editor. They live in Chapel Hill, North Carolina with their faithful canine quadruped, Bailey and a small network of Macs.

Acknowledgments

I would like to thank Gregg and Mary Catherine for putting up with my absence (again!) while I completed another project; Craig & Angelika, for their hard work raising a family like normal people should; Debbie Suggs, for contributing Chapters 11 and 16; Alan Benson, for contributing Chapters 18 and 20; Bailey for keeping me company and alerting me when the FedEx truck pulled up with more page proofs; and my wife Virginia, who continues to remind me when it's time to beam to the planet surface and commune with my people.

Finally, I would like to thank the following people who helped make this book a reality: development editor Martin V. Minner, for guiding the revision of this book; copy editor Judy Flynn, for ensuring it is grammatically correct; proofreader Tom Collins, for catching all those little errors that made it past everyone else (including me); desktop publisher Scott Hosa, for laying it all out and making it look great; acquisitions editor JJ Hohn, for signing me up for this project; traffic coordinator Becky Steele, for chaperoning me through the FTP site changeover; CD-ROM specialist Ginny Phelps, for assembling the Companion CD-ROM; project editor Paul Cory, for keeping it all on track; and all the other Ventana folks whose hard work makes a complicated process seem simple.

—MRB

Contents

PART II
Applications

PART III
Networking

Introduction

Once upon a time, there was a computer that was incredibly easy to use: Macintosh. It was full of youthful innocence, simple elegance, and a kind of conservation of motion that made it impossible to describe any of its operations as complex.

Today, the operating system that started out on the Apple Macintosh is grown up; it's even used on other manufacturers' computers. It has traded innocence for experience, simplicity for sophistication, and singularity for an incredible flexibility. Mac OS 8 provides powerful new features, an improved user interface, extensive additional hardware and network support, and an expanded array of core technologies for software applications. Overall, it improves the way computers can be used, but it does so within the same intuitive framework of previous system software versions.

In *The Mac OS 8 Book*, you'll explore every aspect of Mac OS 8, learning how you can use each feature to be more efficient and productive.

What's in the Mac OS

Any great product improvement keeps the existing product's solid familiar features, adds exciting new breakthrough features, and throws in subtle enhancements for good measure. Mac OS 8 is no exception. Booting up with Mac OS 8 will give even the most sophisticated Mac user a renewed sense of power and possibility as well as that satisfying "out-of-box" experience.

Mac OS 8 features fall into three broad categories:

- **Enhanced ease-of-use features.** The basic characteristics that make the Mac so friendly, such as point-and-click operation of mouse and icons, have been extended so that even more complex tasks—like exchanging data, moving fonts, and changing Control Panels—are now more intuitive. The result is a Macintosh environment that is more intuitive and easier to use and customize.
- **Support for recent hardware advances.** Almost every aspect of Macintosh hardware and peripherals has evolved and improved by several orders of magnitude since the January 1984 introduction of the 128K Macintosh; but until now, the system software has never received the overhaul it needed to exploit this equipment fully. Mac OS 8 has been rewritten to take advantage of the new generation of Macintosh and Macintosh-clone computers based on PowerPC microprocessors, making it the fastest Mac OS ever.
- **Interapplication communication.** The Macintosh has always allowed data to be shared between separate applications with the Clipboard or the Scrapbook. In Mac OS 8, the interaction between applications moved forward light years, not only improving data sharing between programs, but also making it possible for applications to communicate with and control one another.

It would take a whole book to describe everything new in the Mac OS and newer still in Mac OS 8 (hey, there's an idea); but just to whet your appetite, here's a brief listing of specific ways the Mac OS has improved since the earliest versions of the operating system:

- Allowed file sharing between AppleTalk-connected Macs.
- Displayed hierarchical outline-format views of nested files and folders.
- Replaced the Control Panel.
- Eliminated the Font/DA Mover.
- Enhanced MultiFinder and Background Printing functions.
- Expanded application launching options.
- Expanded file-finding capabilities.
- Improved font display and typographic support with TrueType.
- Introduced the ability to store files in more than one place.
- Introduced live Copy-and-Paste of data between applications.
- Provided additional file information in Finder windows.
- Added QuickTime video support.

- Supported faster virtual memory for increased RAM availability.
- Provided support for PowerPC and 68K computers.
- Added Macintosh Drag and Drop to move information, start processes, or place clippings on your Desktop.
- Added hierarchical submenus: automated tasks, recent files, applications and server connections, and so on to the Apple menu.
- Included an underlying macro language, AppleScript; a scriptable Finder; and a set of automation macros.
- Installed a context-sensitive active online help system called Apple Guide.
- Improved the print architecture, making it more powerful, easier, and extensible; eliminates the Print Monitor.
- Supported advanced typographical features and a portable document format with QuickDraw and QuickDraw GX.
- Lets you create Stickie notes, the electronic equivalent of the Post-it note.
- Provided both cross-platform and interapplication file translation.
- Improved overall speed while maintaining compatibility over the wide range of Macintosh models.
- Added additional networking capability through OpenTransport, making connections to the Internet easier.

What's New in Mac OS 8?

Mac OS 8 adds several new capabilities to system software. Some of them were part of separate AppleSoft products, some appeared in third-party utilities, and others are new to Mac OS 8.

Mac OS 8 continues in the Macintosh tradition, providing intuitive features while preserving the "look and feel" of the Macintosh Desktop. Despite the range and depth of these improvements, though, a deliberate effort has been made to retain the Macintosh spirit in commands and design elements. You may not even notice the improvements when you first use Mac OS 8—everything seems like the Macintosh environment you're used to. But closer inspection will show you signs of change almost everywhere. Some of the more notable improvements are:

- A multithreaded, multitasking, PowerPC-native Finder, which is not only significantly faster, but also allows you to perform other tasks while copying files in the background.

- A new "platinum" look and feel that makes the Mac OS easier, not to mention a lot more pleasant, to use.
- Tabbed folders, which give you the ability to drag a folder to the bottom of the screen and hide all but a portion (a "tab") of the folder.
- Spring-loaded folders, which allow you to move or copy items several folders deeper with a single mouse operation.
- The ability to view folder and Desktop contents by small or large icons as well as with single-click buttons.
- An all-new Desktop Pictures option that allows you to use pictures or patterns to decorate your Desktop.
- Better Internet support through faster networking software (Open Transport), built-in modem support (Open Transport/PPP), configuration assistance, and all the applications and utilities you'll need to use just about every aspect of the Internet.
- OpenDoc and Java, which allow you to run new types of programs on your computer.
- A personal Web server built right into the Mac OS to share files and information with anyone on the Internet or your own intranet.
- Viewing files by modification "dates" that are relative, such as Yesterday and Today, as well as by actual dates.
- Contextual help windows, which means you can get help for a particular task or program using Apple Guide more easily than ever before.

Who Should Read This Book?

The Mac OS 8 Book was written for the experienced Macintosh user who is upgrading to Mac OS 8 from previous versions of the Mac OS and for the new Mac OS user who is learning the Mac and Mac OS 8 simultaneously. The information provided in this book will suit users of every 040 or PowerPC model and applies equally to the casual and the habitual user. *The Mac OS 8 Book* addresses the features, capabilities, and requirements that the release of a new generation of PowerPCs and PowerBooks has imposed on the system software. In summary, if you use a Mac, this book is for you.

Experienced Mac OS 8 Users

If you have experience with System 7 or 7.1, this book will help you in the following ways:

- **Describe each new feature in Mac OS 8.** You won't have to play the trial-and-error guessing game in order to understand the system software upgrade fully.
- **Provide specific tips on using Mac OS 8.** I'll go beyond the basics to look at ways you can take advantage of the new Mac OS 8 abilities to improve your productivity and enhance your computing power.
- **Explain ways that Mac OS 8 will alter the way you use the Mac.** There are a number of areas where Mac OS 8's new abilities will alter the way you manage your files and access your applications. To help you make the most of these changes, I'll give you real-world situations that show the results of these features in your work.
- **Clarify how PowerBooks are accommodated in system software.** Mac OS 8 provides features that make PowerBooks both easier to use and more powerful. For PowerBook users, Mac OS 8 helps you improve battery lifetimes between recharges, remotely access other computers, and do file management.

New Mac OS Users

If you're new to the Mac OS, pay special attention to Chapter 1, "System Software Basics." Much of the information in this chapter describes general Macintosh operations, setting the stage for Mac OS 8 features covered in later chapters. You could also consult other resources that focus more on introductory topics, including the reference manuals that came with your Macintosh and *The Little Mac Book*, 4th Edition, by Robin Williams (published by Peachpit Press). For more information, see "Other Sources of Mac OS 8 Information," later in the Introduction.

System 7 Users Who Are Considering Upgrading

If you're a Macintosh user who has not yet upgraded to Mac OS 8, this book will help you in the following ways:

- **Explain all the new Mac OS 8 features.** I'll discuss what's new in a way you can understand, even without hands-on experience with previous versions of Mac OS 8.
- **Give you a clear picture of Mac OS 8's benefits and a few of its drawbacks.** You'll be able to make an informed decision about whether to upgrade now.

- **Clarify Mac OS 8's hardware requirements.** A few Mac OS 8 features are supported only by specific Macintosh hardware configurations. I'll identify those that may require you to upgrade your hardware.
- **Wait patiently on your bookshelf for the day you do upgrade.** At that time, *The Mac OS 8 Book* will provide all the details you need in order to set up and operate your Mac quickly using Mac OS 8.

Apple's System Software Strategy

Apple plans to introduce a dramatically new version of the operating system in the 1997/1998 time frame; it will combine the ease of use of the Mac OS with the industrial strength of OpenStep, a UNIX-style operating system created by none other than Steve Jobs, co-founder of Apple. The current plan is to support and improve the traditional Mac OS at least through the year 2000 but to make many of your favorite applications available on this new operating system as well. The following will be among its most important technologies, but don't be too concerned if you don't know what these terms mean. Computer scientists tend to have a private language the rest of us aren't meant to understand!

- Microkernel architecture
- Multiprocessor support
- Preemptive multitasking
- Full memory protection
- Improved and extended I/O architecture with new bus technologies
- Improved networking
- Advanced graphics
- A new Graphical User Interface (GUI), the reworking of the Macintosh Desktop.

A Word About Versions & Hardware Requirements

Since its initial release, the Mac OS has been enhanced, extended, and updated several times and has been able to run on most hardware platforms. However, Mac OS 8 is limited in terms of hardware requirements. It will run only on the following systems:

- All PowerPC-based Mac and Mac OS clones
- Any 68K Mac with a 68040 processor, with or without an FPU.

This may seem harsh to some, but the benefits of Mac OS 8's internal architecture require that it run on these systems. Anything older, and it just wouldn't work properly. If you have an older Mac, it will most likely accept Mac OS 7.6.x.

What's Inside?

The Mac OS 8 Book is made up of 20 chapters and 2 appendixes.

Chapter 1: System Software Basics

In order to provide a context for discussing Mac OS 8's enhancements and additions, Chapter 1 summarizes basic concepts about the system software and the way it functions on the Macintosh. This information can be used as a review for those who need it and an introduction for first-time Mac users.

Chapter 2: The System Folder

The System Folder (where the operating system is stored) remains a unique and important part of your Macintosh in Mac OS 8, but many changes have been made to the way you use the System Folder and its files. You'll learn about the new System Folder organization and many of the files and folders found there.

Chapter 3: The Finder & Desktop

The Finder gives you tools for organizing and manipulating your disks and files. Mac OS 8's Finder greatly expands these capabilities with new menu commands, more ways to view and manipulate files in Finder windows, additional onscreen help and Apple Guide, improved Get Info dialog boxes, and more. Several improvements since 7.5 are introduced here, including tabbed folders and spring-loaded folders.

Chapter 4: Customizing Your Mac

Mac OS 8 provides all the traditional ways of customizing your Mac that experienced users have come to expect plus several new ways, including Desktop Pictures. You'll learn how to use both the old and new ways to customize your computer, why it's useful to customize your Mac, and how to best use your Mac.

Chapter 5: Managing Your Hard Drive

Several Mac OS 8 features can help you organize your hard drive more efficiently to access your stored data with more speed and convenience. These features include aliases, a Find command (enhanced in Mac OS 8), a new Label menu, and improved support for comments. This chapter shows you how all these features help you control your hard drive and other storage media.

Chapter 6: PowerBook System Software

Chapter 6 looks at the special requirements of portable computing and at PowerBook computers in particular. Mac OS 8 includes a number of convenient utilities like the Control Strip, file synchronization, remote access, and network and Desktop mounting.

Chapter 7: Mac OS 8 & Your Software

The introduction of Mac OS 8 had a direct impact on every software application you use on your Macintosh; this chapter shows you how and why. First, the important issue of Mac OS 8 compatibility and the requirements for the new Mac OS 8-savvy status are discussed. Then we'll look at some new features Mac OS 8 provides to all applications, including the Desktop level, the new status of desk accessories, and ways to launch applications using Stationery Pads.

Chapter 8: Working With Other Types of Computers

One of the things the Mac OS has always done best is work with other types of computers. The earliest Macs were networkable and could talk to many different types of computers, and Mac OS 8 continues this tradition with several options. It has several built-in capabilities that make communicating with PCs an easy task, but if you need more compatibility, there are several third-party software options to let you run just about any operating system on your Mac, including Windows 95 and NT.

Chapter 9: Applications & Memory Management

Additional system software features, together with today's more sophisticated Macintosh hardware and software, put more demands than ever on your Macintosh's memory. This chapter documents two Mac OS 8 features that expand the amount of memory you can make available to your Mac. The chapter also focuses on overall concepts of memory management that relate to Mac OS 8's built-in multitasking and virtual memory.

Chapter 10: Working With Multiple Applications

Mac OS 8 allows you to open and use as many different programs as your Macintosh's available memory can accommodate. This chapter introduces the concepts and capabilities of multitasking and provides examples of how multitasking helps you work more efficiently. Included are discussions of the Hiding commands and the memory implications of using multiple applications. You can now "hide the Finder" so that you no longer lose your place in an application when you click on the Desktop.

Chapter 11: Fonts & Printing

Mac OS 8 uses a powerful graphics engine called QuickDraw. With QuickDraw and QuickDraw GX comes improved and extensible printing capabilities, a new font technology, color matching through ColorSync, and portable documents. Through the Layout Manager, a number of exciting new text effects are possible. QuickDraw GX supports WorldScript and language localization. One area in which Mac OS 8 presents dramatic changes from past system software is font management. This chapter examines all aspects of font management and reviews bitmapped fonts, PostScript fonts, TrueType, and the new QuickDraw GX font technology.

Chapter 12: Interapplication Communication & OpenDoc

Inter-Application Communication (IAC) and OpenDoc are two brand-new Mac OS 8 features that make a significant contribution to sharing data between applications. Inter-Application Communication provides a framework that software developers will use to facilitate automatic data sharing and communication between programs. This chapter also looks at OpenDoc, Apple's compound document technology, and describes OpenDoc's implementation and the effect it will have on your computing style.

Chapter 13: AppleScript

You can save time and reduce errors that occur due to manual entry by capturing common tasks as an automated program. Chapter 13 describes AppleScript, Mac OS 8's macro language, which provides a rich high-level language connection between the Finder and other applications. You will learn how to write and run scripts and how to apply them to common problems.

Chapter 14: Java

Java is now a standard addition to the Mac OS and is proving to be the language that all computers will eventually support. This chapter looks at where it is now and where it will go in the future, and how applications written in Java can be used (and useful) on the Mac OS.

Chapter 15: Multimedia Applications

This chapter looks at the elements of the Mac OS that make it a multimedia giant, including QuickTime and QuickTime VR, QuickDraw 3D, and its impressive speech capabilities. The Mac OS remains the operating system of choice for multimedia programmers, game developers, and makers of CD-ROM applications.

Chapter 16: File Sharing

When you're running Mac OS 8, you can share any folder or volume from your hard drive with any other computer on your Macintosh network. This chapter looks at the many advantages of the File Sharing feature, including granting others access to your shared files, controlling access privileges to those files and folders, and monitoring the use of your shared data by other network users.

Chapter 17: Working on a Network

This chapter looks at the other side of the File Sharing coin—ways you can access data from other Macintoshes on your network. Included is information on using AppleShare file servers and logging on to your own Mac hard drive from another network computer. The IAC feature of Program Linking is also reviewed.

Chapter 18: Internet Connectivity

Mac OS 8 provides an unmatched level of Internet connectivity "right out of the box." You'll learn how to use several Internet software packages to connect to the Internet: Open Transport to connect from a local area network (LAN) and Open Transport/PPP to connect with a modem.

Chapter 19: Personal Web Server

One of the greatest additions to Mac OS 8 is Apple's personal Web server. This chapter will tell you everything you need to know to initialize and configure the Web server so you can share the contents of your Mac with anyone on the Internet or intranet. You'll learn how to use Apple Personal NetFinder instead of traditional HTML to make your Web server look and feel more like the Mac OS, and you'll learn how to use your Mac's File Sharing features to provide password protection to secure areas on your Web server.

Chapter 20: Internet Applications & Utilities

Not only does Mac OS 8 come as ready as ever to get you connected to the Internet, but once you're connected, it also provides you with all the applications and utilities you'll need to be an Internaut. This chapter covers Netscape Navigator 3.0.1 for browsing the Web, Claris Emailer for sending and receiving Internet mail, and several utilities to help you compress and decompress files for quicker file transfers.

Appendix A: About the Companion CD-ROM

The Mac OS 8 Book's Companion CD-ROM comes filled with valuable software. This appendix lists the contents of the CD-ROM and includes brief descriptions of each item.

Appendix B: Installing or Updating Mac OS 8

Unless you were fortunate enough to have Apple or your computer dealer install Mac OS 8 on your hard drive, the first thing you must do to get up and running is use the Mac OS 8 installer. Appendix B explains how to use Apple's new installer and helps you understand the options and intricacies of the Mac OS 8 installer. Also included is information on using the installer on an AppleTalk network to install Mac OS 8 from a remote Macintosh.

Online Sources of Mac OS 8 Information

If you have a modem, you potentially have access to vast amounts of information about the Mac OS in all its versions, Macintosh and Power Macintosh computers, and Mac clones. Here is a quick guide to what's available:

- **Online Services**—America Online and CompuServe have excellent Macintosh-related areas. They provide you and your Mac direct access to thousands of other Mac users and to many software and hardware developers.
- **The Internet**—Usenet newsgroups devoted to the Mac are another place to get information about Mac OS 8—try starting with comp.sys.mac.system. You can also find information and Apple software updates at ftp.info.apple.com.
- **The Web**—Naturally, there are many, many Web sites about all aspects of the Mac and the Mac OS. Some of the best are: MacInTouch (http://www.macintouch.com:80/), MacSurfer's Headline News (http://www.macsurfer.com/news/), MacFixIt (http://macfixit.com:80/), and The Macintosh Resource Page (http://www.macresource.com:80/). You can also visit Ventana's Web site (http://www.vmedia.com) to get information on Ventana's other Macintosh titles.

Spending a little time online is often the best way to get a Macintosh-related question answered; you can also browse through detailed information on almost any Macintosh topic and even download useful software utilities or upgrades.

User Groups

It's a great idea to visit your local Macintosh user group. User groups provide local support on virtually every Macintosh topic, from the trivial to the vital, and act as information channels for Apple and Mac OS software manufacturers. The introduction of Mac OS 8 will undoubtedly be the topic of many user-group meetings. You can find a group near you by calling Apple Computer at 800-538-9696, extension 500.

Moving On

Now that you have a better idea about what this book covers, let's move on to Chapter 1, "System Software Basics," where we'll look at how the operating system we know as the Mac OS works and what it can do for you.

PART I

The Operating System

CHAPTER 1

Operating System Basics

Why is the Macintosh so popular? Is it the graphic user interface? Maybe it's that all Macintosh applications use similar menus and commands. Or is it because configuring hardware and peripherals on the Mac is so easy?

The answer, as everyone knows, is all of the above. But while you probably know how easy a Macintosh is to use—it's friendly, consistent, and expandable—you may not know *why*. The reason is because the operating system (OS) that controls the computer also gives it all of these qualities.

The release of Mac OS 8 gives the OS new prominence; the topic was rarely discussed in the past. And though this emphasis is largely due to Apple's marketing agenda, anyone who uses a Macintosh ought to understand the role of the OS and its capabilities, including how to use it most effectively.

This chapter introduces and defines the functions of the Macintosh OS. It also offers a quick tour of Macintosh basics and some of the more common commands and features the OS provides.

This tour is designed for those who are using a Macintosh for the first time and those who'd like a little review before diving into the details of Mac OS 8's features. If you're comfortable using your Macintosh, you can probably skip the "Basic Macintosh Operations" section of this chapter and skim "What Does the Operating System Do?" and "Using the Operating System" before moving on to Chapter 2, "The System Folder."

What Does the Operating System Do?

What makes the Macintosh smile when you turn it on? Why does the disk icon appear on the Desktop when you insert a floppy disk? How are fonts shared among all your applications? The answer to each of these questions is the same: the operating system does it.

The operating system (abbreviated OS, which computer geeks pronounce to rhyme with *boss*) has three main responsibilities: it controls the hardware built into your Macintosh or Macintosh clone (and any peripherals you have connected), it provides common elements and features to all your software applications, and it lets you manage your disks, files, and directories. Let's briefly look at each of these areas:

- **Hardware control.** In order for your Mac to work, its RAM, disk drives, video monitor, keyboard, mouse, printer, and scanner (or other peripherals) must be collectively managed. Saving files to disk, drawing images on the screen, and printing are examples of hardware control managed by the OS.
- **Common software elements.** Every Macintosh software application has common elements, such as menus, dialog boxes, and support for fonts. These common elements are delivered to software applications from a "software toolbox" in the OS. Apple assures consistency among applications and spares software developers the difficult task of programming these elements by centrally providing them and including conventions for their use as part of the operating system.
- **Disk and file management.** The Finder, which is a part of the OS, provides the ability to format disks, lets you find, copy, move, rename, and delete files, and displays icon and text-based information about disks and files. The Finder also allows you to launch other applications and acts as a "home base" when you start up or after you quit other programs.

Even with the new generation of Reduced Instruction Set Computing (RISC) microprocessors in the Power Macintosh computers, the Mac OS can run the library of software written previously for Complex Instruction Set Computing (CISC) microprocessors, albeit more slowly than software specially written for the Power Macintosh. (CISC-based Macs are also called 68K Macs after the 680x0 series of Motorola microprocessors.) Much of Mac OS 8 is now PowerPC native, including the Finder, and is therefore much faster than previous versions of the operating system.

Without the OS, each application would have to provide its own self-contained operating features for running the hardware and managing your disks and files. There would be no continuity from one application to the next, and software programs would be far more complex, as well as time-consuming and costly to develop.

Fortunately, Mac OS 8 performs all these tasks well, allowing developers to focus on unique and sophisticated programs while leaving the rest to Apple. Figure 1-1 illustrates the central role of the OS.

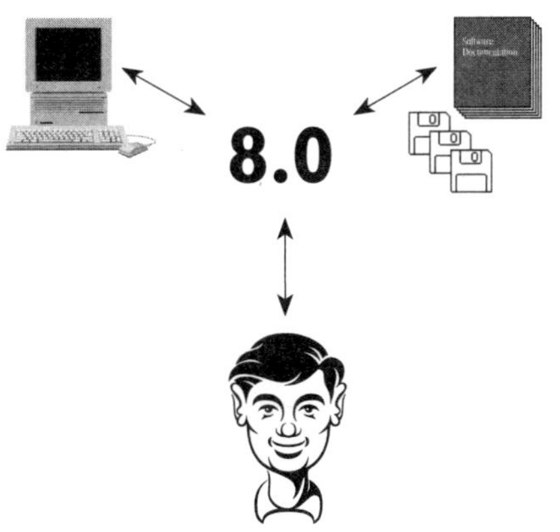

Figure 1-1: The OS provides the link between you, your Macintosh, and your software.

Parts of the Operating System

The most prominent files that make up Mac OS 8 are the System file and the Finder, but printer and network drivers, Control Panel devices, Extensions, and resources (fonts, desk accessories, sounds, function keys) are also part of the OS. All operating system files are found in the System folder, which is described more fully in Chapter 2. The following list summarizes the functions of these components:

- **System file.** The System file is involved in the most important and most frequently used aspects of the OS. It also acts as a framework to which other parts of the OS can connect. The System file helps the Mac start up and provides many of the dialog boxes, menu bars, commonly used icons, and code that help applications manage memory and other hardware resources. The System file also contains resources, including sounds and keyboard layouts.

- **Finder.** The Finder is a program designed to help you control your disks, drives, and files. It puts a "human face" on an otherwise complicated program and is thus the heart of the user interface that makes the Mac OS so user-friendly. It provides utility features such as formatting disks, printing disk catalogs, and deleting files; it's also a "home base" for sorting and working with files and launching other applications. Beginning with Mac OS 8, it is multithreaded and PowerPC native.
- **ROM.** A vital part of the Macintosh operating system is stored in read-only memory (ROM) chips on the computer's logic board. ROM-based software handles start-up and many basic aspects of Mac hardware control. The OS looks at your computer's ROM and adds or updates missing OS instructions so that what loads in memory is the latest and greatest OS. Sometime in 1997, Apple will release a new motherboard design called the PowerPC Platform (PPCP) that will eventually eliminate the dependency of the Mac OS on the ROM.
- **Printer drivers.** Printer drivers are small conversion programs that change data from its original format into a format the printer can digest and output. Printer drivers are selected in the Chooser and "run" with the Print command. QuickDraw GX significantly changes and improves the Macintosh print architecture, making it extensible through third-party programs and making it easier for developers to write printer drivers. This new feature is described in Chapter 11, "Fonts & Printing."

  Apple provides printer drivers for most Apple printers and output devices, but other vendors offer printer drivers that allow the Macintosh to be used with output devices that Apple drivers don't necessarily support. If you are having printing difficulties, check with your printer vendor to determine if you have the latest version of a printer driver that is compatible with Mac OS 8.
- **Network drivers.** Network drivers are also accessed using the Chooser Control Panel. They help your Macintosh communicate with network file servers, print services, remote modems, and other network devices. Apple provides network drivers for AppleTalk, Ethernet, and Token Ring network communications. Many other network drivers are provided along with third-party Macintosh network hardware. Network drivers are found in the Extensions folder and are often classified as Extensions. The network drivers just described are part of Mac OS—other drivers are distributed by third-party software and hardware vendors.

- **Extensions.** Because Macintosh OS is modular, it can be enhanced, modified, or extended by small files that temporarily become part of the OS every time the Mac is started up. These files are called Extensions. (***Note:*** They were called INITs in previous versions of the OS.) The icons for many Extensions appear across the bottom of your screen at start-up.

  Examples of important Apple OS Extensions in Mac OS 8 are Apple Guide, AppleScript, AppleShare, AppleTalk, File Sharing Extension, LaserWriter 8, QuickDraw 3D, QuickTime, and Speech Manager. Most specialized peripheral devices (for example, printers, monitors, CD-ROM players, and networks) normally come with a customized Extension file.

Extensions are what Apple uses to "extend" the OS without having to release a major new OS upgrade. Thus, when QuickTime was first released in 1990, it appeared as an Extension. As Extensions are improved and stabilized over time, they are often added directly to the OS; their functional code is added to the System or Finder file. Finally, when OS code becomes routine and standardized, what initially started out as an Extension may eventually end up encoded in the OS itself.

Extensions sometimes conflict with one another, with your regular applications, and with the OS. As a means of circumventing Extension conflicts, you can control which Extensions load at start-up as well as the order that they load. The new Extension Manager Control Panel, which is described in more detail in Chapter 2, "The System Folder," provides a means for doing this.

  Many Extensions are provided with the OS, but there are many others created independently by third parties. Most Extensions add some new feature or capabilities to the OS. For example, Ram Doubler and Speed Doubler replace certain elements of the Mac OS to increase performance, and StuffflIt Engine boosts compression and decompression times for the StuffIt program.

- **Control Panels.** These are mini-applications that provide additional functionality for some aspect of the OS, an Extension utility, or a hardware peripheral. Control Panels provided along with the OS control your Mac's memory, internal clock, colors, file and Web sharing, and many other system attributes. At the system level, Control Panels work much like Extensions, but they feature an interface that offers the user control over certain variables in the device's function. In some cases, a program you purchase will ship with both an Extension and a Control Panel.

You might ask, what is the difference between Extensions and Control Panels? In reality, not much. Often these two types of files do many of the same things. Developers use Control Panels when they want to allow you to make changes; otherwise they use Extensions. Settings you make to your system with Control Panels are stored until changed again. Therefore, if you remove those Control Panels from your System folder, the settings can't be changed.

- **Desk Accessories.** These are also independent files, and in all versions of System 7, they operate just like normal applications. (In previous versions of the OS, desk accessories were special files run in their own single layer of memory and accessed only from the Apple Menu.) Desk accessories (DAs) provide utility functions not built into the OS. DAs provided as part of the OS include the Chooser, Alarm Clock, Calculator, and Key Caps, to name but a few.

Using the Operating System

The Mac OS is used almost constantly from the moment you turn on your computer. To further help you understand its role, let's take a look at a few of the tasks it controls or assists:

- **Start-up.** From just a moment after the power is turned on, your Macintosh's OS controls the start-up process, loading any available Extensions, Control Panels, and fonts and verifying that your hardware is functioning properly and loading the Finder.

  Only the System, Finder, and Enabler files are mandatory for your Macintosh to start up. The additional components are important, but not required. You can prepare an emergency disk with just those three components and use that disk should your computer not start up properly. You can then copy over additional components from disk as required. See your Mac's documentation to learn how to create an emergency boot disk for your specific model of Mac or Mac clone.

- **File management.** When you manipulate windows and icons in the Finder and on the Desktop, your actions are translated from the onscreen graphic display into actual changes to the files on disk. But files aren't stored on disk as cute little icons; they're simply strings of magnetic 1s and 0s. It's the OS that turns them into meaningful text, beautiful graphics, stirring sounds, and moving images.

- **Application launching.** When you run a software program, the OS accesses the computer and sees to it that the correct portions of the file are read from disk, that the available memory is properly managed, and that data files (and sometimes temporary work files) are created and maintained on disk.
- **Font usage.** Every time a font is used on the Macintosh, whether it's a bitmapped, PostScript, TrueType, or QuickDraw GX outline font, the OS provides character information, including the way it should look in any particular size and style.
- **Dialog boxes.** The OS provides the basic format of almost every dialog box used on the Macintosh. For Open and Save As dialogs, the OS also supports the scrolling file listing and reading or writing files.
- **Printing.** An application must pass its data through one of the OS's printer drivers so it can be converted into a format the printer can understand. After this, the OS communicates the file to the printer and in some cases receives feedback from the printer during output.
- **Screen display.** The OS is responsible for producing the display that appears on your Macintosh screen. Applications communicate the display information to the OS using something called QuickDraw, which converts this information and draws it on the screen.
- **Networking.** Nearly every aspect of communication between the Mac and its peripherals is controlled by the OS. This includes data transfer from the disk to the AppleTalk port (and other ports), the timing of network communications while other software is being run onscreen, cabling, and two-way communications with sophisticated printers, modems, and storage drives.

So as you can see, almost any task you perform on your Macintosh—from the smallest mouse click to the largest data transfer—relies on the OS. Fortunately, you don't need to understand the technical intricacies of how the OS performs its tasks in order to use your Macintosh. But it is useful to have an appreciation for the range and depth of the OS's functions.

Basic Macintosh Operations

We'll now turn from technical descriptions of the OS to the easiest and most fundamental aspects of using the Macintosh. This section looks at the things you need to know in order to use the Macintosh efficiently. It also defines terms you'll encounter throughout the book. This information is intended primarily for those who are using Mac OS 8 in their first experience on the Macintosh.

The Graphical User Interface

The first and most fundamental requirement for using the Mac OS is understanding its graphical user interface. Instead of communicating your commands in words, you select pictures—or icons—that represent words. The icons, along with windows and menus, represent Macintosh hardware and software functions and features. And you use the mouse cursor to communicate with the Macintosh. (Yes, you'll use the keyboard too, but we'll assume you've already mastered that device.)

Let's look at each of these elements individually:

Icons

These are small graphics (drawings) that appear on the Macintosh screen; they represent items such as disks and folders (the icon actually looks like a disk or folder, as shown in Figure 1-2).

Figure 1-2: Disk and folder icons.

Various versions of icons are used to represent files stored on your disks. The icon tells you what kind of file it is. An example file icon and document file icon for the application BBEdit (a text editing program) are shown in Figure 1-3.

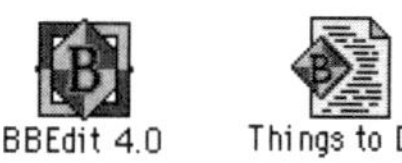

Figure 1-3: Standard application and document file icons.

But many application and document files use custom icons. A collection of custom application and document file icons appears in Figure 1-4.

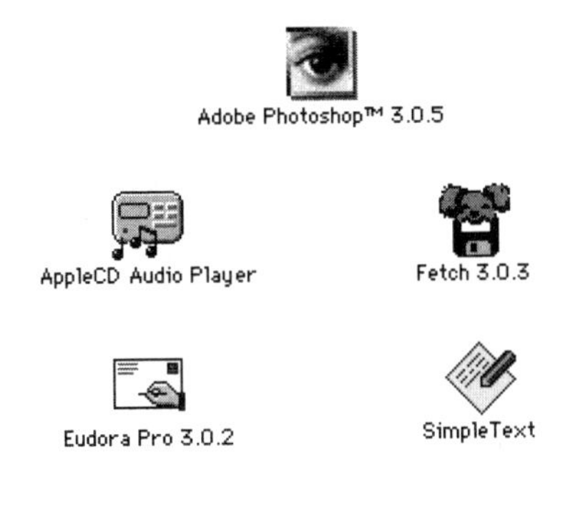

Figure 1-4: Custom application and document file icons.

Windows

When a Macintosh file is opened, its contents are displayed in a window. The most common type of window looks like the one shown in Figure 1-5; it includes a *title bar* at the top and scroll bars on its right and bottom edges. You can move a window around (by dragging its title bar), close a window (by clicking the close box in its upper left corner), and change the size of a window (by dragging the size box in its lower right corner).

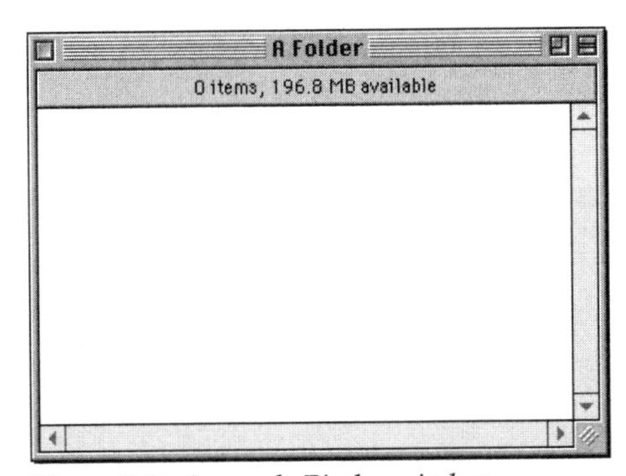

Figure 1-5: A sample Finder window.

However, there are other types of windows, including *dialog boxes.* A sample dialog box is shown in Figure 1-6. These small specialized windows usually present a set of options that allow you to customize a command or activity.

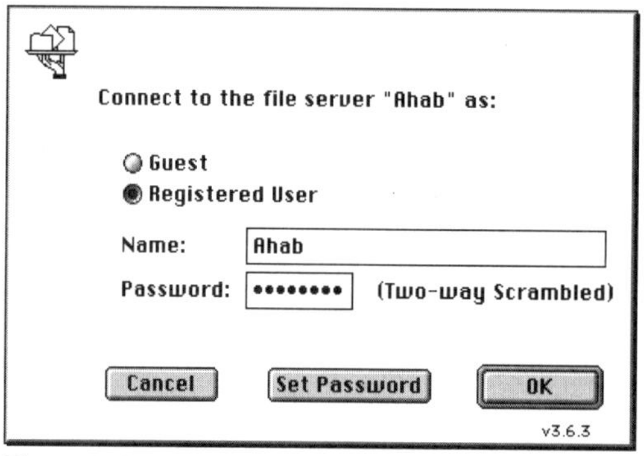

Figure 1-6: A sample dialog box.

There are four common kinds of dialog box options. Small round *radio buttons* present a set of mutually exclusive choices. Small square *check boxes* present a set of choices you can select in any combination. An *option box* is a small area where you type in your choice. Some options provide a set of alternatives in a *pop-up menu;* you can click on the one you want with the mouse.

Some dialog boxes don't present options but simply provide information. Usually this information is feedback concerning a command or action you're engaged in or a message from one of your hardware devices. These are called *alert dialog boxes,* or simply *alerts;* a sample is displayed in Figure 1-7.

Figure 1-7: An alert dialog box.

Another type of window used in some software applications is called a *palette.* Its called a palette because it "floats" on top of document windows and can't be obscured by them. Unlike an ordinary dialog box, which disappears after you've selected options or dismissed it, palettes may remain open for the duration of a work session. A palette presents a set of icons that represent tools you can work with, or sometimes it presents a text list of commands or options you can choose from. Figure 1-8 shows a few palettes from the image editing program Adobe Photoshop.

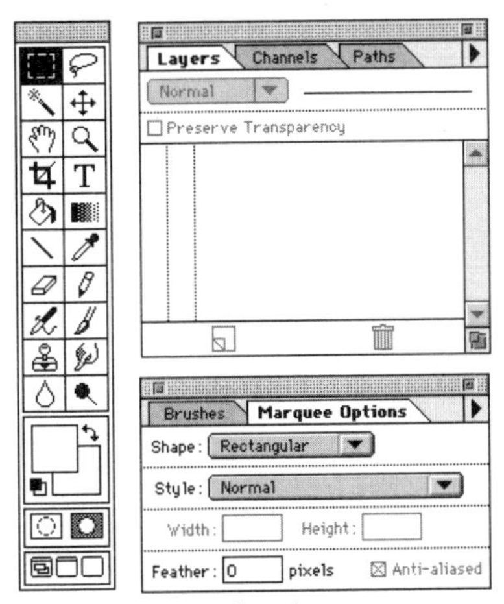

Figure 1-8: Sample palettes.

Menus

Most commands in Mac OS applications are presented in menus displayed along the menu bar at the top of the screen. Commands are usually grouped logically, with logical names that provide clues about what they're used for. The menu bar is the most distinctive element of the Macintosh. The now familiar Chicago font was specifically designed for the purpose of attractive screen display on the original Macintosh but has been replaced by a new font called "Truth" in Mac OS 8.

In Mac OS 8, menus drop down and stay open until you make a menu selection or click somewhere else on the screen. This way, you don't need to hold down the mouse while navigating the menu.

Menus drop down when the mouse is clicked on the menu name and stay down until you make a menu selection or click somewhere else on the screen; this feature is new to Mac OS 8 but was previously available using third-party utilities. As you drag the mouse down, each command is highlighted as it's selected. Releasing the mouse while the command is selected executes that command; to give you feedback, the selection command flashes two or three times. (There will be more about using the mouse later in this chapter.)

There are four basic types of menu commands. Some commands execute as soon as they're selected. Others toggle the status of some features on and off. Command names that end with an ellipsis (...) bring up a dialog box of related options.

A fourth type of menu option is a hierarchical submenu of commands. Holding the mouse button down lets you select one of these normal, toggling, or ellipsis subcommands. Figure 1-9 shows an example of a hierarchical menu.

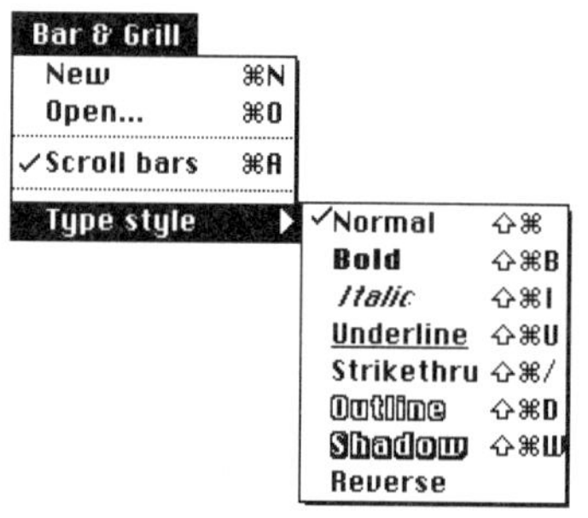

Figure 1-9: Four command types.

The Mouse & Cursors

All these graphic elements interact with your Macintosh via mouse manipulation. Operating the mouse is simple enough: you move the mouse on your desk and the mouse cursor moves onscreen accordingly. Only the motion of the mouse on your Desktop produces a change in cursor position, making the mouse a *relative* pointing device. (Some devices like graphics tablets are *absolute* pointing devices, as each point on their surface maps to a point on your screen.) The type of cursor that appears at any given time depends on the item to which you are pointing, the software you are using, the commands you have chosen, and the keys you have pressed on the keyboard. When you are working in the Finder, the mouse cursor will be the left-facing arrow.

Arrow cursors appear whenever you're pointing to the menu bar, regardless of the application being used. Macintosh applications also use the arrow cursor to select and manipulate objects. Other common cursors are shown in Figure 1-10.

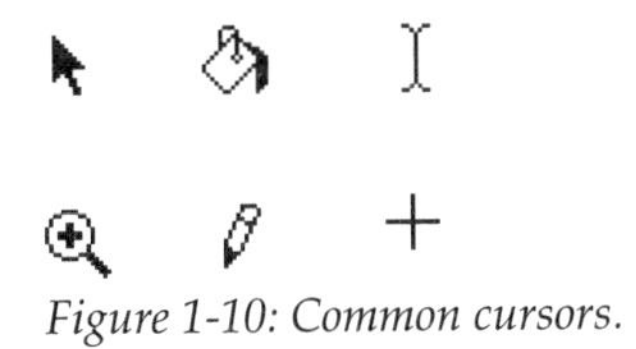

Figure 1-10: Common cursors.

There are five common actions you can make with the cursor. These actions manipulate icons, invoke Macintosh commands, and control application tools:

- **Pointing.** Positioning the cursor over a particular icon or other object or window element. If the cursor is an arrow, the arrow's tip marks the specific point. Other cursors have their own "hot spots," or specific points of action.
- **Clicking.** Quickly pressing and releasing the mouse button. In most cases, the click executes when the button is fully released, not while it's pressed. Mouse clicks select objects, including icons, buttons, and dialog box options.
- **Double-clicking.** Pressing and releasing the mouse button twice in rapid succession. Most beginners don't double-click fast enough to prevent the Macintosh from interpreting them as two single clicks instead of one double-click. Double-clicking controls many Macintosh actions, like opening icons to display their windows. The sensitivity with which the operating system responds to double-clicking can be changed using the Mouse Control Panel.
- **Pressing.** Holding down the mouse button while a command or action is completed.
- **Dragging.** Moving the mouse—and therefore the cursor—while the mouse button is pressed (held down). This action usually moves an item or causes the active cursor tool to be used while the mouse button is down (such as when you are drawing a line with a pencil tool).

Files & Folders

Once you understand icons and windows, and you're comfortable working your mouse, you're ready to put all that knowledge and skill to work. One of the most important tasks will be manipulating files on the Desktop.

There are many different types of files—including applications, data documents, OS files, utilities, fonts, and dictionaries. To keep all these files organized, you'll put them into *folders*. You can create new folders to hold any type of file whenever you like using the File menu's New Folder command. You can also create folders inside other folders to establish a hierarchical arrangement of files and folders, as shown in Figure 1-11. If you've worked on other types of computer systems, folders are directly analogous to directories or subdirectories.

To reposition files or folders—add them to a folder, or copy them to another disk or hard drive—point to the icon of the file or folder you want to manipulate, click and hold the mouse button, drag the file onto the destination icon, and release the mouse button. If you drag files to a different folder on the same disk, the files are *moved* (they now appear only in the new location, not in the old location). If you drag files to a different disk, or to a folder on a different disk, they're *copied* (they appear—and exist—in their new location and in the old location).

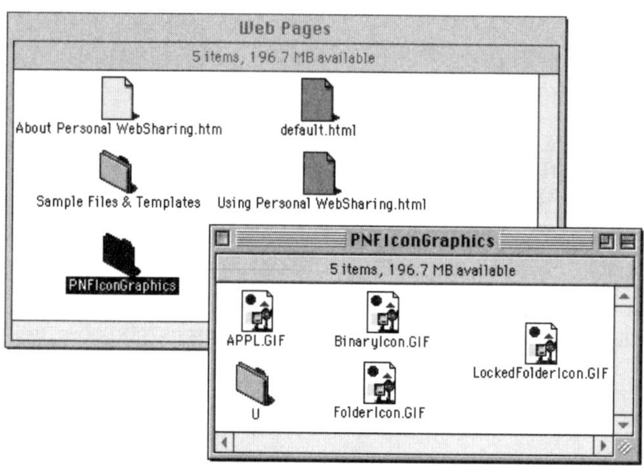

Figure 1-11: In this example, the U folder is inside the PNFIconGraphics folder, which is inside the Web Pages folder.

Floppy Disks

Two types of floppy disks are supported by the Macintosh: 800K floppies, (sometimes known as regular or double-density or DD) and 1.44MB floppies (sometimes called high-density or HD). Most Macs can use either disk type, but some older models can use 800K disks only. You can tell the difference between the two by the number of small windows at the top of the floppy disk: 800K floppies have one window; 1.44MB floppies have two. High-density disks usually have a distinctive HD logo stamped on the lower left corner, near the shutter. As older Macintosh models recede into history, 800K floppy disks are used less often. A good rule of thumb is that if your Apple Macintosh is capable of Mac OS 8, then you'll most likely have a high-density floppy drive. All Mac clones have this type of floppy drive.

Before using a floppy disk for the first time, it must be *formatted*. This erases the disk and prepares it for use. (If the disk has been used before, formatting erases whatever is on it, making the data unrecoverable.) Formatting creates cylindrical sections (with magnetic lines) on the floppy's surface and writes a directory or table of contents for the disk, thereby lowering somewhat the actual capacity of the floppy disk.

When you insert a new floppy disk, the Macintosh can tell that the disk has never been used and asks if you want to format it. You can reformat a disk at any time, which will delete all its files, by inserting the disk, selecting its icon, and choosing the Erase Disk command from the Special menu. The Erase Disk dialog box is shown in Figure 1-12.

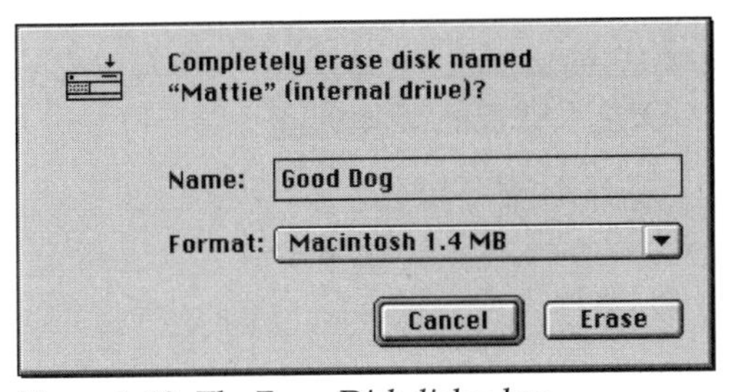

Figure 1-12: The Erase Disk dialog box.

With Mac OS 8 installed, you are given the additional options (enabled by the PC Exchange Control Panel) of formatting your floppy disk as a DOS disk for an IBM PC or PC clone or as a Pro-DOS disk for Apple II family computers. A DOS disk appears on your Desktop in Mac OS 8 with the letters PC in the disk icon. It will operate correctly in an IBM PC. Be careful to format the floppy disk as you intend, as it's easy to forget and use your previous format setting.

Macintosh Utilities

There are several built-in utilities you use frequently when you're working on the Macintosh:

The Chooser

This desk accessory is an electronic switchbox that lets you select from printers, networks, and file servers to which your Macintosh is connected. The Chooser, shown in Figure 1-13, appears when its name is chosen from the Apple menu. Icons representing the devices that may be available are on the left side of the Chooser. Selecting an icon brings up a list in the right side of the dialog box of available devices. Selecting the name of the device you want connects your Macintosh to that device.

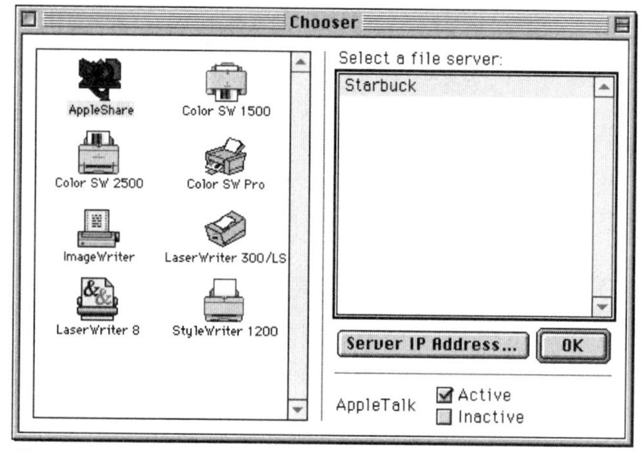

Figure 1-13: The Chooser.

Control Panels

Several of the Control Panels in the Control Panels folder, which is accessed via the Apple menu, are used to specify basic settings and preferences for your Macintosh. Mac OS 8 reworks several of the Control Panels, consolidating functions that were previously separated and adding new functionality.

- The **General Controls Control Panel** is used to change a number of Desktop behavior characteristics. As with earlier versions of this Control Panel, you can change the number of times a menu command blinks when selected and the frequency with which an insertion point blinks. It also allows you to choose whether or not you want to show the Desktop when in another application, view the Launcher at start-up, and display an improper shut-down warning. The settings for system and application folder protection and the location to which a new document is saved are also found here. The General Controls Control Panel is shown in Figure 1-14.

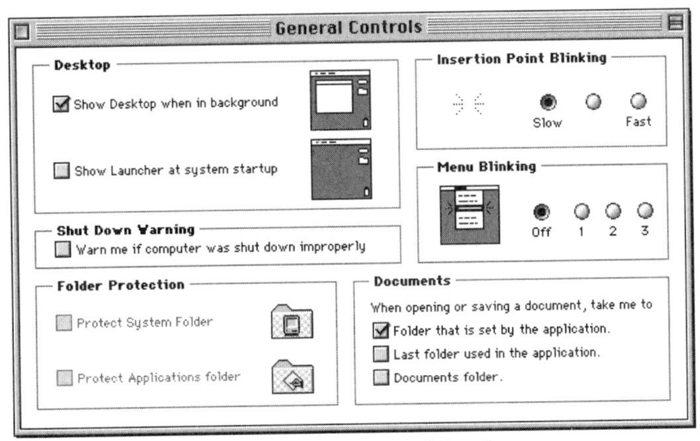

Figure 1-14: The General Controls Control Panel.

- The **Date & Time Control Panel** is used to set the system date and time of your computer, as well as the time zone. This is the date and time that appear in your menu bar (optionally set here) and are used to time-stamp file creation or modification times. It is also used by many applications to do maintenance and updates (for example, to find "today" in a calendar program). The Date & Time Control Panel, included in System 7.1 and later, is shown in Figure 1-15.

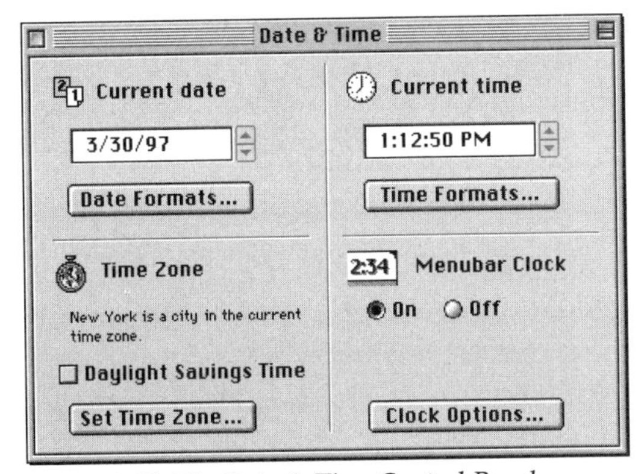

Figure 1-15: The Date & Time Control Panel.

Dates and times are a central function of your computer's bookkeeping. You normally set these parameters once, and then an internal battery runs the clock under its own power. If you are seeing erratic time behavior, it could be that your battery has run down.

- The **Desktop Pictures Control Panel** is used to choose the color or pattern of your Desktop, as well as to select a picture for your Desktop. Mac OS 8 adds an extended set of several dozen patterns, many of which can be found in previous versions of the Mac OS. These new patterns are sure to please you; they are what discriminating Desktops are wearing these days. The Desktop Pictures Control Panel is shown in Figure 1-16. In version 7.5 and earlier, patterns were set in the General Control Panel, and in System 7.5.3, they were set in the Desktop Patterns Control Panel.

Figure 1-16: The Desktop Pictures Control Panel.

- The **Monitors & Sound Control Panel** is used to define your monitor's display of colors or gray values, resolution (if you have a multi-resolution monitor), and sound preferences. It also lets you set the relative position of each monitor if you have more than one connected to your Macintosh. The Monitors & Sound Control Panel is shown in Figure 1-17.

  Changes made to a monitor's color or resolution go into effect immediately. Another feature that PowerBook owners are sure to appreciate is the ability of PowerBooks with external monitors (such as the 160, 180, and 500 series) to be put to sleep with the external monitor attached.

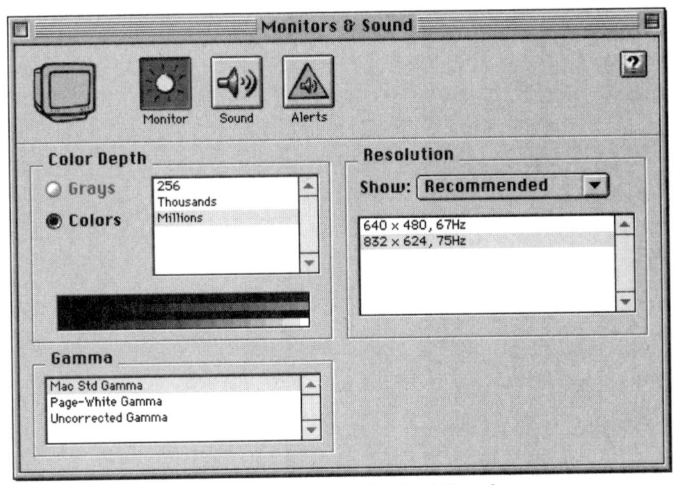

Figure 1-17: The Monitors & Sound Control Panel.

- The **Mouse Control Panel** is used to define the speed of your onscreen cursor relative to how fast you move the mouse and the amount of delay between clicks, which determines if two clicks will be interpreted as two separate mouse clicks instead of one double-click. A PowerBook-specific Control Panel lets you make similar adjustments to the Track Pad, the PowerBook's equivalent of a mouse. The Mouse Control Panel is shown in Figure 1-18.

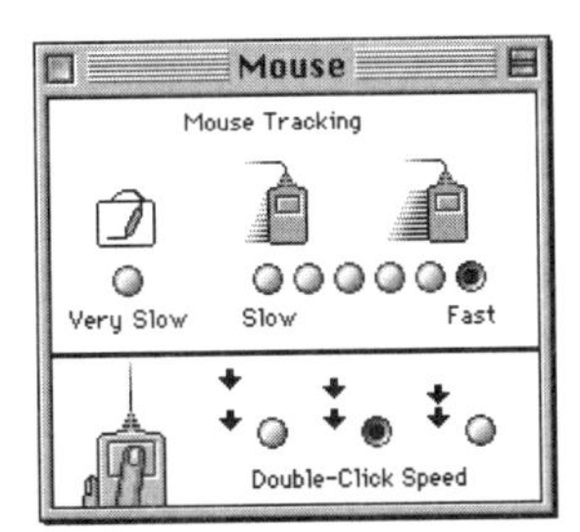

Figure 1-18: The Mouse Control Panel.

- The **Keyboard Control Panel** lets you set the character set of your keyboard. You can also use this panel to control the repeat rate for keystrokes. The Keyboard Control Panel is shown in Figure 1-19.

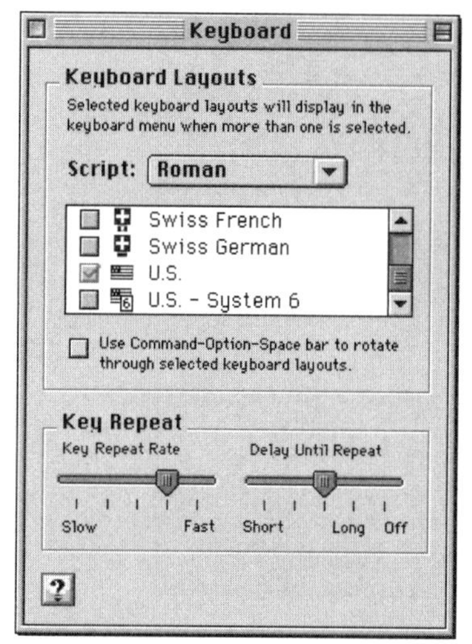

Figure 1-19: The Keyboard Control Panel.

Two Control Panels, the Text and Numbers, are used in Mac OS 8 to support foreign language text and number formats, respectively. For example, the Text and Numbers Control Panels settings enable SimpleText's (the text editor included with Mac OS 8) stylized text, graphics, and language scripting support. The Text and Numbers Control Panels include the following features:

- The **Text Control Panel** offers two simple options: Script and Behavior. A script is a method of writing characters, such as left to right for the Latin or Roman language or right to left for Hebrew or Arabic. A script also defines what constitutes a word (delimiting characters). Behavior specifies the character set, which is often, but not always, country dependent. In the United States we use ASCII; England uses a different character set; and so on. Behavior affects sort order and letter case. The Text Control Panel is shown in Figure 1-20.

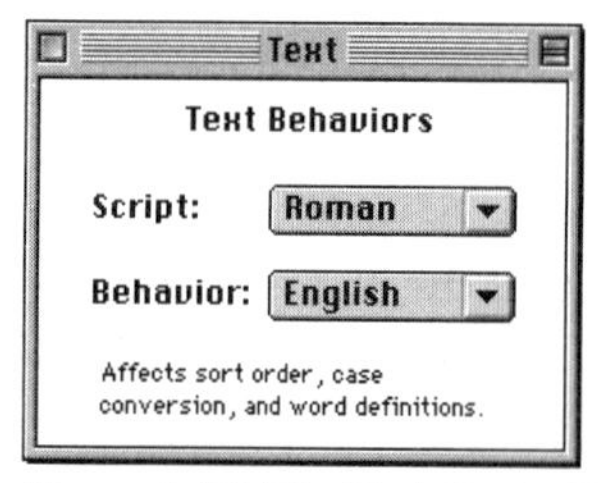

Figure 1-20: The Text Control Panel.

- The **Numbers Control Panel** lets you specify a format by country. You can also set separators and currency symbols. The Numbers Control Panel is shown in Figure 1-21.

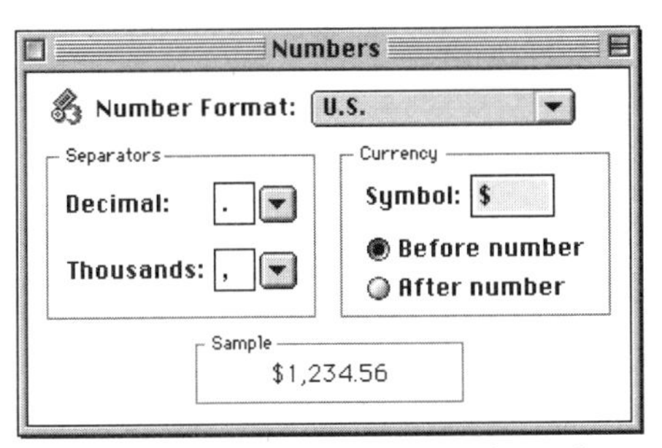

Figure 1-21: The Numbers Control Panel.

There are several other important Control Panels that affect the way you interact with the Mac OS, but we'll discuss them in Chapter 3, "The Finder & Desktop," and Chapter 4, "Customizing Your Mac."

Data Transfer Methods

The Macintosh OS provides a simple built-in method for transferring text, sounds, graphic elements, and even movies from one location to another—the Clipboard. You can use the Clipboard to move items within a document or from one document to another—even if the documents were created by different software applications. The metaphor of the Clipboard is continued with the commands used to manipulate it: Cut, Copy, and Paste, which can be found on the Edit menu.

Since you never see the information being transferred, it's easy to make mistakes with Clipboard operations. Even when you're careful and check the contents of the Clipboard using the Show Clipboard command common to most applications, Clipboard transfers are at least a two-step operation; checking adds a third step. Mac OS 8 uses another more direct method for moving information about: Macintosh Drag and Drop. With Drag and Drop, you click and drag information about. Most users will find *spring-loaded folders*, a new variation of Drag and Drop, to be one of the best major new features of Mac OS 8. It's probably the feature you'll think about least, but the one that will save you the most time. In its way, it's every bit as important a metaphor as Cut and

Paste. When you drag an item such as a document, folder, or application onto a folder or hard drive containing subfolders, just hold the item over the folder or hard drive until it "springs" open. You may continue to drag the item and hold it over folders that subsequently appear, as well as navigate backward through the hierarchy of subfolders to the point at which you began.

Drag and Drop can even move data to the Desktop as clipping objects: text as text clippings, graphics as picture clippings, sound as sound clippings, and video as video clippings. The old Clipping Extension that manages the actions used to be a separate Extension to the OS, but is now part of the OS itself. Clippings can be used by any other file—just drag and drop it. Drag and Drop capability is being added to applications that are upgraded to take advantage of Mac OS 8. In the OS, the Clipboard, Note Pad, Find File, and SimpleText take advantage of Drag and Drop. Drag and Drop also starts processes like printing (drag and drop a file to a printer icon) or opening files (drag and drop a file onto an application icon). We'll pay particular attention to Macintosh Drag and Drop as we proceed through the book, repaying your reading with tremendous time savings.

Cut & Paste: Using the Clipboard & the Scrapbook

You never access the Clipboard directly; instead, you manipulate the contents of the Clipboard using the Cut, Copy, and Paste commands. These commands are used so commonly that it's a good idea to remember their keystroke equivalents: Command+X for Cut, Command+C for Copy, and Command+V for Paste. The Cut, Copy, and Paste commands provide you with the following capabilities:

- **Cut.** Removes the selected objects from their current location and places them on the Clipboard, replacing the previous Clipboard contents. (The Clipboard can contain only the result of the last Cut or Copy command.)
- **Copy.** Places the selected objects on the Clipboard, but leaves them in their current location as well. The objects that are copied replace the previous contents of the Clipboard.
- **Paste.** Places a copy of the objects currently on the Clipboard into the current document at the cursor location. Using the Paste command does not remove items from the Clipboard; you can paste the same item repeatedly.

There are many ways to use the Clipboard. The most common is to move an element—like a paragraph or graphic item—from one place to another in the same document. To do so, you select the element, choose the Cut command, position the cursor at the new location, and choose the Paste command.

The Clipboard is also used to move elements between different documents, even elements created by different applications. For example, to move a chart from a file you created with your spreadsheet into a word processor file:

1. Open the spreadsheet and choose the chart. Use the Copy command, since you want to leave the chart in the spreadsheet even after it has been moved to the word processor.
2. Open the word processor, or switch to it if it's already open. Open the document that will receive the copied chart. You can quit the spreadsheet, but it's not necessary. (Details on opening and switching between several applications are presented in Chapter 10, "Working With Multiple Applications.")
3. Position the cursor in the word processor file where you want the chart placed. Choose the Paste command.

Chances are that if you can select some information, you can copy it to the Clipboard and move it about. In addition to simple ASCII text, the Clipboard supports stylized text and various graphics formats. The Clipboard even supports sound and QuickTime video.

If you want to remove selected items without affecting the Clipboard, use the Clear command or the Delete key. Since the Clipboard can hold only one item and is not saved out to a file, it is overwritten whenever it is modified. Sometimes when you have a large selection on the Clipboard, you can tie up Macintosh memory you need for other programs. To free up that memory, clear the Clipboard or copy a single character to it.

It's easy to forget the contents of your Clipboard. Some applications have as a menu item a command called Show Clipboard. Its placement varies. In the Finder, this command is found in the Edit menu; Microsoft Word places it in the Window menu; other programs place it on a View menu. In the Finder, the Show Clipboard command is enabled by the Clipboard file placed at the top level of the System folder. Selecting this command opens a window that lets you view the Clipboard's contents and tells you what kind of data it contains. Figure 1-22 shows an example.

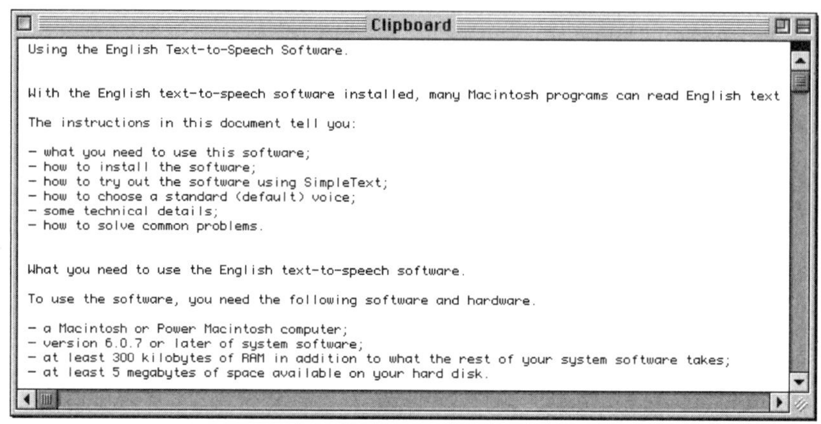

Figure 1-22: The Clipboard window.

Another related Macintosh tool is the Scrapbook, a desk accessory found on the Apple menu that can hold a catalog of text and graphic elements you use frequently or need to move from one document to another. The Scrapbook saves data to a file and thus represents permanent storage (until you modify the data). Elements are moved into or out of the Scrapbook via the Clipboard and the Cut, Copy, and Paste commands previously described. A Scrapbook displaying a single element is shown in Figure 1-23.

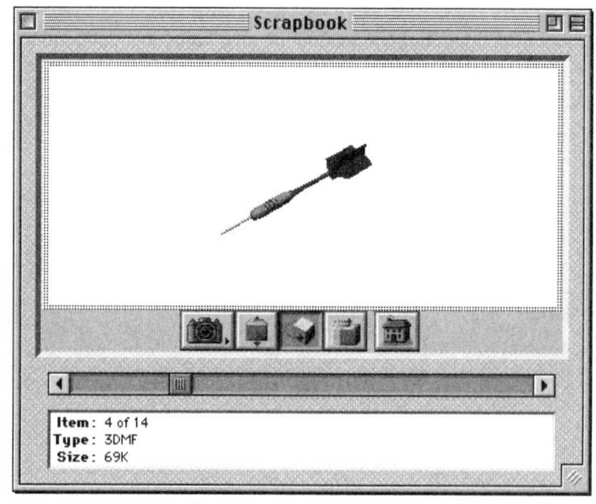

Figure 1-23: The Scrapbook.

For example, if you need to use a set of icons throughout a magazine layout you are creating, you could transfer them all into the Scrapbook and access them from there as needed. To do so, you would follow these steps:

1. Open the file containing the icons. Select one icon, and choose the Copy command to move it to the Clipboard.
2. Open the Scrapbook, and choose the Paste command to move the icon on the Clipboard into the Scrapbook. The Scrapbook automatically creates a new page each time you paste in a new element.
3. Go back to the file containing the icons, select another icon, and again use the Copy command to move it to the Clipboard. Access the Scrapbook again, and paste in the new icon. Repeat this process until the Scrapbook contains all the needed icons.
4. Open your page layout program, and as each icon is needed, open the Scrapbook, locate the icon, and use the Copy command to transfer it from the Scrapbook onto the Clipboard. Set the cursor at the location where the icon is needed, and choose the Paste command to transfer the icon into your layout. Repeat this procedure until all icons are in place.

The Scrapbook was enhanced for Mac OS 8, as it has been for most major system upgrades. Now the Scrapbook not only supports new sound, video, and 3D Meta File (3DMF) formats, it also gives you information about the type of item, the size in bytes, and the dimension in pixels. Best of all, the Scrapbook is Drag-and-Drop enabled. Let's now look at this great feature: Drag and Drop.

Macintosh Drag & Drop

Drag and Drop is a technique for sharing data between documents, files, and applications. Various aspects of drag-and-drop behavior have been around for some time now. In versions of System 7, you could drag a file icon onto an application, and if the application could open that file and translate it, it would. For example, when Macintosh Drag and Drop was used with the System 7 Pro Finder and Macintosh Easy Open (a System Extension), any file dragged onto an application could be automatically translated and opened provided that the capability was set up beforehand.

Mac OS 8 extends Drag and Drop so that you can print files by dragging them to a printer icon on your Desktop (a feature of QuickDraw GX covered in Chapter 11). The most important extension of Drag and Drop is the ability to transfer data within a file, between files, and even to the Macintosh Desktop. Drag and Drop, which used to be monitored by the Drag Manager Extension, is now part of the OS itself.

Macintosh Drag and Drop is a terrific method for data exchange because it is intuitive. If you've used drag and drop in other applications (like Microsoft Word 5.x), then you are familiar with the basics. Select the data and drag it to a new location. It moves an outline of your selected data to the new location and completes the data move when you release the mouse button. An example of moving text within a document is shown in Figure 1-24 using Apple's text editor, SimpleText.

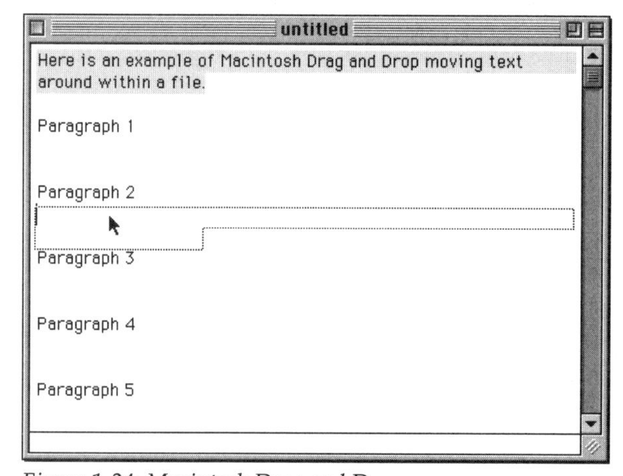

Figure 1-24: Macintosh Drag and Drop.

SimpleText is a text editor that opens files containing simple ASCII text, stylized text, and graphics in the PICT format. It replaces TeachText and expands upon it by allowing basic text editing, as well. You could think of SimpleText as a basic word processor; it even records and plays sounds and speech. SimpleText will open the Read Me files that often accompany new software. These files tell you about late-breaking information that couldn't be included in the manual. Whenever you are trying to open an unknown file on your Macintosh, try SimpleText first.

One very nice feature of Mac OS 8 is the ability to drag and drop selections to the Macintosh Desktop. The resulting objects are called *clippings* and are given a default filename, such as text clipping, to indicate the data type. You can edit the filename using standard Macintosh editing techniques. Click on the filename, type a new name, and press the Return key to change the name. Some clippings are shown in Figure 1-25.

To use clippings, simply drag them to where you want them in another file. Clippings are a convenient way to add logos or headers to documents, glossary items, or other items you might have stored in your Scrapbook. Clippings are tracked and managed by the new Clippings Extension. You may want to consolidate your clippings within a single folder on your Desktop to reduce clutter.

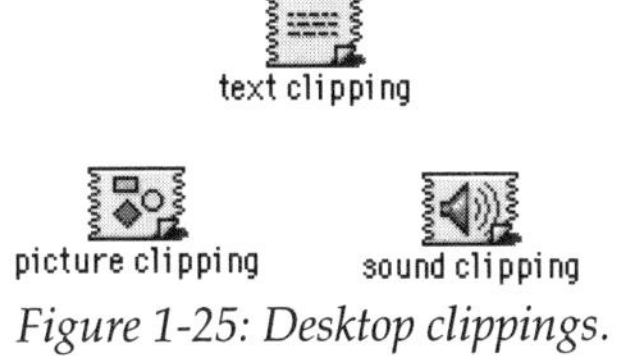

Figure 1-25: Desktop clippings.

Mac OS 8 has a desk accessory called Stickies that you can find on the Apple menu. An example is shown in Figure 1-26. With Stickies, you can create windows of text that float on your Desktop. They resemble the paper version found in most offices and homes that are stuck to desks, lamps, doors, and refrigerators as reminders. You can scroll the text using the arrow keys and collapse the windows to a single bar.

Stickies supports cut, copy, and paste and can import and export text; it even supports Drag and Drop. Stickie Notes can be different colors and any rectangular size down to a single line. When you're done with a note, you can close it and save it to a file or simply delete it.

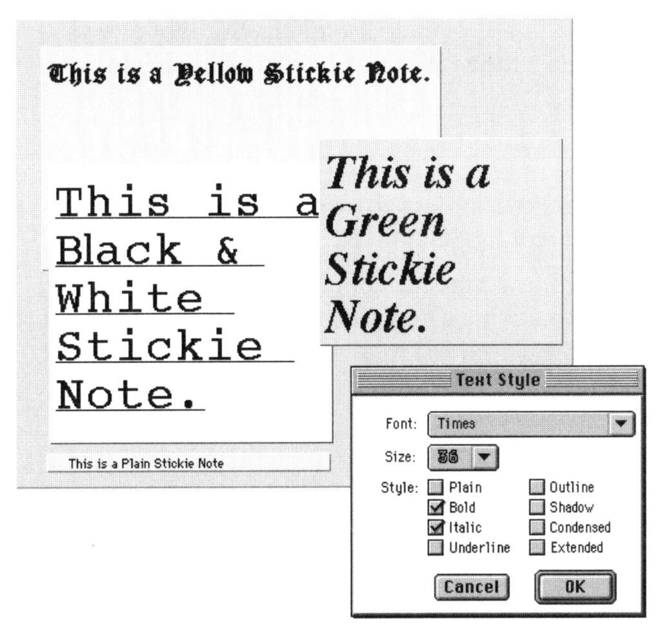

Figure 1-26: Several Stickies and the Text Style formatting dialog box.

Another older desk accessory called Note Pad can place a single window on your Desktop. You can move from page to page by clicking on the dog-ear of the notepad. Note Pad, an example of which is shown in Figure 1-27, has been part of Mac OS from its inception.

Figure 1-27: Note Pad.

Moving On

The OS is the core of what we think of as the Macintosh. The OS makes it possible for the computer to interact with other programs. It also helps in controlling Mac hardware and peripherals. The OS standardizes the Macintosh and allows software developers to produce high-quality applications.

Some of the features the Mac's OS provides to the user are:

- Icons, windows, and dialog boxes.
- Mouse controls and menus.
- Windows and palettes.
- The Clipboard and the Scrapbook.

In Chapter 2, we'll examine the contents of the System folder. We'll find out just exactly what all those items are and why they shouldn't stray from their homes.

CHAPTER 2

The System Folder

There's one folder on every Macintosh hard drive that's distinct from all the others—the System Folder, home of the operating system and many other important files. The System Folder is given special treatment by the operating system, by other software applications, and by you as a Macintosh user.

While you can arrange files on your hard drive (and all other hard drives, referred to as volumes, mounted on your Desktop) to suit your personal needs, you can only change the organization of the System Folder in certain ways. That's because of the fundamental role software in the System Folder plays in the operation of your Macintosh.

In January 1984, when version 1.0 of the system software was released with the Macintosh 128K, the System Folder contained 22 items that consumed only 225K of disk space. Using System 6 on a Mac with a normal assortment of applications and utilities could easily result in a System Folder containing 100 files or more, and the total size of the System Folder can easily soar above one megabyte. In System 7, you can barely fit just the System and Finder files and an Enabler file on a single 1.44MB floppy disk. A packed System Folder could run between 10MB and 50MB in size. Figure 2-1 shows what the contents of the System Folder looked like in an older version of OS. Note that everything is just heaped together instead of placed into specific folders.

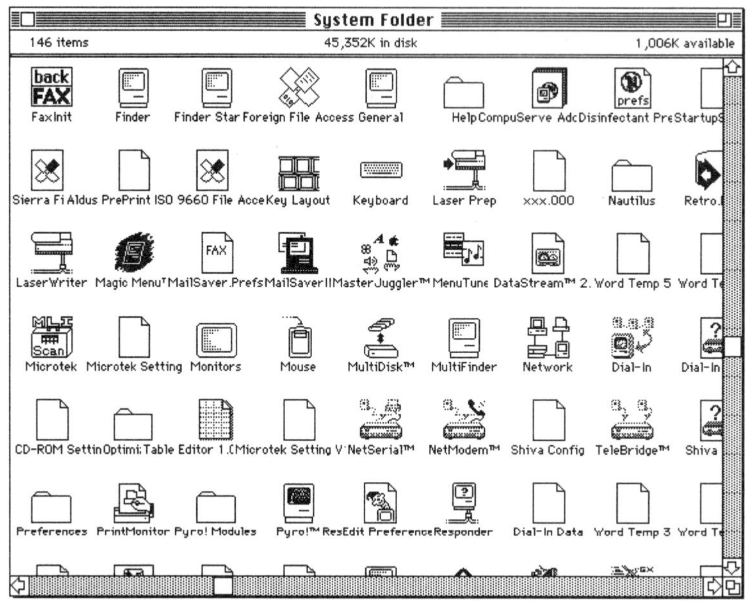

Figure 2-1: A large, messy System 6.0x System Folder.

The main problem with such a large System Folder is the resulting lack of organization, as shown in Figure 2-1. A crowded System Folder is slow to open at the Desktop, and finding what you want in the maze of files is a slow and tedious process.

Increasing complexity has been partially responsible for the growth of the operating system software, but a more direct cause has been the growing number of nonsystem software files that reside in the System Folder. These include third-party fonts, sounds, desk accessories, FKEYs, Control Panels, and Extensions. Adding these files has placed obvious demands on disk space and has also resulted in chaotic System Folder organization and some measure of system instability.

System 7 did little to reduce the pace of System Folder growth, but it did provide new methods of maintaining System Folder organization. It also introduced a few basic means of avoiding the instability caused by the old System Folder organization.

In this chapter, we'll look at the System Folder organization under Mac OS 8 and offer some suggestions to help you effectively manage this important resource.

The Mac OS 8 System Folder

In Mac OS 8, the System Folder includes a number of predefined subfolders, each of which is designed to hold a specific type of file. This organizational system, created when Mac OS 8 is installed, greatly reduces the potential for clutter (see Figure 2-1 for a good example of clutter). The actual number of items in the System Folder depends on the components chosen for installation above and beyond the core OS. See Appendix B, "Installing or Updating Mac OS 8," for exactly what options are available for installation. The System Folder includes many subfolders, including the following (depending on which components you install in addition to the OS):

- Apple Menu Items
- Application Support
- Claris
- Control Panels
- Control Strip Modules
- DataViz
- Desktop Printers
- Editors
- Extensions
- Fonts
- Launcher Items
- Preferences
- PrintMonitor Documents
- Shutdown Items
- Startup Items
- Text Encodings

Additionally, when you use the Extension Manager Control Panel to turn Extensions, Control Panels, or other System Folder items off, you will see the following folders:

- Control Panel (Disabled)
- System Extensions (Disabled)
- Extensions (Disabled)

These folders are created "on-the-fly" (which is computer-speak for *automatically*) by the Extensions Manager program; the folders that are created depend upon what you turn off. A display of the most basic parts of the Mac OS 8 System Folder is shown in Figure 2-2.

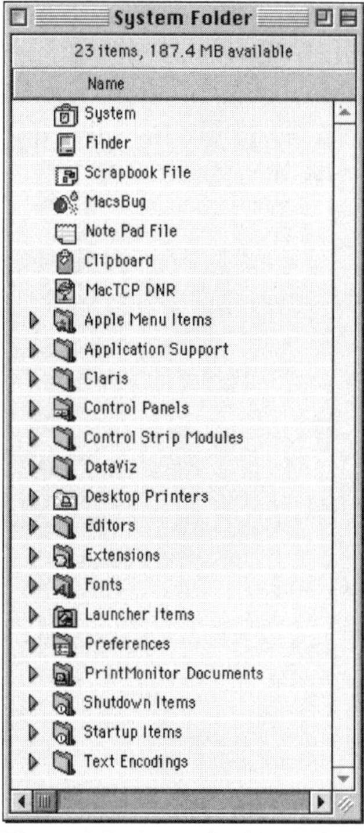

Figure 2-2: A standard Mac OS 8 System Folder.

In some ways, the new System Folder is more complex than the old one. Fortunately, as we'll see, Apple has built in an "invisible hand" to help make sure that System Folder files are always located correctly.

Because the new System Folder and subfolders are so important to the operation of your Macintosh, it's important to understand what type of files should be placed in each folder. The following section describes the folders and provides some basic tips for organizing and using them.

The Apple Menu Folder

One of the best things about the many utilities and small applications that come with Mac OS 8 (that used to be known as desk accessories) is their accessibility, via the Apple menu, from inside any application. In System 7, the convenience of the Apple menu was extended beyond desk accessories to include applications, documents, folders, and even aliases to volumes. And best of all, this powerful new Apple menu was completely customizable.

When Mac OS 8 is installed, the Apple System Profiler, Calculator, Chooser, Connect To, Find File, Graphing Calculator, Jigsaw Puzzle, Key Caps, Note Pad, Scrapbook, SimpleSound, Stickies, and Shutdown applications appear in the Apple menu. Additionally, the Automated Tasks, Control Panels, Desktop Printers, and OpenDoc Stationery folders or folder aliases appear in the Apple menu. (An alias is like a pointer to an original file or folder, and you can always tell an alias from the original because it is italicized and often contains the word *alias* at the end of the file or folder name.) If you open the Apple Menu Items folder inside the System Folder, these are exactly the files you find inside, as shown in Figure 2-3.

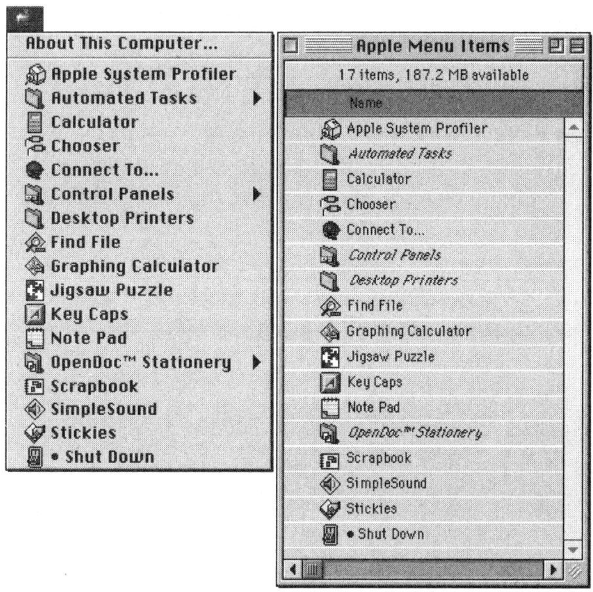

Figure 2-3: The Mac OS 8 Apple menu and Apple Menu Items folder (as configured by the Installer).

Longtime Macintosh users will note the loss of the venerable Alarm Clock desk accessory from the Apple menu in Mac OS 8. It was replaced by the Date & Time Control Panel, now easily accessible from the Control Panels submenu. The Alarm Clock was the preferred method for changing the system date and time in several whole-number versions of system software. Prior to 7.5, you could also change the date and time from within the General Control Panel.

Some people (like me!) prefer to rearrange the Apple menu to make it easier to find things. To modify the contents of the Apple menu, add or remove files or aliases to the Apple Menu Items folder. The Apple menu is updated immediately and displays the first 50 items (alphabetically) contained in the Apple Menu Items folder. The only item you can't remove is the About This Computer option, which is always the first choice in the Apple menu when you are in the Finder.

To make frequently used folders and applications more easily accessible, you can add aliases to the Apple Menu Items folder. For example, you can add aliases to applications, documents, folders, and volumes. Each item will be much easier to access from the Apple menu than by using traditional double-click methods. Choosing an item from the Apple menu is equivalent to double-clicking on the item's icon. The selected application or Control Panel will run, or the selected folder or volume will open.

To avoid moving the file, folder, or volume icon from its original location, most of the files added to the Apple Menu Items folder should be aliases rather than original files. In the Apple Menu Items folder, the filename remains displayed in italics, but it appears in standard font in the Apple menu—you can't tell by looking at the Apple menu that the file in the Apple Menu Items folder is an alias.

Because the Apple menu displays files alphabetically, you can reorder the menu items by modifying their names with numerical or alphabetical prefixes. A list of the available prefixes appears in Figure 2-4.

(space bar)	. (.)	œ (Op-Q)	¶ (Op-7)	ª (Op-9)
! (Sh-1)	/ (/)	w (W)	ß (Op-S)	º (Op-0)
“ (Op-[)	= (=)	z (Z)	® (Op-R)	Ω (Op-Z)
” (Op-])	? (Sh-/)	[([)	© (Op-C)	¿ (Sh-Op-/)
# (Sh-3)	@ (Sh-2)	] (])	™ (Op-2)	¡ (Op-1)
$ (Sh-4)	å (Op-A)	^ (Sh-6)	≠ (Op-=)	¬ (Op-L)
% (Sh-5)	A (Sh-A)	` (`)	∞ (Op-5)	√ (Op-V)
& (Sh-7)	æ (Op-')	{ (Sh-[)	≤ (Op-,)	ƒ (Op-F)
‘ (Op-])	B (Sh-B)	} (Sh-])	≥ (Op-x)	≈ (Op-X)
’ (Sh-Op-])	c (c)	~ (Sh-`)	¥ (Op-Y)	∆ (Op-J)
((Sh-9)	ç (Op-c)	† (Op-T)	µ (Op-M)	… (Op-;)
) (Sh-0)	E (Sh-E)	¢ (Op-4)	∂ (Op-D)	– (O--)
* (Sh-8)	f (f)	£ (Op-3)	∑ (Op-W)	— (Sh-Op--)
+ (Sh-=)	G (SH-G)	§ (Op-6)	π (Op-P)	÷ (Op-/)
- (-)	ø (Op-0)	• (Op-8)	∫ (Op-B)	

Figure 2-4: The list demonstrates, from top to bottom and left to right, the special characters that can be used to alphabetize files in the Apple menu and the keys you press to access them.

The result of using some of the prefixes is shown in the Apple menu pictured in Figure 2-5, in which applications, folders, desk accessories, Control Panels, documents, and volumes are ordered separately. This example shows groups of folders for commonly used applications in the middle, with elements of the OS in the top, and miscellaneous items in the bottom of the Apple menu.

Figure 2-5: Files are arranged in this Apple menu using filename prefixes.

To some extent, the inclusion of the Recent Applications, Recent Documents, and Recent Servers folders in the Apple menu obviates the need to add commonly used items to the Apple menu. However, if you find that a favorite item disappears every now and then from the submenu in one of these folders, by all means add its alias to the Apple Menu folder for permanent inclusion.

The Control Panels Folder

Control Panels are control devices (cdevs) and applications (appcs) that used to appear in the System 6.0x Control Panel desk accessory. In System 7, a Control Panel is a small, independent application launched by double-clicking on its icon. Many Control Panels in Mac OS 8 function just like applications in that they are launched, have menu options, and are quit like other applications. An example Control Panels folder, whose contents are shown as buttons, is shown in Figure 2-6.

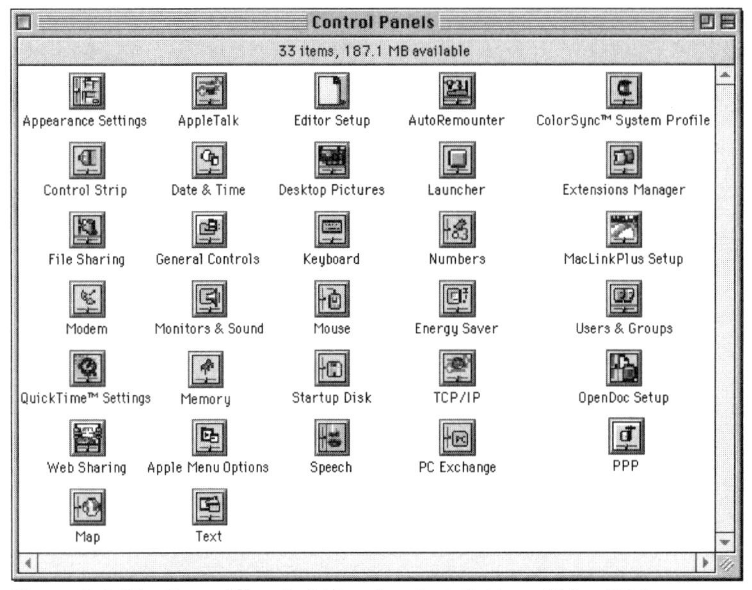

Figure 2-6: The Control Panels folder of an installation of Mac OS 8.

Control Panels are stored in the Control Panels folder, which itself is stored inside the System Folder—mainly because Control Panels often contain special resources (like Extensions) that must be run during start-up. If the Extensions portion of the Control Panel isn't loaded at start-up, the Control Panel may not function properly.

If you want to keep a copy of any Control Panel in another location, create an alias and move the alias to your preferred location. You could, for example, store aliases of frequently used Control Panels in the Apple Menu Items folder or in a folder containing other utility applications. Figure 2-7 shows several Control Panels opened at the same time.

The Extensions Folder

As mentioned previously, Extensions (INITs), printer drivers, and network drivers are major contributors to System Folder overcrowding. In System 7, these files, which have invaded System Folders in epidemic proportions since the introduction of System 6.0, have a home in the Extensions folder. Your Extensions folder may become quite crowded, as exemplified by Figure 2-8, but at least you can find your more important system files without having to wade through all of your Extensions.

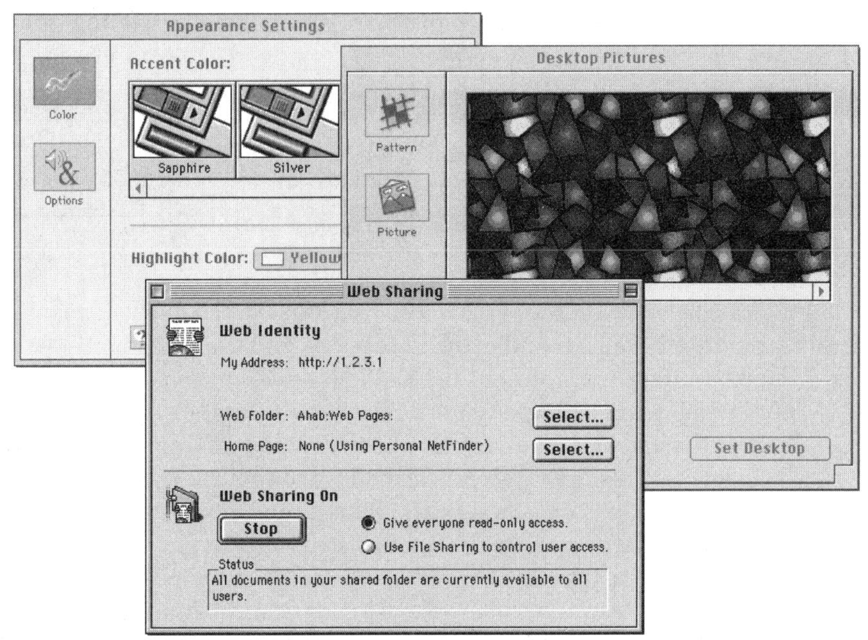

Figure 2-7: Control Panels appear in independent windows.

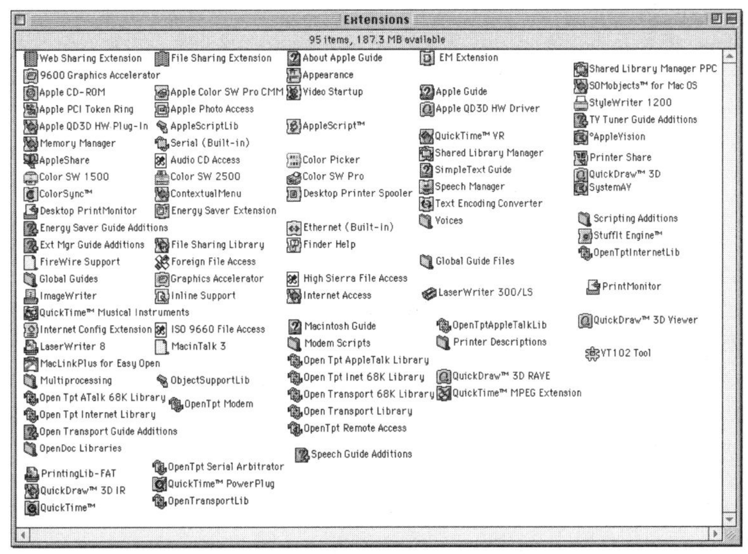

Figure 2-8: The Extensions folder holds Extensions, printer drivers, and network drivers.

Most INITs add features to the Mac's OS, thereby extending its capabilities—hence the name Extensions. Drivers extend system software capabilities in a less dramatic but important way.

The Extensions folder can become quite crowded in Mac OS 8, inviting the View by Name view.

During start-up, the system software looks in the Extensions folder and executes the items found there. Extensions and Control Panels that aren't stored in the Extensions or Control Panels folders won't execute at start-up and won't operate properly until they're correctly positioned and the computer is restarted. Some, but not all, Extensions will appear as icons at the bottom of your start-up screen, as will some Control Panels.

Because Extensions and Control Panels modify or enhance the system software at start-up, a newly installed Extension or Control Panel may cause your Macintosh to crash. Crashes can occur if the item is incompatible with the system software, another Extension or Control Panel, a certain combination of Extensions and Control Panels, or even an application that you use. The range of problems you can encounter is the stuff of legend.

If you experience a compatibility problem, such as sudden or unexplained freezes or crashes, suspect an Extension conflict first. To test the theory, try turning off your Extensions. Hold down the Shift key while restarting your Macintosh. This will disable all Extensions and allow you to remove the incompatible file from the System Folder.

When you restart or start up with the Shift key held down, the words "Extensions" Off will appear under "Welcome to Mac OS." As soon as these words appear, you can release the Shift key, and the computer will start up without executing any of the items in the Extensions folder or the Control Panels folder.

In the good old days of System 6 you could resolve Extension conflicts by adding or removing Extensions one at a time from your System Folder until the offending Extension (or combination) was found. Often, you could avoid conflicts by changing the loading order by simply renaming the Extension (changing ATM to ~ATM, for example).

Various third-party utilities were introduced to automate the process of turning Extensions on and off, changing the loading order, or creating Extension worksets. The best-known of these products is Cassidy & Green's Conflict Catcher, which you should purchase if you are having a significant start-up problem or otherwise suspect an Extension conflict.

The Mac OS loads Extensions first, then Control Panels, then the contents (if any) of the Startup Items folder. All items are loaded alphabetically.

In Mac OS 8, the number of Extensions has become so overwhelming that Apple felt compelled to expand the capabilities of the Extensions Manager Control Panel shown in Figure 2-9. Click the checkmark off to remove an Extension, System Extension (one found in the System Folder, not the Extension folder), or Control Panel. Disabled items are placed into the Extensions (Disabled), System Extensions (Disabled), or Control Panel (Disabled) folders. You can create sets of enabled and disabled Extensions as well as get information about an item by clicking on it once, as in the following example, which shows a set called My Settings with the Apple Menu Options item selected to display more information. You will still need to reboot your Macintosh to effect the new system configuration.

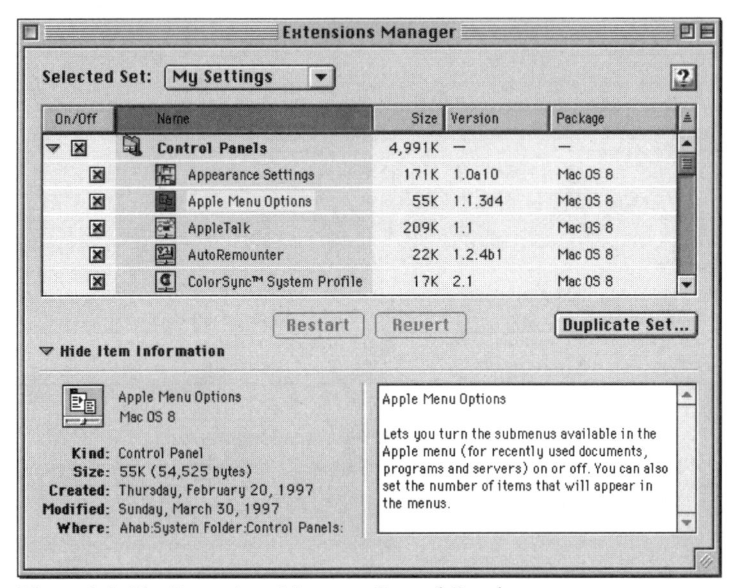

Figure 2-9: The Extensions Manager Control Panel.

The Fonts Folder

Support for a wide range of typefaces has always been an important characteristic of the Macintosh, but Apple is still trying to figure out an elegant way of handling fonts in its system software.

The Fonts folder, introduced in System 7.1, holds PostScript screen fonts and printer fonts as well as TrueType and QuickDraw GX fonts. After screen fonts or TrueType fonts are added to the Fonts folder, they become available in all subsequently launched applications. Fonts moved out of the Fonts folder, or into subfolders of the Fonts folder, are no longer available to applications.

All aspects of working with Fonts in System 7.0 through Mac OS 8, including the Fonts folder, are described in detail in Chapter 11, "Fonts & Printing."

The Preferences Folder

Preferences files created by application programs and utilities also became important contributors to System Folder growth under System 6.0x. Starting with System 7, these files are stored in the Preferences folder, shown in Figure 2-10.

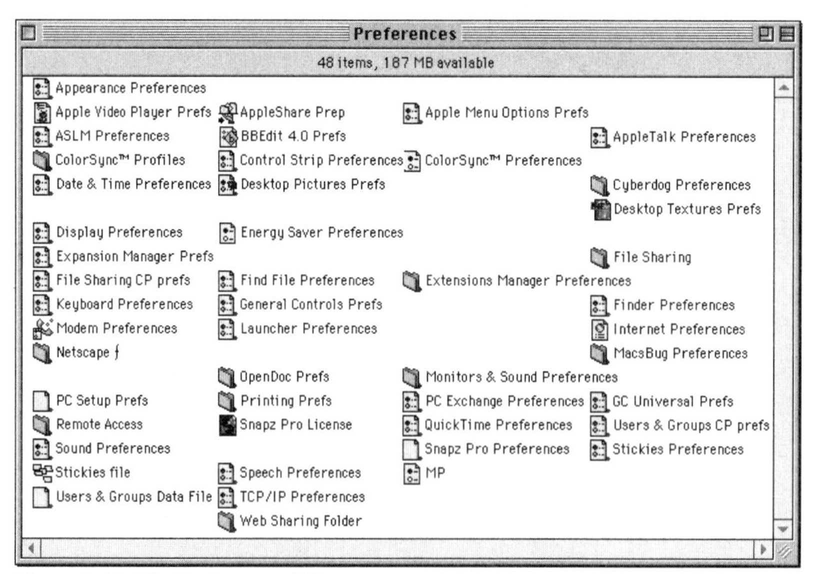

Figure 2-10: The Preferences folder.

As a user, you shouldn't have to do anything to the Preferences folder or its files. Your applications should create and maintain these files automatically. However, you might want to check this folder occasionally and delete the preferences files of unwanted applications or utilities that you've deleted from your drives. This will speed up the time it takes for your computer to start up and free up some space on your hard drive.

If you have made changes to a preferences file and want to go back to the default condition you had when you first installed an application, you can try removing the preferences file from the Preferences folder (but don't delete the file until you're sure you haven't lost any important settings). You can also try locking a preferences file (through the Get Info properties of a file) to prevent the contents of the file from being overwritten. This works in certain circumstances, but not all.

The Startup Items Folder

Applications, documents, folders, and volumes in the Startup Items folder automatically run (or open) each time your Macintosh is started or restarted. This folder takes the place of the Set Startup command found in the Special menu of previous system software versions. As with the Apple Menu Items folder, most of the icons in the Startup Items folder will probably be aliases, as shown in Figure 2-11.

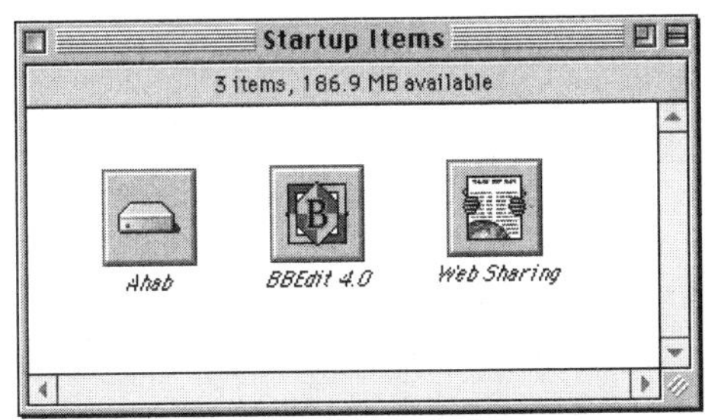

Figure 2-11: The Startup Items folder with alias icons that will be launched or mounted at start-up.

While the Startup Items folder's main purpose is to open applications and documents, it's also a good place to put folder and volume icon aliases. These aliases will be opened, or mounted, at start-up—a simple but useful function. Of course, before mounting a networked volume, a password may be requested.

The System File

The System file remains the centerpiece of Macintosh system software, overseeing all basic Macintosh activities and assisting every application and utility that runs on the Macintosh. As a user, you can remain blissfully ignorant of most of the work performed by the System file. However, you should understand the System file's traditional role as home to fonts, desk accessories, FKEYs, sounds, and keyboard resources.

When stuffed with these items, a single System file in the days before System 7 could grow to 600K or larger—often much larger. This overload often resulted in an unstable System file that would easily and frequently become corrupt, making the annoying and time-consuming effort of deleting and rebuilding the System file necessary.

The release of System 7 provided some relief to bulging System files by providing the Apple Menu Items folder (described earlier in this chapter) as the new default home for desk accessories (DAs) and by allowing DAs to be converted into stand-alone applications that can be stored anywhere on your hard disk (as described in Chapter 7, "Mac OS 8 & Your Software"). As a result of these two changes, DAs are no longer stored inside the System file.

Fonts, on the other hand, remained in the System file in System 7.0, although in System 7.1 and later they moved to the new Fonts folder, as described earlier in this chapter. For more information about fonts, see Chapter 11.

System File Access

Before System 7, the only way to add or remove fonts, desk accessories, FKEYs, or sounds was to use specialized utilities such as the Font/DA Mover or ResEdit. In System 7 and Mac OS 8, the System file's contents can be manipulated directly. You can open the System file by double-clicking on it as if it were a folder, and a window opens, displaying icons for the fonts, sounds, and keyboard configurations it currently contains, as shown in Figure 2-12.

While the System file is open, any font, sound, and keyboard files will appear as individual icons. Double-clicking on any of the icons will open the resource file, playing the sound or displaying a font sample, as in Figure 2-13.

Sounds (but not Fonts) and keyboard files can be added to the System file by simply dragging their icons into the System file window, the same way files are dragged in or out of any normal Mac folder. (All other applications must be closed before adding to the System file.) To remove fonts or sounds, drag their icons out of the open System Folder window and into another folder or volume or directly into the Trash.

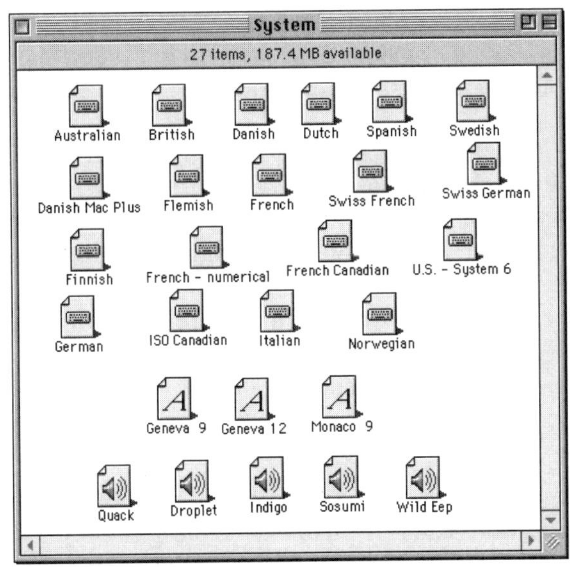

Figure 2-12: An open System file window.

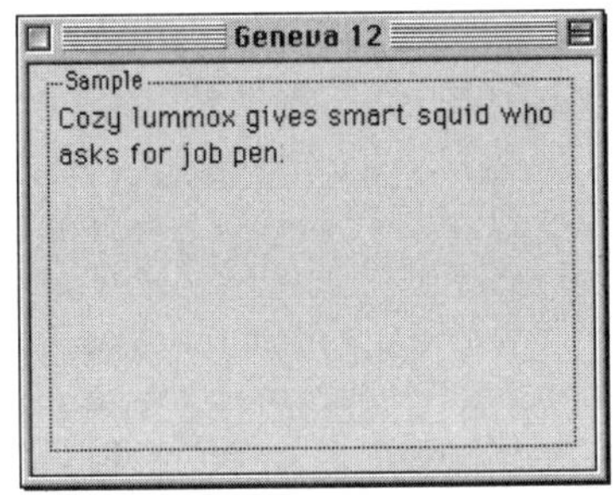

Figure 2-13: Both bitmapped and TrueType fonts can be installed in the System file in Mac OS 8.

Modifying the System Folder

The System Folder and its subfolders are created by the Installer when you first install Mac OS 8, and at that time, all system software files are placed into their proper locations. The System Folder is constantly modified, however, as you install other software applications or perform other common tasks on your Macintosh.

There are several types of files added to the System Folder after the initial installation: fonts and sounds, system Extensions (which add functions to the system software), and miscellaneous files that enable other software applications to function properly.

System Extensions modify the way the system software works or extend the options provided by system software features. They include Extensions, Control Panels, and printer or network drivers. There are hundreds of examples of Extensions and drivers that modify your system software. SuperClock, Pyro, Vaccine, DOS Mounter, NetModem, Mail-Saver, Autographix, PageSaver, and After Dark are a few of the most popular. You've probably added files of this type to your System Folder.

Many applications store miscellaneous files in the System Folder—files that don't interact directly with the system software. They're placed in the System Folder for other reasons:

- **Safety.** The System Folder is the only "common ground" on a Mac hard drive that applications can rely on in every configuration.
- **Simplicity.** The Macintosh operating system can easily find the System Folder regardless of what it's called and where it's located. This allows applications quick access to files stored in the System Folder.
- **Security.** The System Folder is a safe place for applications to add files because most users are not likely to disturb files in their System Folder.

To improve further upon the safety factor of placing files in your System Folder, you can enable the Protect System Folder option found in the General Controls Control Panel. This feature essentially locks the folder so that changes can't be made to it. If you create a folder called the Application folder, then you can use the Protect Application Folder option in the same Control Panel. Files in a protected folder cannot be removed or renamed. Changes to files (such as preferences files) can occur, however.

Some of the many application-related files (or folders) that use your System Folder as a safe storage place are Microsoft Word's Word Temp files (later versions of Word store temp files in the Word folder), the PageMaker and FreeHand Aldus folder, and StuffIt's Encryptors, Translators, Claris translators, and Viewers.

Printer font files are also in this category. Printer fonts are placed in the Fonts folder so they are available when needed for automatic downloading to a PostScript printer and so they can be found by Adobe Type Manager. They can also be in the System file as well, but you should try to keep them in the Fonts folder. Printer font files are usually the most space-consuming files in the System Folder, when loading in the System file—30K to 50K each. Although utilities like Suitcase II and MasterJuggler make it possible to store printer and screen fonts in other locations, many people choose to keep them in the System Folder anyway. It's the preferred location when you have a static set of fonts that you normally work with.

Adding Files to the System Folder

There are several ways that files may be added to the System Folder after its creation:

- **By the Apple Installer.** To add additional printer drivers, network drivers, or keyboards, you can rerun the Apple Installer application at any time. The Installer adds the selected files to your System Folder, placing them into the proper subfolders.

  You don't have to use the Installer to add drivers or files from the system software disks; you can drag-copy files directly from these disks into your System Folder.

- **By application software installers.** Many software applications use installation programs that copy the software and its associated files to your hard drive. Installers that have been specifically written or updated for compatibility with Mac OS 8 can place files correctly into the Mac OS 8 System Folder or subfolders.

  Older installer applications often place all files directly in the System Folder, ignoring the subfolder structure. In these cases, the application may require that the files remain as positioned by the installer. However, most Extensions should be moved to the Extensions folder, and Control Panels should be moved to the Control Panels folder—regardless of how they were originally positioned. Although all Extensions should be placed in the Extensions folder or Control Panels folder, most items of this nature located directly in the System Folder will be executed at start-up.

- **By software applications.** Historically, many software applications read and write temporary and preferences files to the System Folder. Others use the System Folder for dictionaries and other ancillary files. Applications updated for System 7 should properly read and write files in the System Folder and its subfolders.

  Older applications not rewritten for System 7 may not use the subfolders, but files placed directly in the System Folder will be accessed properly and won't cause any problems for your system software or other programs. In the interest of further System Folder simplification, new program releases will address subfolder location.

- **By you—the Macintosh user.** Since some programs and utilities don't use installer applications, many files must be placed into the System Folder manually. These files can be dragged onto the System Folder icon or dragged into an open System Folder window.

When files are dragged onto the System Folder icon, the Mac OS automatically places them in the System Folder or correct subfolder. This helps you add files to the System Folder correctly if you are adding them manually, even if you know nothing about the System Folder structure.

Before positioning files, the Helping Hand informs you it's at work and tells you how it's positioning your files, as shown in Figure 2-14. The Helping Hand works only when files are dragged onto the System Folder icon.

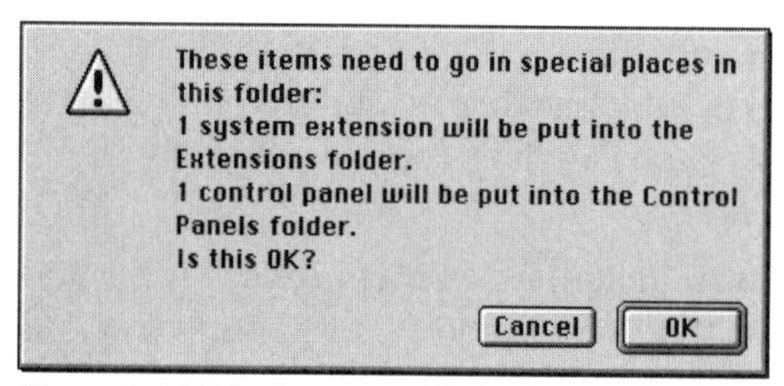

Figure 2-14: The System Folder's Helping Hand makes sure files are positioned properly.

Of course, once files are in the System Folder, you can reposition them freely. The Helping Hand will not affect the movement of files within the System Folder.

You can also avoid the action of the Helping Hand by dragging files directly onto the System Folder and navigating the subfolders using the spring loaded-folder feature. When you drag files this way, you can place files into any System Folder subfolder, or into the System Folder itself, without interference.

Deleting Files From the System Folder

For the most part, files in the System Folder can be deleted just like any other file, by dragging them into the Trash. However, some files cannot be deleted because they're "in use." "In-use" files include the System file, the Finder, any Extensions or Control Panels with code that ran at start-up, open Control Panels, and any temporary or preferences files used by open applications.

To delete the System file or Finder, you must restart the Macintosh using another boot disk. To delete an "in-use" Extension or Control Panel, move the file out of the Extensions or Control Panels folder, restart the Mac, and then delete the file. To delete open Control Panels or temporary or preferences files of open applications, simply close the Control Panel or application and drag the file to the Trash.

Moving On

Working in the System Folder used to be like playing with a house of cards, but as we've seen, Mac OS 8 brings new order and stability to this important part of your hard drive. The subfolders that are especially useful:

- The Apple Menu Items folder lets you customize your Apple Menu.
- The Extensions folder contains all the Extensions and drivers that add features to your Mac and the system software.
- The Control Panels folder holds special "mini-applications" that set preferences for system software features, utilities, and even hardware peripherals.
- The Startup Items folder lets you determine which files and applications are opened each time your Mac is turned on.

In Chapter 3 we'll examine two important aspects of the operating system, the Finder and the Desktop, both of which provide the interface and tools that help control the disks and files you use on the Macintosh.

CHAPTER 3

The Finder & Desktop

Most people don't think of the Finder as a software application, but it really is—just like your word processor, spreadsheet, or graphics program. But while each of those other applications is dedicated to the creation and manipulation of one specific type of data, the unfortunately named Finder focuses on helping you manage your disks and files.

It does this by providing you with the well-known Macintosh Desktop, with icons for each disk, drive, folder, and file plus the Finder menus and the Trash. The Finder lets you view and modify the contents of your disks and drives in many different ways and allows you to launch other applications or Control Panels. Most people think of the Desktop as the Finder, but the Desktop is really a window you use to view into the Finder.

Mac OS 8 introduces many enhancements to the Finder, providing more information about your disks and files, more consistency in commands and features, and additional customizing capabilities. Fortunately these benefits came without a change in the Finder's familiar interface—if you were comfortable working in System 7.x, you'll have no problem adjusting to the new Finder and taking advantage of its expanded capabilities.

This chapter starts by examining the Finder's menu commands and then looks at Finder windows. Other features in Mac OS 8's Finder, such as Apple Guide, Balloon Help, the Trash, and the Get Info dialog box, are also covered, as well as features new to Mac OS 8, including spring-loaded folders and tabbed folders.

This chapter is not, however, the only place in this book where you'll read about new Finder capabilities. Many Finder features are introduced in this chapter and then elaborated on in other chapters where the context is more appropriate. For example, aliasing, the Find command, and the Label menu are discussed in Chapter 5, "Managing Your Hard Drive." The About This Computer command is described in detail in Chapter 9, "Application & Memory Management." The Sharing command is explained in Chapter 16, "File Sharing." You'll be directed to more detailed discussions of these features throughout this chapter.

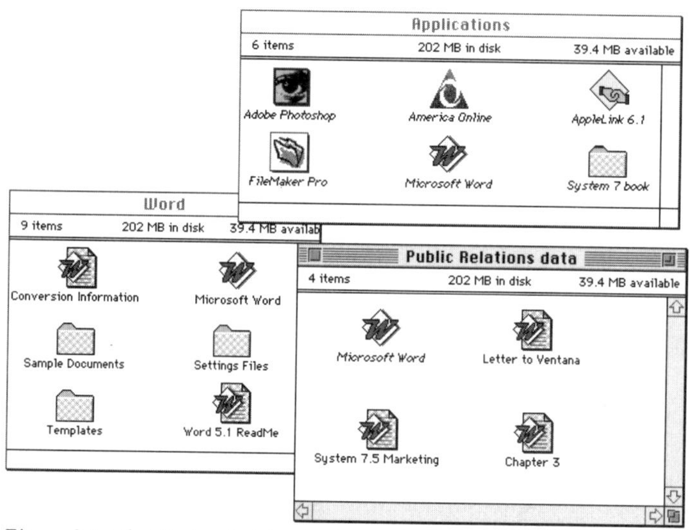

Figure 3-1: The Finder Desktop in System 7.0.1.

Figure 3-1 shows the Finder Desktop in System 7.0.1. In Figure 3-2, which shows the new Finder Desktop, you may notice a few new Desktop elements:

- A new Help menu in place of the Balloon Help icon.
- The removal of the Label menu.
- Tabbed folders.

Of course, the first thing you may have noticed is the change in the overall appearance of the interface. The way the OS draws windows has changed to offer a more appealing 3D look.

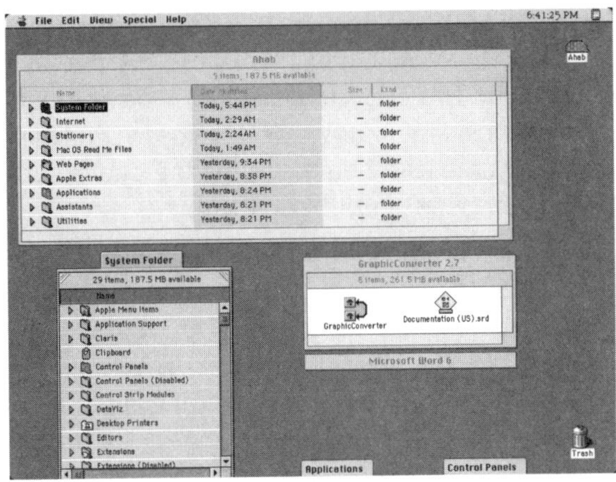

Figure 3-2: The Finder Desktop Mac OS 8.

New Finder Menus

A good way to become familiar with any new or upgraded application is by taking a quick tour through its menu bar and menu commands. We'll use this approach to start learning about the Finder. Figure 3-3 shows the Finder menus and commands as they appear on most systems when Mac OS 8 is first installed. Your menus may vary slightly depending on your hardware configuration and option settings.

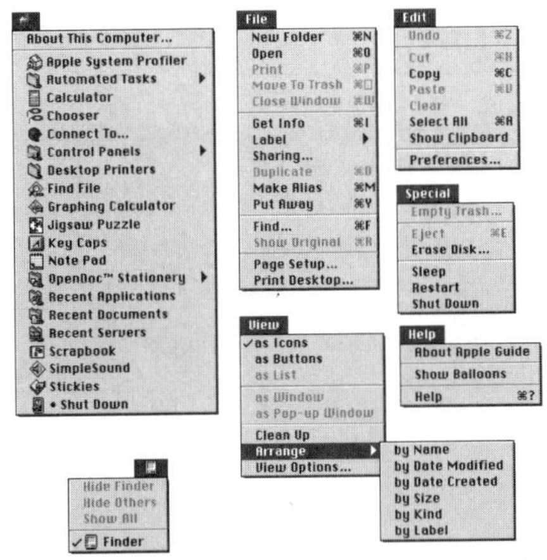

Figure 3-3: The default Finder menus in Mac OS 8.

Most of the Finder commands are unchanged in name or position from System 7.x, and most work the same today as they did previously. To save space (and avoid boring you), this section focuses only on commands new to Mac OS 8's Finder or previous commands that have been improved or upgraded. The new commands are listed on the following pages in the order they appear in the menus, from left to right on the menu bar:

- **About This Computer (Apple menu).** The dialog box this command brings up displays information about your computer such as available physical memory, virtual memory, and open applications. (More information about this dialog box appears in Chapter 9.) This menu choice used to be called About This Macintosh, but since several companies now make Mac-OS-compatible clones, Apple changed the name of this option.
- **Recent Documents, Recent Applications, and Recent Servers submenus (Apple menu).** Selecting one of these commands displays a list of your most recently used files, applications, and servers, allowing you to launch a file or application or mount a server. This is a tremendous time-saver, one you are likely to use frequently in your daily work.

  The submenus are controlled by the Apple Menu Options Control Panel shown in Figure 3-4. Using this panel, you can turn submenus on and off and set the number of recent files, applications, and servers you want your Macintosh to remember. Your most recently used item replaces your least recently used item in the list. In computer jargon, it's "first in, first out." If you use an item more than once, the date of last use determines its position in the stack.

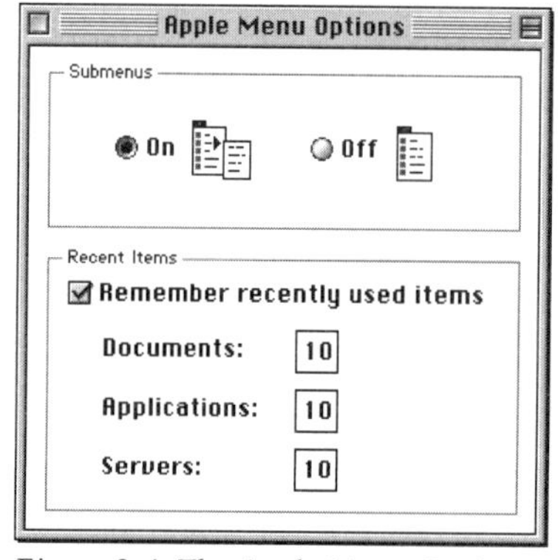

Figure 3-4: The Apple Menu Options Control Panel.

- **Move to Trash (File menu).** This command allows you to throw a selected item into the Trash without having to drag it there. To use this command, select an item to delete by clicking on it once; then choose this command or use the keyboard equivalent (Command+Delete).
- **Label (File menu).** The Label menu has moved from being a menu unto itself to being a submenu under the File menu. It works just as it has in several previous version of the OS; only its location has changed. See the Edit | Preferences option later in this list for more information on how to configure the names and colors of the labels.
- **Find (Apple, File menu).** The Find command replaces the Find File desk accessory of pre-System 7.5 system software versions. The Find command can search for files by filename, size, creation date, label, and so on, and when files matching your search criteria are located, the Finder opens a window containing the file (or files) and selects the file's icon. Using the Find Again command (Command+G), you can repeat the last search, locating and displaying the next file matching the current search criteria.

  Finding a number of items that match the search criteria with the Find command prior to 7.5 was a time-consuming procedure with Find and Find Again (and Find Again). In Mac OS 8, the Find dialog box ends a search by displaying the Found Items dialog box showing *all* of the documents, applications, or disks that match the search criteria (see Figure 3-5). Just double-click on the name to go to the location of your selection. Finding items is covered in much greater detail in Chapter 5.

  Note that the Found Items dialog box is Macintosh Drag and Drop enabled; this means you can drag a file onto your Desktop or into a window to move it, onto an application icon to open it, to a printer icon (with QuickDraw GX installed) to print it, and so on. Figure 3-5 shows an example of this window.
- **Show Original (File menu).** The Show Original menu option is identical to the Reveal Original option of System 7.x., which allows you to select an alias and then find its original file, folder, or application. In older versions of the OS, one could also click an alias, choose Get Info from the File menu, and then click a button entitled Find Original. This option is no longer available in Mac OS 8 when you select Get Info on an alias.
- **Preferences (Edit menu).** The Edit menu is rearranged to move the Show Clipboard menu choice up one notch in the menu to make room for the Preferences menu option, shown in Figure 3-6. The Preferences option takes the place of System 7.x's Views Control Panel and the Label menu. It also adds choices on how the Finder is presented and the spring-loaded folders are configured.

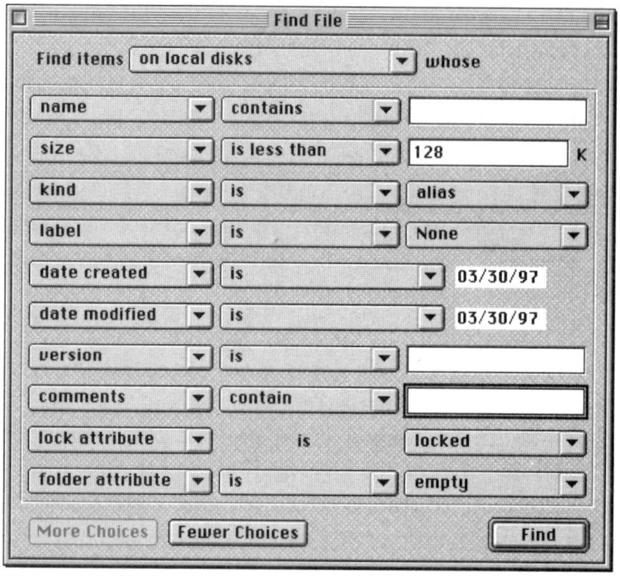

Figure 3-5: The Find dialog box with all its choices visible.

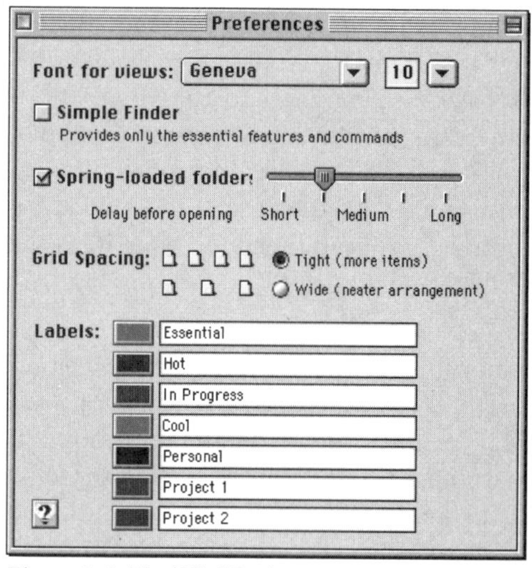

Figure 3-6: The Edit | Preferences menu takes the place of several others and adds new features.

- **View menu**. Perhaps one of the more dramatic changes found in the Mac OS 8 interface is the change to the View menu. Shown in Figure 3-7, there are three ways you may view the contents of a folder—as icons, as buttons, or as a list—which you can select and modify in the View Options menu choice at the bottom of the View menu.

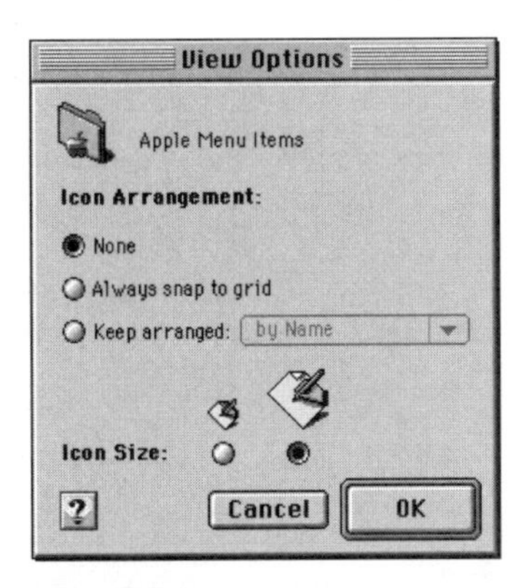

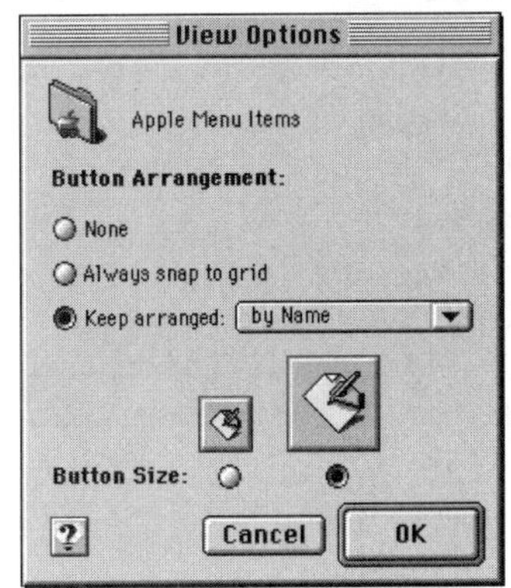

Figure 3-7: The View menu provides several new ways to view the contents of a folder or hard drive.

In addition to viewing the contents of a folder or hard drive as icons, buttons, or lists, Mac OS 8 introduces yet another way to view folders and their contents: the pop-up window, three of which are shown in Figure 3-8 (two minimized and one opened). When a folder is dragged to the bottom of the screen, it turns into a tabbed pop-up window, only one of which is able to "pop up" at a time. You can resize the window or "bring it back" as a normal window by lifting it up or out with the resizing corners on either side.

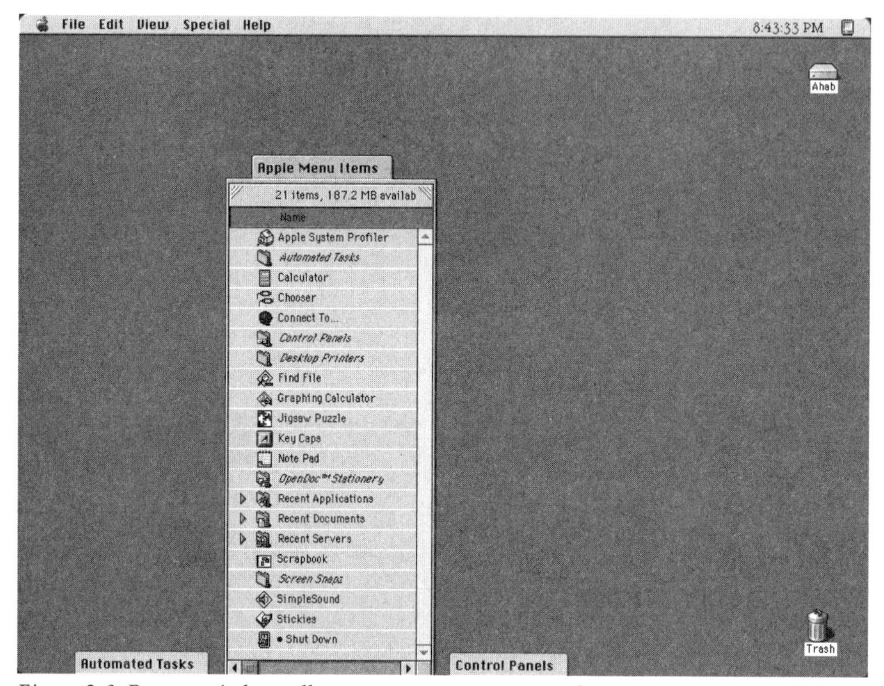

Figure 3-8: Pop-up windows allow you to manage your Desktop more efficiently.

- **Clean Up (View menu).** The Clean Up menu option has been moved from the Special menu, where it was called Clean Up Window. This option performs the same task as before, which is helping to unclutter icons, and has just been renamed and moved to the View menu.
- **Arrange (View menu).** The Arrange menu option is available when viewing the contents of a folder or hard drive by Icons or by List, and in the latter case, the menu option is called Sort List. If viewed by Icons, the options are to Arrange by Name, Date Modified, Date Created, Size, Kind, or Label. If viewed by List, the Sort List options are by Name, Date Modified, Size, and Kind.
- **Special**. The Special menu is the same as before with two minor exceptions. First, the Clean Up Window option found in earlier versions of the Mac OS has been moved to the View menu and renamed Clean Up. Second, the remaining items in the Special menu have been regrouped so that Sleep, Restart, and Shut Down all appear at the bottom of the menu in a single grouping.

- **Help menu.** Another big change in Mac OS 8 is the removal of the Balloon Help icon from next to the Application menu. However, although it is now its own menu, the contents of the menu are pretty much the same as the Balloon Help menu of earlier versions of the OS. You may select Show Balloons to activate Balloon Help, or you may select Help (or press Command+?) to open Apple Guide, the Mac OS's main method of providing help to users, shown in Figure 3-9.

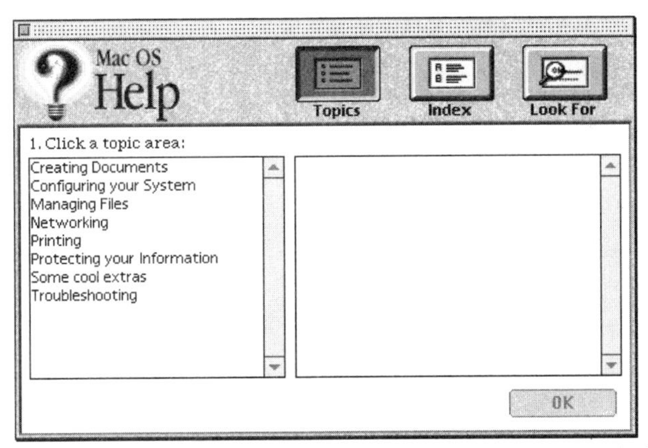

Figure 3-9: You can still choose Apple Guide and Balloon Help from the newly named Help menu.

Both Apple Guide and Balloon Help are available at all times in your applications, not just in the Finder. The quality and quantity of help you get in either help system is determined by whether and how well the developer of your software chose to implement it.

The Show Balloons command turns on context-sensitive help balloons that pop up as you point to menu commands, dialog box options, icons, and other Macintosh screen elements. To turn balloons off, select the Hide Balloons command. (More on the Help menu is presented later in this chapter.) Beginners seem to like Balloon Help, whereas more advanced users hate it.

In System 7.5 and beyond, Apple Guide has become the de facto standard help system. Simply choose the Help command from the Help menu or press the Command+? keystroke to open Apple Guide. (Don't forget to hold down the Shift key to type a question mark character.) Apple Guide can also be customized.

- **Application menu.** The Application menu is located in the upper right corner of your screen and is used as the primary method of switching between open applications. It's available at all times, not just when you're using the Finder. The Application menu is shown in Figure 3-10.

  The name of every open application will automatically appear in this menu. To switch from one application to another, choose the name you want from the Application menu, and that application and its windows immediately appear.

Figure 3-10: The Application menu.

Note that in most cases only your current application, the one selected with a check mark in the Application menu, is actually running and processing. There are some processes like printing and communications that can run in the background, but there are others that do not.

The Macintosh saves the status of your other applications and processes in memory so that it can return to them, a feature called multithreading. Moving between applications (and threads) is called context switching. Running applications sessions concurrently, called multitasking, is being written into system software gradually. We'll have more to say about this in subsequent chapters, particularly in Chapter 7, "Mac OS 8 & Your Software," and Chapter 9, "Application & Memory Management."

Using the various Hide commands, you can use the Application menu to temporarily hide all windows from the current application or all windows except those of the current application, thus reducing the onscreen clutter that can result from running multiple applications at once.

If you've lost your place on the Desktop and menus have changed, check the Application menu to see what program is active in the foreground. This is a common beginner's mistake: clicking on the Desktop and switching to the Finder.

You may also "hide the Finder," a feature enabled in the General Controls Control Panel. The default condition is to show the Desktop in the background. Just click off the Show Desktop When in Background check box (found in the Desktop section) to hide the Finder and prevent losing your place when working in an application. When the Finder is hidden, you do not see any icons on the Desktop like the Trash, disk or drive icons, or folders.

Finder Windows

As a disk and file management tool, the Finder's menu commands play only a small part. Most of the time you move, copy, delete, arrange, and open files by using the mouse to directly manipulate icons on the Desktop and in Finder windows. In Mac OS 8, your ability to see and manipulate files and folders in windows was dramatically improved over the capabilities you had before System 7. The basic attributes of Finder windows, however, have not changed:

- Windows are created each time a volume or folder is opened.
- Each window has a title bar, zoom box, and close box.
- Windows can be freely positioned by dragging their title bars.
- Windows can be resized by dragging on the resize box.
- Windows display the files and folders contained in a single volume or folder.
- The window display is controlled via the View menu.

The improvements to the Finder in System 7 and then Mac OS 8, however, gave you more control over windows, a more consistent user interface, and a wider range of display options:

- The font, icon size, and information displayed in Finder windows are customizable.
- Keyboard commands let you navigate windows and select files without using the mouse.
- Smart zooming opens windows only enough to display their content.
- The contents of any folder or subfolder can be displayed in hierarchical format in any window.
- Hierarchical levels allow files in different folders to be manipulated simultaneously.

It's easy to get lost when you have a number of windows open on your screen. Most applications have a Window menu for just such occasions, but the Finder does not. It's particularly a problem on PowerBooks or Macs with very small displays. There are two features in Mac OS 8 that offer some help with window clutter. First, what used to be called WindowShade in System 7.5.x is now built into the OS. System 7.5.x included a version of WindowShade, formerly a shareware program. Using WindowShade is easy; just click twice on the title bar to reduce the window to its title bar only. Or, click once on what is known as the WindowShade widget (see Figure 3-11). Double-click again on the "minimized" window's title bar or click once on the widget to return the window to its full size. An example of a minimized window created by WindowShade is shown in Figure 3-11 along with the maximized window.

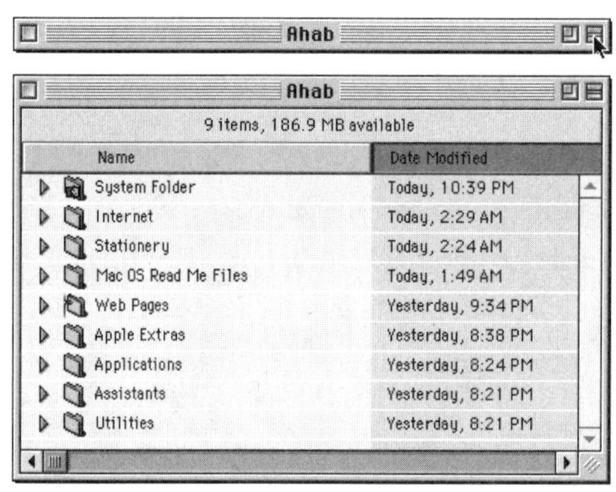

Figure 3-11: Using the WindowShade feature can help clean up a cluttered Desktop.

There used to be a Control Panel for customizing a few aspects of the WindowShade feature, but this capability is now part of the OS itself and cannot be customized or turned off.

Another improvement in Mac OS 8, which we've already seen, is the pop-up, or tabbed, folder feature, which allows you to minimize a folder or hard drive at the bottom of the screen (see Figure 3-8 for an example). This is a very handy feature that has been available to Mac OS users through commercial and shareware utilities for some time, and Apple has finally gotten around to including it into the OS itself. To use a pop-up window once it has been minimized, click on the title bar area once to open it up and click on it again to minimize it.

These and other new features and improvements to the operation of Finder windows are discussed in detail later in this chapter.

Finder Preferences

In older Finder versions, the presentation of text and icons in Finder windows was preset and could not be modified. Text was always listed in Geneva 9 point, and icons appeared in preset sizes in each icon view. In System 7, the Views Control Panel provides a variety of options that let you control the information and the way it's displayed in Finder windows. In Mac OS 8, the ability to view the contents of a folder or hard drive is much more flexible and customizable, not to mention more a part of the core OS rather than in the form of a Control Panel or Extension add-on.

Several elements of the Finder are configurable in the Edit | Preferences menu, as we've seen earlier. This menu takes the place of one half of the Views Control Panel and all the Label menus in System 7.5.x. In addition to allowing you to change the system font, grid spacing of icons, and labels, you can select the Simple Finder option and control the spring-loaded folder option. Figure 3-12 shows a customized Finder Preferences window; let's look at each of these elements in more detail.

Changes in Finder Preferences take effect upon closing the Preferences window.

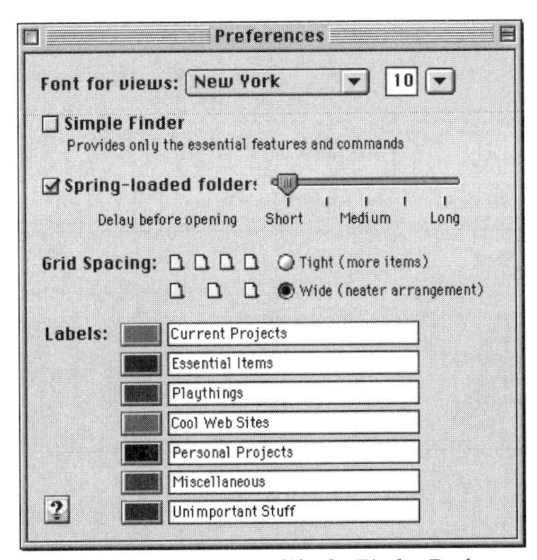

Figure 3-12: You may modify the Finder Preferences to suit your tastes.

There are five elements to the Finder Preferences menu option. The first is the Font for Views, a typeface and type size option that controls the display of text in all Finder windows. A Font drop-down menu presents the names of all installed fonts; you may select the one you want for all Finder windows. Use the size drop-down menu to select the point size for the text display. If you want to use a point size not available in the pop-up menu, type the size you want directly into the Size option box. Figure 3-13 shows several examples of different font sizes as viewed through the Finder.

Although it's appealing to be able to choose from such a wide range of fonts and sizes, you may want to stick with the default, Geneva 9 point. While it doesn't look very good in print, it provides the most legible font for onscreen display purposes.

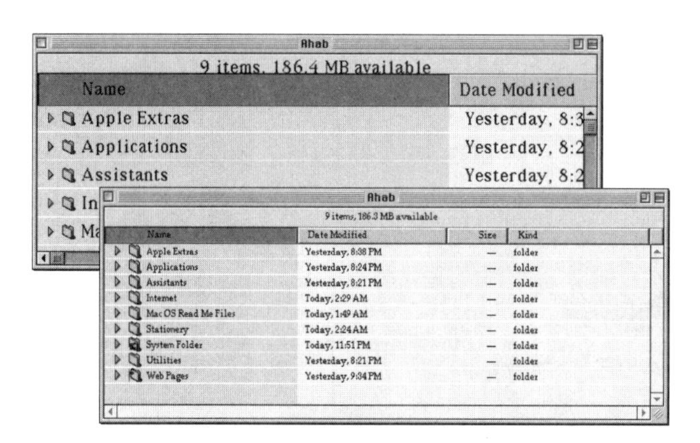

Figure 3-13: Finder windows in various fonts.

The second element in the Finder Preferences menu option is called Simple Finder. Checking this option will remove many of the menu options as well as all but one of their keyboard equivalents. This feature may be useful in certain settings such as elementary schools, learning situations like teaching labs, and if you want to let your children have a go at your computer. It simplifies the Finder by temporarily limiting the Finder menu choices and allows you to restore all the complex features by simply unchecking this menu choice.

The spring-loaded folder option (not to be confused with the pop-up folder feature) is a variation on the drag-and-drop capability of the Mac OS. The sliding rule lets you set the amount of time the OS will wait to spring open a folder onto which you have dragged an item such as a file or folder. Once it springs open, you can drop the item there. If you hold an item over a subfolder, that folder will spring open as well. To navigate backward, move the folder that is being relocated outside of the highlighted folder into which it is currently located (but not dropped). To start completely over, drag the item to the Desktop without letting go and hold it over the hard drive's icon. For example, Figure 3-14 shows an alias being moved two levels deeper from the Desktop into the hard drive and into a folder entitled Internet.

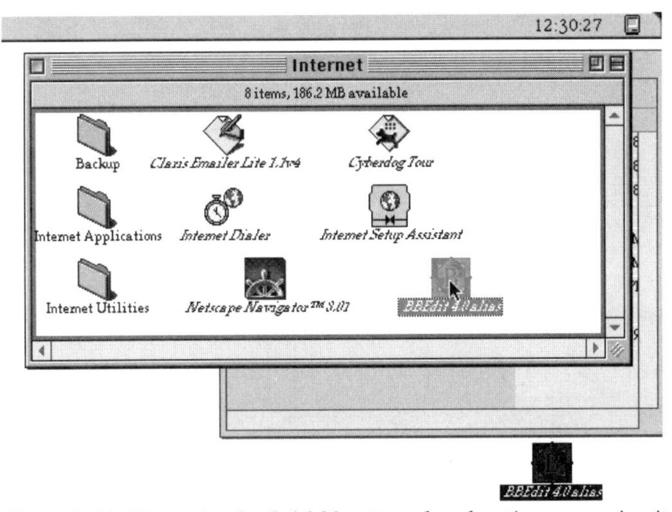

Figure 3-14: Use spring-loaded folders to make relocating or copying items much easier.

The next Finder Preference you may select is for the amount of space between items when viewed by icon or by button (but not by list). This feature is very handy if you like to view folders containing dozens or hundreds of items but are concerned with how much space is available on your monitor to display these items. If "desktop real estate" is limited, you should choose Tight

Grid Spacing. This will instruct the OS to leave as little space between icons as possible if you choose the Clean Up command from the View menu. Conversely, selecting the Wide Grid Spacing option will allow the OS to space icons further apart and prevent them from overlapping, which looks neater. Figure 3-15 shows an obvious example of wide-versus-narrow spacing.

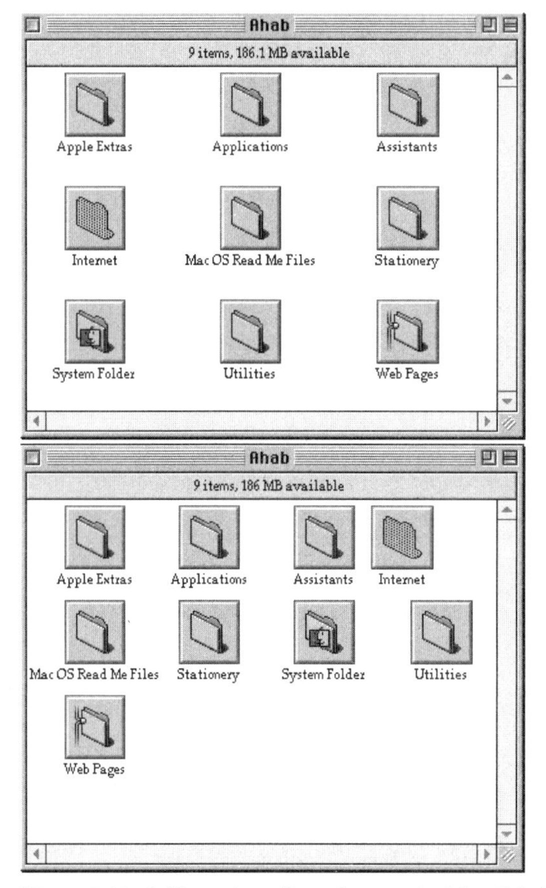

Figure 3-15: Grid spacing affects the way the Mac OS places icons and buttons on the Desktop.

The last Finder Preference you may configure is Labels. The new Label menu is in some ways similar to the Colors menu used in System 6.0x; it allows you to specify colors for file and folder icons. A few important improvements have been added to this colorization process since then, however.

You can now color-code your files by specifying a classification title for each color. In addition, color labels are supported by the View menu and Find command, so you can use label categories as part of your hard-disk organization and management strategy. We'll look at an example of this in just a few minutes, but for now go ahead and type in a few meaningful (or non-meaningful!) phrases in the space provided.

The View Menu

The Finder's View menu, like View menus in past Finder versions, determines how information is displayed in the current active window. Previous versions of the View menu let you display files and folders by icon, small icon, name, date, size, kind, and color. In System 7, the View menu provides all these view methods except for color but adds View by label, version, and comment. Mac OS 8 goes even further and adds several new viewing features, buttons, and pop-up windows. Moreover, most of the options formerly found in the Views Control Panel are now found in the Finder's View menu. The three type of views available in Mac OS 8 are:

- As Icons
- As Buttons
- As List

Each time you apply a View menu command to a particular window, that window's display is arranged according to the selected format (by icon, by button, by list), and it retains that view format until a different View menu command is applied to it. When a window is closed and later reopened, it always appears in the same display view it had before it was closed. There's no way, unfortunately, to change the View option for all open or closed windows since the View menu controls each window independently.

View as Icons

In Mac OS 8, you may no longer view the contents of a folder by name only. There will always be an icon of some type (either large or small) associated with an item. The particular view command that's selected determines what View Options are available, as shown in Figure 3-16.

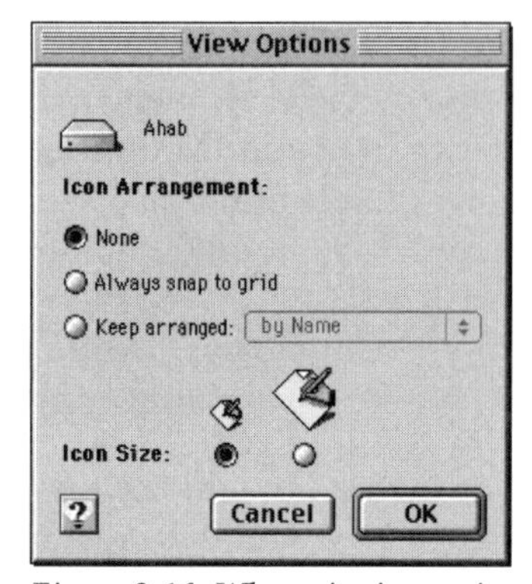

Figure 3-16: When viewing an icon, change the View Options settings for a folder or the Desktop to suit your preferences.

The following items may be found in the View Options menu for one or more of the three types of views.

- **Icon Arrangement: None**. This option tells the Finder that items in a particular folder are not to be arranged in any predetermined way.
- **Icon Arrangement: Always Snap to Grid**. The Always Snap to Grid option forces any repositioned icons or buttons to automatically snap to the nearest point on an invisible grid. This is the same invisible grid used by the Clean Up command and will result in either tight or wide baseline alignment depending on whether the Tight Grid or the Wide Grid option is chosen in the Finder Preferences (described earlier). The concept of keeping files always grid aligned in this way may sound appealing, but it can be disconcerting when the Finder grabs and relocates files while you're trying to position them. In most cases, it's probably better to leave this option off and use the Clean Up command to correct any icon alignment problems in Finder windows.
- **Icon Arrangement: Keep Arranged**. This option tells the Finder that items in a particular folder are to be arranged according to either name, date created, date modified, size, kind, or label. This may seem a bit odd at first because you can tell the Finder to arrange a group—not a list—of items by a criteria such as name or date created. The result is that the icons or buttons are listed in a particular order, left to right or top to bottom, like a list.

For example, Figure 3-17 shows the contents of a hard disk viewed as small icons but ordered by the date their contents were last modified. The result looks like a combination of a list and a window of icons.

Figure 3-17: Viewing the contents of a hard drive by small icons and date modified.

When viewing by icon, the following options are available under the Keep Arranged option under the View | View Options menu:

- **By Name.** This command sorts files and folders alphabetically (A through Z), from top to bottom, as shown in Figure 3-18.
- **By Date Modified.** This command sorts files by the date they were modified, with the most recently updated files at the top of the list. This view is useful when you're looking for files that are much older or much newer than most of the other files in a certain folder.
- **By Date Created.** This command sorts files by the date they were created, with the most recently updated files at the top of the list. When you copy a file or folder from another source, it will retain its original creation date.
- **By Size.** This command sorts files in descending size order. Otherwise, folders are grouped alphabetically at the end of the list. Commonly, the By Size command is used to find files known to be either very large or very small or to locate large files that could be deleted to free up space.
- **By Kind.** This command sorts files alphabetically by a short description based on the file type, a four-letter code assigned by the developer or application creator. Document files associated with a particular application program include the name of their application, using Word 5.1 document or HyperCard 2.2 document, for example, as the kind. Common file kinds include Alias, Application Program, Chooser Extension, Database Extension, Desk Accessory, Document, Folder, and System Extension. Viewing files by kind is useful if you know the kind of file you're looking for and if the window containing that file has many different files in it.

- **By Label.** This command sorts by the label name given to the file with the Label command. Labels, as discussed in Chapter 5, group files according to some user-defined scheme. For example, you might have a group of files that all relate to personal (nonbusiness) issues, a group relating to one project you're working on, and so on. In any case, this command lets you sort the files in the current window according to labels previously applied. Files are arranged as they appear in the Label menu. Unlabeled files appear at the bottom of the listing.

View as Buttons

The View as Buttons option has the exact same viewing options as the View as Icons option, except you may choose to view by small or large buttons instead of small or large icons. Figure 3-18 shows the View as Buttons | View Options configuration window.

When viewing items as buttons, you only have to single-click them to open or launch them.

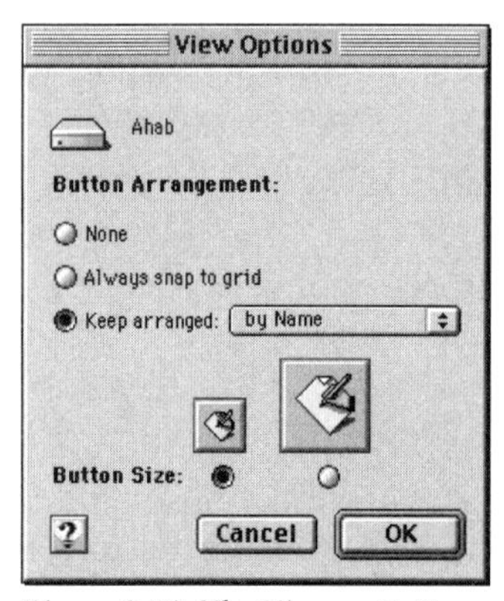

Figure 3-18: The View as Buttons option works exactly like the View as Icons option.

Even when viewing the contents of a folder or hard drive as buttons, you can still arrange them by date created, size, label, and so on. In Figure 3-19, the contents of the hard drive named Ahab are viewed as buttons and arranged by name; the names are listed left to right and top to bottom.

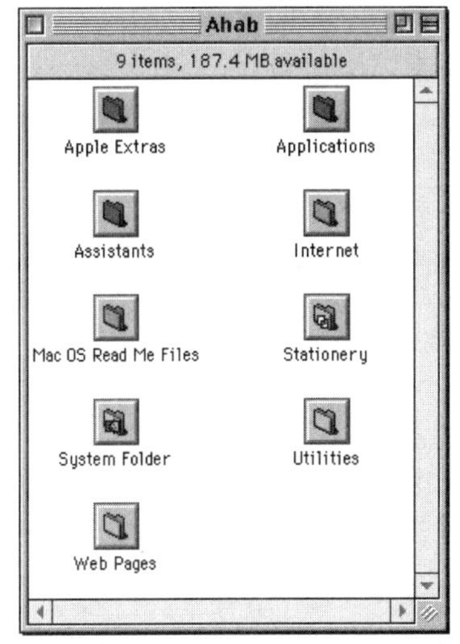

Figure 3-19: Viewing as buttons arranged by name.

View as List

Finally, a different set of View options becomes available when you are viewing the contents of a folder or hard drive as a list. These options, shown in Figure 3-20, are very similar to those found on previous versions of the Mac OS, especially System 7.5.x.

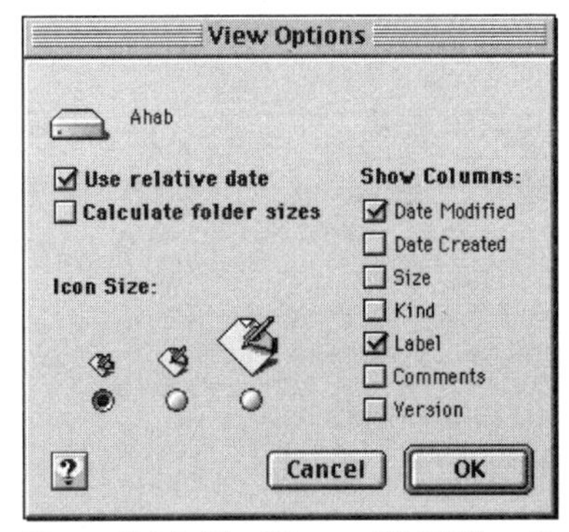

Figure 3-20: The View as List | View Options configuration window.

A few options are different when viewing as lists, including:

- **Use Relative Dates**. Documents created or modified recently will be listed as Today (time) and Yesterday (time), and all others will be listed as Date (time). This is helpful when you have a long list of documents and you want to quickly find the ones you've recently modified.
- **Calculate Folder Sizes**. Checking this option will cause the number of items in a window's subfolders to be calculated and displayed in the list view. Don't check this option unless you have to because it might slow down the performance of your computer dramatically.
- **Show Columns: By Comment.** This command sorts files alphabetically by the text contained in their Get Info dialog box comment fields. Displaying comment text in Finder windows is a major new file management feature, but it's useful only if the first characters of the comment are significant or if you just want to separate all files that have comments from those that don't. Files without comments are placed at the top of any windows using the View menu's By Comment command.
- **Show Columns: By Version.** Useful only for application files, this command sorts by the software developer's assigned version number. Ancillary application files (e.g., dictionaries and references) and data files you create do not have this type of version number.
- **Icon Sizes**. In addition to the small and large icon and button sizes, when you select View as List, you can also select a medium-sized icon. Figure 3-21 shows the hard drive Ahab viewed as a list and arranged by date modified.

Ahab

9 items, 187.7 MB available

Name	Date Modified	Label
System Folder	Today, 12:40 AM	–
Apple Extras	Wed, Apr 9, 1997, 2:46 PM	Essential
Internet	Wed, Apr 9, 1997, 2:43 PM	Project 1
Stationery	Wed, Apr 9, 1997, 2:37 PM	–
Web Pages	Wed, Apr 9, 1997, 2:37 PM	–
Applications	Wed, Apr 9, 1997, 2:32 PM	Essential
Assistants	Wed, Apr 9, 1997, 2:30 PM	Essential
Utilities	Wed, Apr 9, 1997, 2:30 PM	–
Mac OS Read Me Files	Wed, Apr 9, 1997, 2:29 PM	Project 1

Figure 3-21: Viewing the contents of a hard drive as a list.

Hierarchical List Views

This important feature displays as a list the contents of any folder without opening a new folder window. In previous versions, the only way to view and manipulate folder contents was to open the folder, thereby creating a new window. In System 7 and Mac OS 8, you can display any folder contents by clicking on the small triangle that appears to the left of the folder icon. The contents then appear, indented slightly beneath the folder icon, as shown in Figure 3-22.

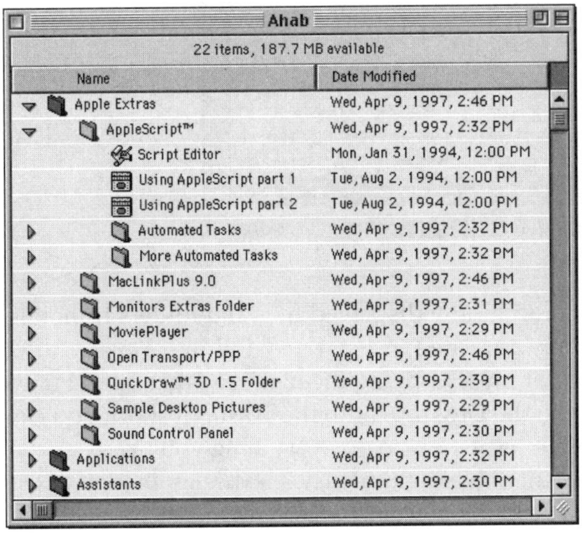

Figure 3-22: A Finder window with hierarchical display.

This display is a hierarchical view because it allows you to see the contents of several levels of nested folders (folders inside of folders) at one time simply by clicking on the triangle next to the appropriate folder. (Alias folder icons, which are discussed in Chapter 5, appear without a triangle and cannot be displayed hierarchically.) Figure 3-23 shows a window in which the aliased folder Apples & Oranges is not displayed hierarchically.

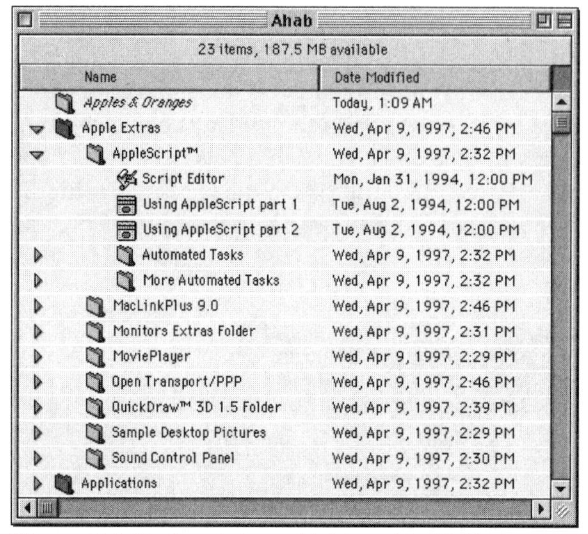

Figure 3-23: Finder window with hierarchical folders open.

You can drag hierarchically displayed files and folders from one location to another just as if they appeared in separate windows. You can also drag files or folders to other volumes (copying the files), to other open Finder windows (moving the files), to the Desktop, or to the Trash. In short, you can take advantage of the hierarchical view to do everything you need.

The primary benefit of hierarchical views is the elimination of Desktop clutter, since there's no need to open a new Finder window for every folder you want to open. In addition, hierarchical views allow you to select and manipulate files and folders from different hierarchical levels at the same time, which was not possible in previous Finder versions because each time you clicked the mouse in a new window, the selection in the previous window was released.

Figure 3-24 illustrates this ability, showing three different files and a folder, each on a different hierarchical level. The files and folder in this selection can now be copied, moved, trashed, or manipulated like any single file. To select files and folders at multiple levels of the hierarchy at the same time, hold down the Shift key while clicking on the filenames.

To collapse a folder's hierarchical display, click the downward pointing triangle next to the folder icon again; the enclosed files and folder listing disappear. When you close a window, the hierarchical display settings are remembered and will reappear the next time the window is opened.

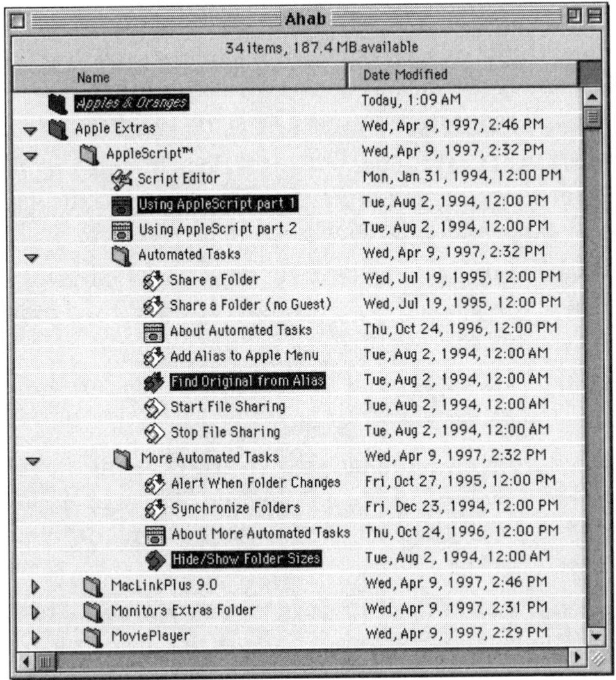

Figure 3-24: The Finder window showing multiple nested folders open with four files selected.

Of course, you can still open a new window for any folder rather than display its contents hierarchically. Simply double-click on the folder icon rather than the triangle. Or select the folder icon and then choose the Open command from the File menu.

Navigating From the Keyboard

Even though the Mac OS relies primarily on its graphical interface and the mouse, there are many times when you need keyboard control. A variety of keyboard shortcuts can now be used to select files, move between file windows, and manipulate icons. The keyboard commands that follow are available in all Finder windows and on the Desktop:

- **Jump to filename.** Typing the first few letters in a filename selects that file. For example, if you want to select a file named Budget, when you type *B*, the first filename starting with a *B* is selected. When the *u* is typed after the *B*, the selection will be the first filename starting with *Bu*, and so on. You must not pause between letters, or the Mac will interpret each additional letter as the first letter of a new search. If you don't know an exact filename, type an *A* to cause the display to scroll to the top of the list, an *L* to scroll to the middle, or a *Z* to scroll to the end.

- **Select next alphabetical filename.** This is done by pressing the Tab key. All files visible in the current window, including those displayed in hierarchically open folders, are included in this selection.
- **Select previous alphabetical filename.** Press Shift+Tab. This is useful when you press the Tab key one time too many and need to back up one step in reverse alphabetical order.
- **Select next file.** Down, Left, and Right arrow keys select the next file or folder icon in the respective direction.
- **Open selected folder.** Command+Down arrow opens the selected file or folder unless the selected file or folder is already open, in which case this key combination brings its window to the front. Command+O will also work.
- **Open selected file or folder and close current window.** Press Command+Option+Down arrow. If the selected file or folder is already open, this key combination brings its window to the front and closes the current folder or volume window. Command+Option+O will also work.
- **Open parent folder window.** Press Command+Up arrow. If the selected file or folder is already open, this key combination brings its window to the front.
- **Open parent folder window, close current window.** Pressing Command+Option+Up arrow closes the current window.
- **Edit filename.** Press Return. (Filenames can also be opened for editing by clicking the cursor on the text of the filename.) You can tell the name has been selected for editing when its display is inverted and a box is drawn around the filename. Once the filename is open for editing, the backspace key deletes characters and the Right and Left arrow keys position the cursor. Pressing Return again saves the filename changes and returns the name to an inverted display.
- **Make Desktop active.** Command+Shift+Up arrow makes the current window inactive and the Finder Desktop active.
- **Throw item into the Trash**. New to Mac OS 8 is the ability to throw one or more selected items into the Trash by pressing Command+Delete.

The following keyboard commands are available only when working in Finder windows viewed as lists (By Name, Size, Kind, Version, Label, or Comment):

- **Expand hierarchical display.** Command+Right arrow hierarchically displays the folder contents.
- **Expand all hierarchical displays.** Command+Option+Right arrow hierarchically displays the contents of the current folder and all enclosed folders.
- **Collapse hierarchical display.** Command+Left arrow collapses the hierarchical display of the current folder.
- **Collapse all hierarchical displays.** Command+Option+Left arrow collapses the hierarchical display of the current folder and all enclosed folders.

Dragging Files Between Windows

Another feature of Mac OS 8 lets you select and move a file from an inactive window. In Finder versions previous to System 7, as soon as an icon was selected, the window containing that icon became the active window and was brought forward. This created a problem when that window overlapped and obscured other folder icons. In the Finder, any visible icon in any window can be selected and dragged to a new location without the source file window becoming active, as shown in Figure 3-25.

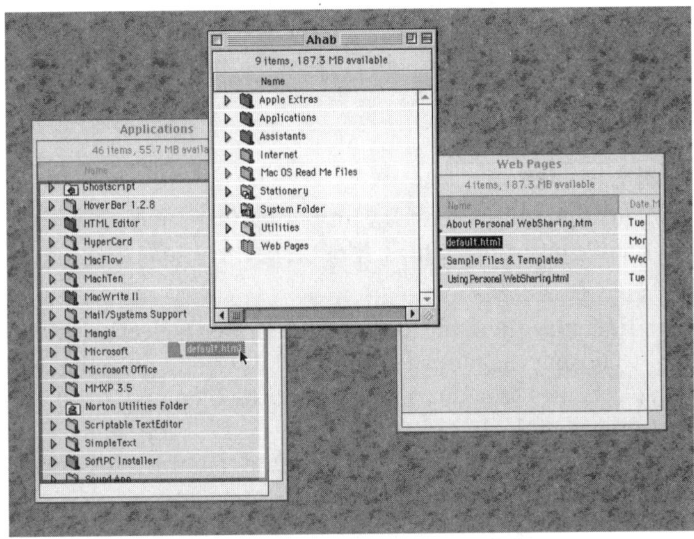

Figure 3-25: Dragging files between overlapping windows.

This feature is more clearly described by an example. Suppose we want to drag a file or folder from the Web Pages window into a folder called Applications. This would be impossible in Finder versions older than System 7 without repositioning the Applications window; as soon as the default.html file was selected in the Web Pages window, the Web Pages window would become active, which would add a step to the process.

To move a Finder window without making it active, hold down the Command key while dragging the inactive window's title bar.

In Mac OS 8's Finder, however, we can simply point the mouse to the item to be moved from the Web Pages window and hold the mouse button down while dragging the icon over the Ahab window on its way into the Applications window. As long as the mouse button is not released, only a single mouse movement is required to move the file.

However, this method cannot be used to move more than one file at a time. To move multiple files from Web Pages to Applications, the Ahab window would have to be repositioned. To move a Finder window without making it active, hold down the Command key while dragging the inactive window's title bar.

In order to give the user more feedback, when you drag items over and into a window, the inside of the window that will contain the item becomes outlined. This feature first appeared in System 7.1 and System 7 Pro and is preserved in Mac OS 8.

Working With Multiple Files

To perform any operation on one or more files in a window or on the Desktop, first select the file or group of files. Most aspects of selecting files in Mac OS 8 are the same as in System 7.x.

- **Immediate marquee selection.** The marquee (selection rectangle), created by clicking the mouse button and dragging with the button pressed, now selects files as soon as any part of the filename or icon is inside the selection rectangle. In previous versions, files were not selected until the mouse button was released, and only files completely contained in the selection rectangle were selected.

- **Marquee selection in all views.** Previously, the marquee could be used only in By Icon or By Small Icon views or on the Desktop. In System 7.5, marquee selection is supported in all Finder windows; for example, you can drag-select in the By Name or By Date views. In Mac OS 8, you can use the marquee selection when windows are viewed as icons, lists, and buttons, as shown in Figure 3-26.

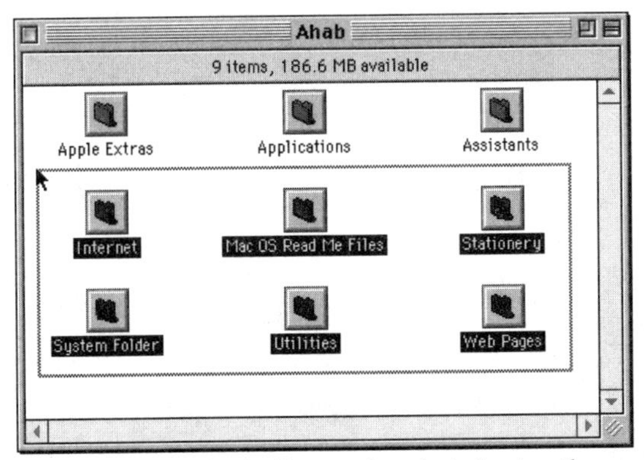

Figure 3-26: Multiple files can be selected using the marquee, even when files are listed by name.

- **Shift select.** Use the Shift key while drawing a marquee to select noncontiguous sections of any Finder window.
- **File dragging.** It's still possible to drag files by clicking on their names. To open a filename for editing, click on a filename and wait a few seconds for a box to appear around the filename. To move a button, you must drag it by the title, not the actual button.
- **Finder scrolling.** When dragging with a marquee, the Finder window scrolls automatically as soon as the cursor hits one of its edges, as shown in Figure 3-27. This is very useful when selecting in Finder windows displaying icons.

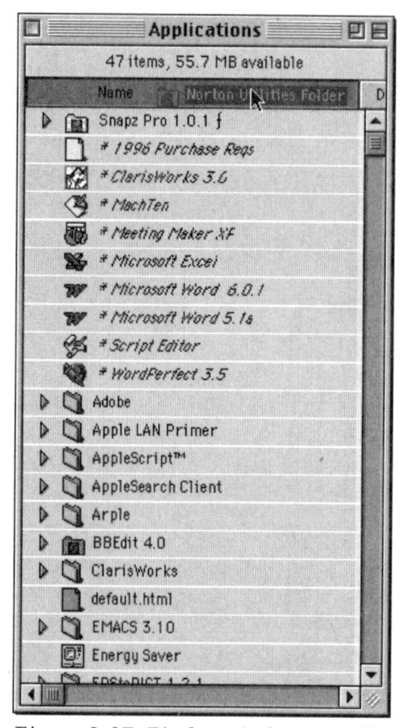

Figure 3-27: Finder windows scroll automatically when items are dragged past their edges.

Title Bar Pop-Up Menu

While hierarchical window views make it easy to move down the folder hierarchy, there's also a new way to move up the folder hierarchy—via a pop-up menu that appears in the title bar of any window when you hold down the Command key and click on the folder's name in the title bar.

Figure 3-28 shows the pop-up menu for a folder named ClarisWorks, which is inside the Applications folder, which is on the hard drive named Skipper. This pop-up menu displays the current folder's parent folder names and the volume on which the current folder is located.

Selecting a folder or volume name from this pop-up menu opens a new Finder window that displays the folder or volume contents. If a window for the selected folder or volume is already open, that window is brought forward and made active. This feature is a real time-saver when hunting files down in the Finder.

Holding down the Option and Command keys while selecting a folder or volume name from the title bar pop-up menu causes the current window to be closed as the new folder or volume is opened, helping you avoid a cluttered Desktop by automating the process of closing windows that aren't being used.

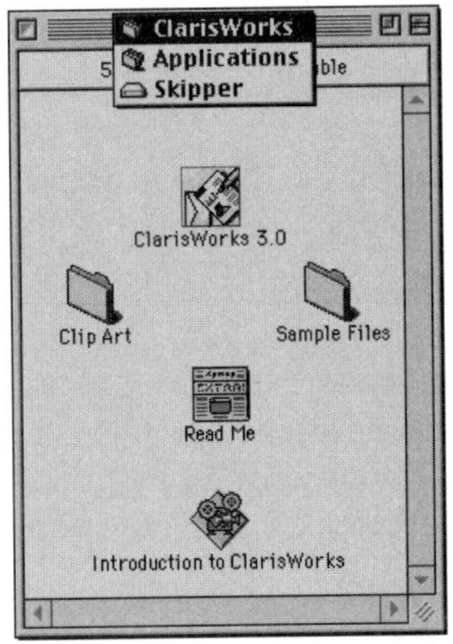

Figure 3-28: You can navigate backward through your hard drive by holding down the Option key while clicking the mouse on the title bar.

Holding down the Option key also closes windows in several other situations:

- **Folders.** While opening a folder by double-clicking on its icon at the Finder, the current folder will close as the new one is opened.
- **Windows.** While clicking the close box in any Finder window, all Finder windows close.
- **Applications.** While launching an application, the window in which the application icon appears closes.

Improved Zooming

To resize an open window, you can either drag the size box in the lower right corner or click in the zoom box in the upper right corner of the window's title bar (to the left of the WindowShade widget). The zoom box expands the window size just enough to display the complete file list or all file and folder icons; it no longer opens the window to the full size of the current monitor unless that size is necessary.

Cleaning Up Windows & Icons

As in previous system software versions, the Clean Up command rearranges icons in Finder windows or on the Desktop to make them more orderly and visible. Several new Clean Up options were added in System 7, however, to help arrange icons in specific situations or to create custom icon arrangements.

These options appear in place of the standard Clean Up command depending on the current selection and whether you're using the Shift, Option, or Command key:

- **Clean Up Desktop.** When you're working with icons or buttons on the Desktop (not in a Finder window), the View | Clean Up command normally reads Clean Up Desktop and will align icons to the nearest grid position.
- **Clean Up All.** Holding down the Option key, however, changes the command to Clean Up All, which returns all disks, folders, and volume icons to neat rows at the right edge of your primary monitor. (Again, this command is available only on the Desktop, not in Finder windows.)
- **Clean Up Window.** When you're working in a Finder window, the Clean Up command is dimmed when the View command is set to anything other than By Icon or By Small Icon. When By Icon or By Small Icon is selected, the Clean Up Window command appears and arranges all icons in the current window into either aligned or staggered rows depending on the settings in View | View Options (as discussed earlier).

  Figure 3-29 shows a folder called HTML Templates before and after the Clean Up command was used.

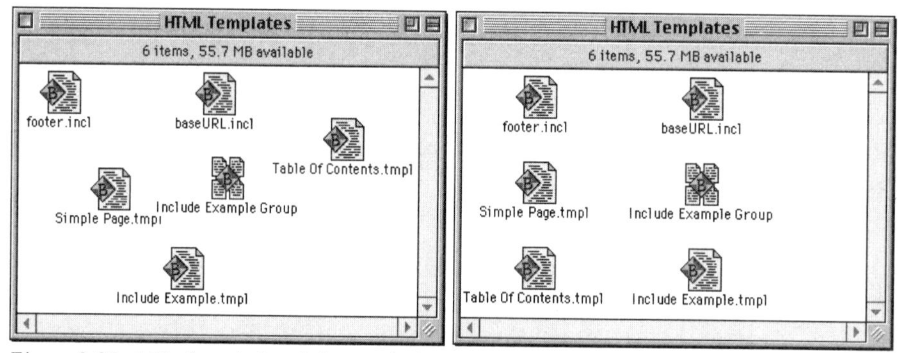

Figure 3-29: A Finder window before and after using Clean Up Window.

- **Clean Up By Name (By Size, and so on).** Holding down the Option key while selecting a Finder window lets you arrange icons by filename, size, date, comment, label, or version. The specific option presented is the one selected in the View | View Options menu Arranged by Icon or when the By Small Icon command was chosen.

To arrange icons by size, for example, select the respective windows for the icons you want to affect, choose By Size from the View menu, choose By Icon (or By Small Icon) from the View menu, and then hold down the Option key while choosing Clean Up By Size.

- **Clean Up Selection.** While a specific file or group of files is selected, holding down the Shift key activates Clean Up Selection, which will reposition only the selected files.

The Help Menu

When System 7 was introduced, it included several features that were often touted by Apple as primary benefits of their new system software but that have in fact turned out to be either impractical, poorly implemented, or just plain useless. The new Help menu and Balloon Help, for example, were major disappointments. While some novice users seem to actually like Balloon Help, the great majority of Macintosh users actively hate it.

Balloons are passive and don't lead you through complex task assistance. Apple took so much heat on Balloon Help that they rethought the entire issue. In System 7.5, Apple's solution to increasingly difficult software is Apple Guide, an active context-sensitive help system that is the result of several years of work. In Mac OS 8, the help system that uses Apple Guide has been renamed Mac OS Help (it used to be called Mac OS Guide), but it functions the same as it did under System 7.5. It is accessible under the new Help menu, which replaces the old Apple Guide menu, both of which are shown in Figure 3-30.

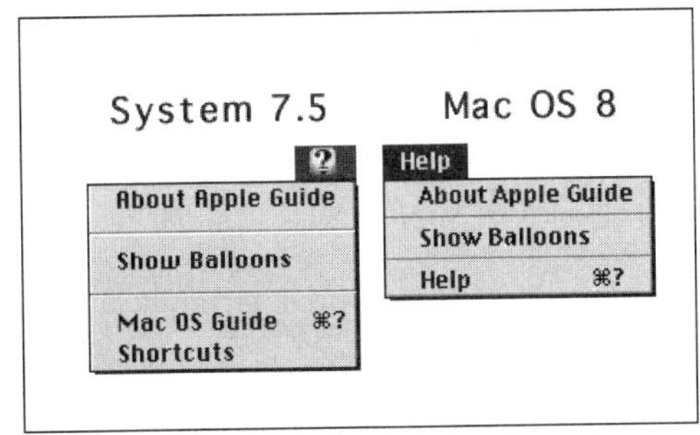

Figure 3-30: The old and new Help menus.

Apple takes the issue of help one step further in Mac OS 8 with the introduction of contextual help, which saves you, the user, from having to search for help on a topic. Instead, you can now Control+click on an item and choose

Help from a pop-up menu. Most programs haven't yet incorporated this ability, but look for future revisions of your favorite applications to take advantage of this new feature. Before we look at this, however, let's review the main help features in the Mac OS.

Mac OS Help & Apple Guide

Mac OS Help uses Apple Guide to help users help themselves. The Apple Guide opens in its own window at the lower left corner of the screen when you choose the Help command (Command+? keystroke) from the Help menu. Arranged by topic, it provides interactive help to common questions. Onscreen visual devices lead the user through an established procedure: menu commands are flagged in red, radio buttons and check boxes are circled with coach marks, and so on. All the while, Apple Guide instructs you on the next step. Apple Guide will even scroll windows to guide you to a feature. Figure 3-31 provides an example. If you make a mistake, Apple Guide tells you so and instructs you on how to correct it. Pretty cool, huh?

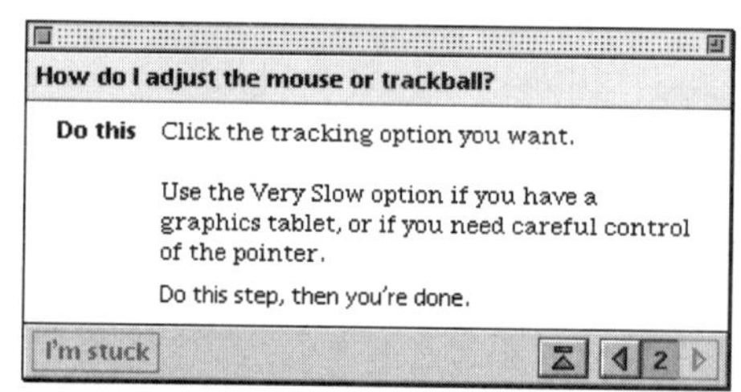

Figure 3-31: An Apple Guide instruction and coach mark.

Apple has enough confidence in Apple Guide to use it to "write down" the Mac OS manual to under 100 pages. Instead of giving you step-by-step instructions in the manual, you are sent to the topic and question in Apple Guide that gives the required procedure. Since Apple Guide is implemented as a developers' toolkit, it will undoubtedly improve in content and operation over time. Most developers use Apple Guide in their programs. In this book, you may have noticed an Apple Guide icon leading you to the important topics of interest in appropriate sections.

With the Apple Guide window open, click the Topics button to see a list of areas covered in Apple Guide. Topics are general categories. Clicking a topic brings up a list of common task-oriented questions in the right-hand scroll box, as shown in Figure 3-32. Double-click on a question to begin the active help process.

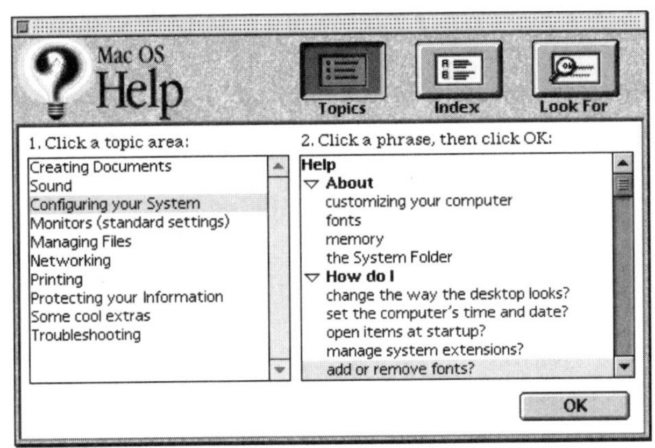

Figure 3-32: A Topics list in Apple Guide.

If you know what you want but don't see the right question, there are a couple of other ways to get into Apple Guide. You can see a list of keywords by clicking the Index button. The third button, Look For, lets you search Apple Guide for a keyword without having to browse the list of keywords or questions. What you see in Apple Guide depends upon the application that is active at the moment. Most applications ship with enabled Apple Guide systems and offer updated Apple Guides over the Internet.

Once a task is selected, the window opens up to display information and show you the first step in the task. An example is shown in Figure 3-33. The selected question appears at the top of the window, information appears in the center, and arrow buttons lead you forward and backward in the process. Sometimes you will see the I'm Stuck button; clicking it shows you information related to the task. To return to the Topics list, click the Up arrow button.

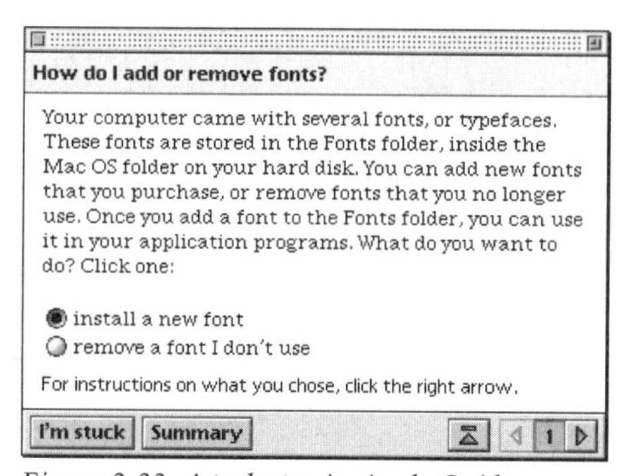

Figure 3-33: A task step in Apple Guide.

Once a step is completed, click the Next button (the Right arrow button) to proceed to the next step. You will get an error message if you made a mistake. Arrows dim when there is no next or previous step in the process.

The Guide window is a special kind of floating window that is always available at the top of your screen. Chances are that you will want to recover the display area (referred to as "real estate" in computer-speak) to see other items while keeping Apple Guide around for additional help. You can move the Apple Guide window by dragging its title bar. To minimize the window (shown in Figure 3-34), click the minimizer box in the upper right corner of the title bar. You can restore the window to full size by clicking on the minimizer box again. Or, click on the Right arrow button to open the window fully and go to the next step. Apple Guide can be closed by clicking the Close box at the upper left corner of the title bar.

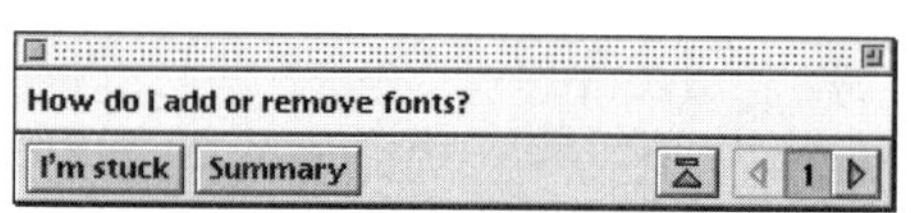

Figure 3-34: A minimized Apple Guide window.

Apple Guide and AppleScript form a powerful combination. You can embed AppleScript functionality in an Apple Guide help system to actively assist users. For example, if you are supplying a FileMaker Pro database system to a client, you can place buttons in the Apple Guide window that open files or perform other operations. The button launches an AppleScript macro and commands FileMaker through AppleEvents to perform the task. Even the Finder in System 7.5 is scriptable and susceptible to being managed through an Apple Guide help system. We'll have more to say about AppleScript in Chapter 13.

Balloon Help

Balloon Help gives Macintosh software applications the ability to provide onscreen context-sensitive information. It works by selecting the Show Balloons command under the Help menu, which causes a help balloon to be displayed when the arrow cursor is positioned over any menu command, window element, dialog box option, tool, or icon. This help balloon provides a brief description of that command, element, or icon function, a few examples of which are shown in Figure 3-35.

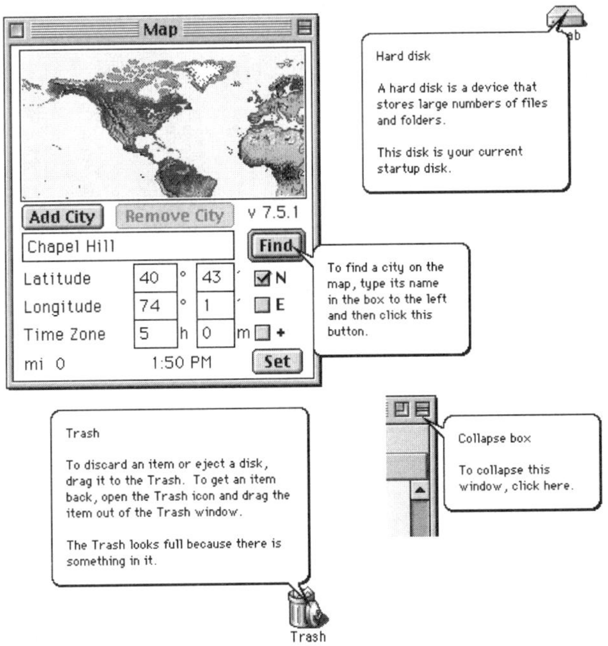

Figure 3-35: A sampling of the Finder's help balloons.

After the Show Balloons command has been chosen under the Help menu, it changes to the Hide Balloons command, which can be used to turn off the display of help balloons.

Balloon Help Limitations

In theory, Balloon Help makes it easier to learn new applications and refresh your memory when accessing infrequently used commands or dialog box options. However, these balloons can appear only in applications that have been written or upgraded specifically for System 7 or higher (including Mac OS 8) and in which Balloon Help has been specifically implemented.

In those programs that do offer Balloon Help, the information provided may be too limited or too generic to be truly helpful. This appears to be caused by the limited amount of space available for balloon text and limited efforts from developers. Always check with the documentation that comes with your software for more information and help.

A bigger problem is the annoying way that help balloons pop up from every element your cursor points to once the Show Balloons command has been chosen. Someone wishing to take advantage of Balloon Help is unlikely to need assistance on every single object, command, and element but instead would like to read the one or two help balloons relevant to a single, specific problem. Unfortunately, Apple's current "all-or-nothing" implementation of Balloon Help leads to a very distracting display that tends to encourage many users who might occasionally benefit from Balloon Help to instead stay away from it completely.

Contextual Help

Mac OS 8 introduces a new way to get help on a specific item; it is called contextual help. Instead of opening Mac OS Help and using the Topics, Index, or Look For features to invoke an Apple Guide session, you can now get help for an object such as an application, document, folder, alias, or hard drive by Control+clicking on the object. Figure 3-36 shows examples of getting contextual help on these types of objects.

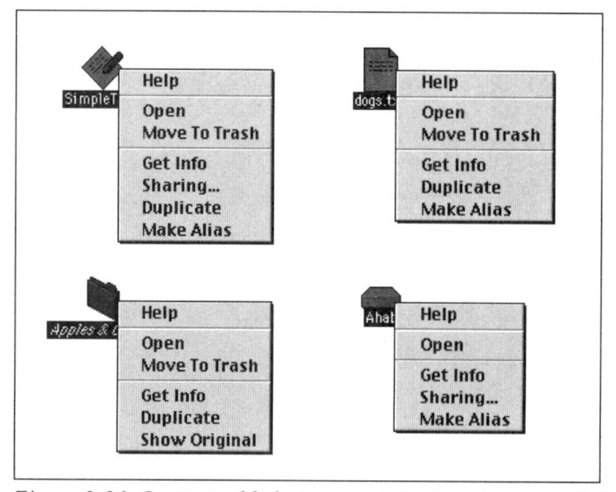

Figure 3-36: Contextual help is a great shortcut to getting help on an item.

Many of your favorite software titles may not have yet been programmed to take advantage of this type of help, but look for them to include it in the near future. When they do, you'll be able to click the Help entry at the top of the pop-up menu and get more information on the item. Figure 3-37, for example, shows the Apple Guide help entry for the SimpleText program.

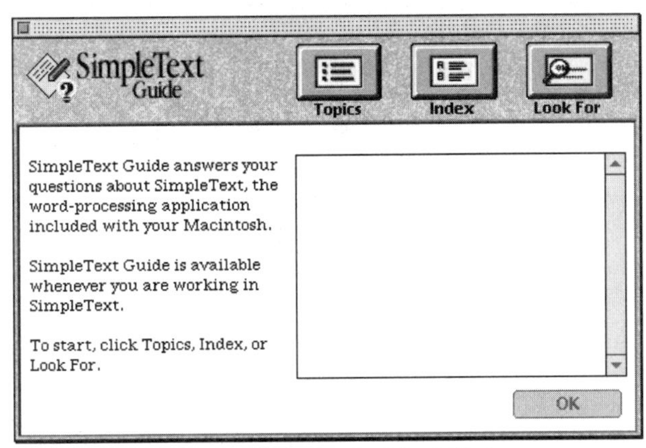

Figure 3-37: Contextual help for the SimpleText program.

Finally, contextual help is also available from within a program. Under System 7, the Apple Guide menu provided access to help that may or may not have been provided as part of the program. In Mac OS 8, however, this menu has been moved to the Help menu, although it provides the same information. Figure 3-38 shows the options available under the Help menu for the popular HTML editor called BBEdit.

Figure 3-38: Look to the new Help menu for links to Apple Guide help.

Trash & Empty Trash

The big news in System 7 was that the garbage collector no longer came without being invited—the Trash is emptied only when the Empty Trash command is chosen from the Special menu. In previous versions of the system software, the Trash was automatically emptied when any application was launched or when the Macintosh Restart or Shut Down commands were selected. In Mac OS 8, items remain in the Trash until Empty Trash is selected, even if the Mac is shut down. Figure 3-39 shows the contents of the Trash in a hierarchical list.

Trash

7 items

Name	Date Modified
Apple Extras	Wed, Apr 9, 1997, 9:08 AM
About the Mac™ OS	Wed, Apr 9, 1997, 8:54 AM
AppleCD Audio Player	Wed, Apr 9, 1997, 8:57 AM
AppleScript™	Wed, Apr 9, 1997, 8:57 AM
MoviePlayer	Wed, Apr 9, 1997, 8:53 AM
Sound Control Panel	Wed, Apr 9, 1997, 8:54 AM
Apples & Oranges	Today, 1:09 AM

Figure 3-39: The Trash window displays files currently in the Trash.

When the Empty Trash command is accessed from the Special menu or by pressing Control+click on the Trash icon, a dialog box appears asking you to confirm that you want to delete the current Trash files. This dialog box appears regardless of what files the Trash contains and tells you how much disk space will be freed by emptying the Trash, as shown in Figure 3-40.

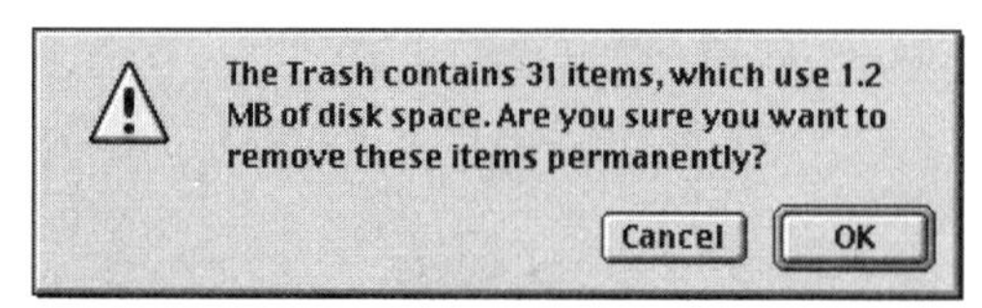

Figure 3-40: The Empty Trash? dialog box.

Trash Tips

While using the Trash is straightforward, there are several less-obvious aspects you'll want to know about:

- **Avoid Trash warnings.** If you hold down the Option key while choosing Empty Trash, the confirmation dialog box will not appear and the Trash will be emptied immediately.

- **Disable Trash warnings.** You can also disable the warning dialog by selecting the Trash, choosing the Get Info command, and deselecting the Warn Before Emptying option, shown in Figure 3-41. Of course, this will make it easier to delete application and system software files accidentally, so this option should be deselected with caution.

Figure 3-41: The Trash Info dialog box.

- **Retrieving Trashed items.** Any time before the Empty Trash command is chosen, items inside the Trash may be recovered and saved from deletion. This is done by double-clicking on the Trash icon and dragging the file icons you want to recover out of the Trash window and back onto the Desktop or onto any volume or folder icon.
- **Freeing disk space.** Only when the trash has been emptied and this command is chosen is disk space released. In previous systems, dragging items to the Trash alone was sufficient to cause disk space to be freed—although not always immediately.
- **Repositioning the Trash.** In System 7.5, you can reposition the Trash on your Desktop and it will stay there even if you reboot. It's no longer automatically returned to the lower right Desktop corner each time you reboot. This is helpful if you use a large monitor or multiple monitors.

Don't be in too much of a hurry to empty the Trash. Do it every so often when you need to recover disk space but give yourself a chance to retrieve mistakenly trashed items first. Once the Trash is emptied, deleted files can still often be recovered. You will need to use one of several third-party undelete utilities such as Symantec Utilities for the Macintosh, Norton Utilities, or Central Point Software's Mac Tools, among others.

The Get Info Dialog Box

As in previous Finder versions, selecting any file, folder, or drive icon and choosing the Get Info command from the File menu or the contextual pop-up menu brings up an Info dialog box (usually called a Get Info dialog box) that displays basic information and related options. The Mac OS 8 Get Info dialog box for the text editing program BBEdit, as shown in Figure 3-42, is only slightly different from those in previous Finder versions.

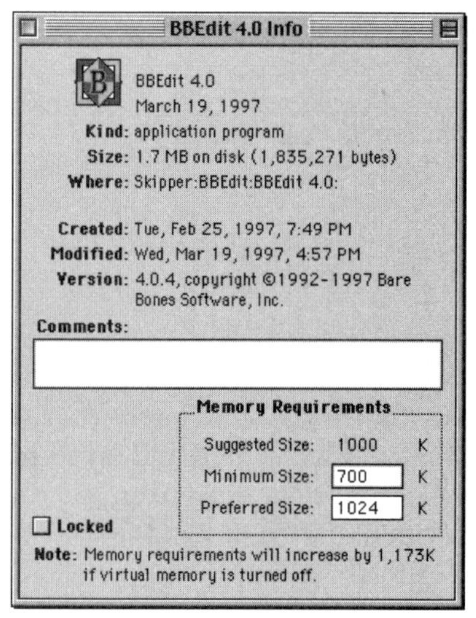

Figure 3-42: The Get Info dialog box for files.

There are now five different versions of the Get Info dialog box—one each for files, folders, applications, volumes, and alias icons. Options may differ among versions, but the basic information each provides is the same:

- **Filename.** The exact filename that appears on the Desktop, which cannot be changed from within this dialog box.
- **Icon.** Appears to the left of the filename, providing a visual reference for the file.

  You can customize the icon of almost any data file, application, or volume by pasting a new icon on top of the existing icon in the Get Info dialog box. To change an icon, copy any MacPaint or PICT graphic onto the Clipboard, select the icon you want to replace in the Get Info dialog box (a box will appear around the icon, indicating its selection), and choose the Paste command from the Edit menu. If the picture is too large to fit into the icon frame, it is scaled down. Close the Get Info dialog box and the new icon will appear in the Finder window or on the Desktop. Likewise, you can copy and paste any icons between Get Info boxes.

- **Kind.** Provides a brief description of the selected file. For data files, this usually includes the name of the application that created the file.
- **Size.** The amount of disk space that the file consumes.
- **Where.** The location of the selected file, including all folders enclosing it and the volume it's on.
- **Created.** The date and time the file was created. The date is reset when a file is copied from one volume to another or if a new copy is created by holding down the Option key while moving a file into a new folder.
- **Modified.** The date and time the contents of the file were last changed.
- **Version.** Lists the software application's version number. No information on data files, folders, or volumes is provided.
- **Comments.** System 7 vastly improved its support for adding comments to this Get Info dialog box field. In System 7.5, comments can be displayed in Finder windows, and you can use the Find command to locate files by the comment text. A complete discussion of comments is provided in Chapter 5, "Managing Your Hard Drive."

Several other options appear in some Get Info dialog boxes:

- **Locked.** Makes it more difficult to change or delete the selected file. The Locked option appears for data files, applications, and aliases. Locking ensures that unwanted changes are not accidentally made to data files that should not be altered. Locked data files can be opened, in most applications; but changes cannot be saved unless you use Save As to create a new file.

  Locked files are also spared accidental deletion since they must be unlocked before they can be emptied from the Trash. If you try to delete a locked file, the dialog box shown in Figure 3-43 appears. It's important to note, however, that locked files will be deleted from the Trash without notice or warning if you hold down the Option key while you choose Empty Trash from the Finder's Special menu.

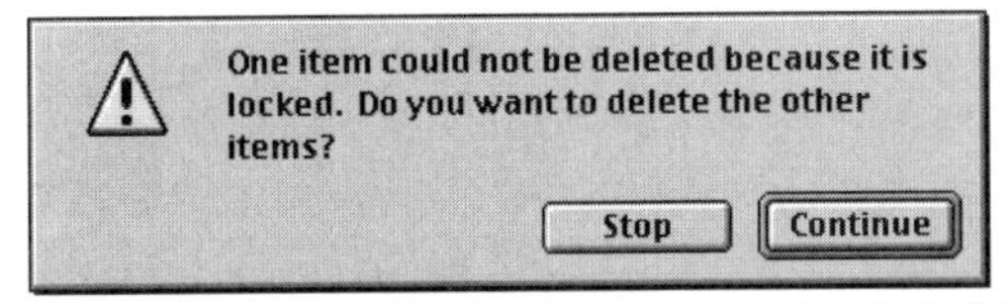

Figure 3-43: The warning that appears when locked items are placed in the Trash.

- **Memory.** Appears only for application files and includes Suggested Size, Minimum Size, and Preferred Size. Suggested Size specifies the application developer's recommendations for the amount of memory to be allocated to the program when it's opened. The Minimum Size setting is the least amount of RAM required to open the application, and the Preferred Size indicates the amount of RAM the user wishes to allot the application. (A discussion of these options is presented in Chapter 9, "Applications & Memory Management.")
- **Stationery Pad.** Available for data files only, this turns the selected document into a template. (A template is a master document on which new documents are based.) With this option, each time the selected document is opened, a copy of the file is created, and any changes or customizations are made to this copy, leaving the original Stationery Pad document available as a master at all times. (A complete discussion of Stationery Pads is provided in Chapter 7.)

Get Info for the Trash

The Trash Info dialog box, shown in Figure 3-44, contains two important pieces of information and one useful option. The dialog box lists the number of files and the amount of disk space they consume, which lets you know how much space will be freed by the Empty Trash command. It also lists the date when the most recent item was placed in the Trash.

Figure 3-44: The Trash's Info dialog box.

The Warn Before Emptying option, which is a default, causes a confirmation dialog box to display when the Empty Trash command is selected (shown in Figure 3-45). If you don't want the dialog box to display each time the Empty Trash command is chosen, deselect the Warn Before Emptying option. But without this warning dialog box, you increase the risk of permanently deleting files you may want later.

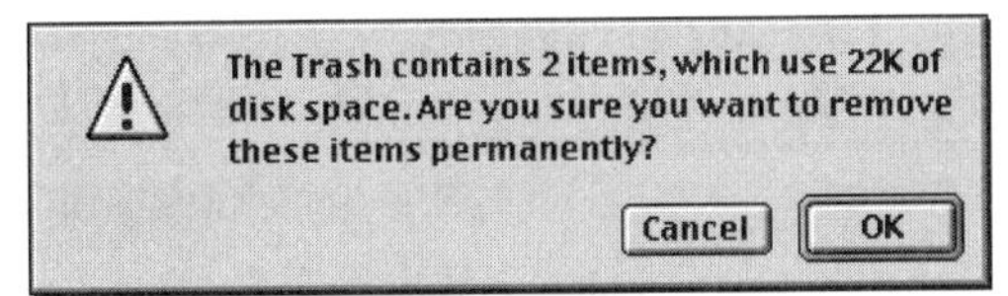

Figure 3-45: The Empty Trash confirmation dialog box.

Get Info for Alias Icons

The Get Info dialog box for alias icons is different in several ways from the one used by standard files. First, the version information normally displayed beneath the dates is replaced with the path and filename of the original file, as in Figure 3-46.

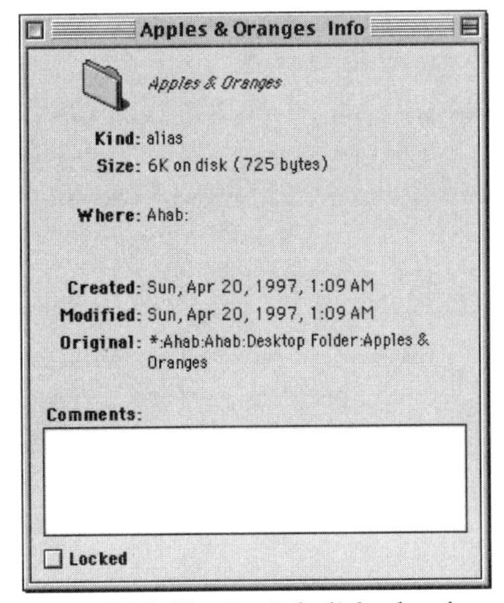

Figure 3-46: The Get Info dialog box for an alias icon.

Also, the Get Info dialog box no longer includes the Find Original button that locates the disk or folder containing the original file (from which the alias was made). Mac OS 8 includes what used to be known as "secret Finder features"; although they have been present in the Finder for some time, they were not made active features until now. To find the parent item to which an alias belongs, press Command+R (for *reveal*). This command can open the disk or folder window and select the original file icon. If the disk or volume containing the original file is not available, a dialog asks you to insert the disk containing the original file, or in the case of a network volume, the volume will be mounted. The contextual pop-up command (Control+click) for this feature is named Show Original.

The Comments and Locked options are available for aliases, behaving exactly as they do for any other files. The Stationery Pad option, however, is not available for alias icons.

Moving On

The Finder is the most visible part of the Macintosh system software; as we've seen in this chapter, it gives you powerful and intuitive tools to manage the disks and files you're using with your Macintosh:

- The new Finder menus
- The many ways you can see and manipulate data in Finder windows
- The new Help menu, Apple Guide, and Balloon Help
- The Trash and Empty Trash commands
- The Get Info dialog box, in its many forms

Next, in Chapter 4, "Customizing Your Mac," we'll look at the various elements in Mac OS 8 that you can use to customize your Mac, as well as a few third-party utilities that are very inexpensive and can add a lot of features to your computer.

CHAPTER 4

Customizing Your Mac

Without a doubt, the main reason for the fierce loyalty among Mac users is the ability to customize the Mac OS and thereby make it easier to use. The Mac has always been customizable, and Mac OS 8 makes it even easier than before to personalize your Mac. After all, you didn't purchase the Mac OS to be locked into using the same computer day after day, did you? The Mac OS lets you change the way you interact with your software, which makes the Mac experience like no other.

In this chapter, we'll look at some elements of the Mac OS that not only are configurable but also will enhance your experience using it.

Changing Appearances

There are numerous features, Control Panels, and Extensions used by Mac OS 8 that allow you to configure and customize your Mac. We've seen several of them in earlier chapters, and I'll go over them here again; we'll look at them as tools to allow you to manipulate the Mac OS interface to best suit your needs, and not just as features of the Mac OS. If you're like me, however, you'll probably do a lot of experimenting and change things from time to time anyway. Who wants to be stuck with the same interface day after day? The majority of these configuration options are found in the Control Panels, so let's start there.

Appearance Settings

The Appearance Control Panel takes the place of the old Color and WindowShade Control Panels. Shown in Figure 4-1, the Appearance Control Panel has two configuration tabs for now. Later in 1997, Apple will introduce a third item to this Control Panel that will allow you to change the way windows, dialog boxes, and progress bars are drawn onscreen. These appearances, called themes, were to have shipped in Mac OS 8 in 1996 as part of the old Mac OS 8, code-named Copland. A bit later in this chapter, we'll look at a shareware utility called Kaleidoscope that achieves the same effect.

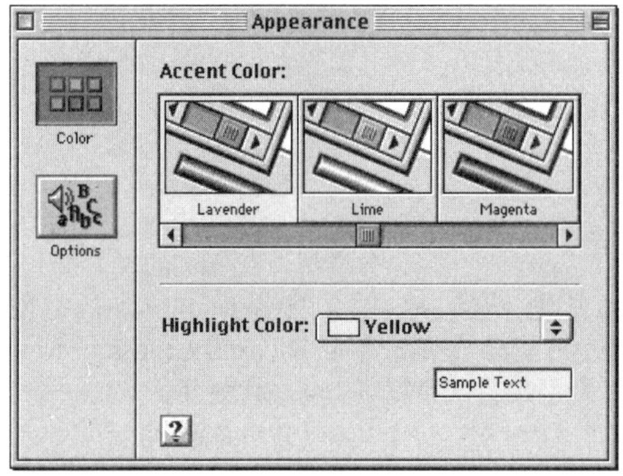

Figure 4-1: Begin customizing your Mac's appearance with the Appearance Settings Control Panel.

The first section allows you to select the color the Mac OS uses to highlight selected text, as in Figure 4-2.

The second section of the Appearance Control Panel, shown in Figure 4-3, allows you to configure a few options for the collapsing windows feature (formerly WindowShade) and the default system font. You can also choose to revert to the old System 7 appearance in place of the OS 8, or platinum, appearance.

There are many differences between the old and the new appearances. For example, Figure 4-4 shows the title area of two folders, one with the old appearance and one with the new. Notice that the newer appearance adds what used to be known as the WindowShade widget on the right side of the title bar. You can single-click this to collapse a window or expand a collapsed window instead of double-clicking on the title bar.

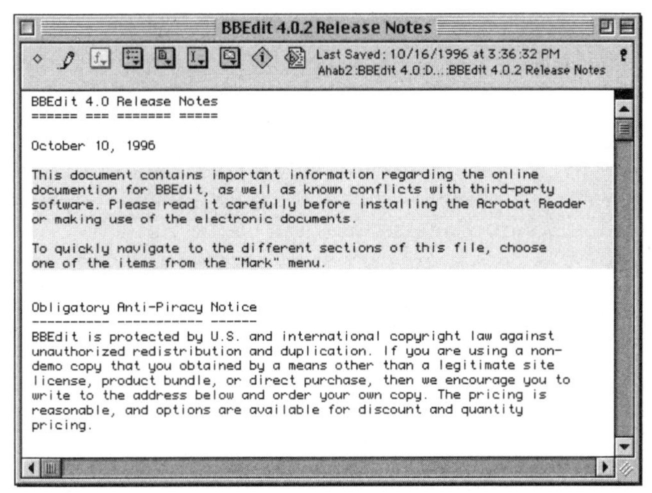

Figure 4-2: Choose a highlight color that's easiest on your eyes.

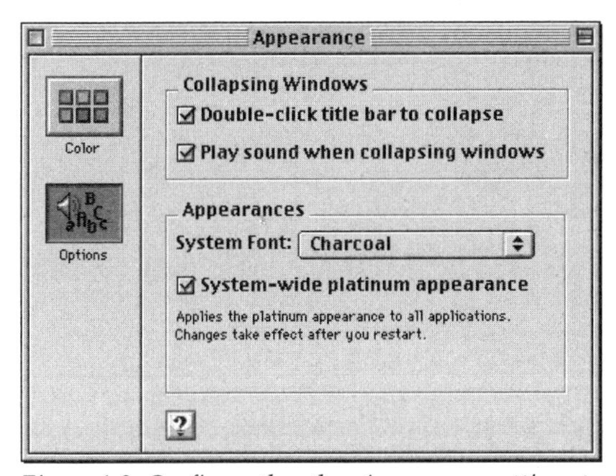

Figure 4-3: Configure the other Appearance settings to suit your tastes.

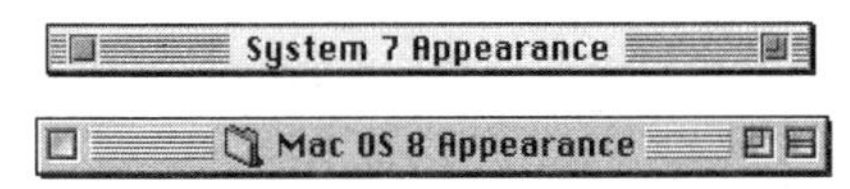

Figure 4-4: You can select between the old (System 7) and the new (Mac OS 8) appearances.

Apple Menu Options

The Apple Menu Options Control Panel provides a couple of neat ways to save you time. First, it makes the Apple Menu hierarchical, allowing you to select an item, such as a document or application, that is nested several layers deep with the single click of the mouse. This is one of the popular features of the Mac OS that has been mimicked in many other operating systems. The Apple Menu Items Control Panel is shown in Figure 4-5.

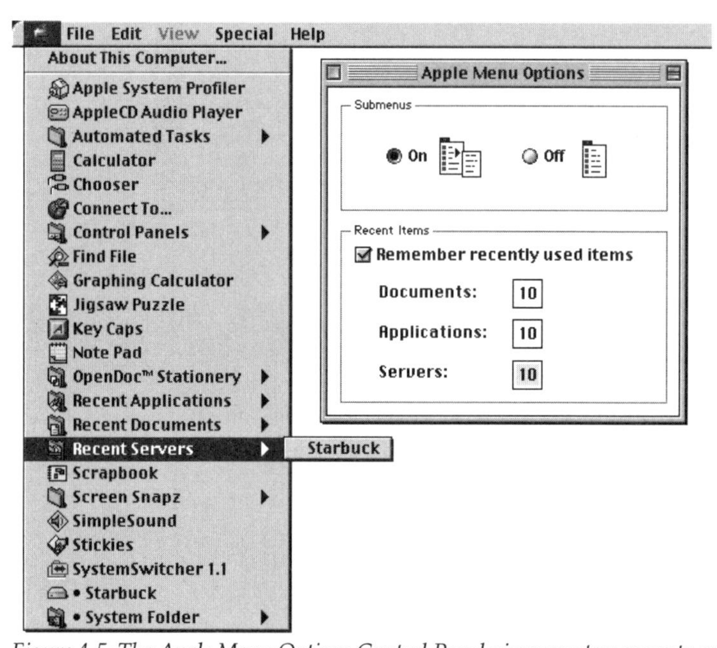

Figure 4-5: The Apple Menu Options Control Panel gives you two ways to customize your Mac.

You can set the number of remembered documents, applications, and servers to whatever number you'd like, but a high number has a few drawbacks—a slower response to the hierarchical menu feature as well as more system RAM required by the OS to store information about these items. If your system is low on memory or is slow in general, try not to use this feature to see if your performance improves.

Desktop Pictures

There are several freeware or shareware utilities that perform the same task as the Desktop Pictures Control Panel, but none does so at such as low cost to the Mac OS. Where other utilities use an extension, Desktop Pictures is a Control Panel that doesn't consume nearly as much RAM. Moreover, since Desktop Pictures gives you the ability to control both patterns and images on your Desktop, it is one of the most used Mac OS customization utilities.

The top button of the Desktop Pictures Control Panel controls the 50 or so Desktop patterns that come as part of Mac OS 8. These patterns are small images in the native PICT format that are tiled (repeated over and over) to create the illusion of being one large image, much like sheets of wallpaper pasted together to cover a wall. The Notes pattern, shown in Figure 4-6, is only 256 X 64 pixels in size and takes up only 19K of disk space.

Figure 4-6: One of the most popular features of the Mac OS has been the Desktop patterns that come as part of the Mac OS.

If you want to use something more elaborate, try one of the handful of sample Desktop pictures that come with Mac OS 8. This is the first time such pictures have been included as part of the OS, and they are very impressive. For example, Figure 4-7 shows an image of Glacier National Park by Scott Melnick, which is also a very small image (72K).

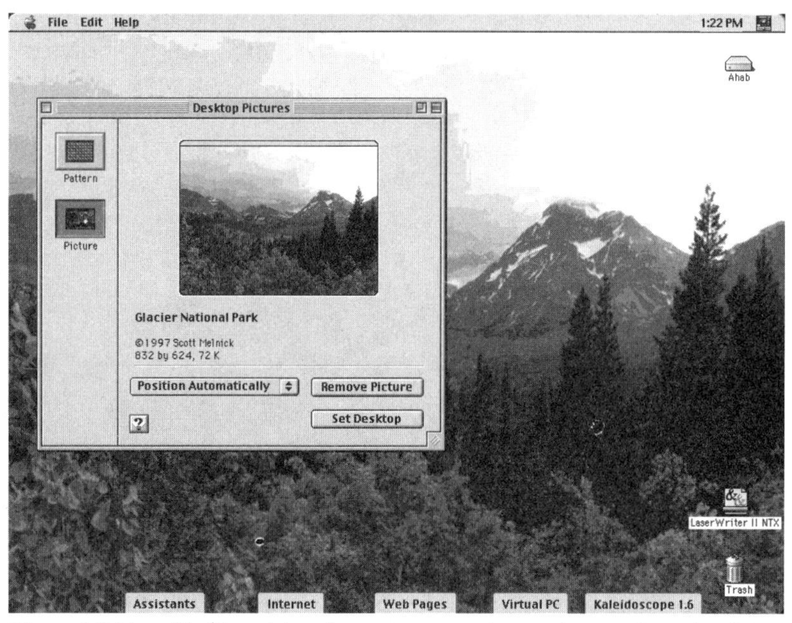

Figure 4-7: Try a Desktop picture for an even more impressive way to customize your Mac's Desktop.

You can use you own pictures on the Desktop if you'd like. Just open the Desktop Pictures Control Panel and select a new image. There's only one real consideration to take into account when doing this, however, and that is the size of your image. If, for example, you have a monitor that is capable of displaying a maximum resolution of 832 X 624 pixels and you have an image that is only 640 X 480 pixels, the image won't completely fill the screen. You can attempt to compensate for situations like this using the positioning options. Figure 4-8, for example, shows the options that are available for positioning your image. Start by choosing the Position Automatically option, which should take care of most images.

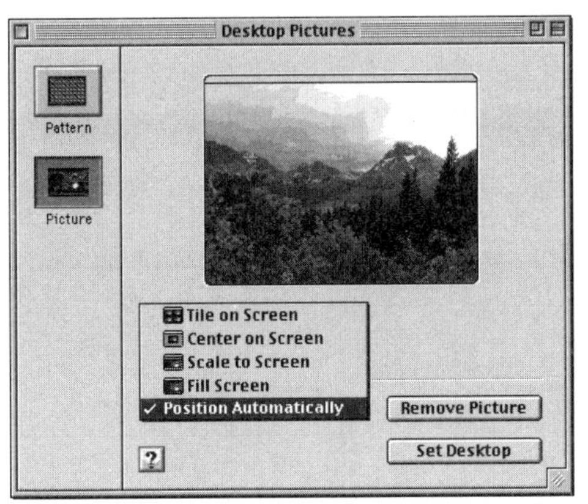

Figure 4-8: Use the positioning options to assist you in customizing your Mac's Desktop.

General Controls

One of my favorite ways to customize my Mac is to hide the Desktop when it is not active by using the Control Panel called General Controls. This option is especially helpful if you tend to have multiple applications active at the same time and lots of clutter on the Desktop, creating an unruly scene, as in Figure 4-9, for example.

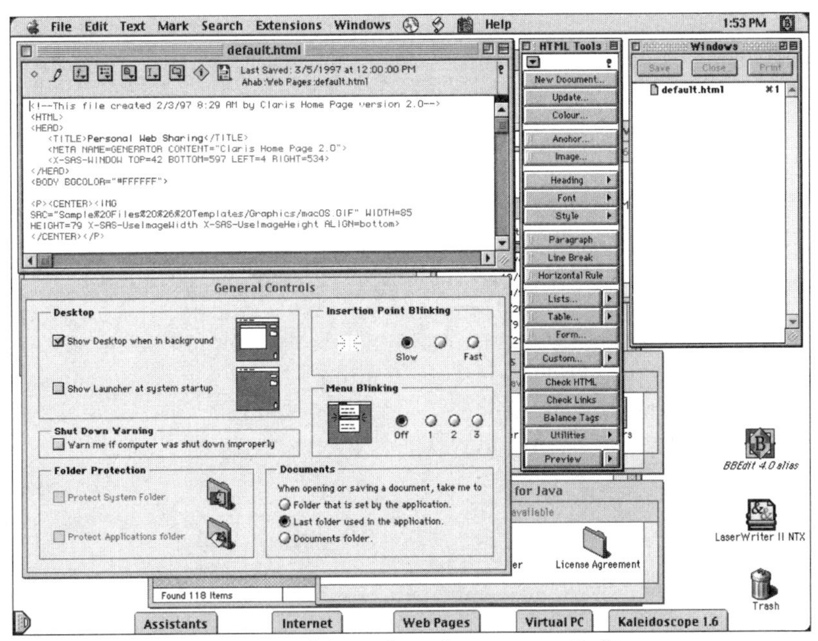

Figure 4-9: You can use General Controls to clean up your Desktop.

Notice how hard it is to see what's going on? To clear things up, open General Controls and deselect the Show Desktop When in Background option. This will cause the Desktop to be invisible unless selected, as in Figure 4-10, which shows the exact same information as in Figure 4-9 except that the Desktop is hidden.

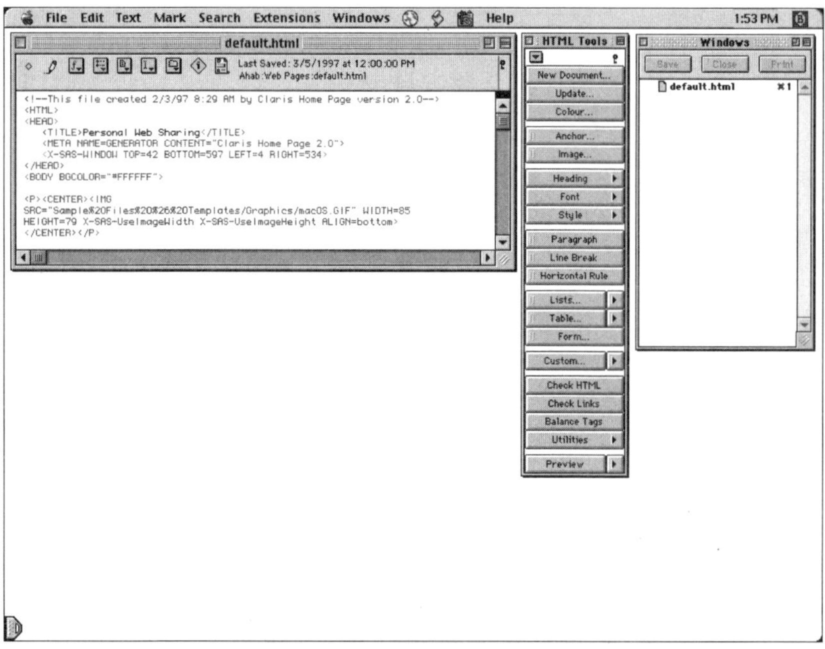

Figure 4-10: Hiding the Desktop can help unclutter your screen.

One final thing you can do with General Controls that can help speed things up for you, albeit in a small way, is to disable menu blinking by selecting the Off radio button. When you select something from the Apple menu, menu blinking gives you an additional visual clue by blinking the selected menu item one, two, or three times before opening the selected item. This is nice; I know that I've selected something when it's blinking. However, it performs unnecessary processor cycles and takes a noticeable time to complete. Disabling this option will speed things up a bit.

Monitors & Sound

You cannot only customize how your Mac looks, but how it displays information on your monitor and how it sounds as well. This is another one of the great reasons the Mac OS is so popular with users and has been copied in other operating systems. Humans like to get feedback, and the Mac OS is glad to give it.

The Monitors & Sound Control Panel is where you go to customize several features, and depending on what type of monitor you have, your options may look slightly different from what you see here in Figure 4-11. In the figure, for example, you see the three main areas in which you can customize how your computer displays the information it receives from the Mac OS.

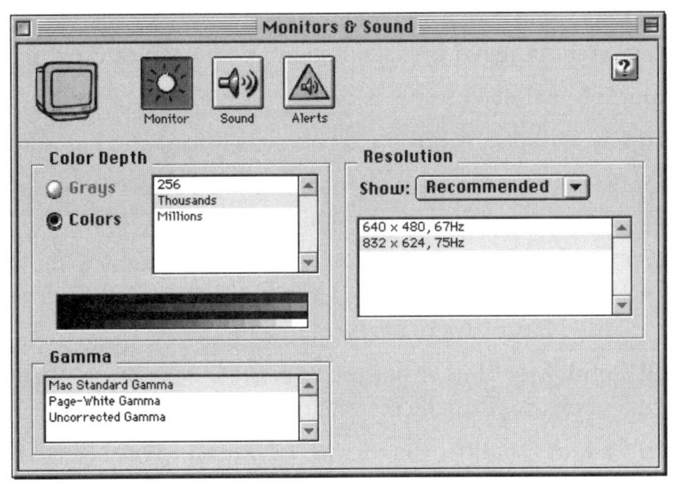

Figure 4-11: Choose the Monitors & Sound Control Panel to customize sound and display features.

The number of colors your monitor can display will depend on the amount of video RAM (also called VRAM) and the type of display. Most monitors that ship with new computers are capable of displaying millions of colors, but if you don't have enough VRAM, you might only be able to display thousands or 256 colors. A good rule of thumb is to set your monitor to display thousands or millions of colors if it is capable to do so, but not 256 (see Figure 4-11). If you have a PowerBook, which we'll talk about more in Chapter 6, you can reduce the number of colors in order to save battery consumption.

The amount of VRAM also affects the ability of multiresolution monitors to display multiple resolutions. For example, if your Mac has a monitor that is capable of displaying a maximum resolution of 1024 X 768, you will need 2MB of VRAM. If you only have 1MB of VRAM, however, the higher resolution setting will not be visible in the Monitors & Sound Control Panel. A variation on this theme goes like this: if you are able to select a higher resolution, the number of colors available to be displayed will decrease. So, to set your monitor's colors and resolution, you'll need to strike a balance between the abilities of your system and the task you're performing to choose the best settings.

The Sound portion of Monitors & Sound allows you to customize how your Mac plays and records sound. As you can see in Figure 4-12, you can select many different options, including:

- **Sound Out Level.** Determines the output level of your Mac when you have speakers plugged into your sound port (standard on all Macs).
- **Computer Speaker Volume.** Sets the volume level of sound.
- **Sound Out Balance.** Adjusts the balance of right and left output.
- **Computer Speaker Balance.** Adjusts the balance between right and left speakers, if attached. If not, this option is not functional.
- **Sound Output.** Identifies the hardware source to which audio signals are sent. All Macs have internal speakers, so the default is built-in unless you've added hardware to perform this function.
- **Sound Input.** Identifies either the internal CD player or the microphone (internal or external) as the source for incoming sound.
- **Sound Output Quality.** Sets the rate of output to the selected sound output device.

As with displays, you should customize your sound settings as necessary, and don't be afraid to tinker and explore your computer's options. It's a Mac, after all!

Finally, the Alerts section, shown in Figure 4-13, is probably the single most familiar, customizable element of your Mac's interface, except perhaps the Desktop patterns. Longtime Mac users will remember this feature as what made us say to our friends, "Hey, come look at this. My Mac thinks it is a duck!" Now, of course, you can purchase sample sounds or download them from the Web, so your computer might have Bart Simpson talk back to you or Captain Kirk beam you aboard instead of just quacking at you.

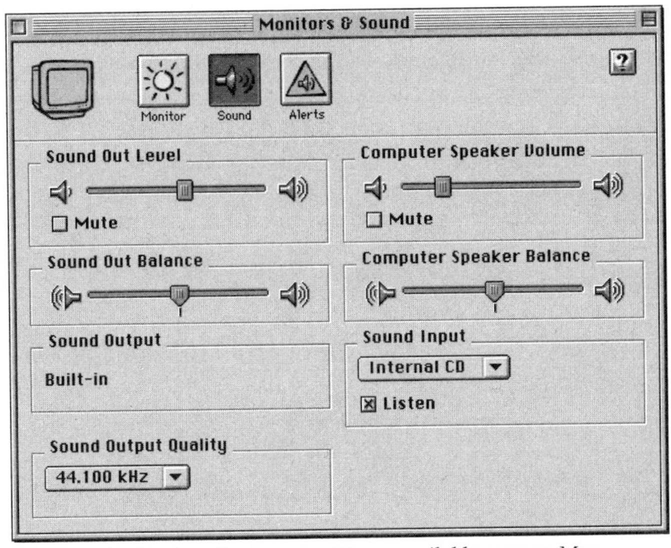

Figure 4-12: Explore the Sound settings available to your Mac.

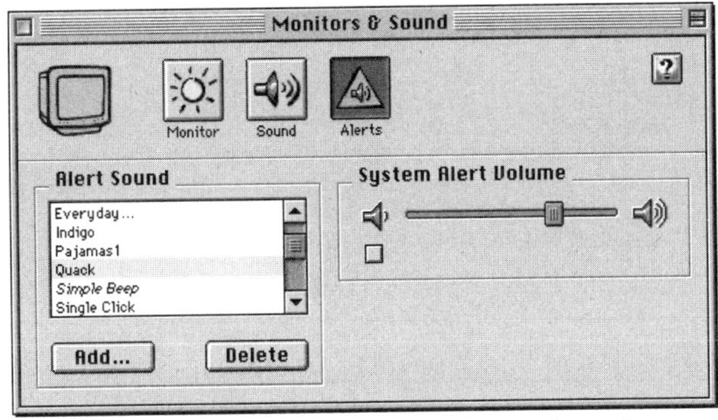

Figure 4-13: Choose a custom alert message to make getting your attention a bit more interesting.

Energy Saver

Finally, you can customize your Mac with the Energy Saver Control Panel. Now, you may not think of this Control Panel as a customization feature, but it has two features that can be quite useful.

First, the Sleep Setup portion of the Energy Saver Control Panel, accessible through the Sleep Setup button shown in Figure 4-14, gives you the ability to tell the Mac OS when the computer should revert to a power-saving mode or to tell it to shut itself down after a specified period of inactivity. You can specify that the entire computer be shut down or that the display and/or hard drive go into sleep mode.

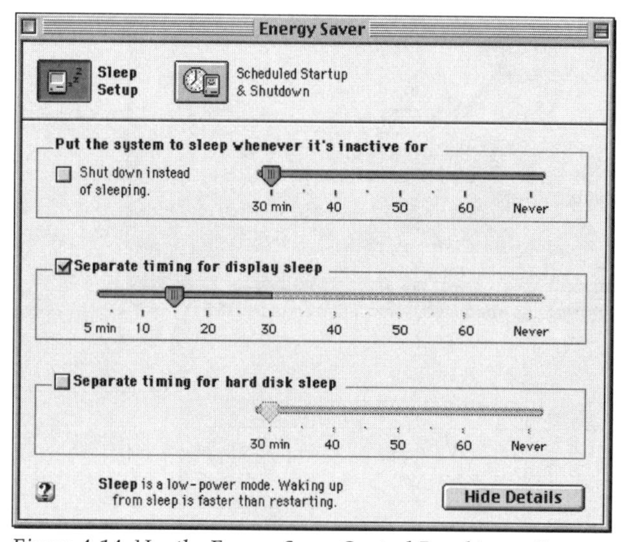

Figure 4-14: Use the Energy Saver Control Panel to configure your Mac to sleep or shut down.

Finally, you can customize your Mac to automatically start up or shut down at designated times in the Scheduled Startup & Shutdown portion of the Energy Saver Control Panel, shown in Figure 4-15.

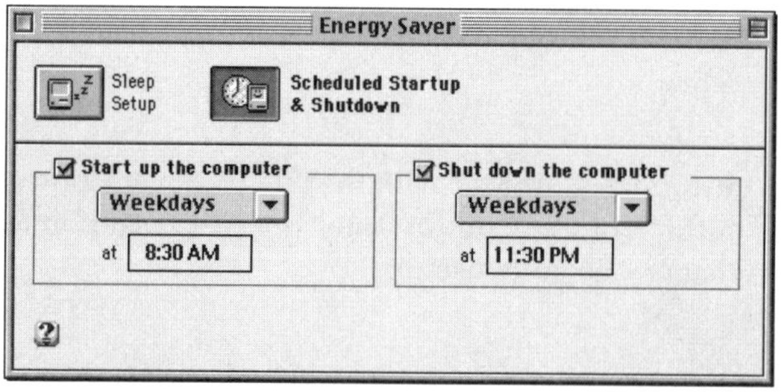

Figure 4-15: Schedule your Mac to start up or shut down automatically using the Energy Saver Control Panel.

You can control the exact hour and minute of the operation as well as configure it for the following days:

- Weekdays
- Weekends
- Every day
- Monday
- Tuesday
- Wednesday
- Thursday
- Friday

You can use this feature to have your computer automatically shut down if you've left it on unintentionally. You can also have it start up automatically to perform a task in conjunction with an item in your Startup Items folder, such as checking your e-mail every morning of the work week.

These are the major customization features that are part of Mac OS 8, but there are thousands more that are available to help with just about every task you can imagine, and then some.

Third-Party Utilities

There are so many freeware and shareware utilities for the Mac OS out there that it's hard to keep track of them. Fortunately for us, there are several enterprising individuals and companies that have created Web sites to track these software titles and make them available for downloading. The best places I've found include the following:

- **Yahoo.** http://www.yahoo.com/Computers_and_Internet/Software/Platforms/Macintosh/Shareware/
- **The MIT HyperArchive.** http://hyperarchive.lcs.mit.edu/HyperArchive/Abstracts/Recent-Summary.html
- **Shareware.com.** http://www.shareware.com/SW/Selections/Index/

I've chosen a few programs that are very useful, very cool, and very cheap. You can use them to customize your Mac in many ways.

Kaleidoscope

By Greg Landweber, Frederick J. Bass, and Amargosa Software, Inc.
http://www.kaleidoscope.net
Shareware

If you haven't already seen Kaleidoscope from Greg Lanweber, then you've probably seen another of his shareware applications called Aaron. Aaron gives earlier versions of the Mac OS some of the look and feel of Mac OS 8, specifically the "platinum" appearance. Kaleidoscope, on the other hand, can give the Mac OS any number of appearances much in the same way that the next release of the Mac OS plans to do.

Kaleidoscope consists of a Control Panel and a folder of Kaleidoscope themes that go in your Extensions folder. Once you restart your Mac, you can open the Kaleidoscope Control Panel and select a new appearance "on the fly," meaning the changes go into effect immediately. Figure 4-16 shows the Control Panel with the default theme.

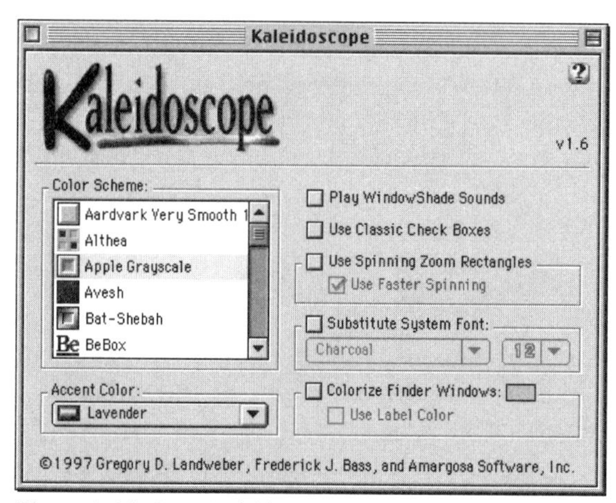

Figure 4-16: Open Kaleidoscope to change your Mac's appearance.

To change the appearance on your Mac, just select one of the six or so themes that comes with Kaleidoscope or any that you may have downloaded from the Web. The theme goes into effect immediately, although some icons may not appear correctly until you have restarted your computer. In addition to selecting a theme, you can select from these options, some of which will not be available when using certain themes:

- **Accent Color.** Replaces the color selected in the Color box under the Appearance Control Panel.

- **Play WindowShade Sounds.** Replaces the check box in the Collapsing Windows section under the Appearance Control Panel. If selected, it plays a swishing sound when you click the collapsing window (WindowShade) widget.
- **Use Classic Check Boxes.** Substitutes a check box for the new checkmark in Mac OS 8.
- **Use Spinning Zoom Rectangles.** Causes a window to zoom closed when the close window (Command+W) command is issued. It gives more of a visual clue that a window has been closed and in which direction the parent folder is located.
- **Substitute System Font.** Replaces the font selected under the Appearances section of the Appearance Control Panel.
- **Colorize Finder Window.** Allows you to select a custom color to replace the default white for a window's content area as well as to select a Label color as defined under the File | Label menu in the Finder.

Kaleidoscope can really enhance the look and feel of your Mac, and the great thing about it is that people are constantly creating new themes every week. Figure 4-17, for example, shows three of my favorite themes: BeBox, The NeXT Copland, and Onyx (from top to bottom).

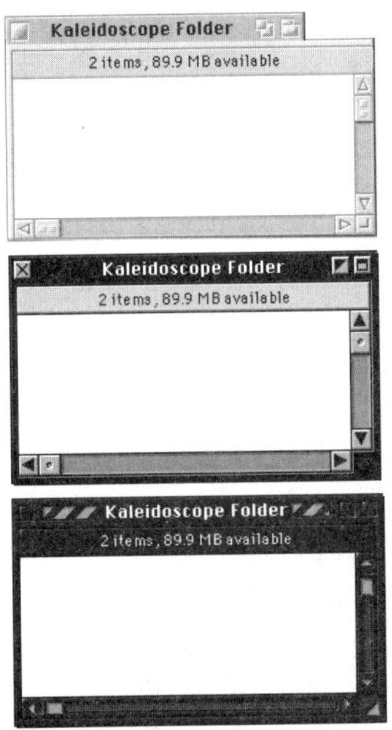

Figure 4-17: Customize your Mac with one of these three very distinctive Kaleidoscope themes.

Of course, you can always switch back to the Mac OS 8 or System 7 color scheme, but my guess is that you'll find one that you'll like better. For a list of links to vast collections of Kaleidoscope themes on the Web, visit the Kaleidoscope home page and link to the theme archive.

GoMac

By Proteron, LLC
http://www.proteron.com
Shareware
I often have so many applications open at the same time that I'm always looking for a utility that will allow me to switch between them easily. A new, customizable utility called GoMac adds a program bar at the bottom of the screen that does this and more. Figure 4-18 shows what GoMac looks like under Mac OS 8.

Figure 4-18: Install GoMac to add a customizable program bar at the bottom of your screen.

In addition to adding a program bar to identify all of your open applications and easily switch between them, GoMac adds several configurable options that make accessing data and applications on your Mac more flexible. GoMac uses a Start menu in the lower left corner of your screen to store links to your most recently accessed applications, documents, and servers and to your hard drive(s). Figure 4-19 shows several applications, including the Finder, that are selectable through GoMac's program bar.

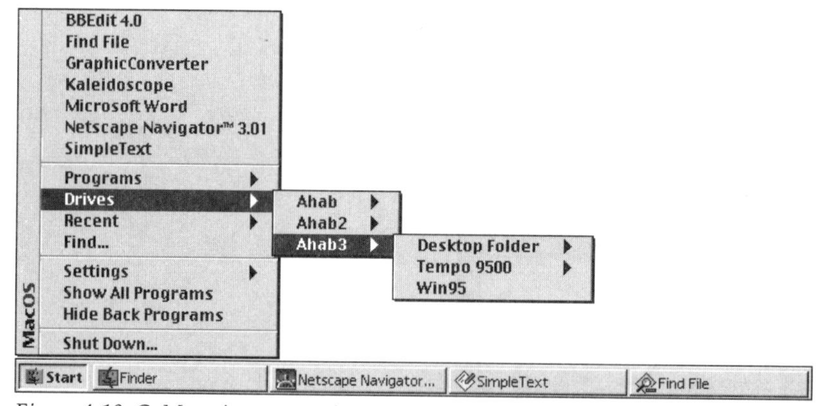

Figure 4-19: GoMac gives you easier access to your computer.

GoMac works like an upside-down Apple menu, but with many more options. For example, Figure 4-20 shows the two main configuration tabs in the GoMac Control Panel, where you'll choose most of your configuration options.

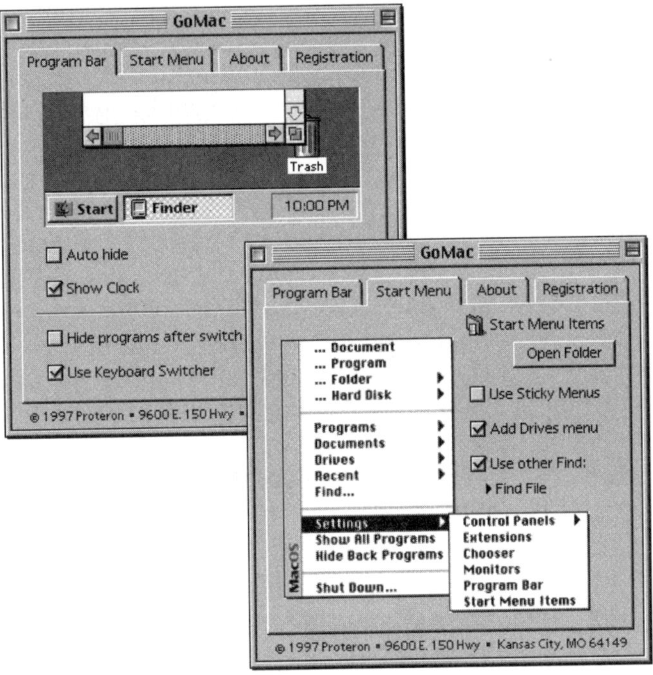

Figure 4-20: Customize GoMac's program bar to optimize access to your computer.

In addition to providing easy access to files and folders, GoMac can hide itself until you drag your mouse over it. This way, it takes up less space on your Desktop. You can also display a clock and pop-up calendar by selecting the Show Clock check box. On the Start Menu tab, you can configure GoMac to store aliases of your favorite applications, documents, and folders. In Figure 4-19, I've included several of my favorite applications in the Start menu, including BBEdit, GraphicConverter, and Navigator. The Start menu contains much of the same information found in the Apple menu, including recently accessed applications, documents, and servers. It also gives you access to a find-file utility of your choice as well as giving you easy access to your hard drive(s). The Start Menu tab can be a real time-saver and can be configured to your liking.

AMICO

By Dennis Chronopoulos
http://www.shareware.com
Shareware
If you want to stick with your Apple menu, there is a great utility called AMICO, which stands for Apple Menu Items Custom Order. This utility lets you create customized groups within the Apple menu that are more intuitive to access and remember. The Apple menu normally displays the contents of the Apple Menu Items folder (located in the System folder) in alphanumeric order. You can do a small amount of customization by inserting blank spaces to force an item to go to the top of the Apple menu when you click on the Apple icon, or you can preface an entry with a bullet (Option-8) to make it last in the list.

AMICO is an Extension that tells the Mac OS to look for certain characters in the Apple Menu Items folder and to change how items in the folder are displayed when the Apple menu is activated. For example, you can insert dividers, reorder the contents of the Apple Menu so they are no longer listed alphanumerically, and format dividers.

Figure 4-21 shows an Apple menu and an Apple Menu Items folder that have been customized to display groups of folders in distinctive sections of the Apple Menu. Each was customized with AMICO.

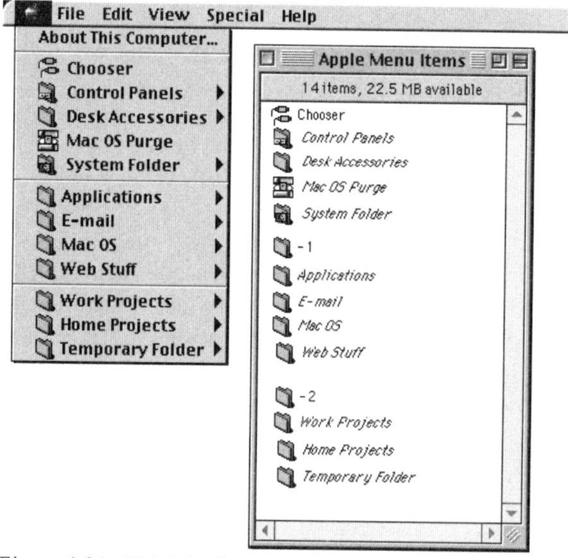

Figure 4-21: AMICO allows you to customize the Apple menu in several very useful ways.

There are several ways to apply such customizations. AMICO looks at how the Apple Menu Items folder is displayed in the Finder and then applies the appropriate changes:

- By Name
- By Date Modified
- By Size
- By Kind
- By Icon (small or large)

In Figure 4-21, the contents of the Apple Menu Items folder are displayed by small icon in the Finder, which causes AMICO to display the contents of the Apple menu in literal order rather than alphanumeric order. Figure 4-22 shows the View Options (under the View menu) for the Apple Menu Items folder in Figure 4-21.

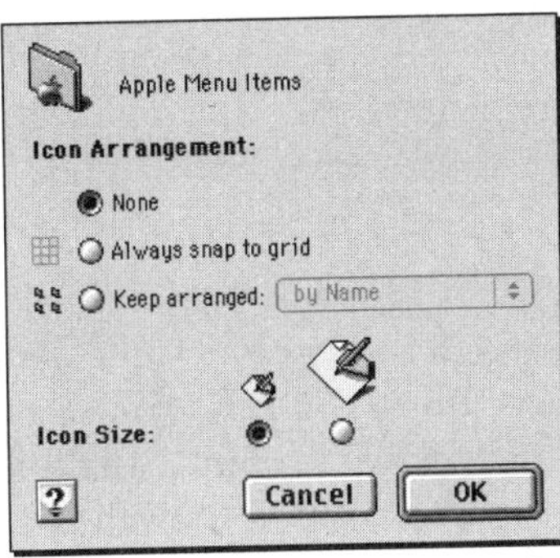

Figure 4-22: Changing the View Options affects how the Apple menu appears.

You can also choose to insert custom dividers as names rather than horizontal rulers. In the menu in Figure 4-23, for example, I've replaced the two dividers in Figure 4-21 with named dividers which can appear in bold, underlined, or italicized text (or all three). The only drawback to this approach is that the divider names are grayed out, which makes them a bit harder to read.

I've always found the Apple menu that comes with a new installation of the Mac OS a bit cluttered, and the very first thing I do is customize the daylights out of it. GoMac and AMICO are two answers to the same question: How can I customize my Mac to make it easier to organize and find information? Give them both a try, and don't forget to register your copy if you decide to keep using it.

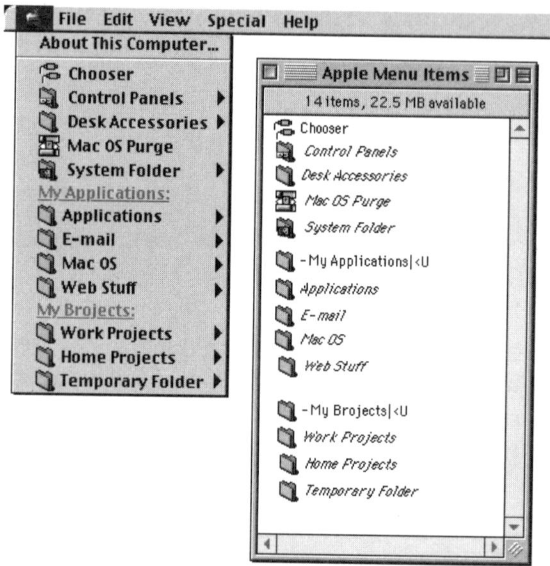

Figure 4-23: Use AMICO to customize your Apple menu..

Moving On

Using the Mac OS for the first time is kind of like driving someone else's car—when you get in the driver's seat, the first thing you do is adjust the mirrors and seats so that you're comfortable. The Mac OS is unique among operating systems in this respect because there's a lot you can do to tweak and customize the interface. Apple builds much of this ability right into the interface, but even more customization can be done through the thousands of third-party utilities, most of which are available on the Internet.

In the next chapter, we'll look at the commands and options that are available through the Mac OS to help you manage your hard drive.

CHAPTER 5

Managing Your Hard Drive

As we've seen in Chapter 3, the Finder provides a comprehensive set of commands and features that help you manage disks and files. The Finder does not, however, require that you organize your electronic files in any particular way; it's still up to you to decide the best way to arrange your files.

For related information, see "Files" and "Disks" in Mac OS Help.

File management is an interesting challenge: you must balance your available storage space with the quantity and size of files you need to keep available, and you must design a logical arrangement that will allow you to quickly locate the files you need.

Fortunately, Mac OS 8 provides several file management tools, including the Make Alias command, the Find command, and the Label menu. These commands will affect the way you store files on your hard disk—and on floppy disks, removable cartridges, network file servers, or any other storage devices. In this chapter, we'll take a look at these features and how they can help you organize your hard drive.

Aliasing

Wouldn't it be nice to be in several places at one time? Imagine, for example, that while you are hard at work earning your paycheck, you could also be lying on a beach enjoying the sun. And if being in two places at once sounds appealing, how would you like to be in any number of places at one time? For example, you could be at work earning a living, at the beach getting a tan, at the library reading a book, and on a plane bound for an exotic destination—all at the same time.

Mac OS 8 extends this convenience to your electronic files through a feature called *aliasing*. Aliasing is perhaps one of the most significant improvements the Mac OS has offered the average Macintosh user. It removes the single largest constraint—space limitation—from the task of organizing files and thereby makes it easier to take full advantage of your software applications and data files.

Basic Aliasing Concepts

In simple terms, an *alias* is a special kind of copy of a file, folder, or volume. Unlike copies you might create with the Duplicate command or other traditional methods, an alias is only a copy of the file, folder, or volume *icon*.

To understand this distinction, think of a file icon as a door; the file that the icon represents is the room behind the door. As you would expect, each room normally has just one door (each file has one icon), and opening that door (the icon) is the only way to enter the room. Another way to think of aliases is as bookmarks that you may use to find your place in a book. Aliases are not new, however. They are used on UNIX computers and are called symbolic links. More recently, Microsoft implemented aliases in the Windows 95 and NT operating systems and called them shortcuts. Figure 5-1 shows two folders that contain the same aliased file, default.html, which resides in the Web pages folder.

Creating an alias is like adding an additional door to a room; it presents another entrance, usually in a location different from the existing entrance. Just as you wouldn't have two doors to the same room right next to each other, you won't usually have two icons for the same file (the original and an alias) in the same location. This is the first important feature of an alias: it can be moved to any folder on any volume without affecting the relationship between the alias and its original file. In fact, the link between an alias and its original file is maintained even if both files are moved.

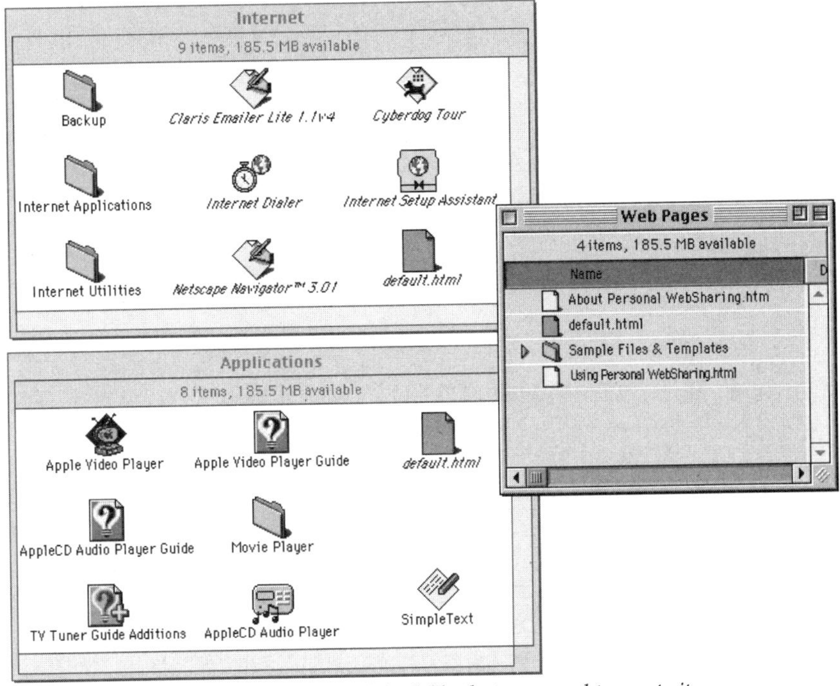

Figure 5-1: Each alias points to the original file that was used to create it.

Another key feature of an alias is that it requires only about 1K or 2K of disk space, regardless of the size of the original file. That's because the alias is a copy of the icon, not a copy of the file itself. The alias's small size is an important attribute since it consumes very little storage space.

Details about these and other aspects of aliases are provided later in this chapter, but before getting too far into the technical aspects, let's take a quick look at a few practical ways to use aliases:

- **To make applications easier to launch.** Since double-clicking on an application's alias launches that application, aliases make applications easily accessible.

  For example, you can keep one alias of your word processor on the desktop, another in a folder full of word processing data files, and yet another alias in the Apple Menu Items folder. You could then launch this application using the icon that is most convenient at the moment. Figure 5-2 shows a folder containing aliases to my favorite applications.

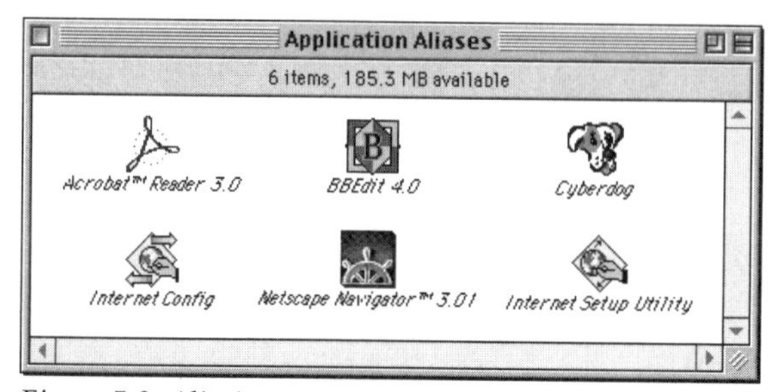

Figure 5-2: Aliasing an application makes it more convenient to launch.

- **To organize data files more logically.** You can keep alias copies of data files in as many folders as they logically belong in.

  If, for example, you keep a spreadsheet file with information on your income taxes in a folder along with all the spreadsheets you've created during that year, you could also keep an alias copy of that same spreadsheet in a personal finances folder, in another tax file folder, and in a general accounting folder.

  Storing alias copies in multiple locations, as in Figure 5-3, has several benefits. First, it lets you quickly locate the file you're looking for because there are several places to find it. It's also easier to find files because they can be stored along with other files they're logically connected with. Finally, archival storage lets you move the originals off the hard drive, saving disk space while still allowing access to the file via aliases.

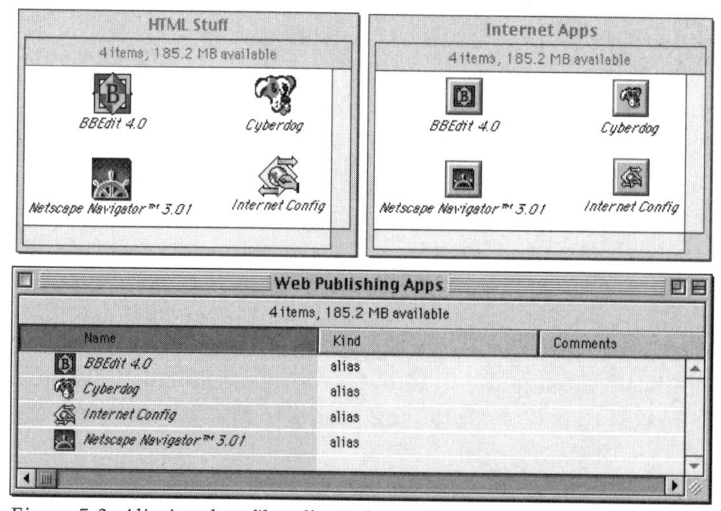

Figure 5-3: Aliasing data files allows them to be stored in multiple logical locations.

- **To simplify access to files stored on removable media.** Keeping aliases on your local hard drive from floppy disks, removable hard drives, CD-ROMs, and other removable storage media lets you locate those files quickly and easily.

  When an alias of a file stored on removable media is opened, the Mac OS prompts you to insert the disk (or cartridge) that contains the original file.

- **To simplify access to files stored on network servers**. Placing aliases of files from network file servers on your local hard drive is another way to quickly and easily locate the files no matter where they're stored.

  When an alias of a file stored on the network server is opened, the Macintosh automatically connects to the server, prompting you for necessary passwords.

Creating & Using Aliases

To create an alias, select the file, folder, or volume icon and:

1. Choose the Make Alias command from the File menu.
2. Press Command+M
3. Press Control and click the mouse on the file and select Make Alias.

An alias icon will then appear with the same name and icon as the original followed by the word *alias*, as shown in Figure 5-4.

Figure 5-4: Creating an alias of a hard drive named Skipper.

For the most part, alias icons look and act just like other files, folders, or volumes. You can change the filename of an alias at any time; changing the filename doesn't break the link between the alias and its original file (see Figure 5-5). Changing a filename is like changing the sign on a door; it doesn't change the contents of the room behind the door.

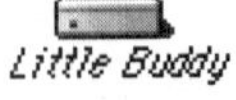

Figure 5-5: Renaming an alias doesn't break the link to the original item.

You've probably noticed that alias filenames appear in italic type. This is always true, even when they're listed in dialog boxes (*except* when aliases are listed under the Apple Menu). The italic type helps you distinguish the alias files from the original files, as in Figure 5-6.

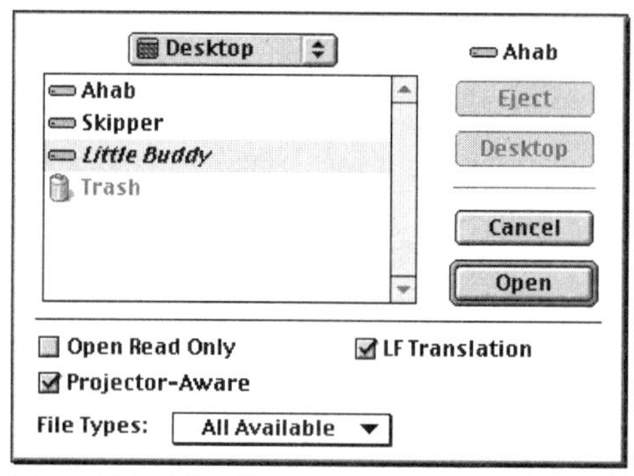

Figure 5-6: Alias filenames appear in italics in dialog boxes.

As mentioned earlier, alias icons can be moved to any available folder or volume without losing the link they maintain to the original file. This is the magic of aliases and the key to their utility. No matter how files are moved, the links are maintained.

Original files can also be moved, as long as they remain on the same volume, and they can be renamed without breaking the link with their aliases. When the alias icon is opened, the Mac OS finds and opens the original file.

To illustrate how this automatic linkage is maintained, assume you have a file called 1997 Commission Schedule, which is stored in a folder named Corporate Documents. You created an alias of this file, moved the alias into a folder called 1997 Personal Accounting, and renamed the alias 1997 Commissions (see Figure 5-7).

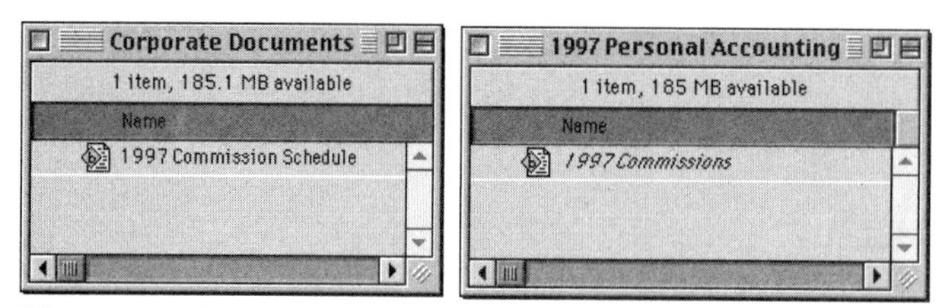

Figure 5-7: Files and aliases as originally named and positioned.

Later, you decide that this file will contain only data for the first six months of 1997, so you rename the original file 1997 Part 1 and put it in a new folder named Jan-June Stuff inside the Corporate Documents folder (see Figure 5-8).

Even though both the original file and the alias have been moved and renamed since they were created, double-clicking on the 1997 Commissions file (the alias) will open the 1997 Part 1 file.

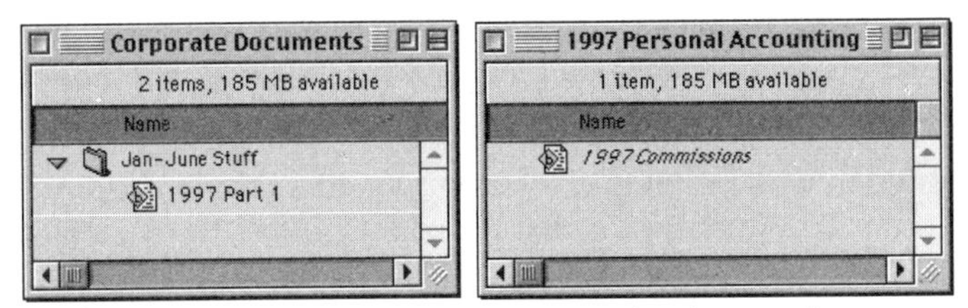

Figure 5-8: Files and aliases after being moved and renamed.

Advanced Aliasing Concepts

Once you understand the basic concepts of aliases and begin using them, you may have questions, such as: How many aliases can one file have? Is it possible to alias an alias? What happens when an alias's original file is deleted? The answers to these and other questions follow:

- **Multiple aliases.** There is no limit to the number of aliases you can create from a single file, folder, or volume.

  When multiple aliases are created, alias names are designated by numbers to distinguish them from existing alias names. The first alias of a file named Rejection Letter is named Rejection Letter alias; the second, Rejection Letter alias 1; the third, Rejection Letter alias 2; and so on until the earlier aliases are renamed or moved to different locations. These alias numbers have no significance beyond serving to avoid filename duplication.

- **Aliasing aliases.** You can create an alias of an alias, but this causes a chain of pointing references: the second alias points to the first, which points to the original. In most cases, it's better to create an alias directly from the original file.

  If you do create a chain and any one of the aliases in the chain is deleted, all subsequent aliases will no longer be linked to the original file. To illustrate this problem, assume an alias named New Specs alias was created from an original file named New Specs, and then New Specs alias alias was created from New Specs alias (see Figure 5-9).

Figure 5-9: Creating an alias of an alias creates a chain that can be broken if one alias is deleted.

At that point, each of these files can be repositioned and renamed and the alias links will be automatically maintained. However, if the New Specs alias file is deleted, New Specs alias alias will no longer be linked to New Specs. You can reestablish the link be creating a new alias of New Specs named New Specs alias.

- **Deleting aliases.** Deleting an alias has no effect on the original file, folder, or volume. It simply means that in order to access the item that the alias represented, you'll have to access the original item or another alias.

  You can delete aliases in any of the ways you delete normal files: drag the alias to the Trash and then choose the Empty Trash command or delete the alias using some other file deletion utility.

- **Moving original files.** The link between an alias and its original file is maintained regardless of how the original is moved on one volume, but links are not maintained when you copy the original file to a new volume and then delete the original file. In other words, there's no way to transfer the alias link from an original file to a copy of that original file.

  If you're going to move a file from which aliases have been created from one volume to another, and you must delete the original file, all existing aliases will be unlinked and therefore useless. You could create new aliases from the original file in its new location and replace the existing aliases with the new ones, but you'd have to perform this process manually.

- **Deleting original files.** Deleting a file from which aliases have been made has no immediate effect; no warning is posted when the file is deleted. But when an attempt is made to open an alias of a file that's been deleted, a dialog box appears informing you that the original file cannot be found. There's no way to salvage a deleted file to relink with this alias, so in most cases you'll want to delete the orphaned alias.

  The exception to this rule is when the original file is still in the Trash. In this case, if you try to open an alias, a dialog box will inform you that the file cannot be opened because it's in the Trash. If you drag the original from the Trash, it's again available to the alias.

- **Finding original files.** Although an alias is in many ways a perfect proxy for a file, there are times when you'll need to locate the alias's original file—for example, if you want to delete the original file or copy the original onto a floppy disk.

  To locate the original file for any alias, simply select the alias icon in the Finder and choose Show Original from the Finder's File menu; then press Command+R or choose Show Original from the contextual pop-up menu. The original file, folder, or volume is selected and displayed on the desktop. If the original file is located on a removable volume that's not currently available, a dialog box appears prompting you to insert the disk or cartridge containing that file. If the original file is located on a network file server, the Macintosh attempts to log on to the server to locate the file, prompting for any required passwords. Figure 5-10 shows the path information to the original item, not the alias itself.

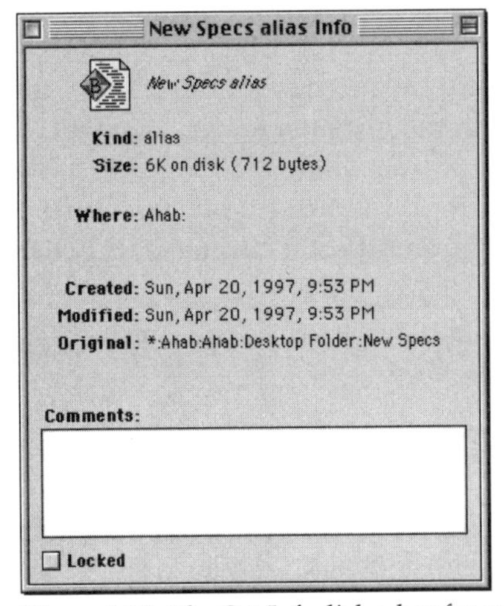

Figure 5-10: The Get Info dialog box for an alias.

  If the selected alias is an alias of an alias, the Mac OS will find the original file, not the alias used to create the current alias.

- **Replacing alias icons.** As introduced in Chapter 3, "The Finder & Desktop," new icons can be pasted into the Get Info dialog box for any file. This is also true of alias icons. Replacing the icon of any alias has no effect on the icon of the original file.

Aliasing Folders or Volumes

So far, most of this section has focused on aliasing in relation to application and data files. But almost without exception, aliasing works the same way for folders and volumes. Folder aliases are created, renamed, repositioned, deleted, and linked to their originals in exactly the same way as the file aliases previously described:

- Aliasing a folder creates a new folder icon with the same name as the original, plus the word *alias*.
- The name of an alias folder appears in italics on the desktop or in dialog box listings.
- Folder aliases can be renamed at any time. Of course, an alias cannot have the same name as an original or another alias while in the same location.
- Folder aliases can be moved inside any other folder or folder alias or to any volume.
- When an alias folder is opened, the window of the original folder is opened. Aliasing a folder does not alias the folder's content. For this reason, the original folder must be available anytime the folder alias is opened. If the original folder is on a volume that's not currently mounted, you'll be prompted to insert the volume, or the Macintosh will attempt to mount the volume if it's on the network.
- Deleting a folder alias does not delete the original folder or any of its contents.

But there are some unique aspects of folder aliases:

- When a folder alias is displayed hierarchically in a Finder list window or the Apple Menu (see Figure 5-11), it cannot be opened hierarchically (no triangle appears to its left) because the folder alias has no contents, strictly speaking. You can open the folder alias by double-clicking on it to open a new Finder window.
- Anything put into a folder alias, including files, folders, and other aliases, is actually placed into the original folder. The folder alias has no real contents; it's just another "door" to the original folder.

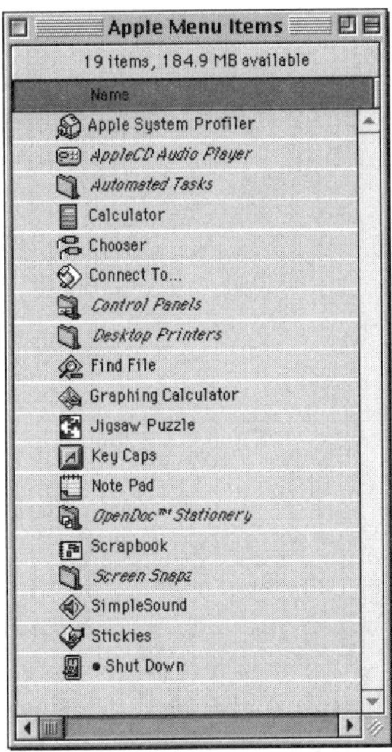

Figure 5-11: Alias folders are commonly used in the Apple Menu.

Volume aliases are similar to file aliases but have some of the same characteristics as folder aliases:

- Opening a volume alias mounts the original volume if it's not already available. If the original volume is not currently mounted, you'll be prompted to insert the volume, or the Mac OS will attempt to mount the volume if it's on the network.
- Opening a volume alias displays the Finder window of the actual volume and the contents of this window.
- Aliasing a volume does not alias the volume contents, just the icon of the volume itself. Figure 5-12 shows a collection of aliased volumes.

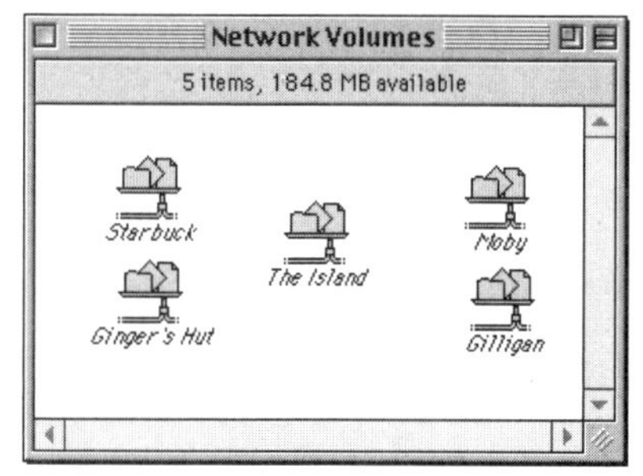

Figure 5-12: Alias volumes stored in a folder.

Using Aliases

Aliases have a multitude of uses. The following are some of the more interesting possibilities:

- **Alias applications.** The easiest way to launch an application is to double-click on its icon. But many of today's applications are stored in folders containing a morass of ancillary files—dictionaries, color palettes, Help files, printer descriptions, and so on. Amid all this clutter, it's hard to locate the application icon in order to launch it. Aliasing allows easier access, as shown in Figure 5-13.

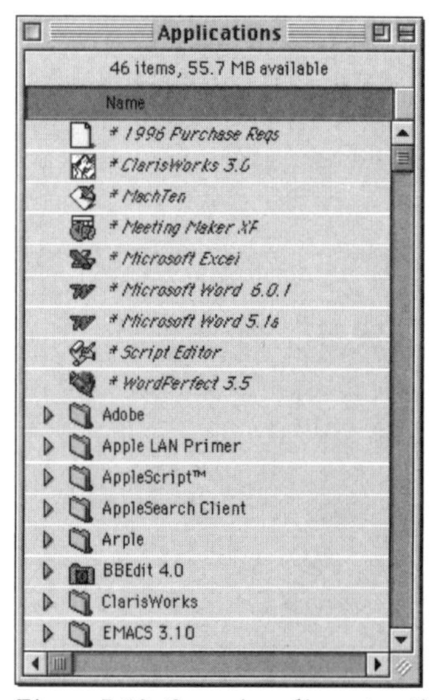

Figure 5-13: Grouping aliases together helps organize access to your recently used applications.

The most straightforward way to simplify application launching is to alias each of your applications inside the Apple Menu Items folder of your System folder. You can then launch the applications by simply choosing their names from the Apple Menu. Keep in mind that the Recent Applications folder may make this a less practical approach than in previous versions of system software.

Or, instead, you might group your application aliases into folders and then alias these folders and place them in the Apple Menu. Doing it this way takes two steps instead of one, but this method leaves room in your Apple Menu for other folder, volume, and file aliases. Of course, you could leave a few applications that you use extensively directly in the Apple Menu, but since the Mac OS shows hierarchical menus for any folder in the Apple Menu folder, the former approach is preferable.

You can also put application aliases, along with groups of documents created with the application, on your desktop. But since double-clicking on any document will launch the application anyway, this is not really very useful.

- **Multiple data file aliases.** To avoid having to remember all the places where a frequently used file is stored every time you want to use it, you can use aliases to store each data file in as many places as it logically fits—anywhere you might look for the file when you need it later.

  Suppose, for example, you write a letter to your boss about a new idea for serving your company's big client, Clampdown, Inc. Depending on your personal scheme, you might store this letter, along with other general business correspondence, in a folder pertaining to Clampdown, Inc., or you might even have a file where you keep everything that has to do with your boss. Using aliases, you can store the file in all these locations and in a folder containing all work you've done in the current week, as illustrated in Figure 5-14.

- **Aliases of data files from remote or removable volumes.** You can store hundreds of megabytes worth of files on your hard drive, regardless of how big it is, by using aliases. Keeping aliases of all the files you normally store on removable disks or drives and all the files from network file servers that you occasionally need to utilize lets you locate and open the files by simply searching your hard drive (at the Finder, in dialog boxes, or using a search utility) without the cost of hard-drive space.

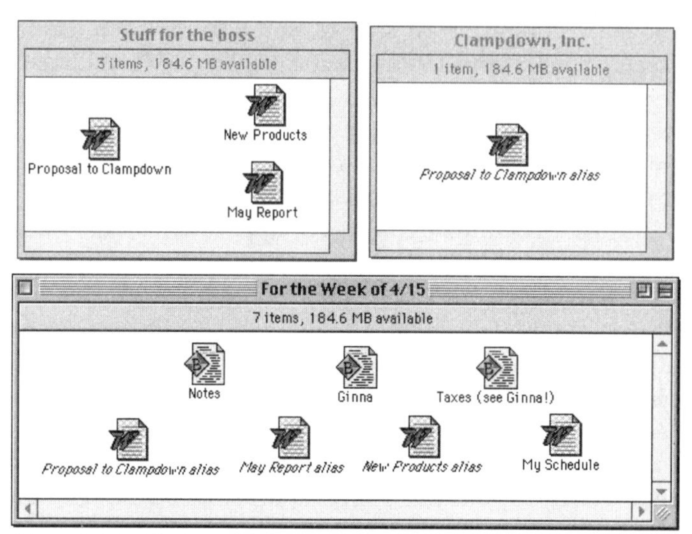

Figure 5-14: Aliasing a file into multiple locations.

This is perfect for storing libraries of clip-art files, downloadable fonts, corporate templates, or other infrequently used file groups. Storing these aliased files on your hard drive, as shown in Figure 5-15, lets you browse through them whenever necessary. The hard drive will automatically mount the required volumes or prompt you for them when they're needed.

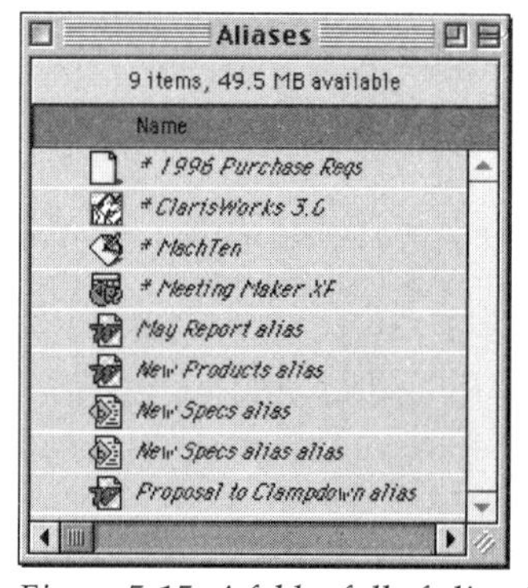

Figure 5-15: A folder full of aliased utility files stored on a removable volume.

- **Trash alias.** You can alias the Finder's Trash and store copies of it in any folder. Dragging folder files to the Trash alias is the same as dragging them to the actual Trash. Files trashed in this way will not be removed until you choose Empty Trash from the Special menu, and they can be retrieved by simply opening the Trash (or an alias of it) and dragging the file back onto a volume or folder.
- **Removable cartridge maps.** Create a folder for each removable cartridge, drive, or floppy disk. Alias the entire contents of these volumes and store the aliases in the volume's folder. Then you can "browse" these volumes without mounting them. You may also want to keep other aliases of files from these volumes in other locations on your drive.
- **Network file server volume maps.** Create a folder called Network and place an alias of each remote volume inside that folder. You can then log on to any remote volume by simply double-clicking on the volume alias. This eliminates the need to access the Chooser, locate the file server, and locate the volume every time you want to use the volume. Of course, you'll be prompted for any required passwords.
- **Hard drive alias.** If you work on a large AppleTalk network, put an alias icon of your hard drive on a floppy disk and carry it with you. If you need to access your hard drive from another location, all you have to do is insert the floppy disk containing your hard drive alias into any Macintosh on the network, double-click on the alias icon, and your hard drive will be mounted via AppleTalk.

Aliasing Summary

Aliases have many uses, including the following:

- You can alias any file, folder, and volume icon or the Trash.
- To create an alias, select the desired icon and choose Make Alias from the Finder's File menu, press Command+M, or choose Make Alias from the contextual pop-up menu.
- An alias initially takes the same name as its original file with the word *alias* appended.
- Alias names always appear in italics, except in the Apple Menu.
- Aliases can be renamed at any time. The standard Macintosh 32-character name limit applies.
- Aliases can be moved to any location on the current volume or any other volume.

- An alias is initially given the same icon as its original. The icon can be changed in the Get Info dialog box.
- An alias requires only a very small amount of storage space.
- The link between an alias and its original is maintained even when the files are renamed or repositioned.
- Deleting an alias icon has no effect on its original file, folder, or volume.
- Copying an alias to a new location on the current drive (hold down the Option key while dragging) is the same as creating a new alias of the original file—it does not create an alias of an alias.
- Press Command+R after selecting an alias to locate its original.
- Opening a folder alias opens the window of the original folder.
- Opening a volume alias opens the window of the original volume.

The Find Command

Regardless of how well organized your electronic filing system is, it's impossible to always remember where specific files are located.

To solve this problem in the past, Apple provided the Find File desk accessory (DA) to let you search for files—by filename—on any currently mounted volume. Find File locates the files and lists them in a section of its window. Once a file is found, selecting the filename reveals the path of the located file along with other basic file information, as shown in Figure 5-16. Using this information, you can then quit the Find File DA and locate the file yourself, or Find File can move the file to the desktop where it's easy to access.

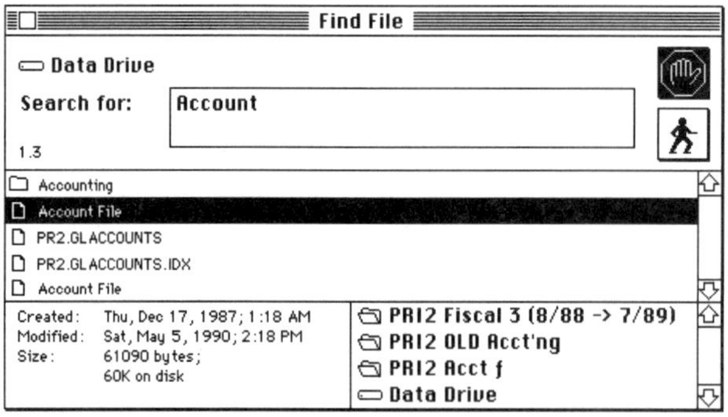

Figure 5-16: The Find File desk accessory.

Beyond Find File, other file-finding utilities have also been available for quite some time. Most of them let you search for files not only by filename but also by creation date, file type, creator, date modified, file size, and other file attributes. Norton Utility's Fast Find is one example. Like Find File, most of these utilities locate matching files, display the path information, and let you return to the Finder and use or modify the file as required. (There is also a class of utilities that search inside files to find matches to text strings, such as Retrieve It!, GOFer, and OnLocation, to name but a few.)

In System 7, a new Find command was added to the Finder. This command and its companion command, Find Again, significantly improve on the Find File desk accessory. And System 7.5 significantly improves on the Find command by returning all matches to a search in a new Found Items dialog box, thereby eliminating repetitive Find Again searches. Because these new commands are built into the Finder, they offer important advantages over other file-finding utilities.

In Mac OS 8, a new version of the Find command is present that gives you even more choices when searching for files on your Mac. A new search engine behind the scenes also makes searching for files much faster. Let's look at the latest version of the Find command and compare it to the older versions of the Find command so you can get an idea of what you could do under older versions of the Mac OS and what you can do now.

Using the Find Command

The Find command is located in the Finder's File menu, and the actual program itself is in the Apple Menu. In previous versions of the Mac OS, the Find command consisted of both a program named Find File and an Extension named Find File Extension, which worked together to search for items on your, and other, hard drives. In Mac OS 8, however, the Find File Extension has been eliminated but it still uses the Find File program user interface found in System 7.5.x. The new Find File is many times faster than previous versions due to the new multithreader, PowerPC-native Finder

Because the Find File program is an actual application, you may find it necessary to increase the amount of memory dedicated to the application if you have numerous files or large hard drives. More memory is required to search larger numbers of files. Figure 5-17 shows the Find File application's Get Info window, which is located under the Apple Menu and has the default memory allocation bumped up from 280K to 350K.

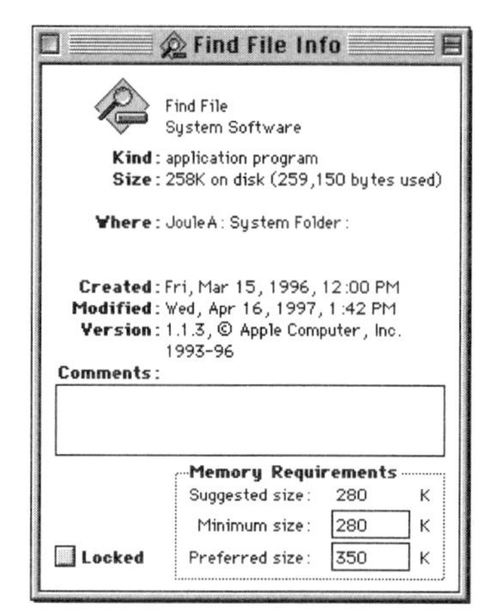

Figure 5-17: The Find File application's Get Info window.

The Find File application is launched by either selecting it from the Apple Menu or pressing Command+F; both options present the window shown in Figure 5-18.

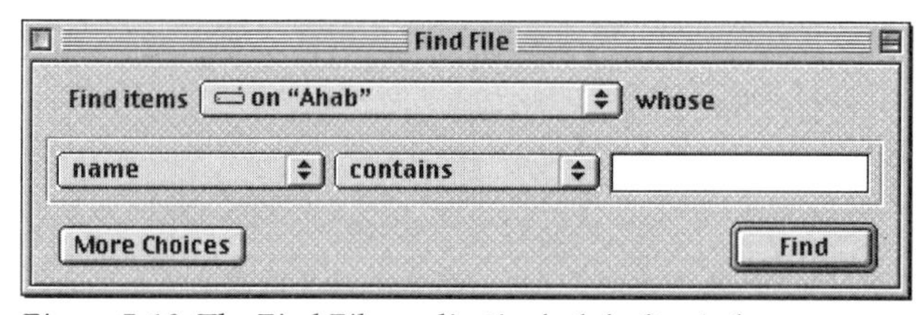

Figure 5-18: The Find File application's default window.

The File Find window defaults to a "simple search" window, but you can ask the Find File application to do a very complex search as well. We'll get into that a bit later in the chapter, but for now let's start with the basics. Using the basic Find dialog box to locate files by name, you can enter the complete filename or only the first portion of the filename:

- **Enter a complete filename.** If you know the complete name of the file you're looking for, enter it into the Find option box. In most cases, only the correct file will be found, but if you make even a slight error in spelling the filename, the correct file will not be found. This is not the most efficient way to execute a file search.

- **Enter only the first portion of a filename.** Entering the first few characters of the filename is the most commonly used and usually the most efficient filename search method. This locates all files whose names begin with the characters you've specified. The exact number of characters you should enter will depend on the circumstances; the goal is to enter enough characters to narrow the search down but not so many that you risk a spelling mistake and therefore a chance of missing the file.

  For example, if the file you wanted to locate is named Archaeology Report, specifying only the letter *A* would yield a huge number of files to sort through. On the other hand, entering six or seven characters could allow filenames with spelling errors, such as Archio or Arhcae, to escape the search. Decide on the number of characters according to how common the first few characters are among your files and how well you remember the filename. In this example, searching for files starting with Arc would probably be the best strategy.

After specifying the search criteria, click the Find button to start the search. The search starts with the start-up drive and proceeds to search any other volumes you specify (more on that in a minute). If the search will take more than a few seconds, a Progress dialog box appears. In versions of the system software prior to System 7.5, when a file matching the search criteria is located, a Finder window is opened and the file is displayed. In Mac OS 8, however, the entire search results are displayed in a second window, as in Figure 5-19, which shows a search for any item on the boot drive Ahab that contains the letters *a p p l e*.

Notice the Items Found window is divided into two parts. The upper part lists the search results, which may be viewed by name, size, kind, or the date an item was last modified (but not created). To change the view, just click on Name, Size, Kind, or Last Modified to rearrange the search results.

The path to an item is displayed in the lower half of the Items Found window. For example, the first item displayed in Figure 5-19 is named About Apple Guide, which is an Apple Guide document located in the Extensions folder, which is inside the System folder, which in turn is on the hard drive named Ahab. At this point, you can use or modify the found file as required. If the selected file is not the one you wanted, or if after modifying the selected file you want to continue searching for the next file that matches the search criteria, choose the Find command (Command+F) again and the Find File window will be made active.

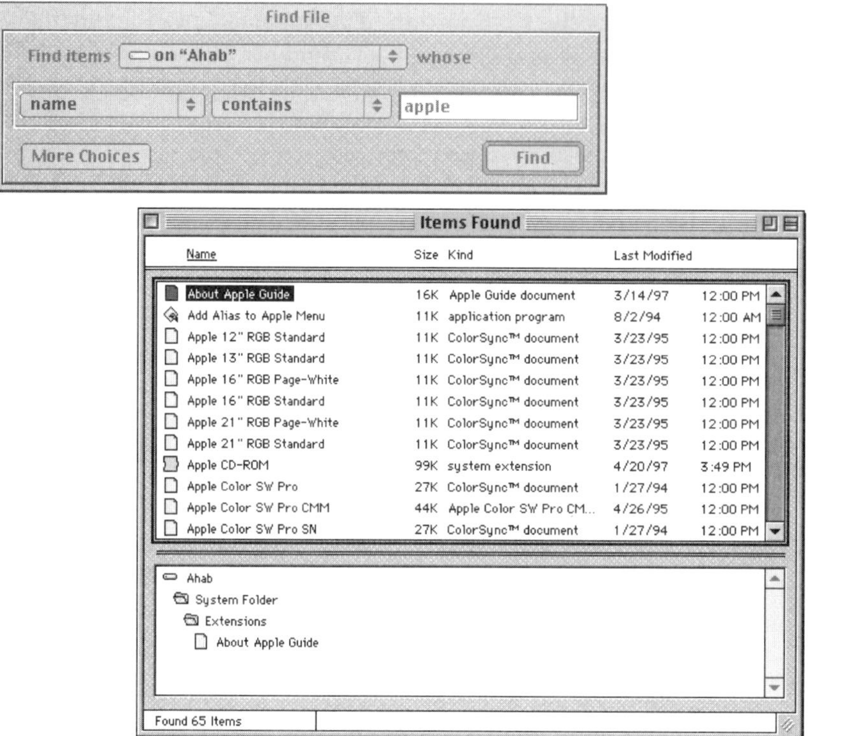

Figure 5-19: The results of a simple search.

The Search options are:

- **On All Disks.** Searches all mounted volumes, including all folders and items that appear on the Finder desktop.
- **On Local Disks.** Limits the search to local disks only, such as internal and external hard drives, floppy drives, and removable media such as Zip drives. Local disks are part of your SCSI chain.
- **On Mounted Servers.** Mounted servers are network-connected volumes. All these volumes show up as their volume names. For example, you might see Macintosh HD as a listing (or whatever name the owner has given to the hard drive).
- **On the Desktop.** Limits the search to the desktop if no volume or folder is selected. If you have multiple hard drives, each Desktop file will be searched.

- **In the Finder Selection.** Confines the search to those items currently selected. Clicking a folder in the Finder and then choosing this option will allow you to search only in that item, whether that be a folder, a hard drive, or a mounted server.
- **On <*hard drive*>.** Confines the search to a particular hard drive or mounted volume.

To see the full dialog box, click the More Choices button in the simple Find dialog box. A single additional criterion appears. Continue to click the More Choices buttons to fully expose the dialog box and have it look like the one shown in Figure 5-20. Click the Find button to initiate the search, or click Fewer Choices to narrow your search options.

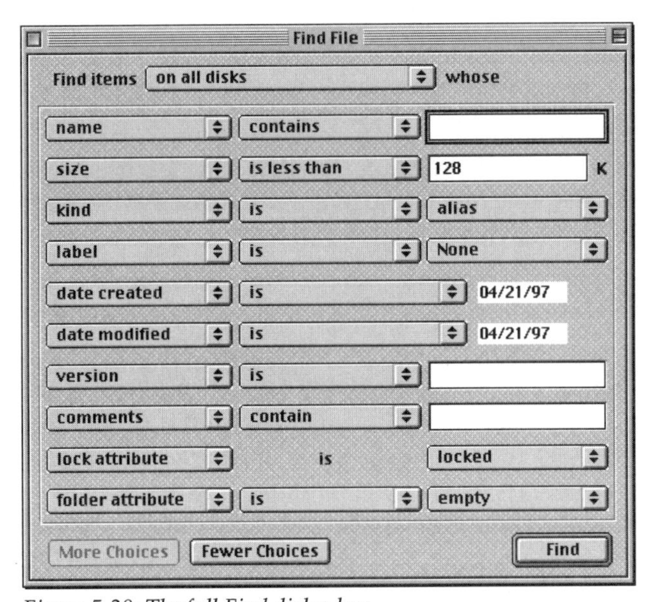

Figure 5-20: The full Find dialog box.

Using Macintosh Drag and Drop, you can do a number of things with selections in the Found Items dialog box after you've executed a search:

- **Open the item's window.** Press Command+E to open the item's enclosing folder, or select the Open Enclosing Folder command from the File menu.
- **Move the file.** Drag the file or folder name to a new location. The item moves to where you drag it. When you drag the item to another disk, it is copied.

- **Open the file.** Double-clicking on a folder or typing Command+O with a folder selected will open the folder. The same actions will open a selected file if the application that created the file is available. You can also drag the filename to an application. If the application can open that file type, it launches (if necessary) and opens the file—translating the file, if needed.
- **Print the file.** Drag the file onto a printer icon on the Finder (if you have one).

Tips for Effective Searches

Here are a few Find Command tips to help you create effective searches:

- Once you close the new Found Items dialog box, the criteria of your search are forgotten. To repeat a search, you'll have to start over.
- Find does not look inside the System file. Items like fonts or sounds that have been placed inside the System file will not be located by the Find command.
- Find locates aliases as well. Any alias that matches the specified search criteria can be found just like regular files. Aliases will appear in italic text in the Found Items dialog box.
- Find also locates folders and volumes. Any folder or volume matching the specified search criteria will be found, just like any other file.
- Use the Search by Kind option to locate all data files created by one specific application. To use the by-kind search criterion, specify the file kind (for example, all HTML documents) that the application assigns to its data files. (See the sample file kinds in Figure 5-21.) To see these additional search types, click the pop-up menu. Items like Folder Type, File Type, and Creator Type appear at the bottom.
- Use Find to do quick backups. After you've used the Find command to locate all files on a volume modified after a certain date, you can drag those files to a removable volume for a "quick-and-dirty" backup. Of course, this procedure shouldn't replace a good backup utility—but you can never have too many backups.

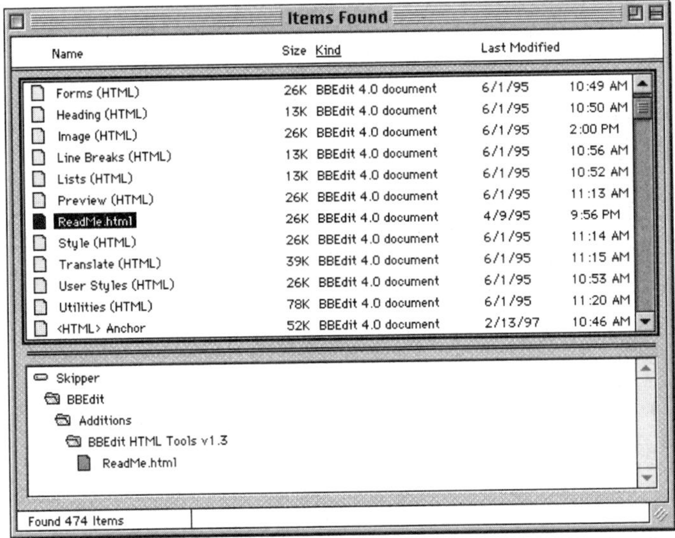

Figure 5-21: The Kind column displays the name of the application that created the file (BBEdit, in this case).

- Use the selected item's search range to perform multiple-criteria searches. For example, the Find command will locate all filenames beginning with *S* that are less than 32K in size and have the Microsoft Word creator type (or any other set of multiple criteria). The first criterion is searched for using the on *<any one volume>* range; then you search for each additional criterion using the selected items range.

Labels

The Label menu is a great tool that helps you categorize your files, identify certain types of files, locate these files, and in some cases, manipulate them as a group.

Configuring Labels

The Label menu is no longer in the Finder menu bar; it's configured using the Finder Preferences option under the Edit menu. Figure 5-22 displays the Finder Preferences and the Labels options. The text and color of your labels are configured in this area.

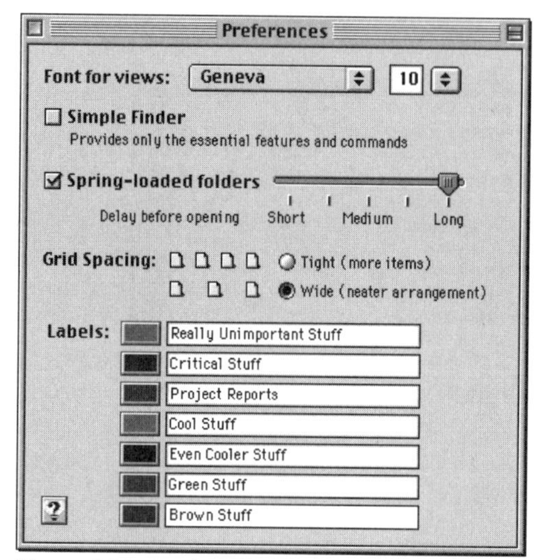

Figure 5-22: Configuring the labels in the Finder Preferences.

To set label text, click in each label text block and enter the name of the label category you want to define. With label assignments, form must follow function; there's no advantage to having label assignments that don't help you use and manipulate your data more efficiently. There are several ways to use labels:

- **To categorize files.** Labels provide an additional level of categorization for files. Files are already categorized by type, creation and modification dates, and related folders, but using labels, you can also classify them by topic, importance, or any other way you choose.
- **For visual distinction.** Color-coding icons helps you quickly distinguish one type of file from another on a color monitor. For example, all applications can be red, making them easier to spot in a folder full of dictionaries, Help instructions, and other files. You can also use the Labels column in Finder windows, which lists label names next to filenames.
- **To facilitate data backup.** You can find all files assigned to a specific label and then copy them to another disk or volume for backup purposes.
- **To indicate security requirements.** When using File Sharing, you can create labels that remind you of the security level of specific folders, files, and volumes.

Using Label Categories

There are many ways to use the available label categories:

- **Categories for logical subdivisions of data files.** If your work is project based, you can specify large projects by individual labels and use one miscellaneous label for smaller projects. You could also have Long-Term Projects, Short-Term Projects, and Permanent Projects labels.
- **Categories for software applications.** You can differentiate launchable applications or label both applications and their ancillary files. You might want a separate label for utility programs, including third-party extensions, control panels, desk accessories, and utilities that are launchable applications.
- **Specify security levels.** If special security is required in your work environment, label one or two folders to identify them as secure. You can then use encryption utilities to safeguard these files; use them carefully with File Sharing or apply third-party security utilities to protect them.

Once labels are defined, you can modify label colors (available only on color Macs). To do so, click on any color in the Labels control panel to bring up the color wheel dialog box, shown in Figure 5-23. Specify the color you want for the label. Because label colors are applied over existing icon colors, weaker colors with lower hue and saturation values (found toward the middle of the wheel) work best.

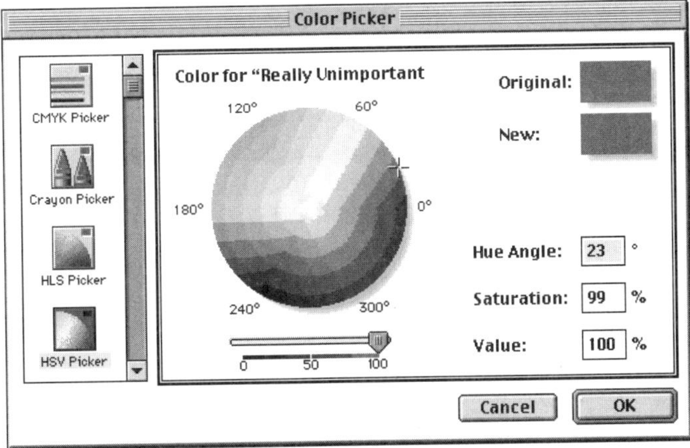

Figure 5-23: Changing a label color using the Apple color wheel.

After you've modified the label names and colors, close the Finder Preferences. The labels and any files or folders affected are then updated. You can reopen the Finder Preferences menu any time you need to reset the text or colors.

Comments

In the past, adding lengthy comments to Mac OS files has been unsatisfactory, to say the least. The main problem was that the comments were likely to disappear every time the invisible desktop file was replaced or rebuilt. Most people stopped using comments when they discovered that they could never be sure how long they'd last. Plus, comments could only be seen by opening the Get Info dialog box, so they were inconvenient to use.

System 7 attempted to breathe new life into file comments, correcting some of their former shortcomings and adding some interesting possibilities that could make comments an important part of working with your Mac OS files. In the Finder, comments have been improved in three important ways:

- **Visibility.** You can now see comments in Finder windows. When the Show Comments option in the Views | View Options preferences is selected (as detailed in Chapter 3), comments will display in Finder windows. This makes them practical to use.
- **Searchability.** The Find command (prior to System 7.5) lets you search for text in file comments, making it possible to locate files by comment entries.
- **Permanence.** Comments are retained when the desktop is rebuilt by holding down the Option and Command keys on start-up.

People will find other productive ways to use these new comment features. One idea is to use comments as cues: keywords or phrases can provide information not already included in the filename, date, kind, or other file information. Client names, project titles, and related document names are a few examples. This additional information would be displayed in Finder windows via the Find command.

Figure 5-24 shows some files with comments added. Complete comments make it easy to see at a glance what these files contain when browsing Finder windows; it also makes the files easy to retrieve with the Find command.

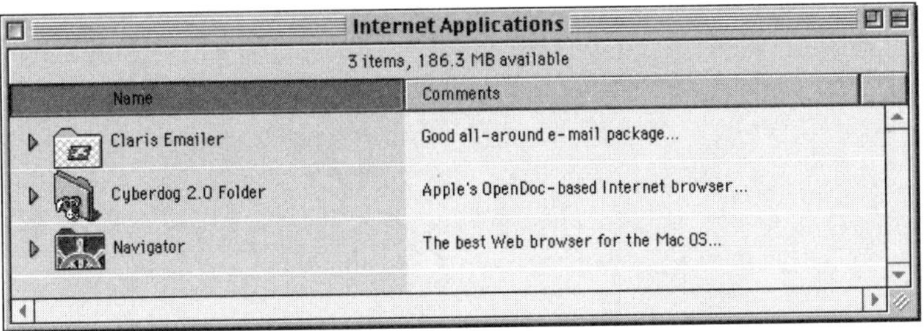

Figure 5-24: A Finder window as it appears when using the Show Comments option.

Moving On

The power and importance of the capabilities introduced in this chapter cannot be overestimated. As you become more familiar with Mac OS 8, you'll use these features frequently:

- **Aliases** help you locate and launch files and access network data quickly and easily.
- **The Find command** will solve your "where is that file?" problem.
- **Labels** make it easier to keep important files organized.
- **Comments** remind you of details about particular file or folder content.

Next, we'll look at the special software and features designed for PowerBook and mobile users.

CHAPTER 6

PowerBook System Software

PowerBook system software support began with System 7.0.1. A suite of simple utilities for controlling your PowerBook's basic functions was included, controlling screen display, measuring battery lifetimes, doing processor cycling, and other tasks. Sensing an opportunity, many vendors rushed in, substantially improving upon Apple's meager offerings with packages like Claris's Power To Go, Connectix's CPU, Norton's Essentials for the PowerBook, Inline Design's PBTools, and so on. Several million PowerBooks later, Apple substantially improved the support that PowerBook owners looked for elsewhere. Some of these features added in Mac OS 8, such as the Control Strip, will doubtless appeal to many people.

PowerBook Issues

The Apple PowerBook 100 series was the most successful introduction of any family of portable computers in history, and Apple has had a string of successes with virtually all of its PowerBooks and Duos since. The PowerBook replaced the ill-fated Portable, and Apple learned volumes from the experience. Millions of Macintosh users have not just supplemented their computing needs but replaced their desktop machines as well. Minimal system software support for the PowerBook series began with System 7.0.1 but has grown stronger over the past three years. Now, with the 240 MHz PowerBook 3400c, you can run the latest Mac OS and benefit from its enhancements.

PowerBook users have different needs than desktop users, including the following requirements:

- **Improved battery lifetime between recharges.** There are various techniques to reduce power consumption, such as slowing down the processor, reducing screen brightness, spinning down hard drives, reducing hard disk input and output (I/O) using a RAM disk, and putting the system to sleep. All these capabilities are supported in system software.
- **Easy connection.** PowerBook users require remote access, automatic remounting of hard drives and network servers upon wake-up, and other connection features for which there is now system support.

  You can use the PowerBook Setup Control Panel shown in Figure 6-1 to connect your PowerBook to another Macintosh as if it were an external hard drive or another Small Computer Serial Interface (SCSI) device.

Figure 6-1: The PowerBook Setup Control Panel.

- **Presentation services.** PowerBooks manage external displays. Video-out is a feature of many models, as is video mirroring. These features are provided in an updated Monitors Control Panel.
- **Spooling of print documents for later printing.** You can store documents to a printer with a Print Later feature, which is enabled by the Assistant toolbox extension. When you try to print to a printer that isn't connected, you will get a dialog box asking if you want the document stored. Printing occurs automatically the next time you connect to that printer.

  The Assistant toolbox, a component of Mac OS 8, supplements your PowerBook support. It adds features such as mouse tracks and fat cursors (in the Mouse panel), a keystroke for instant sleep or hard drive spin down, and some screen dimming. You can add this to earlier system versions by purchasing the PowerBook File Assistance package, which is meant primarily for file synchronization.

- **Peripheral support.** Keyboards, trackballs, trackpads, and other ADB devices are supported. For example, Figure 6-2 shows the two Trackpad settings that are available to allow you to customize your mouse movements.

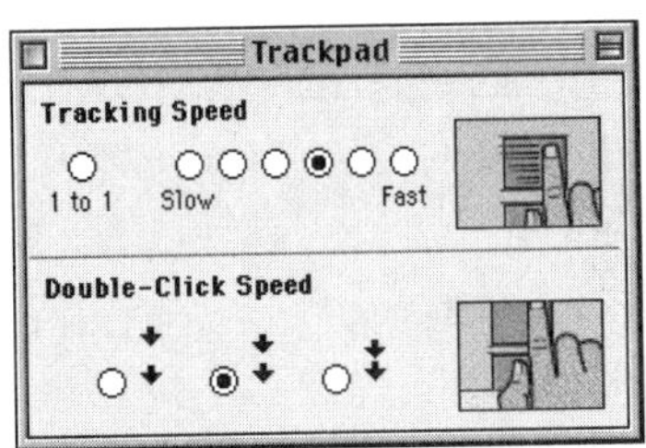

Figure 6-2: Set cursor speed and double-click time in the Trackpad Control Panel.

- **File synchronization.** To update files on a PowerBook with your other Macintosh computers, you can use the Macintosh File Assistant.

Mac OS 8 adds a number of new features that PowerBook users will appreciate, notably a convenient Control Strip utility and the Location Manager. Most other PowerBook utilities have been reworked to a small extent in Mac OS 8 but are virtually the same.

There is much to know about PowerBooks and not enough space in this book to cover it. Two books you might appreciate are *The PowerBook Companion*, Second Edition, by Sharon Zardetto Akker and Bruce Wolfson (Addison-Wesley); and *PowerBook: The Digital Nomad's Guide*, by Andrew Gore and Mitch Radcliffe (Random House). Although both books are good, the Akker/Wolfson book is more up-to-date in this rapidly changing marketplace.

Power/Performance Management

There's a plethora of PowerBooks out there, and some consume more power than others. The power consumption of PowerBooks is a major portability issue, particularly with models using CD-ROM drives and color screens. Luckily, Mac OS 8 employs a number of techniques to reduce power consumption through the PowerBook Control Panel. You can view this Control Panel in its Easy view (Figure 6-3) or in the Custom view (Figure 6-4).

Figure 6-3: The PowerBook Control Panel in the Easy view.

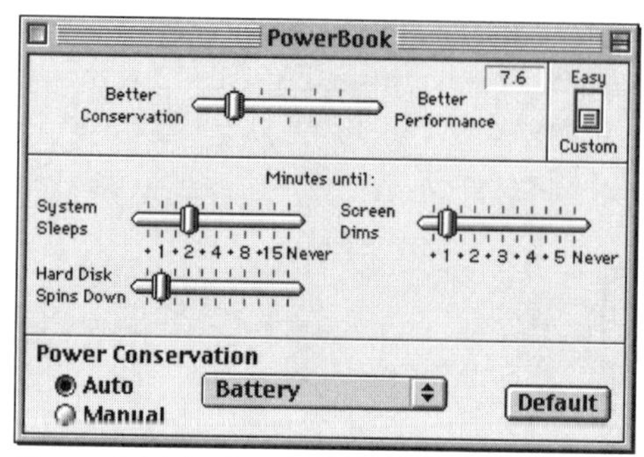

Figure 6-4: The Custom view of the PowerBook Control Panel.

You want easy? Move the Battery Conservation slider to the Better Conservation side to increase battery longevity. Use this setting when you aren't plugged in somewhere. Move the setting to Better Performance when you are plugged in. Your PowerBook translates your settings into the time it takes to dim your screen, spin down your hard drive, and go to system sleep, among other things. As a rule of thumb, when you are on the road, use Better Conservation until you notice performance differences that bother you.

You can monitor your battery's performance by viewing the Battery menu bar item shown in Figure 6-5, which is one of the several items in the Control Strip (see Figure 6-10 for other items in the Control Strip). This battery meter has eight levels that change color as a function of your battery's *voltage* level. When all eight bars are colored, you are fully recharged. Bars go white from top to bottom as your battery depletes. You get 2 warnings about power depletion before your last warning, which is 10 seconds before your PowerBook is sent to sleep.

Figure 6-5: The Battery menu item shown with a nearly depleted battery.

This system of measuring voltage levels is accurate and reliable as far as it goes. What voltage measurements don't tell you is how much time your battery has left. For that indicator, you need to know the lowest voltage level your battery will drop to, your instantaneous power consumption, and the history of power consumption you have had. Anomalies such as which battery you are using, memory effects, unusual power consumption activities, and other factors make learning about your battery's life a difficult proposition. So, the power warnings you get only tell you voltage levels, not how long you have left on a battery.

Battery life is such a valuable measurement that the PowerBook 500 uses batteries with microprocessors in them. These batteries give more accurate measurements in the Battery Monitor section of the PowerBook Control Strip, and an estimated time is given in hours.

Surprisingly, your microprocessor is a major energy draw; it uses about 25 percent of your battery's current. The other major power draw is the display, which depending on its type can consume anywhere from 20 percent (black and white) to 50 percent (color) of your current. Display issues are covered in the next section of this chapter.

Most later model PowerBooks contain a microprocessor capable of lower energy consumption states. In one state, the CPU goes down to a lower clock rate. This feature is called *processor cycling*, and it can save energy when you use it. This state is different from the processor *sleep state*, in which only CPU memory is preserved.

To turn on processor cycling, use the Custom section of the PowerBook Control Panel, and click the Reduced Processor Speed check box in the Options section. Because your processor fires up instantaneously, processor cycling is a good feature to enable when you are on battery power. These and other power consumption routines are part of the Power Manager in the Macintosh toolbox that first appeared in System 6.

Sleep is the condition in which your hard drive is spun down, your screen powered off, and your microprocessor is put in a comatose state. Each component can be put to sleep separately. Sleep is a perfectly safe condition for transporting your PowerBook and storing it for short periods. Depending on the model, your PowerBook can retain contents of memory for two weeks in this condition. A major factor in this equation is the amount of memory you have installed that needs to be refreshed.

You have several ways of putting your PowerBook to sleep in Mac OS 8:

- Choose the Sleep command from the Special menu.
- Press the Command+Shift+Zero keystroke (added by the Assistant toolbox).
- Set the period of inactivity for automatic sleep in the PowerBook Control Panel.
- Click the Sleep Now icon in the Control Strip.

Press any keystroke other than the Caps Lock key to wake up your Macintosh.

Your hard drive is another source of power draw for a PowerBook. It's estimated to consume about 15 percent of your power, on average. You can do some things to improve the power consumption of this element:

- Use memory-resident (RAM) applications that don't require much I/O.
- Press the Command+Shift-Control+Zero keystroke to spin down your hard drive instantly (added by the Assistant toolbox).
- Set the period of inactivity for automatic hard drive spin down in the PowerBook Control Panel (Figure 6-4).
- Click the HD Spin Down icon in the PowerBook Control Strip (Figure 6-10) to spin down a drive instantly.
- Use a RAM disk to limit disk access. This feature is covered in Chapter 9, "Applications & Memory Management," and is part of the Memory Control Panel.

Don't get too carried away with keeping your hard drive spun down. The energy expended in spinning up a hard drive is equivalent to something like 30 seconds to a minute of the hard drive spinning at its rated speed. You need to be in situations in which you don't access the disk more than every two or three minutes at a time for this feature to be valuable.

Similarly, keeping AppleTalk active takes a noticeable amount of power. The serial port must be polled for activity. Using the AppleTalk Control Panel or the Control Strip, you can turn AppleTalk on and off. Another factor is File Sharing, which makes the disk less able to spin down; you can also turn on and off from the File Sharing icon in the Control Strip.

Display Management

You can achieve substantial battery savings by simply turning down your display screen. This savings is particularly true for color Macintosh computers, for which the screen is the major power draw. The PowerBook Control Panel will blank your screen after some period of inactivity but not dim it. You can manually dim your screen using the slider or button on your PowerBook model. If you want finer control, then you need to purchase a third-party utility for that purpose. You may be surprised by the substantial amount of dimming that is possible in low-light conditions.

An external monitor is one of the nicest features of a PowerBook. Many PowerBooks have built-in video support and video-out ports, which are signified by the TV icon on the PowerBook. This is true of the 160, 180, 200, 500, 5300, and 3400 series PowerBooks. You can supplement other models to add video-out through external devices. You can also buy adapters to run a monitor from your SCSI chain or PC card slot with somewhat lower performance quality. A video adapter that will enable you to connect the video-out port to an external monitor is also supplied with your PowerBook.

You can plug in a monitor during sleep or at shutdown. When you start up your Macintosh, the external monitor is powered up. After the start-up icons appear on your PowerBook, the desktop should appear on the external monitor. If the desktop does not appear, open the Monitors Control Panel and drag the menu bar from the icon of your PowerBook screen to the icon of the external monitor.

In Mac OS 8, you can have changes to the external monitor take effect as soon as you shut the Monitors Control Panel. This behavior is enabled by the new Display Manager.

You cannot go into system sleep with your PowerBook when an external monitor is in use. For larger external displays, it is recommended that you leave processor cycling turned on so that your battery can recharge and doesn't get too hot. External screen blanking will occur based on your setting in the PowerBook Control Panel. You can also turn down your PowerBook screen manually. Almost any activity will turn your screen back on.

When working in presentation mode, you may find it convenient to have the same display on your external monitor that appears on your PowerBook. This process is called video mirroring. To turn on video mirroring, use the PowerBook Display Control Panel shown in Figure 6-6.

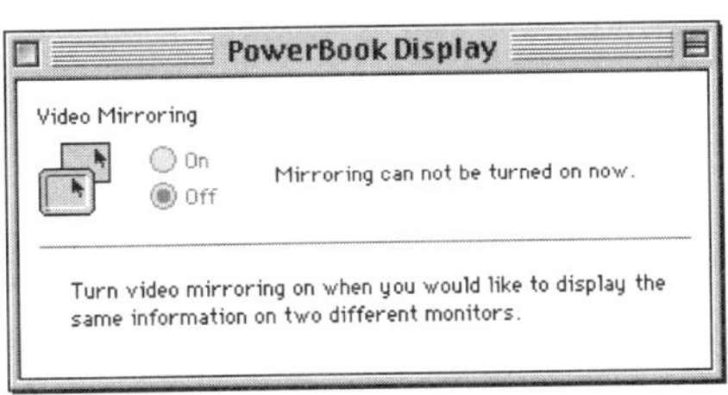

Figure 6-6: The PowerBook Display Control Panel.

Connections, Remounting & Remote Access

System software makes connecting your Macintosh to other drives, Macintosh computers, networks, and phone lines easier. Some of these capabilities are there for you right out of the box. The connection features that are different for PowerBooks are mentioned in this section.

The ability to mount a PowerBook as an external hard drive, the so-called *SCSI disk mode*, is a useful feature. You enable this mode using the PowerBook Setup Control Panel shown in Figure 6-1. A mounted PowerBook can be convenient for file synchronization because SCSI is a high-speed data bus. See "File Synchronization" later in this chapter.

You need to pay special attention to SCSI termination for PowerBook chains; otherwise, you can run into trouble with the SCSI disk mode. Refer to your PowerBook manual or third-party books for more details. Also, you should always shut down your PowerBook before making or breaking SCSI connections.

AutoRemounter is a Control Panel that performs a simple but necessary task (see Figure 6-7). When your PowerBook goes to sleep or disconnects from a network, normally servers and shared volumes are dismounted. AutoRemounter remembers these connections and can automatically remount disks when waking or can require that a password be entered. It is safer to have a password asked for automatically when you are connected to a network and are leaving your PowerBook on.

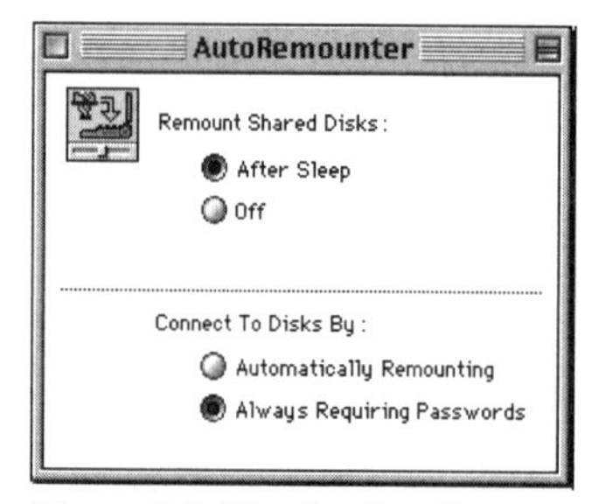

Figure 6-7: Use the AutoRemounter feature to reconnect to shared servers after waking up from sleep.

AutoRemounter first shipped in System 7.1, and it does not work with early PowerBooks (100, 140, 145, and 170). Without AutoRemounter, you need to mount your volumes manually and reestablish network connections.

One of the most useful adjuncts to system software for PowerBooks has finally been included in the Mac OS. It is Apple Remote Access (ARA). ARA is mentioned here in passing because it is a terrific product that can connect you to remote servers via modem while you are on the road, but it is not used much anymore because it has been largely replaced by other networking protocols such as TCP/IP. Apple Remote Access is also sold by AppleSoft in a client version (Figure 6-8) and various server configurations.

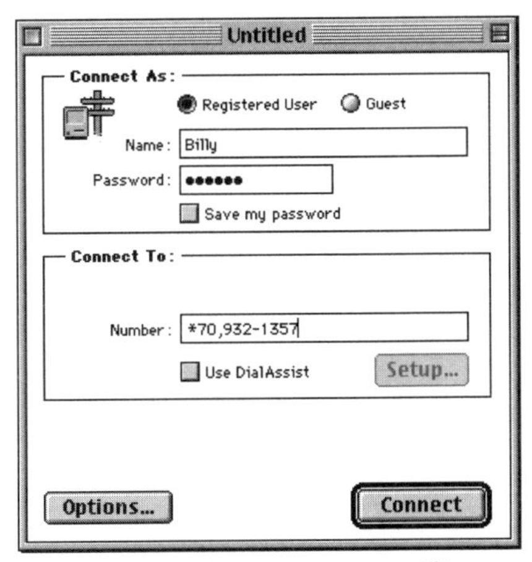

Figure 6-8: Apple Remote Access Client.

You can set up your desktop Macintosh to receive incoming calls and then dial in using ARA. Using the Apple Remote Access MultiPort Server, you can configure a Macintosh to accept several incoming ARA sessions. Some companies also sell dedicated multiline ARA servers that replace a Macintosh and a set of modems.

Once you supply a password or have ARA supply it, you are connected just as you would be in an office. Modem connections are a slow data exchange medium, so without fast modems, ARA is best used as a message exchange medium. For high-speed modems (28,800 baud and above), you can use ARA to do large file exchanges using File Sharing, remote database work with serious data manipulation, and other tasks. ARA can be a good place to try Program Linking.

The PowerBook Control Strip

Because third parties have expressed so much interest in PowerBook utilities and the class of application has been so popular, Apple decided to include an extensible PowerBook utility in Mac OS 8. It's called the Control Strip, and by default it's turned on and visible on your screen. To turn off the Control Strip, use the Control Strip Control Panel shown in Figure 6-9 and choose Hide Control Strip.

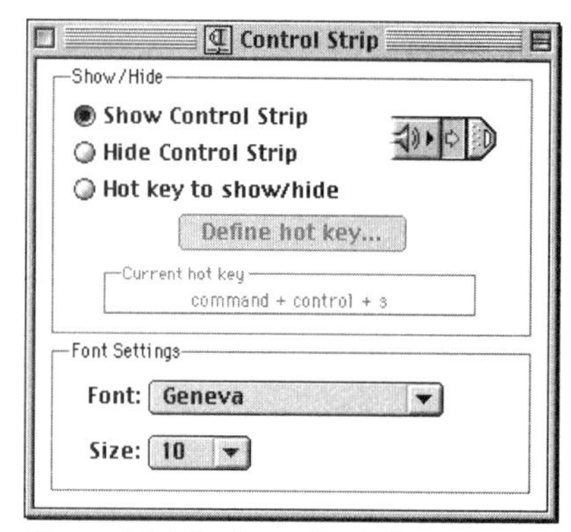

Figure 6-9: The PowerBook Control Strip Control Panel.

The Control Strip, shown in Figure 6-10, is a floating palette that appears as the topmost window on your PowerBook screen, regardless of your current application. It's one of Mac OS 8's nicest small features.

Figure 6-10: The PowerBook Control Strip shown for a PowerBook 5300 series computer running Mac OS 8.

Each icon contains a pop-up menu that enables you to select from a set of options. Most are simple on and off settings, but more commands may be added over time. Some additional Control Strip modules may appear as third-party shareware because Apple has published the needed specifications.

The Control Strip has the following features (from left to right):

- **Close box.** Click to close the strip down to the Control Tab. To remove the Control Strip, use the Control Strip Control Panel shown in Figure 6-9.
- **Scroll arrows.** Use these arrows (on both ends of the strip) to view additional panels that may be hidden.

- **AppleTalk switch.** By turning AppleTalk off, you can save power. This switch duplicates the function found in the Chooser.
- **Battery monitor.** The monitor indicates both voltage and estimated battery lifetime. Icons indicate if the battery is full, discharging, or charging.
- **CD Control.** If your PowerBook sports a CD-ROM drive, you can control the playing of audio CDs from here.
- **File Sharing.** You can manually turn File Sharing on and off using this panel. You can also check to see who's connected. This panel duplicates functions found in the Sharing Setup and File Sharing Monitor Control Panels. Refer to Chapter 16, "File Sharing," for more details.
- **HD Spin Down.** This feature spins down your drive.
- **Location.** This lets you quickly switch between location settings using the Location Manager (see the section entitled "Location Manager" below for more information).
- **Colors**. This feature lets you change the bit depth of your display.
- **Resolution.** This feature lets you change the resolution of your display (for PowerBooks that support this feature, such as the Duo 2300).
- **PowerBook.** Opens the PowerBook Control Panel, and offers quick access to the Better Performance and Better Conservation items.
- **Printers.** Lets you choose between different desktop printers.
- **Sleep Now.** This feature puts your computer into system sleep.
- **Sound volume.** Drag to the sound level you desire. This feature re-creates the Sound slider in the Sound Control Panel.
- **Tab.** Drag the Tab to resize the Control Strip. Click the Tab to shrink the strip to just the Tab. When you are viewing just the Tab, click the Tab to view the Control Strip again.

You will note some differences between Control Strips installed on different models of PowerBooks. For example, only intelligent batteries give time estimates, and only models with video-out capabilities support the video mirroring panel.

You can also remove modules from the Control Strip folder of the System Folder as desired. To shorten the Control Strip, drag the Tab to the left. You can view modules in the shortened strip by clicking the left- and right-facing arrows at the end of the Control Strip. To collapse the Control Strip to just a Tab, click the Close box at the left of the strip.

Don't like the order the icons are in? It's easy to customize the Control Strip just the way you want it. To reorder icons in the strip, Option+click on the item and drag it to where you'd like it to be. To remove an icon from the strip, remove it from the Control Strip Items folder inside your System folder.

File Synchronization

When you use two or more computers for your work, tracking file changes can be tedious. You always want to work with the most current versions of your files and not have to re-create changes. You can do this using a procedure called *file synchronization*. When you create or modify a file, it is time-stamped with the date and time of your system. Then you can replace older files with newer ones, adding new files to folders that didn't contain them.

If you had to track all these changes manually, you probably wouldn't. Therefore, you can use the PowerBook File Assistant for this important task. With this utility (which is part of Mac OS 8 or purchased separately), you can designate files and folders that you want updated. The utility is basic and easy to learn. You only need to connect your two computers directly via a network or with modems to use the File Assistant.

In the PowerBook File Assistant Setup dialog box that you see when you launch the program (see Figure 6-11), you can simply drag and drop files and folders that you want synchronized. You link pairs of items on either side of the arrow into linked sets. You can create as many pairs as you wish and scroll the window to review them. Using the Preferences command from the File menu, you can also link nonmatching named folders.

You can specify whether synchronization is manual or automatic via commands on the Synchronize menu shown in Figure 6-12. Other choices allow you to choose the direction of the updating that you wish to occur. A double-headed arrow will update either file when there are changes. Single-head arrows are most useful when you wish to use the server to update a file on your hard disk.

After you have set up the PowerBook File Assistant, you only need to connect the two computers and run it. The Synchronize Now command (Command+G) begins the process. If you select a manual synchronization, you will need to click the arrow outline to synchronize each pair. For automatic synchronization, you can use AutoRemounter to reconnect shared disks and then place the File Assistant in your start-up disk. Whenever you mount your drives and File Assistant is running, your files are automatically updated.

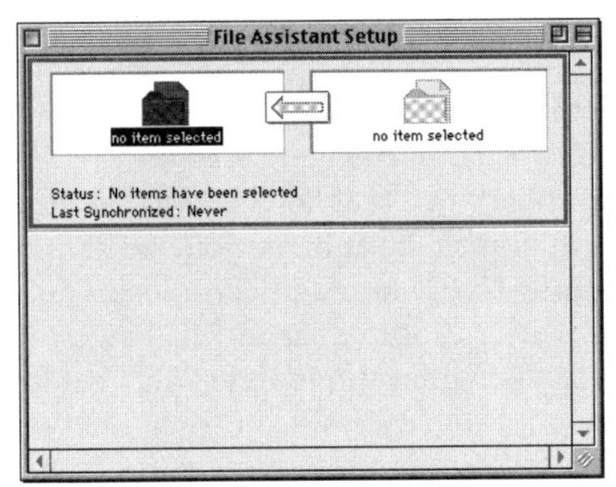

Figure 6-11: The PowerBook File Assistant Setup dialog box.

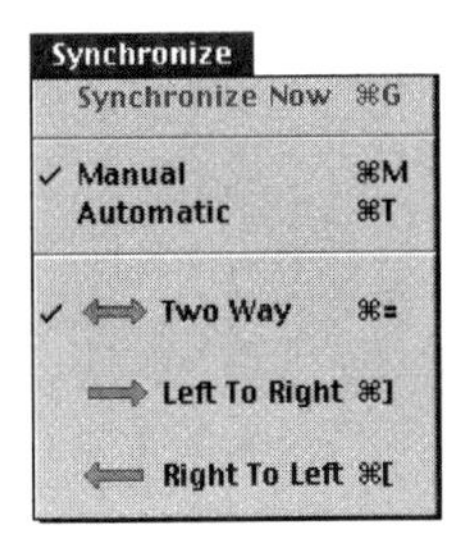

Figure 6-12: The PowerBook File Assistant Synchronize menu.

Three types of actions are monitored by the File Assistant: modifications of files and folders, deletions of missing and moved files and folders, and the replacement of a file with another of the same name. Table 6-1 summarizes the results based on your settings.

Left File	Right File	Result
Changes	Doesn't Change	The right file is updated.
Doesn't Change	Changes	For a two-way update, the left file is updated. For a left-to-right update, there are no changes.
Doesn't Change	Deleted	For a two-way update, you get a message asking you whether you want to delete the left file. For a left-to-right update, the right file is updated.
Deleted	Unchanged	You get a message asking you whether you wish to delete the right file.

Table 6-1: Actions monitored by File Assistant.

Location Manager

As you've noticed, there's a plethora of controls on your Mac, and many of them change depending on where you are. For instance, maybe the printer you use at the office is different from the printer you use at home. Perhaps your office uses an Ethernet-based TCP/IP connection, while at home you use PPP.

Changing all of these settings just to go home can be a major pain, so Apple devised the Location Manager. The Location Manager lets you create a snapshot of the settings you use at particular locations and switch between them. For PowerBook owners, this is one of the coolest features of Mac OS 8. In the old days, you would have to spend 15 minutes fighting with various Control Panels every time you moved to a new place. Now, you can set the Location Manager once, and use the control strip as you walk about.

To make a setting, first you must create a new location. Click the New button in the Location Manager dialog box to do this (see Figure 6-13).

You will be presented with the dialog box in Figure 6-14. Enter a name for the location, and use the scrolling list to specify settings, then select Add.

It takes a while to set everything up, but the task is made easier by the fact that you don't have to set up items you don't care about. For instance, if you don't want to have your AppleTalk settings change, you don't have to specify it. This can save loads of time up front.

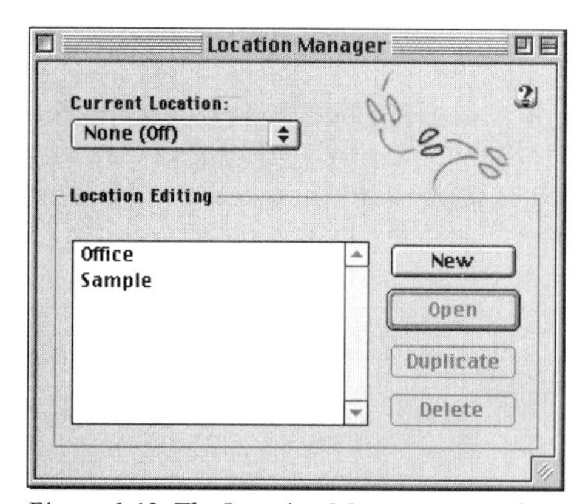

Figure 6-13: The Location Manager Control Panel lets you pick your current location and resets all of your PowerBook's important settings to match.

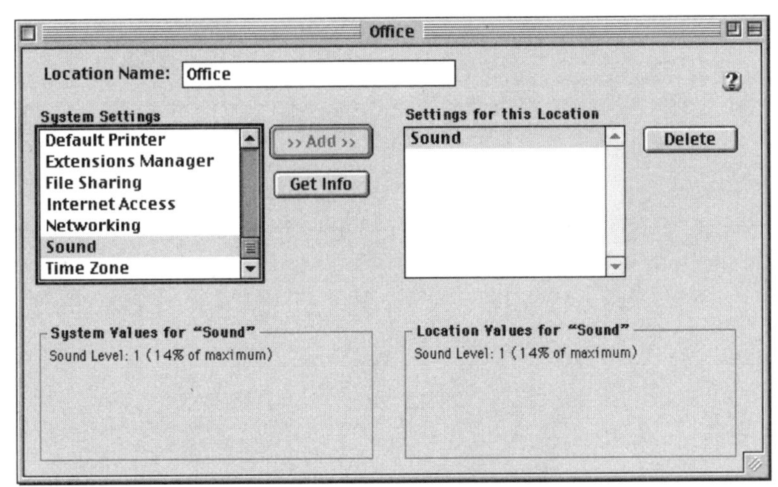

Figure 6-14: You can add nearly any kind of setting to a location. Here, I'm making sure the speaker volume is at a low setting when I'm in the office.

Security

If there's a downside to PowerBook ownership, it's that everyone wants to get their grubby paws on yours. They're so fun and cool that sometimes it seems that everyone wants to borrow it—sometimes without asking!

In case someone tries to boot your PowerBook and poke around, you can protect it with a password of your choosing using the Password Security Control Panel shown in Figure 6-15. Just enter a password into this dialog box, confirm it, and the next time you boot the machine, it'll demand a password before anything will load.

Figure 6-15: You can password-protect your main PowerBook volume with this Control Panel.

Be very careful with the password feature—it's easy to forget a password, and if that were to happen, you'd be out of luck. The only way to recover from a forgotten password is to reformat the hard drive!

Also, if you partition your drive into multiple volumes, keep in mind that only the boot volume is password-protected. A user without the password could hook your PowerBook up to another Mac using the SCSI disk mode and mount any other nonboot volumes. Keep all sensitive data on your boot volume.

Moving On

Mobile computing offers a new way of computing, and the freedom comes with a few limitations and risks. In this chapter, you learned:

- How to make your PowerBook last longer on a battery charge.
- How to connect your PowerBook locally or remotely.
- How to make your PowerBook secure.
- How to connect an external monitor and how to synchronize files and folders.

In the next section we'll look at applications and using them under the Mac OS. In the next chapter, we'll examine Mac OS 8's backwards compatibility with applications designed to run on System 7.x and the Stationery Documents feature.

PART II

Applications

CHAPTER 7

Mac OS 8 & Your Software

Thus far, the Mac OS 8 features we have discussed are those that change the way you organize and manipulate data files on your Macintosh at the OS level. But as important as the OS is, it's not the reason you use a Macintosh. You use the Mac because its software applications—word processors, spreadsheets, databases, graphics programs, and the rest—help you accomplish your work productively.

In this chapter, we'll look at some of the ways Mac OS 8 affects software applications, beginning with the important issue of compatibility. Then we'll see the expanded launching methods, new stationery documents, and Desktop-level enhancements Mac OS 8 provides. Other major enhancements that affect software applications, including data sharing, program-to-program communication, and support for TrueType and PostScript fonts, are discussed in Chapter 10, "Working With Multiple Applications," and in Chapter 11, "Fonts & Printing."

Mac OS 8 Compatibility

It's always exciting to get a new software upgrade—it means more features, better performance, and an easier-to-use interface. But as seasoned computer users know, along with improvements and solutions, software upgrades often introduce bugs and incompatibilities.

System software is particularly susceptible to upgrade-compatibility problems because every Macintosh application is so heavily dependent on the system software. Each application must be fine-tuned and coordinated to work together smoothly with the system. The relationship between system software and an application is like that of two juggling partners, each throwing balls into the air that the other is expected to catch. When system software is upgraded, a new partner replaces a familiar one without changing the routine or allowing time to practice while still expecting each toss and catch to occur precisely.

During the development of System 7, Apple worked hard to ensure that it was compatible with as many existing applications as possible. (The beta version of System 7 in development was distributed to many thousands of people using a variety of applications and Macintosh models.) In fact, Apple claimed that any application running under System 6.0.x would operate under System 7 without alteration as long as the application was programmed according to System 7's widely published programming rules. For the most part, this claim was apparently true.

The majority of major applications were compatible with System 7's initial release, and a great many utility programs were compatible too. Naturally, many utility programs whose functions were to modify or extend the system software itself were not initially compatible.

Now—many years after the introduction of System 7—it's almost impossible to find an application or utility that isn't compatible with System 7. Every program written or updated in that time period has been created or modified with System 7 in mind. Mac OS 8 continues in this tradition of extending system software capabilities while maintaining a high level of backward compatibility with the existing third-party software library.

The introduction of Mac OS 8 brings additional changes and more capabilities to the system software, yielding yet another set of potential problems. Very few programs—again, usually utilities that modify or extend the system—have proven incompatible, however. More likely, you will find that the new capabilities of system software make many programs you currently use in your working environment obsolete.

What Is Compatibility?

Generally speaking, to be considered *compatible*, an application must run under System 7 or higher and provide the same features with the same degree of reliability. But compatibility can exist in varying degrees in different applications. Most compatible applications will launch and provide basic operations under Mac OS 8 and operate correctly in Mac OS 8's multitasking environment.

Applications that are System 7 compatible will probably survive under Mac OS 8, but applications that are System 7 savvy will thrive. These applications are specifically written to take full advantage of System 7, and must do the following:

- **Support multitasking.** Mac OS 8 lets your Mac open multiple applications and process data simultaneously. Applications should be able to operate in both the foreground and the background and should support background processing to the greatest degree possible. (More information on multitasking and background processing appears later in this chapter.)
- **Be 32-bit clean.** Mac OS 8 is a 32-bit operating system, but many older applications were not written as 32-bit applications. The Memory Control Panel in older versions of the OS allowed users to turn 32-bit addressing on or off, increasing software compatibility. In Mac OS 8, applications will run even if they are not 32-bit clean.
- **Support the Edition Manager's Publish and Subscribe features.** The Edition Manager, described in Chapter 12, allows data to be transferred from one application to another while maintaining a link to the original file. Applications must include the basic Publish and Subscribe commands.
- **Support AppleEvents and Core events.** Mac OS 8's Inter-Application Communication (IAC), also described in Chapter 12, defines a basic set of AppleEvents that allow one application to communicate with another.
- **Impose no limit on font sizes.** QuickDraw GX-savvy applications should support all font sizes, from 1 to 32,000 in single-point increments, and others should support fonts up to 127 points. (See Chapter 11, "Fonts & Printing.")
- **Provide Balloon Help.** As described in Chapter 3, "The Finder & Desktop," Balloon Help offers quick pop-up summaries of an application's menu commands, dialog box options, and graphic elements.
- **Apple Guide support.** The ability to work with a customized Apple Guide help system is universal for Macintosh applications. Therefore, all Macintosh applications are intrinsically "Apple Guide aware." Apple Guide support is therefore really dependent on whether developers have added this technology to their products.
- **Be AppleShare compliant.** Mac OS 8 allows any user to access files shared on AppleShare servers or files from other Macintoshes using File Sharing. Applications should operate correctly when launched over an AppleTalk network or when reading or writing data stored on File Sharing or AppleShare volumes (see Chapter 16, "File Sharing," and Chapter 17, "Working on a Network").

- **Support stationery documents.** Applications should be able to take full advantage of stationery documents, a type of document template featured in System 7.x and later. (See "Stationery Documents" later in this chapter.)

Mac OS 8 uses other technologies that "savvy" applications should utilize in order to be truly compatible. These technologies include the following:

- **AppleScript.** Two levels of AppleScript awareness are recognized. An application is called *scriptable* if it can be controlled by an external AppleScript. A scriptable application contains a dictionary of AppleScript programming verbs and objects that are both supported.

  The second level of AppleScript awareness is called *recordable*. A recordable application allows the user to record actions and compose a script reflecting that action using the AppleScript recorder function. Recordable is a lower level of compatibility, more like being "aware." Refer to Chapter 13 for a discussion of AppleScript.
- **Macintosh Drag and Drop.** Drag-and-drop actions can be data transfer within a file, between files, and to the Desktop as clippings. Additional drag-and-drop techniques let the user initiate processes such as opening a file, printing data, and others. No standard for "full" support exists, but programs such as SimpleText, the Scrapbook, Find File, and other system software come closest. Applications may implement any subset of these features.
- **QuickDraw GX implementation.** QuickDraw GX is a portfolio of graphics, fonts, color, and printing routines with broad requirements and upgrade opportunities. Again, no current standard exists for what features a program must include for it to be deemed "QuickDraw GX savvy." At the minimum, most developers would agree that QuickDraw GX font support is a basic requirement because it enables both advanced typographical features and the portable digital document standard that is central to workgroup collaboration technologies.

  Other important QuickDraw technologies are color matching through the ColorSync System Profile Control Panel and advanced printing and peripheral I/O device driver architecture. Extensions and Control Panels are QuickDraw GX savvy when they support Desktop printer icons and enable advanced printing features such as multisided, multijob print processes. Because extensions are system software, most applications should achieve a rapid level of QuickDraw GX awareness by allowing these advanced print options in their respective print dialog boxes. QuickDraw GX is described more fully in Chapter 11, "Fonts & Printing."

Whew! That's quite a list. Of course, you have to be careful not to take the "savvy" label too seriously. Many great applications have been upgraded to take full advantage of Mac OS 8 but cannot be officially categorized as "savvy." The usual reason is that the programs' developers intentionally decided not to implement one or more of the required items because such features were either unimportant or inapplicable for that application. Sometimes developers are using a different programming and interface model in their work.

For instance, many applications don't support Balloon Help or QuickDraw GX. Some vendors will undoubtedly choose to promote their own online help system in place of Apple Guide. Microsoft is also implementing Object Linking & Embedding (OLE), a compound document technology that competes with Publish and Subscribe. Finally, some of the core system software technologies are complex, multifaceted, and still developing—which will make their adoption slow in coming.

Launching

Double-click, double-click, double-click. That's how most Macintosh users launch their software applications. Two clicks to open the drive or volume, two to open the application folder, and a double-click on the application icon to launch the software.

This method can quickly grow wearisome when it means clicking through many volumes and folder layers to reach an icon. As alternatives, a wide range of application launching utilities—including OnCue, NowMenus, SuperBoomerang, DiskTop, and MasterJuggler—have appeared to enhance the Mac OS. With these utilities, you can launch by selecting application names from a list instead of searching through folders for icons. Two-button mice are also available for the Mac OS; they allow you to assign one of the two buttons to perform a double-click when only single-clicked. And as we've seen, Mac OS 8 will allow you to view an item as a button instead of an icon, which is opened using a single click.

Mac OS 8 uses several ways to launch files or applications. You can use the Recent Documents or Recent Applications submenu off the Apple menu (discussed in previous chapters). With the Macintosh Easy Open Control Panel, applications can do transparent file translation, enabling a drag-and-drop-type process. Lastly, the Launcher Control Panel offers an easy way to group applications and documents for easy launching. Any object that can have an alias—files, applications, AppleScripts, servers, and so on—can be added to the Launcher window. Opening that object or starting the process is then just a click away in the Launcher window. We'll look at Macintosh Easy Open and the Launcher in more detail in this section.

In fact, you can now launch applications in all the following ways:

- **Double-click an application icon.** You can double-click an application icon, or the alias of an application icon, to launch that application.

- **Double-click a document icon or its alias.** If the application that created a document is unavailable, the Application Not Found dialog box, shown in Figure 7-1, will appear. To open a document that presents this dialog box, you must either locate the original application or use another application that's capable of opening that type of document.

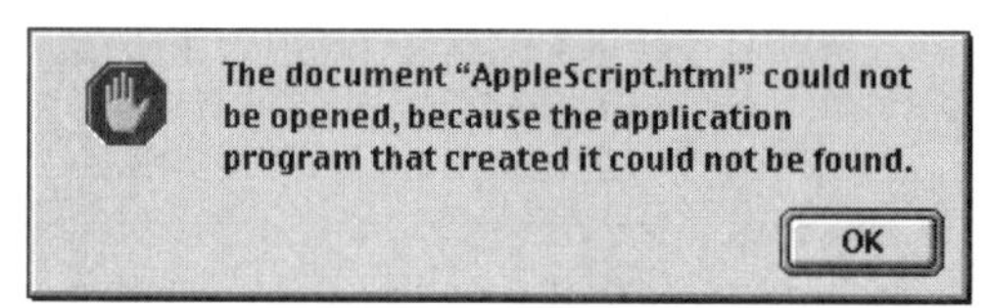

Figure 7-1: The Application Not Found dialog box.

For example, suppose a WordPerfect file displays the Application Not Found dialog box when double-clicked. You could open Microsoft Word and then access the file using the Open command under Word's File menu. Similarly, GraphicConverter can open Photoshop files, and many applications can open TIFF or EPS files. Most applications can open documents of several different file types. The Macintosh Easy Open Control Panel, which is discussed later in this chapter, addresses this problem.

- **Double-click a stationery document or its alias.** Stationery documents are template documents that create untitled new documents automatically when opened. (More about stationery documents appears later in this chapter.)
- **Drag a document icon onto an application icon.** This method of launching will work only when the document is dragged onto the icon of the application that created it.

  If an application will launch, the application icon highlights when the document icon is above it. Application icons will highlight only when appropriate documents are positioned above them, as shown in Figure 7-2.

Figure 7-2: Application icons highlight when you drag documents onto them that they can launch.

- **Add applications or documents to the Startup Items folder inside the System folder.** To automatically launch an application or open a document and its application at startup, add the application or document icon or an alias of one of these icons to the Startup Items folder inside the System folder. This action will cause the application or document to be launched automatically at startup.
- **Choose an application or document name from the Apple menu.** By placing an application or document in the Apple Menu Items folder inside the System folder, the application or document name will then appear in the Apple menu and can be launched by choosing the application or document name.
- **Choose an application or document name from the Recent Document or Recent Application submenus of the Apple menu.** If you've enabled this option in the Apple Menu Options Control Panel (it's on by default) in Mac OS 8, a variable number of your most recently accessed files or applications is added to these submenus, as shown in Figure 7-3. Items are replaced on a last used, first out basis.

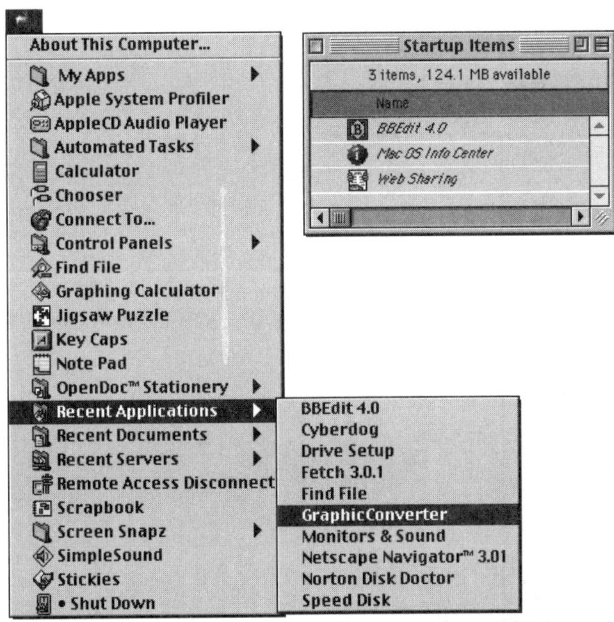

Figure 7-3: Items are launched at startup when you add them to the Startup Items folder (right), or you can select them from the Apple menu (left) to launch them.

Launching Methods

There's no one best way to launch applications. You'll probably find that a combination of methods is the most efficient. Keep the following launching tips in mind:

- **The Apple menu.** Add the applications and documents you use most frequently to the Apple menu. If you use a document or program daily, it will probably stay in the Recent Applications or Recent Documents submenu, so you may not need to put it in the Apple menu. Use your judgment on the best method for organizing your own Apple menu.
- **Alias folders.** Assemble groups of application aliases into folders according to application type; add aliases of frequently used folders to the Apple menu.

  You can choose the folder name from the Apple menu and then choose an item in this folder when it is hierarchically opened. Figure 7-4 shows an Apple menu configured using this method. A blank space (" ") has been added before the name of the "My Apps" folder alias, which forces this folder to group near the top of the Apple menu.

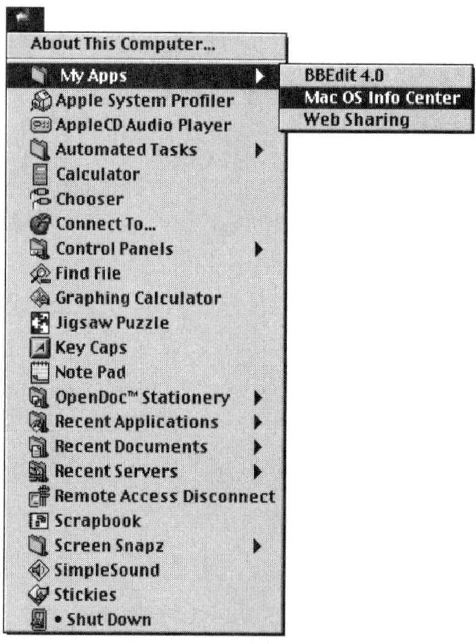

Figure 7-4: Adding folders full of application icons to the Apple menu makes them easy to access.

This method may be less convenient than relying on the Recent Applications submenu or the Launcher window. There's virtually no setup time involved in configuring the Recent Applications submenu, and it's just as convenient. For the same amount of work as adding a folder of aliases, you can configure the Launcher. In fact, if you have already created a folder of aliases or added aliases to the Apple menu, just copy those aliases over to the Launcher Items folder found in your System folder.

- **Double-click icons.** When you're browsing in Finder windows to locate specific files, use the tried-and-true double-click method to launch applications, aliases, documents, or stationery icons.
- **Drag icons onto applications.** If you store documents and applications or their aliases in the same folder, or if you place application icons or aliases on the Desktop, dragging icons onto applications (or drop-launching, as it's called) may prove useful, although double-clicking the document is often easier.

The Launcher

Mac OS 8 adds the Launcher Control Panel as a means of enabling novice users to launch files, applications, or any other item for which you can create an alias in the Finder. If you've ever worked with Apple's At Ease utility, then you will recognize this feature. It's a great time-saver and an absolute boon for novice users and small children.

When you use the Launcher and uncheck the Show Desktop When in Background option (found in the General Controls Control Panel), you can prevent users from switching inadvertently to the Finder with a misplaced click. This can be very confusing to novice users. The combination works well, but it is incomplete in shielding the novice user from the Finder because the Launcher itself will show the Macintosh Desktop when it is in the background.

To open the Launcher, double-click on the Launcher Control Panel or choose its name from the Control Panel submenu under the Apple menu. You can choose to always show the Launcher upon startup by turning on that option in the Desktop section of the General Controls Control Panel, as shown in Figure 7-5. In this same section, you can turn on Finder Hiding.

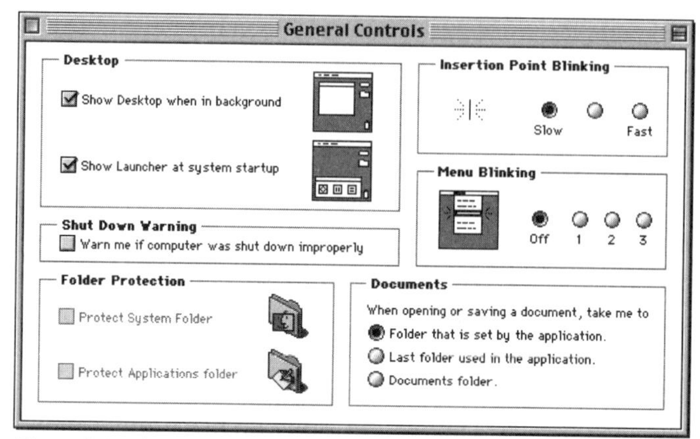

Figure 7-5: The Desktop section of the General Controls Control Panel.

You add items to the Launcher by copying or moving aliases of files, applications, AppleScripts, servers, Control Panels, folders, the QuickDraw GX printer—literally anything you can alias in the Finder—to the Launcher Items folder. This folder is located at the top level of your System folder. You may also create groups with the Launcher by following these steps:

1. Open the Launcher Items folder.
2. Create a new folder be choosing File | New Folder or by pressing Command+N.
3. Rename the folder with a bullet as the first character (Press Option+8 to create a bullet).
4. Add any items you wish to the new folder. Figure 7-6 shows several groups in the Launcher Items folder.

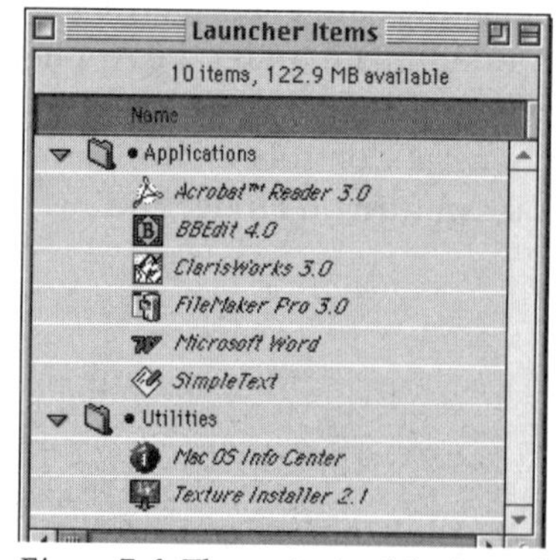

Figure 7-6: The contents of the Launcher Items folder.

You delete items from the Launcher by removing their aliases from that folder. If you have a folder of aliases for applications or have added aliases to your Apple Menu Items folder, you may want to copy or move those aliases to the Launcher Items folder to get started. Figure 7-7 shows what the Launcher looks like using the contents of the Launcher Items folder shown in Figure 7-6.

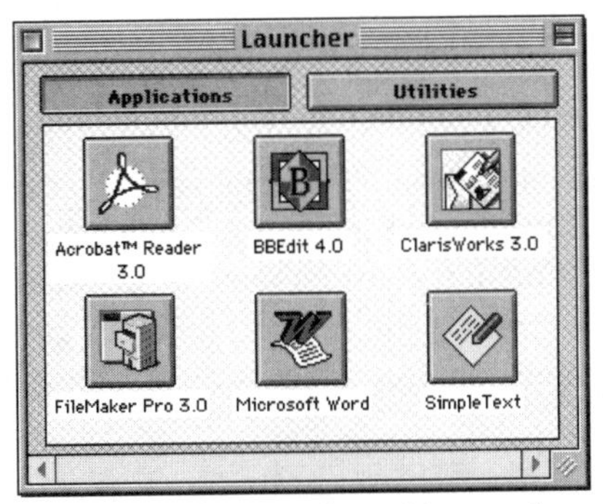

Figure 7-7: The Launcher with several groups.

There isn't much to the Launcher, but it is a tremendous time-saver. Click once on an icon to open the object or start the process. The current Launcher is Macintosh Drag and Drop enabled; that is, you can drag a document onto an application icon in the Launcher. Remember, you can use the WindowShade Control Panel to minimize the Launcher window when it's not in use.

Stationery Documents

Another useful feature in Mac OS 8 is the stationery document. A stationery document is a document that is going to be stationery, and you use them to make an existing document into a template quickly. Templates, as you may know, give you a head start in creating new documents.

For example, the documents in your word processor probably fall into a handful of specific formats—letters, reports, memos, chapters, and so on. Rather than start each document with a new, unformatted file, you can use, for example, the stationery document for a letter, which provides the date, salutation, body copy, closing character, paragraph formatting, correct margins, and other basic formatting.

Template support has been available in several Macintosh applications for some time, but by adding the stationery documents feature, Apple makes templates available in every software package you use to create documents.

Creating a Stationery Document

A stationery document is usually created in three steps:

1. First, you find an existing typical example of a document you commonly create.
2. Then you modify the typical document to make it a good generic representation and save it to disk.
3. Finally, save the document as stationery if possible, or select the Stationery Pad option in the file's Get Info dialog box if not.

For example, to create a memo stationery document, open an existing representative document, like the one shown in Figure 7-8. Although this memo is typical, it does have one unusual element—the embedded graphic. Remove that element because most memos do not call for such graphic elements. The remaining memo elements are left to serve as placeholders.

prize.stny

6/1/97

Dear Ms. DeVine:

This is your lucky day! I am pleased to inform you that your name has been selected in our weekly grand-prize drawing, and you have won a new car and dream vacation valued at $25,000.

In order to claim your prize, please stop by our store and complete a Prize Winner Registration form, available from our Store Manager, Mr. Alan Benson. You will then be allowed to select your automobile and vacation from the prize-winner catalog.

Once you have received your prize, our contest photographer will contact you to arrange to have promotional pictures taken of you and your prizes. (You agreed to such photos in your signed entry form.)

Sincerely,

Laura Black
Store Manager

Figure 7-8: A letter that will become a stationery document.

Before you save the memo stationery document, it's a good idea to edit the text in all placeholders so that they're appropriate to use in final documents. Replace placeholder text with nonsensical data (*greeking*), which helps ensure that no placeholder elements are accidentally used in finished documents. For the memo date, for example, use 0/0/00, and the memo address can read To: Recipient.

You might overlook a date such as 6/1/97 and use it instead of the current date each time you use the stationery document. You're almost certain to notice the 00/0/00 date, on the other hand, when you proofread the document. Figure 7-9 shows our sample memo with generic placeholders inserted.

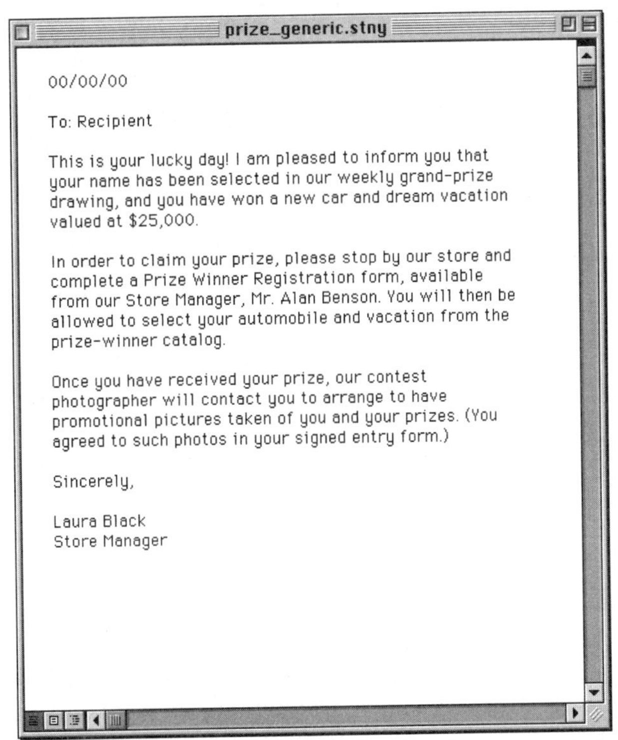

Figure 7-9: After being edited, the stationery document contains placeholders.

After you edit the memo, use the Save As command to save the template document to disk. Use names that are easily identified in Finder windows and dialog box listings: for example, add the letters *stny* to the end of each document name. You're not required to use naming conventions; you'll be able to distinguish stationery documents by their icons alone, but using distinct filenames gives you an extra advantage. See Figure 7-10.

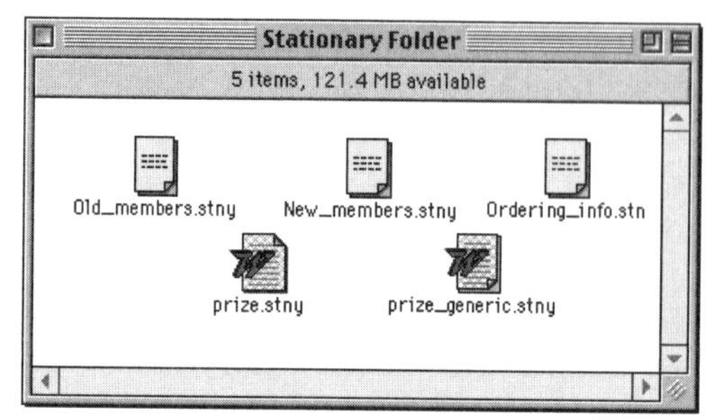

Figure 7-10: A folder full of stationery documents.

There's one final but critical step in creating a stationery document. After you've edited and saved your document, go to the Finder and select its icon. Then choose the Get Info command from the File menu. Click in the Stationery check box in the lower right corner of the Get Info dialog box. Notice that the icon inside the Get Info dialog box changes to show that the document is now a stationery document. After you close the Get Info dialog box, the conversion is complete.

Note: Some applications, such as Simple Text and Microsoft Word, give you the option of saving your documents in stationery documents format. Saving this way may be simpler than digging up the Get Info box, particularly if your document is buried several folders deep on your drive.

The document's icon in the Finder will also be updated to reflect its new status, but the icon that appears depends on the application you used to create the document. These icons are discussed more completely later in this chapter.

Using Stationery

After you've created stationery documents, you can either launch them from the Desktop by double-clicking their icons, or you can open them with the Open command in an application's File menu.

When you launch a stationery document from the Desktop, the document will open in a window that appears to be the original document, but in reality it is a copy of the stationery. You can see this by looking at the title bar area of the window, which will show the document name as Untitled. Because the stationery document file is duplicated and renamed as Untitled when it's opened, if you later decide you don't need this new document, you'll have to manually delete it from your disk. To save the document as a stationery document, choose the appropriate options in the Save As dialog box. For example, Figure 7-11 shows the options available for a SimpleText document being saved as a stationery document.

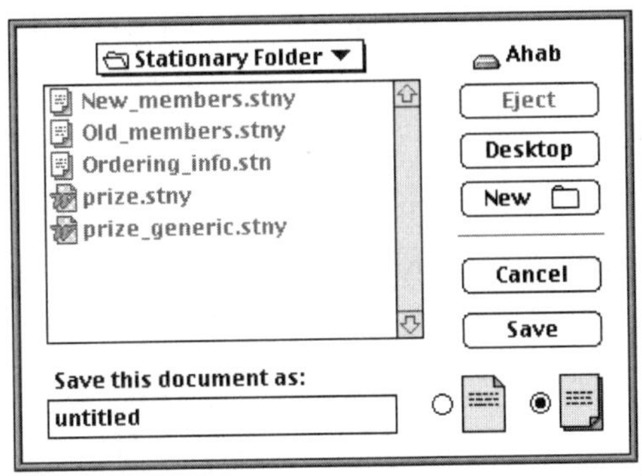

Figure 7-11: An Open dialog box with stationery documents visible.

Note the two document icons in the lower right-hand corner of this figure. The document icon on the left represents a regular SimpleText document, which has one page. The icon on the right, however, appears to have two pages (see the dog-ear tab on the lower-right hand side of the icon). This is a visual signal that the document will be saved as stationery. Once you've opened a copy of a stationery document, you can customize it as required. Be sure to edit all placeholders that you set when creating the stationery document. You can delete unnecessary elements, add new ones, and edit the document in any other way you choose.

Stationery Document Tips

Using Stationery documents may be a new concept to some, so let's review several tips that might be useful:

- **Stationery documents aliases.** Whether they were created before or after the Stationery Documents option was set, aliases of stationery documents access the stationery documents normally. The alias icon displays the stationery documents icon.
- **Stationery documents folder.** Create a stationery or templates folder and keep aliases of all your stationery documents in this folder. Keep the original documents organized as they were originally. This way, it is easy to access stationery documents when you need them. If you use them frequently, you can also put an alias of this folder in your Apple Menu Items folder.

- **Application support for multiple documents.** If an application does not support more than one open document at a time, opening a stationery document from the Finder when the application and a document are already open may not work. In this case, close the open document and then reopen the stationery document using the Open command.
- **Opening stationery documents with the Open command.** Opening a stationery document from inside an application that isn't "Stationery documents aware" may cause problems. An application may open the stationery document itself rather than create a new Untitled copy. When you open stationery documents using the Open command, be sure to use a new filename and the Save As command so that you don't accidentally overwrite your stationery document.
- **Editing stationery documents.** Deselecting the Stationery Documents option in the Get Info dialog box will turn any stationery document back into a "normal" document—it will lose its stationery document properties. You can then edit the stationery document, making changes to your master. After editing and saving this document, reselect the Stationery Documents option in the Get Info dialog box to turn the file back into a stationery document.

The Desktop Level

It is impossible to work on the Macintosh and not hear—and use—the word *Desktop*, as we've seen in Chapter 3. In Macintosh terminology, the word *Desktop* usually refers to the Finder Desktop, which is the onscreen area where volume icons, windows, and the Trash appear. Also, files and folders can be dragged from any mounted volume or folder and placed directly on the Desktop.

In system software versions prior to System 7, the Finder Desktop was ignored by the Open and Save dialog boxes. In these dialog boxes, each mounted volume was discrete, and all files were on disks or in folders, unlike Mac OS 8's Desktop, shown in Figure 7-12.

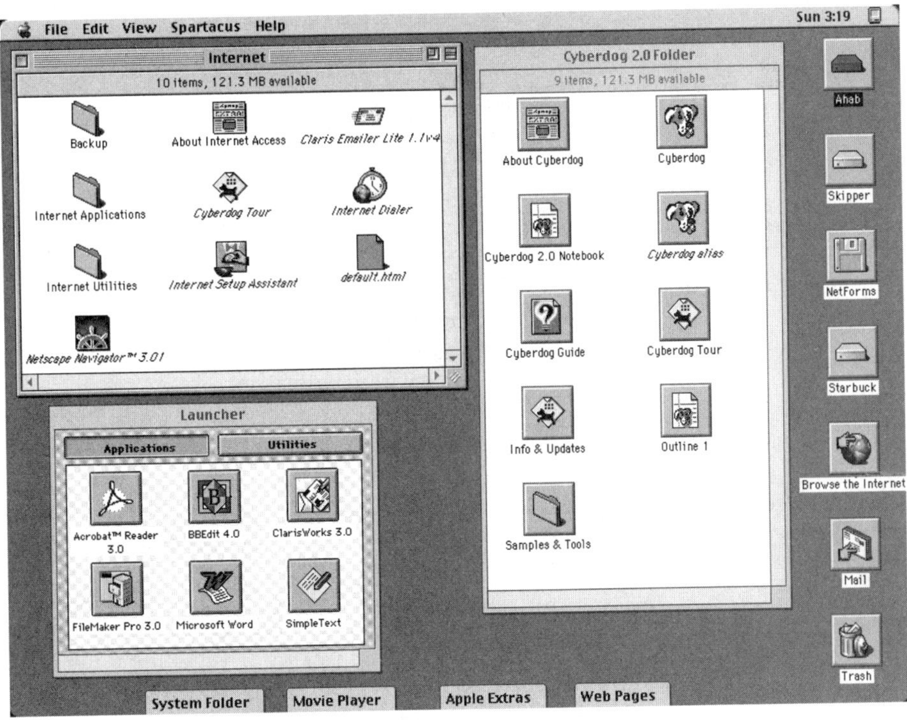

Figure 7-12: The Finder Desktop.

In System 7, dialog boxes provide access to the Finder Desktop and all volumes, files, and folders that reside there. In fact, the Drive button has been replaced with a Desktop button that causes a new Desktop view to appear in the scrolling file listing. This Desktop view displays the name and icon of each volume, file, and folder that exists on the Finder Desktop. In Figure 7-13 you can see the Open File dialog boxes of Systems 6 and 7.

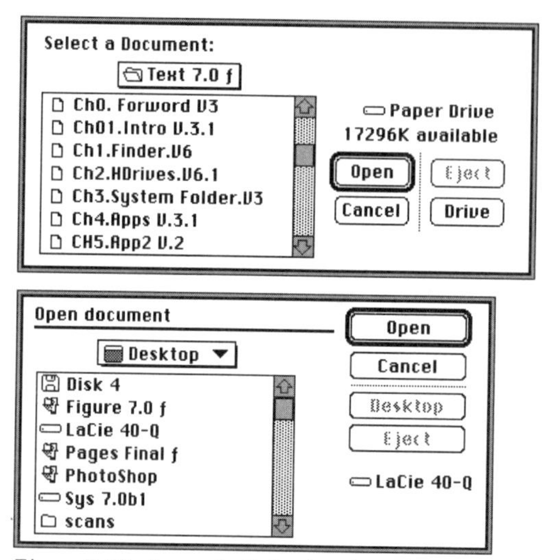

Figure 7-13: A sample dialog box from System 6.0.x (top) and one from System 7 (bottom).

From the Desktop view in these new dialog boxes, you can move into any volume, folder, or file on the Desktop by double-clicking a name in the scrolling list, or you can save files directly onto the Desktop. Once any volume or folder is open, the list of files and folders at that location is displayed, and the dialog box operates normally. Saving a file onto the Desktop causes its icon to appear on your Finder Desktop and leaves you free to later drag it onto any volume or folder. Figure 7-14 shows some of the possible volumes that are available when opening a document on the Desktop. Note the different icons used by the Mac OS to differentiate between hard drives, floppy drives, and network volumes.

Saving files to your Finder Desktop writes the actual data to your boot drive (the drive with your System folder on it). Be careful—saving to the Desktop can get confusing if you use multiple drives or volumes.

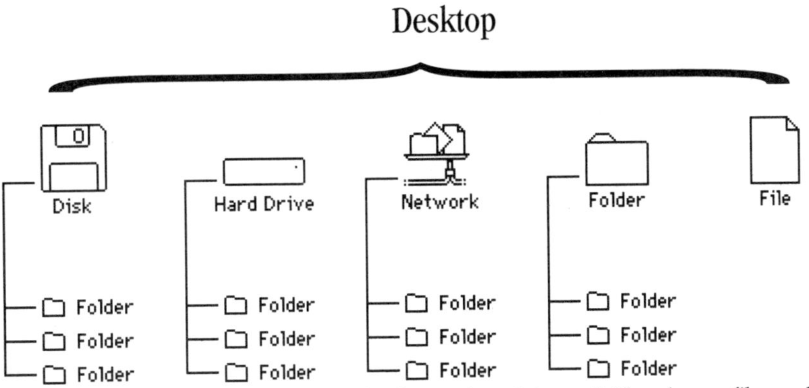

Figure 7-14: The Desktop level offers a bird's-eye view of the available volumes, files, and folders.

Figure 7-15 shows the volumes that are available to the application BBEdit when choosing File | Open on the computer whose Finder Desktop is shown in Figure 7-12.

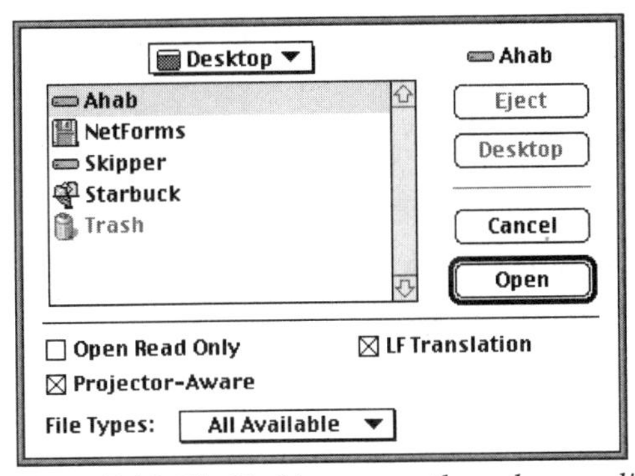

Figure 7-15: The Desktop as seen through an application.

Dialog Box Keyboard Equivalents

In addition to having the new Desktop button, all Open and Save dialog boxes now support a number of keyboard equivalents that make it faster and easier to find and create files:

- **Next or previous volume or drive.** To cycle through available volumes, press the Down arrow key. You can now also cycle backward by pressing the Up arrow key.

- **File listing/Filename options.** In Save As dialog boxes, pressing the Tab key toggles back and forth between the scrolling file listing and the filename option. You can tell which is activated by the presence of an extra black border, and you can also control the active window from the keyboard. (In earlier versions of the system software, pressing the Tab key was the equivalent of pressing the Drive button.)

  When the filename option is active, you can control the cursor position with the arrow keys and, of course, enter any valid filename. When the scrolling file listing is active, use the following keyboard equivalents to locate, select, and manipulate files and folders (see Figure 7-16):

  - **Jump alphabetically.** Typing any single letter causes the first filename starting with that letter, or the letter closest to it, to be selected.
  - **Jump alphabetically and then some.** If you quickly type more than one letter, the Mac OS will continue to narrow down the available filenames accordingly. In other words, typing only the letter *F* will jump you to the first filename that starts with an *F*; typing *FUL* will pass by the file Finder 7 Facts and select the file Fulfillment Info. When typing multiple characters to find files, you must not pause between characters; otherwise, the Mac will think you're starting a new search. Instead of interpreting your second character as the second letter of a filename, it will treat it as the first letter of a new search.
  - **Open folder or volume.** While a folder (or volume) is selected, press Command+Down arrow key to open it and view its contents.
  - **Close folder or volume.** While a folder (or volume) is selected, press Command+Up arrow key to close it and view the contents of its enclosing folder or the Finder Desktop (in the case of a volume).

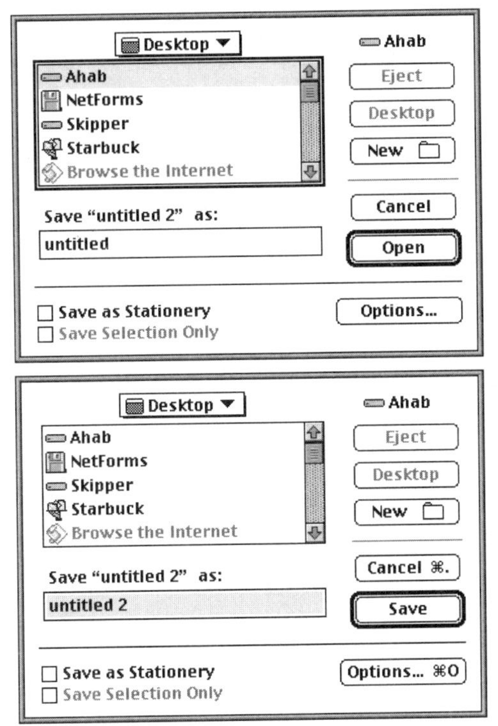

Figure 7-16: A dialog box with the scrolling list active (top) and with the Name option box active (bottom).

Moving On

Even the performance of the oldest Macintosh programs improves when used with Mac OS 8, as we've seen throughout this chapter. Some improvements are dramatic and substantial, whereas others are more subtle or incidental.

Another important aspect of Mac OS 8 that many people take for granted is the ability to work with other types of computers. In fact, the Mac OS is arguably the most flexible operating system on the market due in part to its minority status. To survive, it has had to be compatible with several different types of computers. As we'll see in the next chapter, "Working With Other Types of Computers," the Mac OS gets an A+ on its report card for playing well with others.

CHAPTER 8

Working With Other Types of Computers

Another of the many great things about using the Mac OS is how well it works with other types of computers: the Mac OS is a good network citizen. When the Macintosh was introduced in 1984, there was basically only one other type of computer available, the IBM PC. There are several others available today, but Macs and PC clones account for about 98 percent of the computers in the world. I'd love to be able to tell you that the majority of these people use Macs, but that wouldn't be true. The indisputable truth, however, is that the Mac OS is the easiest operating system in the world to install, maintain, and use in conjunction with other computers. You can take that to the bank. In this chapter, you'll learn about the software and hardware extensions that allow the Mac to be the best possible corporate citizen.

Sharing Data

There are basically only three ways to share data between different computers:

- Network
- Removable media
- Floppy drive

In the early days, when Macs were networked together using AppleTalk and File Sharing (see Section III, "Networking," for all the details), PCs were connected via Sneakernet. To transfer data from one PC to another, you had to put the data onto a big floppy (remember those?), put on your Converse or Adidas sneakers, and walk it on over to the other PC—not very high-tech.

Some of the large, more sophisticated computers also had networking capabilities, but they were out of reach for the average user. Networked computers can transfer and share data directly between computers of the same type with ease. However, different types of computers are often not as successful at sharing data because of the many different ways they communicate. UNIX computers, for example, use many different types of communication methods, called *protocols*, and even though they are all very sophisticated computers, they sometimes can't agree on the protocols to use to effectively communicate. Sharing and transferring data gets even more difficult when you try to get other types of computers together. Computers that use Microsoft Windows, for example, are even more difficult to connect to UNIX computers.

The Internet has been the great equalizer in this respect because it uses the Transmission Control Protocol/Internet Protocol (TCP/IP) suite for most of its communication. Any computer that can use TCP/IP is potentially easier to connect to over the Internet, and we'll discuss this more in Section III.

Today's computing environment also uses a good deal of removable media to store and transfer large amounts of data. We all know about CD-ROM drives, of course, but Macs also use a good deal of other types of removable media such as CD-R (recordable), Zip and Jazz drives from Iomega, and EZ drives from Syquest. These drives are capable of holding between 100MB and 1GB of data. The hardware required to access these types of removable media is very easy to install and use. In most cases they use the Small Computer Serial Interface (SCSI), and since most Macs use SCSI, it's usually just a matter of plugging in the drive.

The good people at Apple decided to make the Macintosh accessible in as many ways as possible, including via the Sneakernet as well as AppleTalk and Ethernet networking. Working well with other types of computers via Sneakernet computers required being able to read floppies formatted by different operatings systems—and the SuperDrive was born.

SuperDrive

In the early days of desktop computing, the only real way to share data—unless you had a Macintosh—was with a floppy disk. The first disks were huge (almost the size of a Frisbee), but they eventually got smaller. In the early 1980s, by the time the Macintosh came along, the disk was small enough to fit in a shirt pocket, and Apple shipped the first Macintosh with a SuperDrive.

The SuperDrive, standard equipment on all Macs except certain PowerBooks (in which it is optional), is capable of reading, writing to, and formatting several types of file formats:

- Macintosh (all makes and models)
- DOS
- ProDOS

These file formats cover about 99 percent of all operating systems on the market or still in use, and transferring data via floppy isn't exactly low-tech or extinct. You can always use a floppy if your network is down or if all else fails. And if you receive a floppy formatted by one of the methods just mentioned, you can just pop in the disk and the Mac OS will take care of the rest because of a piece of software called PC Exchange, which assists the Mac OS in talking to the SuperDrive.

PC Exchange

Mac hardware has had the capability to read PC disks for many years. But in that time, Apple's only software support for this capability was Apple File Exchange, a Font/DA-Mover-like utility that made it possible to copy files from PC disks onto Mac disks or hard drives.

But while everyone else was wondering why PC disks wouldn't just mount at the desktop so files could be dragged to and from disks directly, Apple ignored the issue in release after release of the system software. With PC Exchange, a $79 addition to the Mac OS, Apple finally provided this capability around the time that System 7.1 was released. PC Exchange is compatible with any version of System 7 or later and is now included as part of the Mac OS.

PC Exchange was also shipped as part of the Macintosh PowerBook/DOS Companion package. The Macintosh File Assistant, used for synchronizing files between drives, was also part of the Companion package, and it is discussed in Chapter 6, "PowerBook System Software."

When PC Exchange is installed, a PC disk inserted into a 1.44MB SuperDrive appears on the Mac desktop just like other Mac disks. A PC disk icon is shown in Figure 8-1. Via the PC Exchange Control Panel, you can specify which Macintosh application you want to use to open files from PC disks when you double-click the file or application icon. When you open a PC file from within an application using the Open command from the File menu, you can apply the translators that are part of that program without using PC Exchange in the conversion.

Figure 8-1: A PC floppy disk icon.

Files dragged to PC disks will automatically have their names changed to comply with PC file-naming conventions (eight characters and a three-character extension, also known as the 8.3 rule). Figure 8-2 shows the PC Exchange Control Panel.

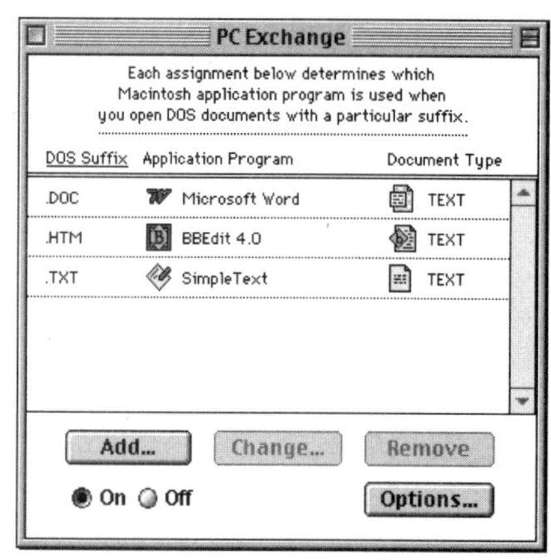

Figure 8-2: PC Exchange Control Panel.

Setting up the PC Exchange Control Panel requires only a few steps. You can add conversions of DOS files to the list in the Control Panel by clicking the Add button. Enter the three-letter extension, select a Macintosh application that you would like to open when that file is used, and then select the type of document you want that application to translate the DOS file into. Any translators are shown in the pop-up menu for the document type. Figure 8-3 shows an example of an .HTM (HTML) file being converted to a BBEdit TEXT file.

Some of the more common translations are the following:

- Lotus 1-2-3 .WKS files to Lotus 1-2-3 (Mac) and MS Excel TEXT files.
- Excel .XLS files to Lotus 1-2-3 (Mac) and Excel (Mac) TEXT files.
- Microsoft Word for Windows .DOC files to Word (Mac) WDBN files.
- PageMaker .PM4 files to PageMaker (Mac) ALB4 files.
- Quattro (DOS) .WK1 files to Lotus 1-2-3 (Mac) and Excel TEXT files.
- Ventura Publisher .CHP files to Ventura Publisher VCHP files.

Use the Open command from within an application to open WordPerfect (DOS) files, since no suffix is assigned to those files.

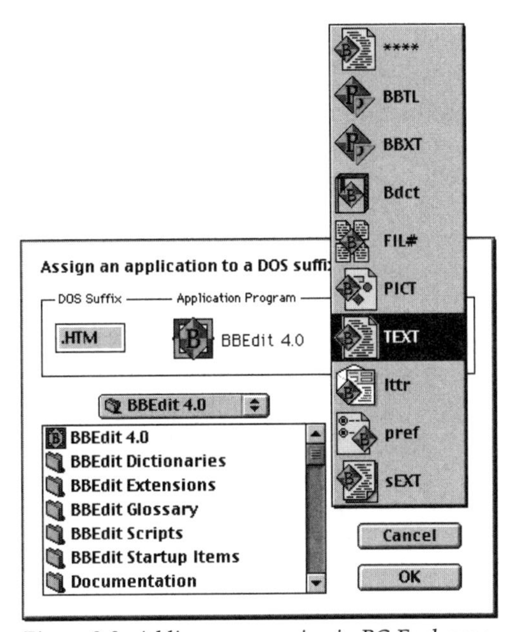

Figure 8-3: Adding a conversion in PC Exchange.

PC Exchange enables you to format a floppy disk as a PC disk using the same Erase Disk command on the Special menu that you use to format a floppy disk as a Macintosh disk. The Erase Disk dialog box is shown in Figure 8-4.

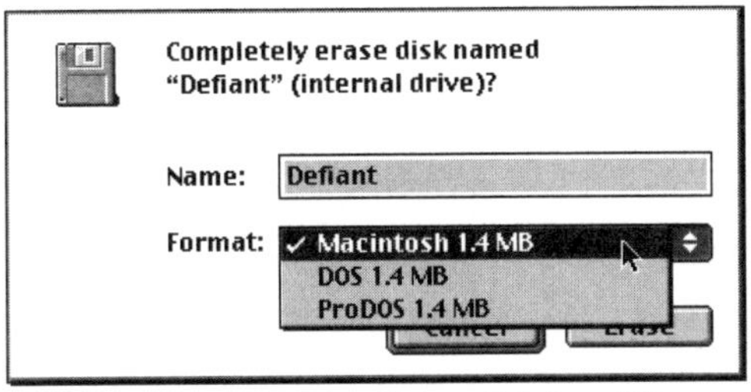

Figure 8-4: Formatting a floppy disk for a PC.

Macintosh Easy Open

Macintosh Easy Open allows your Mac to better communicate with other types of computers by helping you take a file created by one application and open it with another when the original application is not available. Files can be Macintosh, MS-DOS, Windows, or OS/2 files. A set of "translator" files is used to convert the file, and you are prompted to select an appropriate application from a list of possible choices. If you have DataViz translators installed (part of the MacLinkPlus PC package, described next), then Easy Open will work with them.

For example, when someone sends you a PICT file, you can open it in SimpleText. Easy Open works together with PC Exchange to make opening files on your Macintosh easy.

Some Power Macintosh configurations may have Insignia Solutions's SoftWindows or SoftWindows 95. SoftWindows is a native PowerPC application that emulates an Intel 80x86 microprocessor with Microsoft's Windows library. Insignia Solutions licensed the Windows Toolbox directly from Microsoft. Using Easy Open and SoftWindows, you can set up documents to open inside other Windows applications instead of opening in Macintosh applications.

To turn Easy Open on or off, open the Control Panel shown in Figure 8-5.

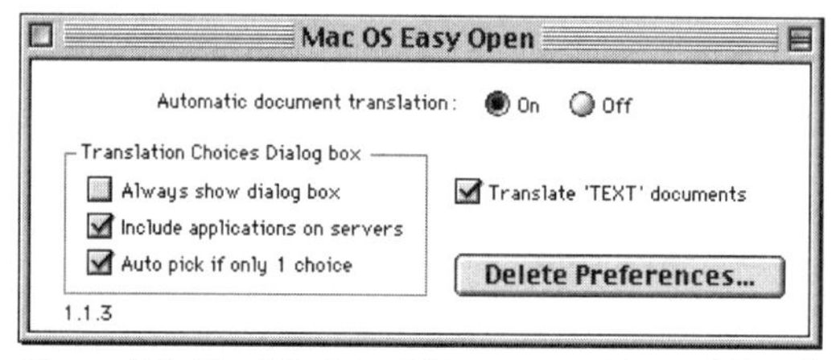

Figure 8-5: The Macintosh Easy Open Control Panel.

You can select the Always Show Dialog Box check box to display the list of compatible applications; otherwise, Easy Open will make a selection for you. When you set the Include Applications on Servers check box, Easy Open will use applications on other Macintosh computers to open your file. An example of the Easy Open selection dialog box is shown in Figure 8-6.

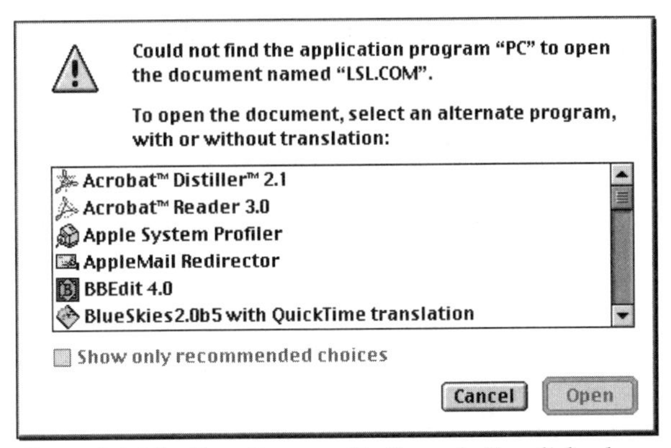

Figure 8-6: The Easy Open application selection dialog box.

MacLinkPlus

Another extension to the Mac OS that helps your Mac live in a Windows world is MacLinkPlus from DataViz. MacLinkPlus is a companion product to PC Exchange that helps you open documents created on Microsoft Windows–based computers even if you don't have the Mac OS version of the application that was used to create the document.

MacLinkPlus is easily configured through MacLinkPlus Setup in the Control Panels, shown in Figure 8-7. In fact, all you need to do is confirm that the default settings are accurate (which they usually are).

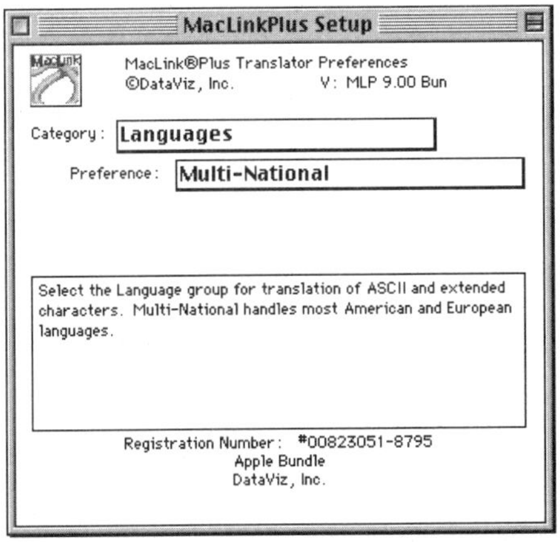

Figure 8-7: Configure MacLinkPlus through the Control Panels.

Next, locate the MacLinkPlus folder on your Mac's hard drive, usually in the Apple Extras folder on the root of your boot drive. To convert a document, just double-click the document and wait a few seconds for the Macintosh Easy Open dialog window, shown in Figure 8-8, to open. It will list the available applications that might be able to successfully translate your document into the appropriate Mac OS application. Make a choice from the scrolling menu and MacLinkPlus will translate the document and launch the appropriate application.

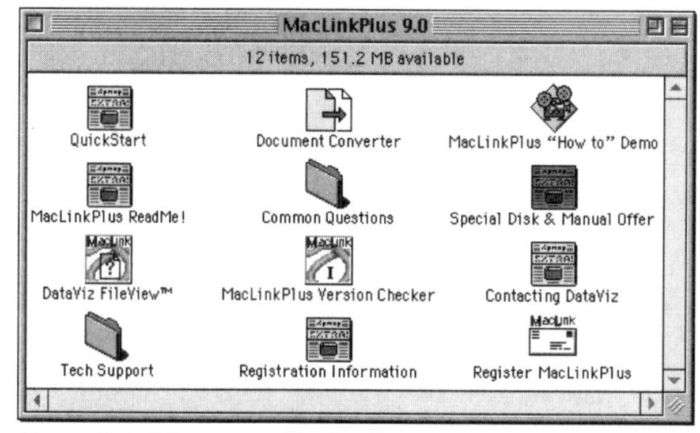

Figure 8-8: Select an application for which a document is to be translated.

Other OS Solutions

Since the majority of computers use operating systems other than the Mac OS, several companies have been making alternative hardware and software solutions for many years. The solutions allow other operating systems to run in place of, or along side of, the Mac OS, including:

- MS-DOS
- Windows 3.x
- Windows 95
- Windows NT
- MkLinux UNIX
- MachTen UNIX

And with the release of Virtual PC in June 1997, your Mac can now run any operating system that can run on the x86 (Intel) platform, which opens an entirely new meaning of cross-platform compatibility.

The first major application to run another operating system was SoftPC from Insignia Solutions, which later created SoftWindows and SoftWindows 95. Insignia's approach has been to create an environment within the Mac OS environment that emulates these operating systems. These programs run as co-operating systems and are launched as applications, which means you can run the Mac OS and all its applications at the same time as another operating system provided you have the necessary RAM and other hardware requirements. For example, Figure 8-9 shows SoftWindows 95 running as an application under Mac OS 8.

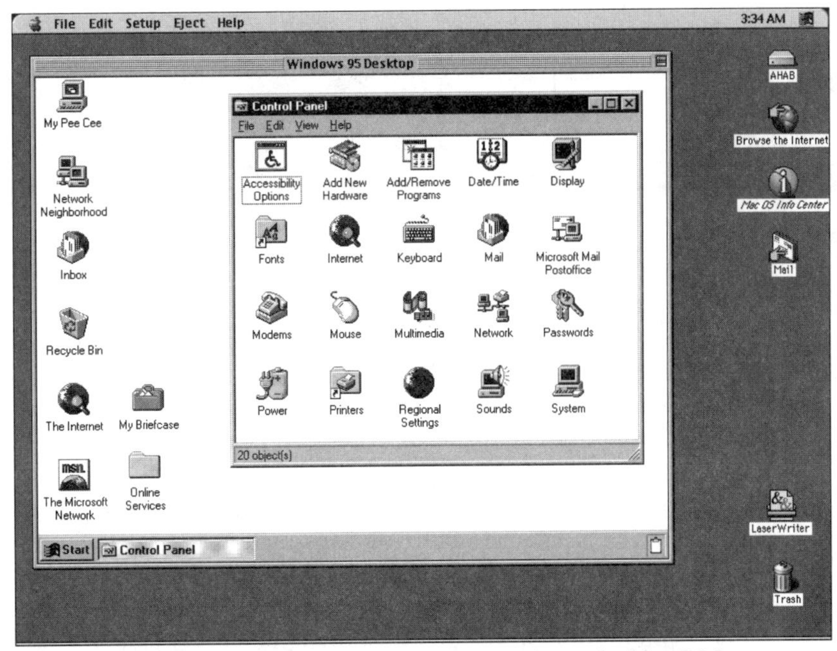

Figure 8-9: Insignia Solutions's SoftWindows 95 running under Mac OS 8.

Having an application like SoftWindows or SoftWindows 95 is the ultimate in compatibility with other computers because you can run not only all your favorite Macintosh applications, but almost any Microsoft Windows application as well, giving you access to about 99 percent of all applications. Not bad, eh?

Because SoftWindows 95 works like many other applications on the Mac OS in terms of installation and configuration, you have the standard pull-down menus that you would have in most other Mac applications. The Setup menu, shown in Figure 8-10, is where you'll configure various elements of SoftWindows that emulate various aspects of a PC.

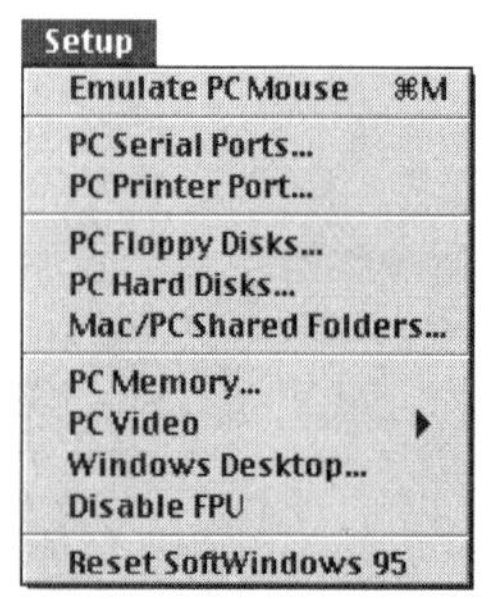

Figure 8-10: Use the Setup menu to configure SoftWindows 95.

SoftWindows and SoftWindows 95 emulate various elements of PC hardware and software, matching the printer selected in the Chooser, for example, to the PC equivalent, usually the LPT1 port.

The newest, and possibly coolest, compatibility software for the Mac OS is Virtual PC from Connectix, makers of Speed Doubler and Ram Doubler. Virtual PC is different from SoftWindows in that it emulates the entire PC, not just a particular version of a Microsoft operating system such as Windows 3.1 or 95. Virtual PC serves as a hardware abstraction layer that emulates a Pentium-based PC and allows you to install any operating system that will run on a PC onto your PowerMac.

The configuration of Virtual PC, shown in Figure 8-11, allows you to easily configure all the elements of a PC as they should be configured on a PowerMac. You can select what hardware devices to use, such as hard drives, CD-ROM players, a floppy drive, sound support, and the like. The options are self explanatory.

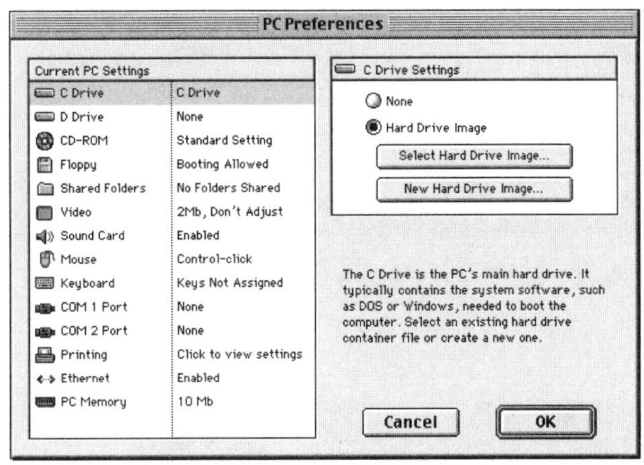

Figure 8-11: Use the Preferences menu to configure Virtual PC to emulate the hardware of a Pentium-based PC.

When installed, Virtual PC boots without an operating system, so the first thing you'll need to do is install one, such as MS-DOS. Figure 8-12 shows a Virtual PC session when running MS-DOS, which takes just a few megabytes of hard drive space to install.

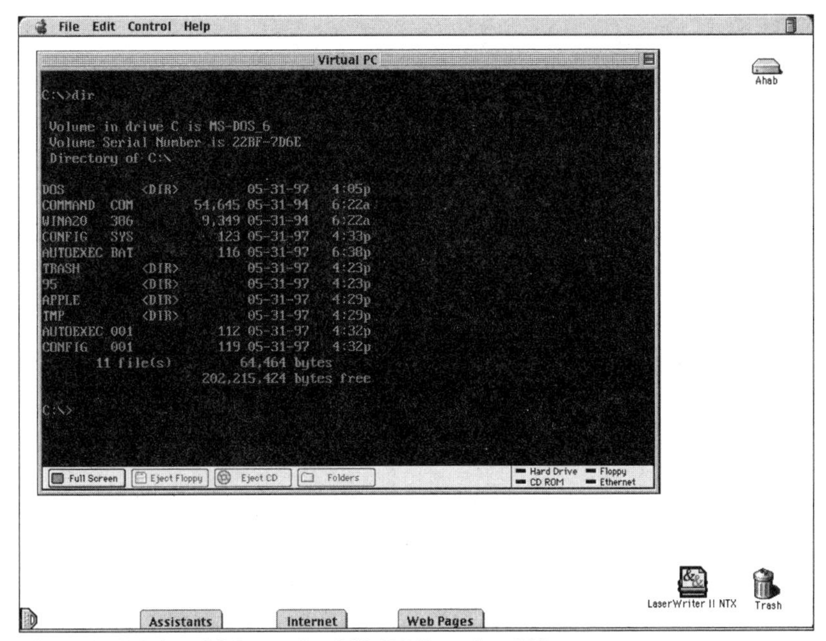

Figure 8-12: Virtual PC running MS-DOS version 6.22.

Many older network and business environments still rely on older versions of the Windows operating system, such as Windows 3.1, shown in Figure 8-13 running on a PowerMac under Virtual PC.

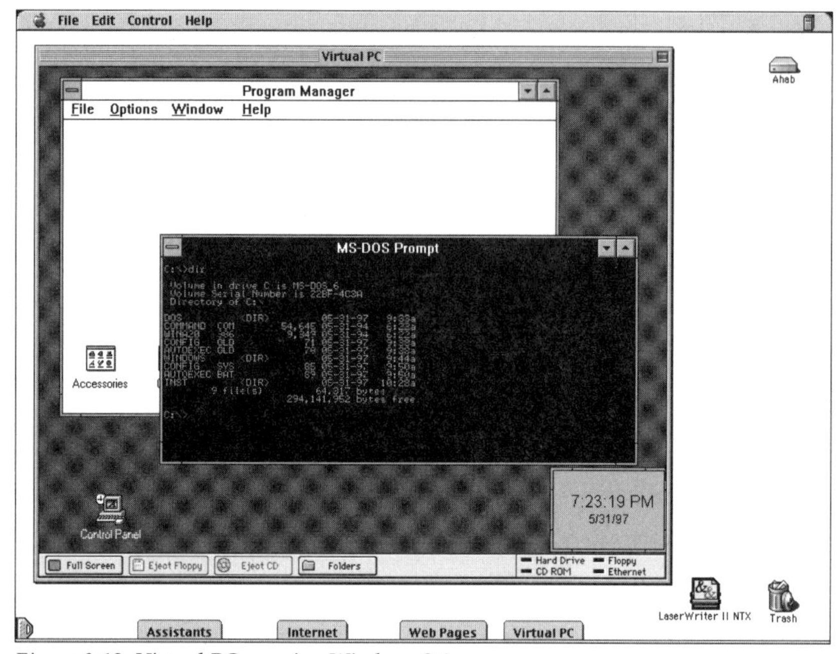

Figure 8-13: Virtual PC running Windows 3.1.

However, because Virtual PC can run any operating system that a Pentium-based PC can run, you can install a more modern operating system such as Windows 95, shown in Figure 8-14.

If you have a very fast PowerMac, you should give one of the software emulation packages such as SoftWindows or Virtual PC a chance. However, if you need more speed, you can always purchase a hardware solution in the form of a DOS card from Apple, Orange Micro, or Radius. You can get a DOS card for well under $1,000 that includes a Pentium processor running up to 166 MHz, 16MB of RAM, an L2 cache, and MS-DOS. You can also get DOS cards with regular Intel, Cyrix, or AMD chips; and, if you want to pay the price, you can get a Pentium Pro 200 MHz and Windows NT. Expect to pay at least $2000 for a system like that, however.

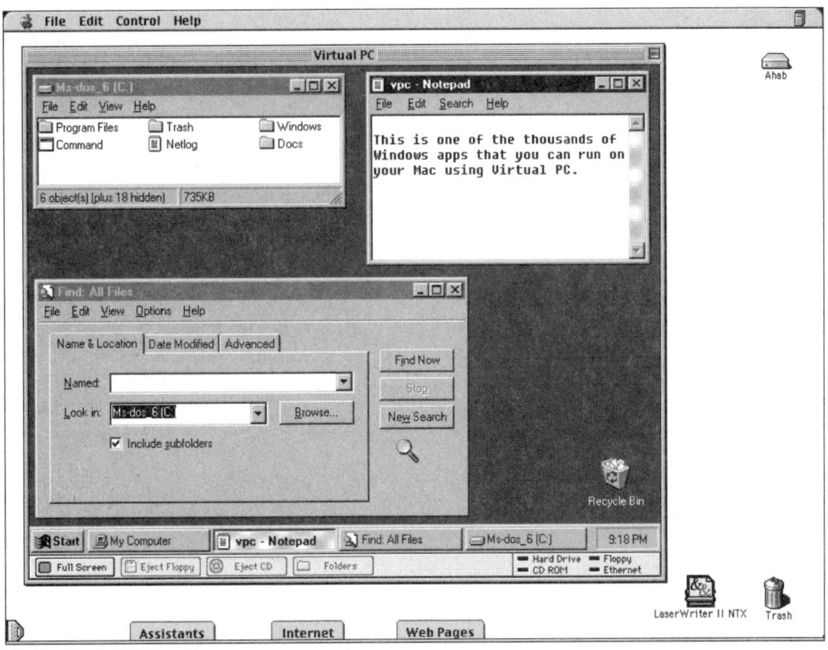

Figure 8-14: Virtual PC running Windows 95.

Moving On

You'll want to choose the road to compatibility that is best for your Mac and for your environment. All Mac OS 8 owners will have the benefits of Apple's SuperDrive, PC Exchange, Macintosh Easy Open, and MacLinkPlus. These tools can help your Mac be a better neighbor with other computers. However, if you need more compatibility, you can always run other operating systems on your Mac or PowerMac, such as Windows and Windows 95. If your Mac is in a network environment dominated by UNIX computers, you can install one of several UNIX-on-Mac solutions, such as MachTen from Tenon Intersystems, which is an application, or MkLinux, a free UNIX operating system that replaces the Mac OS. Whatever your needs, there is probably a good solution to help your Mac better communicate with other computers in your environment.

In the next chapter, "Applications & Memory Management," we'll look at ways in which your Mac uses memory to operate applications and how you can tweak the Mac OS to help your applications run peacefully on your Mac.

CHAPTER 9

Applications & Memory Management

When someone asks you about your Macintosh, you probably say something like, "I've got a PowerMac 7200 with 16 megs of memory and a 500-meg hard drive." It's no accident that the three variables you use to describe your computer are its model name, the amount of installed memory, or random access memory (RAM), and its hard disk size. These are the factors that determine the speed and range of activities you can perform with your computer.

With Mac OS 8, the amount of RAM installed in your Mac is still important, but it's no longer the total measure of memory or the only important memory issue. In this chapter, we look at the overall picture of Macintosh memory, including the new Memory Control Panel options, the About This Computer dialog box, and ways you can configure applications to use memory most efficiently.

Memory vs. Storage

Before we jump into the Mac OS 8's new memory options and their implications, let's clarify the difference between memory (RAM) and storage (disk space). This distinction may be clear to experienced Macintosh users, but if you're not certain you understand the difference, please read this section carefully.

In the simplest terms, memory consists of the chips in your computer where data is temporarily stored while it is being used by the Macintosh. This is in contrast to your hard disk, floppy disks, and other storage devices where data is permanently stored when it is not being used by your Macintosh.

The differences between RAM and storage (hard drives, floppies, and other media) are very important. Both RAM and storage hold data—application programs, system software, and data files—but the similarities end there. RAM stores data electronically on a set of chips, and as a result, these chips "forget" their contents as soon as the power is turned off or the Mac is restarted. Storage devices like hard drives and floppy disks operate magnetically, or by optical technology, and only lose information if it is intentionally erased.

More importantly, the Macintosh can only work with data stored in RAM; it cannot directly manipulate data on any storage device. In order to open an application or file, it must be read from storage and written into memory. Once in memory, the application can be executed or the file can be modified, but to make these changes permanent, the information in RAM must be written back out to the storage device—this is what happens when you choose the Save command.

RAM & You

If we compare the way your Mac uses memory and storage with the way you work and think, perhaps the difference will become more apparent and easier to remember. In this analogy, the computer (and it's processor) plays the part of the human brain, memory (RAM) is equated with our own memory, and floppy and hard disk storage is equated with written or typed notes.

As you know, no information can gain access to your brain without also entering your memory; regardless of whether information originates from your eyes, ears, or other senses, it is immediately put into memory (RAM) so that your brain (the Macintosh processor) can access it. But what do we do with information that we want to use in the future? We transfer it to some storage medium, like paper (disk). This way, we know that when this information is needed in the future, we can transfer it back into memory by reading it. Of course, the fact that humans have both short-term and long-term memory weakens this analogy, but it is generally a useful way to make the distinction between memory and storage.

The Memory Control Panel

One of the realities Macintosh users have to confront is the finite amount of memory available in their computers. Today's software seems to have an insatiable appetite for RAM, and new technologies—like multitasking, 24-bit color and sound, and particularly the Web and Web browsers—intensify the problem. The crusade for additional memory has traditionally encountered certain roadblocks: the operating system's limited ability to address the need for large amounts of memory, the computer's physical limitations, and the high price of memory chips.

System 7 began the process of breaking down these barriers, or at least temporarily pushed them back. The Memory Control Panel was one of System 7's new memory-related features. This Control Panel offers virtual memory, 32-bit addressing, and RAM disk options as well as the disk cache option, which is System 7's version of the RAM cache found in the General Control Panel of earlier systems. All of these elements undergo continual improvement as system software develops. Even when the outward appearance of the Memory Control Panel remains unchanged, you can detect speed enhancements due to underlying changes—particularly in Mac OS 8.

The Memory Control Panel in older versions of the Mac OS doesn't provide the same options on all Macintosh models because of certain limitations at the hardware or software level. When a certain Mac model doesn't support an option, it doesn't appear in the Control Panel. Figure 9-1 illustrates this point with the various Memory Control Panels found in System 7.5.

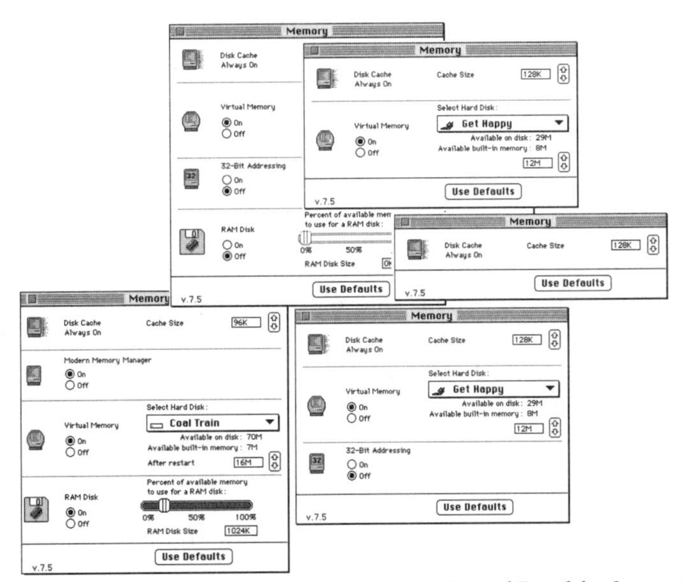

Figure 9-1: The five versions of the Memory Control Panel for System 7.5 that appear on various Macintosh models.

In Mac OS 8, however, the degree of difference in the Memory Control Panel between models of the Macintosh and Macintosh clones is virtually nonexistent. Figure 9-2 shows the Memory Control Panel in Mac OS 8, and the sections that follow describe the different elements of this Control Panel.

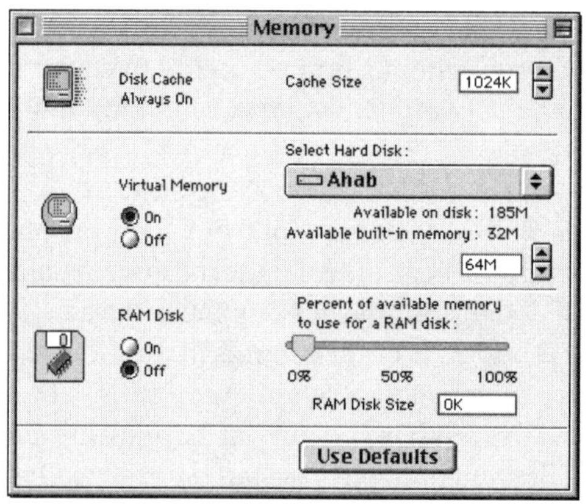

Figure 9-2: The Memory Control Panel for Mac OS 8.

Disk Cache

A disk cache is a small section of Macintosh RAM set aside to store a copy of the most recent data read from disk (or volume) into memory. Storing this copy makes the data readily available when it's needed again. Reaccessing data via the RAM-based cache rather than having to reread it from disk saves considerable time.

By default, your Macintosh uses 32K of cache for every 1 megabyte of RAM installed in your Mac. If you have 16MB of RAM, for example, 512K would be the default cache setting. Using the arrows, you can increase or decrease your disk cache size as required.

For most users, settings between 512K and 1024K are sufficient. Unless you have specific memory limitations, you shouldn't reduce the cache below its default setting since the small amount of memory the cache consumes significantly improves your Macintosh's performance. In most cases, you should not increase the size of your cache too much either, as there is a distinct point of diminishing returns after which more disk cache will actually slow down your Macintosh.

Settings over 1024K or perhaps 2048K should be used only in very specific situations. In situations where large cache allocations aid performance, normally your software's documentation will mention this. For example, Adobe's

Type Manager can use large cache allocations when it is rendering several fonts for a document. The "built" fonts can be stored in memory, and the larger cache is helpful in that circumstance. Most applications use their own internal memory caching scheme and don't rely on the system software's cache for performance enhancement.

The perfect disk cache size is a matter of great debate even among the most technically knowledgeable Macintosh users. Your Macintosh hardware and software configuration and the way you use your Mac have a big effect on your optimal setting, so trial and error is really the only way to find what works best for you.

The Disk Cache option is always on; you may adjust its size downward, but you may not turn it off.

The disk cache has been reworked in Mac OS 8—although you wouldn't know it to look at the Memory Control Panel. A file subsystem cache scheme extends the current file system cache into temporary memory (RAM) when possible. This is of particular benefit to users with a large amount of physical RAM installed. Also, menus are now better cached so that the next time a menu is pulled down, it is drawn immediately. Menu performance varies with CPU speed, but will be most apparent to users with slower machines.

Virtual Memory

Virtual memory is a software trick. It uses space on your hard drive to "fool" the Macintosh into thinking there's more available memory than there really is. Using virtual memory, a Macintosh with only 4MB or 8MB of actual RAM can act like it has 16MB or more. In fact, virtual memory can provide your Macintosh with over 1 gigabyte (1000MB) of memory. This number is one half of the addressable disk space in System version 7.1. System 7.5 has 4GB addressable disk space, half of which is addressable as virtual memory (double the amount of potential virtual memory from earlier versions). Mac OS 8, however, can address up to 1 terabyte (1000 gigabytes) of hard drive space, so you could have up to several gigabytes of virtual memory.

Virtual memory substitutes hard disk space for RAM. One benefit of using this device is that hard drive space is generally much less expensive than actual RAM, and virtual memory can provide access to more memory than is possible with RAM chips alone.

However, using virtual memory has two main drawbacks. First, performance is slower than with real RAM since the mechanical actions required of your hard drive are no match for the electronic speed of RAM chips. Second, virtual memory appropriates hard disk space normally available for other activities. You'll notice a striking difference in hard drive speed on virtual memory when you upgrade to a new drive. An onboard hard drive disk cache (installed RAM) can improve virtual memory performance.

In order to use virtual memory, your Macintosh must be equipped with a 68030 or better processor, but a good rule of thumb is that if your computer is capable of running Mac OS 8, then it can utilize virtual memory as well.

Enabling Virtual Memory

Go to the Memory Control Panel to enable virtual memory, as shown in Figure 9-3. After clicking the On button, the Select Hard Disk option becomes available. From the pop-up menu, choose the hard disk volume on which the virtual memory storage file will be created and stored.

The amount of available space on the selected hard disk is displayed below the hard disk pop-up menu. The amount of free space available determines the amount of virtual memory that can be configured. A virtual memory storage file equal to the total amount of memory available while using virtual memory will be placed on the selected disk. In other words, if your Macintosh has 16MB of actual RAM, and you wish to reach 40MB by using 24MB of virtual memory, a 24MB virtual memory storage file must be created on the selected volume.

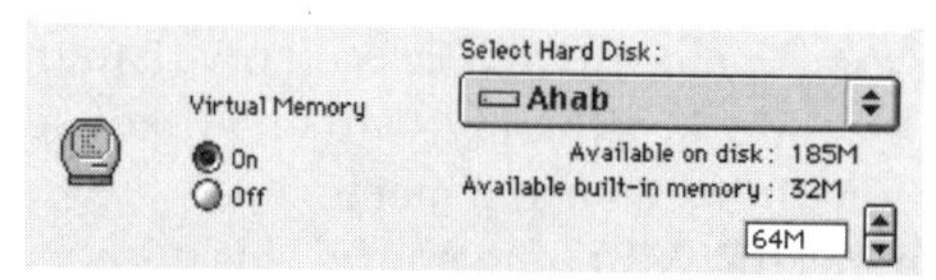

Figure 9-3: The Virtual Memory option in the Memory Control Panel determines the size and location of the virtual memory file.

Appearing below the Available on Disk option is the Available Built-In Memory field, which tells you how much physical RAM is installed and recognized by the Mac OS. If you increase the amount of virtual memory to be used, a field called After Restart will appear. The After Restart option indicates the amount of memory specified, including actual RAM and virtual memory. Click on the arrows to modify this specification. If the After Restart option is not visible, click one of the arrows until it appears.

Any changes made to the Virtual Memory option will not take effect until your computer is restarted. To verify that virtual memory is on, choose the About This Computer command to display the current memory status. (More information on the About This Computer dialog box later in this chapter.)

Virtual Memory Performance

Virtual memory works by moving information between a disk-based swap file and the RAM inside the computer; even when virtual memory is being used, the Macintosh communicates only with the real RAM. This movement of data between hard disk and RAM, technically known as paging, causes the Macintosh to perform slower than it does when using actual RAM alone.

The amount of paging slowdown depends on how much actual RAM is available and how virtual memory is being used. The more available RAM, the less paging interference. The type of activity called for also affects paging: working on multi-megabyte data files and frequent switching between open applications are examples of activities that usually require more paging and therefore decrease performance. Problems with virtual memory show up as poor performance in animation, video, and sound. Games and multimedia content that require large data manipulation are the first to suffer. Virtual memory is a prime energy drain in PowerBook computers.

A good rule of thumb in determining your own RAM/virtual memory mix is that you should have enough actual RAM to cover your normal memory needs and enough supplemental virtual memory to handle occasional abnormally large requirements. If you find that approximately 16MB of RAM let you work comfortably in the three or four open applications you use regularly, but you occasionally need 32MB to open additional applications or work with large data files, then 16MB of real RAM and a combined total of 32MB of RAM and virtual memory would probably be adequate. However, if you don't need an additional 16 MB of virtual memory on top of your 16MB of physical memory, use just one additional MB of virtual memory instead. This will help speed up things a bit and, as with using any amount of virtual memory, your applications won't ask for as much RAM.

Exactly what ratios of real to virtual memory Macintosh users should set has long been the subject of speculation. The final answer is for you to use as much virtual memory as is practical and useful. But remember, physical RAM is fairly cheap these days, and you should have at least 16MB on any model of PowerMac or Mac clone (all clones use the PowerPC chip and are therefore PowerMacs as well). These days, the entry level computer ships with 16MB.

Disabling Virtual Memory

Virtual memory can be turned off by clicking on the Off button in the Virtual Memory area of the Memory Control Panel and restarting your Macintosh. After disabling virtual memory, the virtual memory storage file is deleted from your hard drive automatically, and the space it occupied will be returned to the Mac OS for use by other programs.

What Happened to 32-Bit Addressing?

Older versions of the Memory Control Panel had an option to enable or disable something called 32-bit addressing. This option is no longer present, however, because it is obsolete. In the past, 8MB was the maximum amount of RAM that could be installed (or used) on the Macintosh. This limitation was posed by the way the available memory chips were addressed by the Macintosh system software, including those parts that reside on the ROM chips on the computer's logic board. Newer Macintosh computers of course use newer versions of the ROM chips, allowing much more physical RAM to be installed.

This extended ability to use memory is called 32-bit addressing, referring to the number of digits used in the current memory-addressing scheme. The Mac's older memory scheme is 24-bit addressing, since only 24 digits are used. Power Macintosh computers have 32-bit addressing built in and cannot have it turned off. Therefore, you don't see a 32-bit Addressing section on a Power Macintosh Memory Control Panel in Mac OS 8.

The ROM chips required for 32-bit addressing are 32-bit clean ROMs and are currently included in all shipping Macintoshes and all clones. Certain "older" models, specifically the Plus, Classic, SE, SE/30, Portable, II, IIx, IIcx, and LC, do not have 32-bit clean ROMs and therefore can't normally use 32-bit addressing. The SE/30 and Macintosh II, IIx, and IIcx can be upgraded to 32-bit clean capacity using an extension called MODE32 or the 32-bit addressing system enabler, both of which are available without charge from user groups and online services. Apple used to distribute and support MODE32 but no longer does so. Support for this function is built into later versions of the system software.

In some cases, launching a really old application that's not compatible with 32-bit addressing will cause your computer to crash.

What Happened to the Modern Memory Manager?

Older versions of the Memory Control Panel on PowerMacs have an option called the Modern Memory Manager. When you turn on the Modern Memory Manager option (first introduced in System 7.1.2), you are enabling a memory processing scheme specially written for the PowerPC chip and native applications. RISC-based microprocessors such as the PowerPC (used in all PowerMacs) load so much more of the instruction set into RAM than CISC-based microprocessors (used in all other Macs) that virtual memory, paging, and other memory operations were among the first that were ported into native PPC code.

The Modern Memory Manager contains algorithms that improve memory performance, not only when you are using native PPC programs, but even when you are using older programs operating in 680x0 emulation mode. Just as the introduction of 32-bit addressing caused compatibility problems early on, so did the Modern Memory Manager (it was the single biggest cause of compatibility problems with the PowerMacs).

In Mac OS 8, the Modern Memory Manager has been rolled into the system software and is on by default. It cannot be turned off.

Memory Control Panel Tips

There are several factors to keep in mind when configuring the Mac OS to use memory, both real and virtual. Here are a few tips to keep in mind that may be helpful:

- Use at least the minimum recommended disk cache. The disk cache speeds up operation, so you should leave it set to at least 32K for every megabyte of RAM installed in your Mac. (That means 256K for 8MB, 512K for 16MB, and 1024K for 32MB.)
- Install enough real RAM in your Macintosh. Real RAM chips should provide enough memory to cover your normal daily memory needs—at least 16MB and in some cases, up to 32MB. Although virtual memory can provide inexpensive additional memory, 80 percent of your memory needs should be covered by real RAM. The performance drawbacks of relying too heavily on virtual memory don't justify the relatively small amount of money saved.
- Extend your available memory with virtual memory. Once you've installed enough RAM to satisfy your everyday needs, use the virtual memory to give yourself extra memory to cover special occasional situations, such as working with large color images, animation, or more than the usual number of simultaneously open programs.

Turn off virtual memory when you see performance problems. Some programs, such as games and graphics programs, do considerable data input/output. Virtual memory can degrade performance, and rapid paging can also lead to system crashes. Turn virtual memory off if you are experiencing these conditions.

- Some applications, especially multimedia games, movies, and audio programs, just don't like virtual memory. If these types of programs don't behave properly, check with their instructions for information about possible virtual memory incompatibilities.

Controlling Memory

Once you've determined how much memory you need and made it available to the Mac OS (by installing RAM and by using virtual memory), you'll want to manage that memory wisely and use it economically. Managing your Mac's memory allows you to make sure that each application has enough RAM to operate properly and that enough total memory is available to open as many different applications as necessary.

System 7.5 provides two excellent tools for memory management—the About This Computer dialog box and the Get Info dialog box. We'll look at both of these tools in this section.

About This Computer

In Mac OS 8, the familiar About This Macintosh command has been changed to About This Computer, and the dialog box associated with it has been improved. The About This Computer dialog box provides information about the Macintosh being used, the system software version, installed and available memory, and the amount of memory used by each open application. Figure 9-4 shows the About This Computer dialog box.

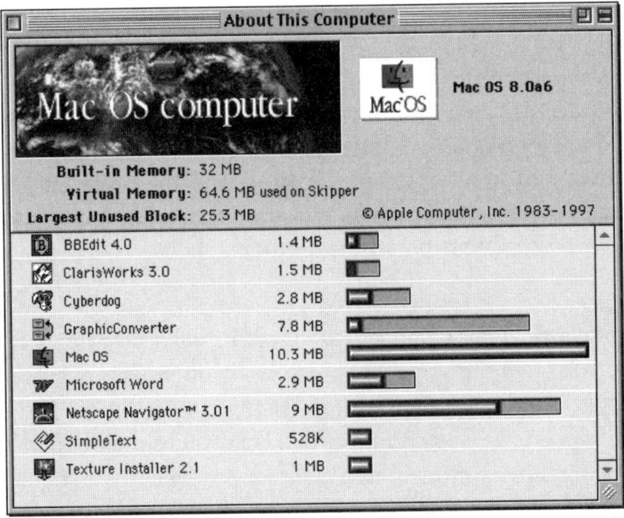

Figure 9-4: The About This Computer dialog box.

The upper section of the dialog box gives the version of operating system currently in use and the following data related to the memory available in your Mac:

- **Built-In Memory.** Displays the amount of physical RAM installed in your Macintosh, not including virtual memory.
- **Virtual Memory.** Documents the total memory available in your Macintosh, including installed RAM plus available virtual memory. The name of the hard disk storing the virtual memory file and the amount of hard drive space being used are listed to the right of the Virtual Memory listing.

  Virtual memory and hard drive designations are set via the Memory Control Panel, described earlier in this chapter.
- **Largest Unused Block.** Calculates the largest contiguous section of memory currently not being used by open software applications. This number is important because it determines both the number and size of additional software applications you can open.

In some cases, the largest unused block will not equal the amount of total memory available less the size of all open applications. That's because as applications are launched and quit, memory becomes fragmented—gaps are created between sections of memory that are used and those that are available. To defragment your memory and create larger unused blocks, quit all open applications and then relaunch them. As they're relaunched, applications will use available memory sequentially, leaving the largest possible unused block.

If you get an out-of-memory alert box and there should be plenty of memory left, you have a fragmented memory situation. This occurs when you launch and quit programs repeatedly. Try and "unlearn" techniques of the past by leaving programs you will use later open and in memory. If you have a fragmented memory problem, try first quitting programs in the reverse order they were opened. If that doesn't do the trick, you will have to restart to flush your Macintosh's memory.

Each software application requires a particular amount of memory in order to be opened successfully. The amount of memory is documented and can be controlled in the Get Info dialog box, as described later in this chapter. When a program is launched, if its memory requirement is larger than the largest unused block, it can't be opened. So you need to know approximately how much memory an application needs.

The lower portion of the About This Macintosh dialog box displays information about each open application, including its name, icon, and amount of memory allocated and used:

- **Application name and icon.** Each open application is listed in alphabetical order along with a small version of its icon.
- **Amount of memory allocated.** Just to the right of the application name, the total amount of memory that was allocated to that program when it was opened is displayed along with a bar graph showing this amount in relation to amounts used by other open applications. The total bar represents total allocated memory; the filled portion of the bar represents the portion of that allocated memory currently in use.

- **Amount of memory used.** In most cases when an application is opened, only a portion of its total allocated memory is used immediately. Usually, some of the memory is used by the application itself, some is used to hold open document files, and some is left over for use by the software's commands and features. Only the memory currently being used appears as the filled-in percentage of the memory allocation bar.

Holding down the option key when choosing the About This Computer command changes the command into About the Finder, the result of which is shown in Figure 9-5. Choosing About the Finder brings up a copyright screen that first appeared in Finder 1.0 in 1984 (waiting a bit will get you a history of the Finder's programmers scrolling across the screen).

Figure 9-5: The secret About the Finder dialog box.

The Get Info Dialog Box

The Get Info dialog box allows you to use the information provided in the About This Computer dialog box to take charge of your Macintosh's memory use. To minimize problems related to memory shortages or better allocate your available RAM to the different applications you want to open simultaneously, you can adjust the amount of memory each program uses.

The memory-related options of the Get Info dialog box are different in older versions of the operating system (such as System 7) and Mac OS 8, so we will examine each of these separately.

Get Info in Version 7.0

The Get Info dialog box's Memory option is shown in Figure 9-6 as it appears in version 7.0. The Memory option has two parts: Suggested Size and Current Size:

- **Suggested Size.** Displays the amount of RAM the developer recommends to properly run the application. You can't change this option, but it's very valuable as a reminder of the original Current Size setting.
- **Current Size.** Specifies the actual amount of RAM that the application will request when it's launched. (By default, the Current Size is equal to the Suggested Size.) You can change the amount of memory that will be allocated by entering a new value in this option and then closing the Get Info dialog box.

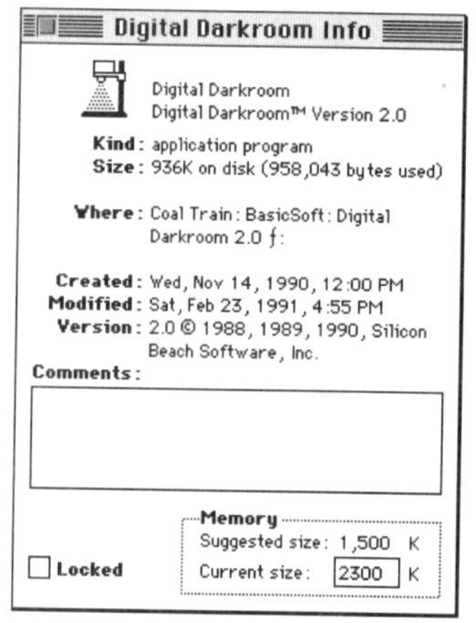

Figure 9-6: An application's Get Info dialog box in System 7.0.

When an application is launched, the program requests the amount of memory specified in the Current Size option. If this amount is available in an unused block, the memory is allocated and the program is opened. You can check the size of the largest available block in the About This Macintosh dialog box, as described earlier.

If the amount of memory requested is larger than the largest available unused block, a dialog box will appear stating that not enough memory is available (shown in Figure 9-7), asking if you want to try to run the application using less memory (shown in Figure 9-8), or suggesting that you quit an open application to create enough free memory (see Figure 9-9).

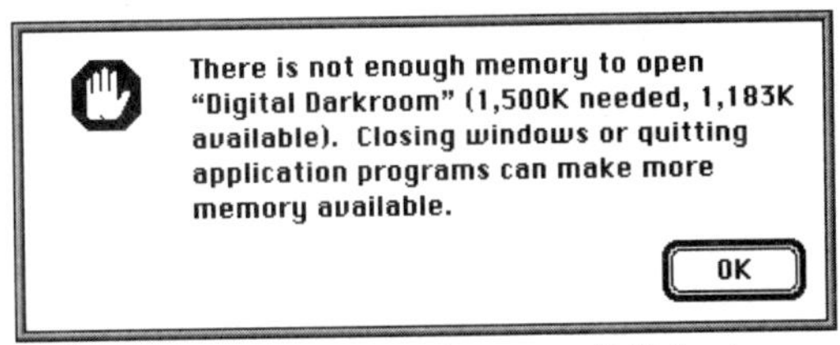

Figure 9-7: The "not enough memory" dialog box.

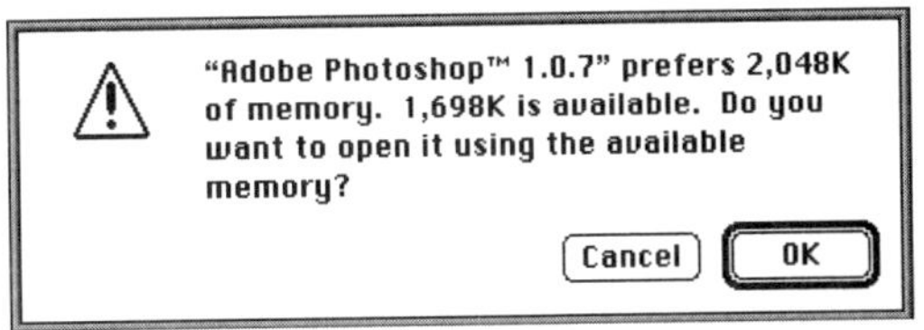

Figure 9-8: The "almost enough memory" dialog box.

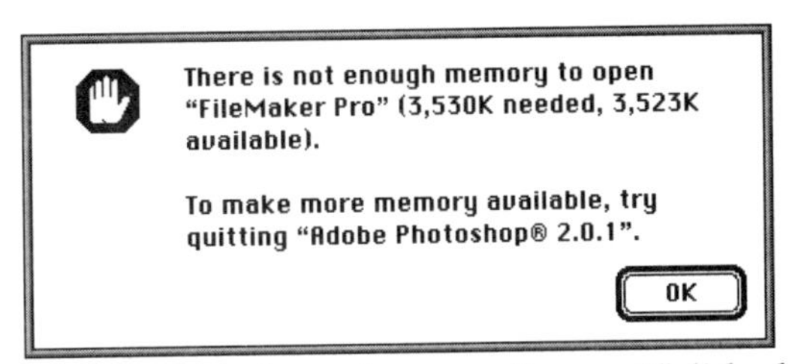

Figure 9-9: The "enough memory if you quit" dialog box.

Get Info in Mac OS 8

In Mac OS 8 (as in System 7.6), the Get Info dialog box's options eliminate the need to change settings for different memory situations; it allows you to set options that determine the amount of memory that will be used depending on the amount of memory available at launch time.

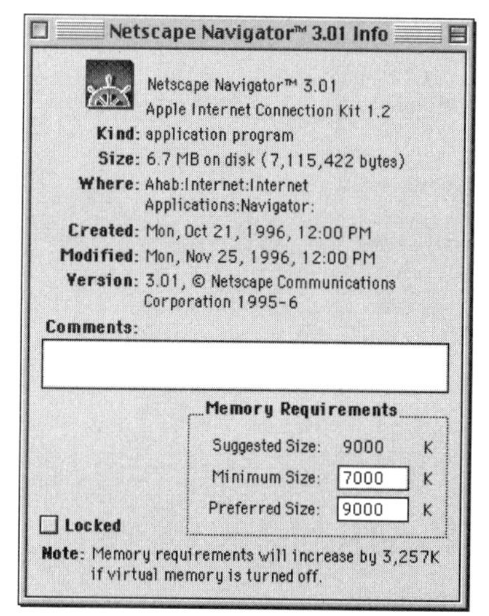

Figure 9-10: An application's Get Info dialog box in Mac OS 8.

The Memory option here has four parts: Suggested Size, Minimum Size, Preferred Size, and Note.

- **Suggested Size.** Lists the amount of RAM the developer recommends to properly run the application. You can't change this option—it's a reminder of the memory requirements as set by the application developer.
- **Minimum Size.** Designates the smallest amount of RAM in which the application will run properly. You can change this option by entering a new value.
- **Preferred Size.** Specifies the actual amount of RAM that the application will request when it's launched. You can change the amount of memory that will be allocated by entering a new value in this option and then closing the Get Info dialog box.
- **Note.** Informs you how much additional memory would be required if virtual memory is turned off. If virtual memory is turned on, this field will be blank.

When an application is launched, the program requests the amount of memory specified in the Preferred Size option. If this amount is available in an unused block, the memory is allocated and the program is opened. You can check the size of the largest available block in the About This Macintosh dialog box, as described earlier.

If the amount of memory requested by the Preferred Size option is not available, but more memory is available than the Minimum Size option, the application will launch using all available memory. If the amount of RAM specified in the Minimum Size option is unavailable, one of two dialog boxes will appear: one offers to quit an open application that has no open files in order to free enough memory to complete the launch (see Figure 9-11); the other one states that not enough memory is available to complete the launch (see Figure 9-12).

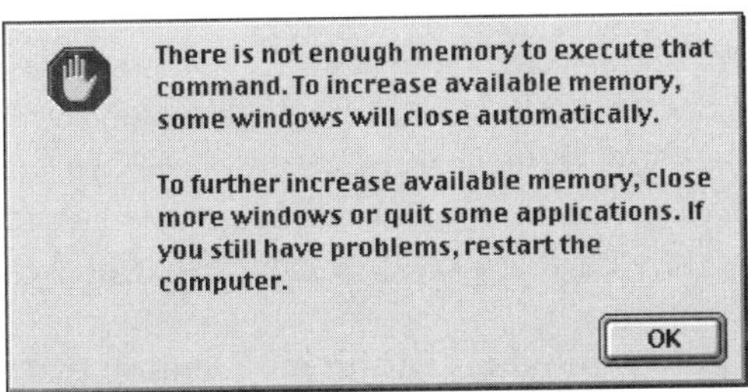

Figure 9-11: The "Not Enough Memory Unless You Quit Another Application" dialog box.

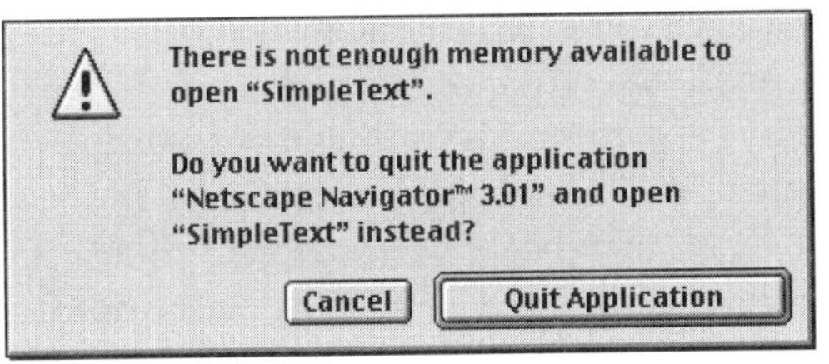

Figure 9-12: The "Not Enough Memory" dialog box.

Setting Memory Options

Optimally, 15 to 25 percent of the space in the memory allocation bar displayed next to an application name in the About This Computer dialog box should remain open, or unused, while the application is running. (As explained earlier, the bar graph displays total allocated RAM in white and the portion of memory actually being used in black.)

Most applications will not use all their allocated memory at all times—usage will vary as commands and features are used. So to determine the actual, average, and maximum amount of memory used, keep the About This Computer window open while you work and monitor the changes in memory used by your applications in the lower half of the screen, shown in Figure 9-13.

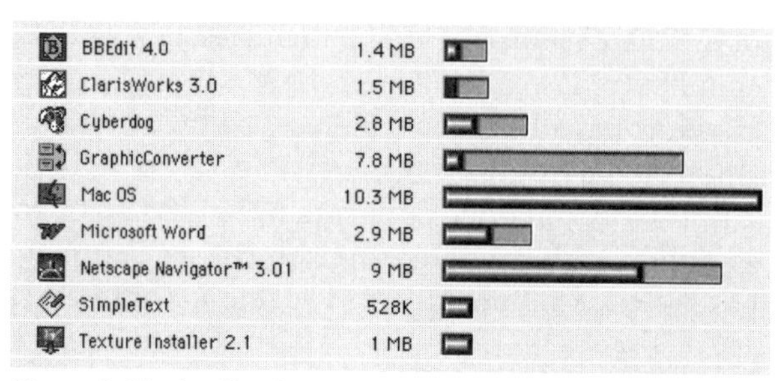

Figure 9-13: Application memory use is documented in the About This Computer dialog box.

Given that 15 to 25 percent unused space is the goal, watching the amount of actual memory used will show if the current memory allocation is too low, too high, or about right. As a result, you may need to increase a program's memory allocation, or you may be able to decrease it. Either of these modifications is done with the Size options.

Increasing memory allocation provides additional memory that can in many cases improve application performance, allow larger and more complete document files to be opened, and reduce or eliminate the possibility of memory-related crashes. These effects are hardly surprising when you consider how an application uses its allocated memory: it must control and manage its own code, data from any open document files, and all data manipulations performed by its commands and features. And it must do all this with an allocated memory that's less than the total size of the application program and its data files, let alone what it needs to manipulate its data. As a result, software must constantly shift parts of its own code and data from open documents back and forth between disk-storage memory and real memory. Providing additional memory minimizes this activity and allows the program to concentrate on operating efficiently.

For most programs, increasing the Current Size or Preferred Size option by 20 to 25 percent is optimal, but if you experience frequent "out of memory" errors in any software application, continue increasing until these errors are eliminated.

Decreasing memory allocation allows you to successfully launch applications with less memory, thereby running more programs simultaneously. This is generally not a recommended practice, but in many cases software will operate successfully using less RAM than the developer suggested.

There is no easy way to determine what the true minimum size should be, although it will rarely be more than 20 percent smaller than the suggested size. Don't be afraid to try it—just be sure to test the application in this configuration before working on important data and save frequently once you begin working. Start by reducing the Current or Minimum Size option by just 5 to 10 percent; if you find that the About This Computer dialog box shows large amounts of unused space, you may be able to reduce the allocation even more.

With the low price of RAM and the ability to use virtual memory, the need for most Macintosh users to reduce these sizes should become less common. Even if you have only 16MB of RAM installed, using virtual memory is preferable to reducing the Current or Minimum Size options. You're less likely to experience crashes or loss of data using virtual memory than with a reduced Current Size. (See the discussion of virtual memory earlier in this chapter.) Of course, the best long-range solution is to add enough RAM to your Macintosh so you won't have to depend on either virtual memory or Memory Requirements reductions.

Moving On

The amount of memory available on your Macintosh determines, in large measure, what you can do with your computer. As we've seen in this chapter, Mac OS 8 has fine-tuned changes made since System 7 that were designed to give you much more control over memory availability and how that memory is utilized:

- Virtual memory lets you "create" memory by using space on your hard drive as if it were RAM.
- Built-in 32-bit addressing makes it possible to access a vast amount of memory.
- The Get Info dialog box helps you control the amount of memory an application uses.
- The About This Computer dialog box provides constant feedback about what's happening with your Mac's memory.

In the next chapter, "Working With Multiple Applications," we'll look at one of the Mac OS's greatest strengths—the ability to launch and operate multiple applications at the same time. This chapter will focus on the multitasking abilities of the Mac OS, the commands and features it supports, and the ways in which you can use multitasking to work more productively.

CHAPTER 10

Working With Multiple Applications

One "exciting feature" of Mac OS 8 is actually an old feature that Macintosh users have been using for more than 10 years. Known as MultiFinder in previous system software versions, this feature lets you do the following:

- Run multiple applications at once.
- Switch between open applications as necessary.
- Leave one program working while you switch to another.

MultiFinder was a separate utility file kept in the System folder of previous system software versions. Because the MultiFinder utility file is no longer used, the name MultiFinder is not appropriate. In this book, the set of abilities that allows you to open multiple applications simultaneously will be called *multitasking*. Other people and publications may continue to refer to them as MultiFinder features, or you may also hear them described as the Process Manager. Some may avoid using any specific name, simply referring to the features as part of the system software or the Finder.

Technically speaking, there are two kinds of multitasking: cooperative and preemptive. Mac OS 8 provides cooperative multitasking, which means that all open applications have equal access to the Macintosh's computing power. In cooperative multitasking, applications are responsible for "letting go" of the microprocessor, whereas in preemptive multitasking, system software assigns a *time slice* to each application and shuttles processing between each running application. Time slices occur so frequently that each application appears to be running in real time.

Some purists consider preemptive multitasking, which ascribes priority to specific applications or tasks, to be the only "real" multitasking. You find preemptive multitasking in more "robust" operating systems such as UNIX, where each computer supports multiple users. Apple is slowly migrating the system software toward full multitasking and memory protection.

The distinctions between cooperative and preemptive multitasking are unimportant—and probably uninteresting—to most Macintosh users. Faster hardware and more memory make running multiple applications much more practical, however. For convenience, we'll use the term *multitasking* to describe the Mac's ability to open and operate multiple applications simultaneously.

What Is Multitasking?

Multitasking allows several programs to be opened and used simultaneously. You can have your word processor, Web browser, and graphics package all running at the same time, and you can switch between them freely. It's even possible for an application to continue processing information while you're using another application. Figure 10-1 shows Netscape Navigator, GraphicConverter, and BBEdit running simultaneously.

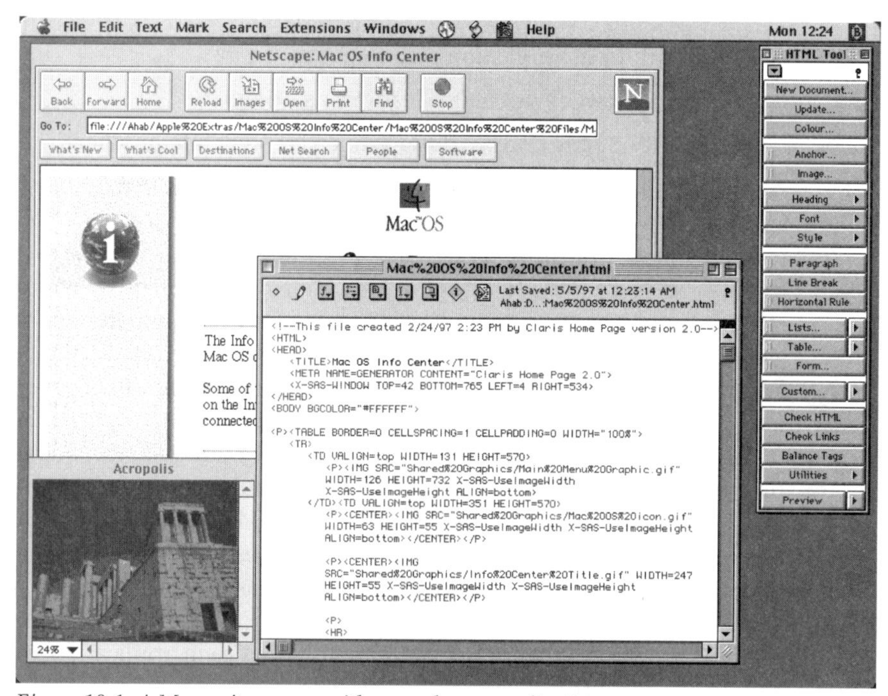

Figure 10-1: A Mac as it appears with several open applications.

Multitasking is a fantastic productivity booster, allowing you to use time and resources with maximum efficiency. For example, you're working in your word processor when you receive a telephone call from your mother. She wants to know whether she'd be better off investing the $10,000 she just won playing bingo in a 10-year CD paying 8.25 percent, or if she should sink it into T-bills paying 6.15 percent tax-free. To help dear old Mom out of her dilemma, you need access to a spreadsheet. So you quit your word processor, launch your spreadsheet, perform the necessary calculations, offer your advice, quit the spreadsheet, launch the word processor, reload your file, and say good-bye to Mom.

Following this approach is fine—of course you want to help your mother—but all the time it took to quit your word processor, launch the spreadsheet, quit the spreadsheet, relaunch the word processor, and reload your file could have been avoided. Multitasking would have allowed you to run your spreadsheet without quitting your word processor.

This example points to one of the most obvious benefits of multitasking—the ability to handle interruptions with minimum loss of productivity. For most people, interruptions are an unavoidable part of working, and whether they're in the form of a ringing telephone, a knock on the door, an urgent e-mail message, or your own memory lapses (you forgot to print that report and drop it in the mail), the least disruption possible is the key to productivity.

The second major benefit of multitasking is its ability to use two or more applications together to complete a single project. To prepare a mail merge, for example, you can export data from your database manager, prepare the merge lists, and then execute the merge. In most cases, the raw data exported from your database will require some cleaning up before it's ready to be merged, and often you'll encounter a minor data formatting problem that requires you to repeat the whole export and data cleanup process. But by using multitasking, you avoid the delay and frustration of quitting the word processor to return to the database and then quitting the database to return to the word processor.

Suppose you need to read reports and view database or spreadsheet data while preparing presentation graphics, update graphic illustrations in a drawing package before importing them into a page layout, or use an optical character recognition package to read in articles for storage in a database? In these and many other cases, quickly switching from one application to another and using the Mac's Cut, Copy, and Paste commands allow transfer of information between applications that can't otherwise share data.

The third benefit of multitasking is the most exciting—and certainly the one yielding the largest productivity gains: multitasking supports background processing. Therefore, an open application can continue to process data even when you switch away from that application to work in another. Any task that ties up your computer, forcing you to wait for it to finish, can probably benefit from background processing. Common examples are printing, downloading files from the Internet, making large spreadsheet calculations, and generating database reports. Examples of background processing and ways you can take advantage of this tremendous capability are discussed later in this chapter.

MultiFinder in System 6.0.x

If you're familiar with MultiFinder from earlier versions of the system software, you'll find only a few differences between MultiFinder and the multitasking features of System 7 and Mac OS 8. The most notable difference is that multitasking is always available and, unlike MultiFinder, cannot be turned off.

If you didn't use MultiFinder in previous versions of the system software, it was probably for one of the following reasons:

- **Insufficient memory.** MultiFinder required 2 megabytes of RAM (at a minimum) and 4 or more megabytes of RAM to be useful. The same is true of the multitasking capabilities of Mac OS 8, although the recent lowering of RAM prices and the addition of virtual memory in Mac OS 8 make having insufficient memory less of an issue than in the past. (Mac OS 8 memory requirements are discussed later in this chapter, and in Chapter 9, "Applications & Memory Management.")

  As the system software has continued to grow, so too has Mac OS 8's memory appetite. In Mac OS 8, the current recommended minimum RAM for basic system software is 8MB in a 68k Mac and 16MB in a Power Macintosh. This increase is more associated with additions of numerous features (extensions, Control Panels, and the like) than it is with the memory management requirements of multitasking.

- **Reputation.** MultiFinder had a reputation for instability. Many people believed that using MultiFinder made the Macintosh prone to frequent crashes. As often happens with software and hardware, this reputation was undeserved—the rumors of crashes were not based on the real facts.

  When MultiFinder was first released, many applications crashed when they were launched under MultiFinder. Crashing was not the fault of MultiFinder; it was usually because the application had not been written according to Apple's programming rules. Once these incompatible applications were made MultiFinder-compatible, almost all problems vanished.

  Another problem—again not MultiFinder's fault—was the increasing use of start-up programs, which caused a memory conflict in the System Heap (an area of RAM used by the operating system), often resulting in crashes when using MultiFinder. This problem was easily cured with utilities such as HeapFix or HeapTool, which are freely available from user groups and bulletin boards. In any case, this type of problem is not apparent in System 7.

- **Complexity.** MultiFinder was considered too complex by many novice Macintosh users. This perception was understandable—after all, MultiFinder was offered as a virtually undocumented utility program. A Macintosh user had to be somewhat adventurous just to turn it on and learn how to use it. For the majority of users who didn't spend their free time attending user groups, browsing on CompuServe, or reading about the Macintosh, MultiFinder seemed intimidating and too risky.

In System 7 and later, Mac OS 8, multitasking was seamlessly integrated into the system software, making the simultaneous use of multiple applications a fundamental part of the working routine. Everyone who uses the Macintosh should take the time to learn, understand, and benefit from this powerful tool.

Multitasking in Mac OS 8

The ability to keep multiple programs in memory and recall them from the background to the foreground has been part of Macintosh system software since before MultiFinder. This kind of behavior is called context switching. An application in the background is suspended at its last point of execution. Context switching is not multitasking because only one process is running at a time. In technical parlance, your Macintosh stores the different threads of execution—but only a single thread in one application can execute.

Background processing started in System 6 and continued into Mac OS 8. Many lower-level I/O (input/output) functions have been enabled, allowing you to print, communicate, and display data in the background while a single application runs in the foreground. This is the beginning of multitasking: your Macintosh can run multiple processes, but it limits which types of processes can be concurrent. In this manner, the Macintosh is single-threaded because only one thread operates for the foreground and for any processes running in the background. That is, only one process is running at a time and your Macintosh CPU cycles between foreground and background tasks. This is commonly referred to as time slicing.

System 7.5 introduced the Thread Manager (compatible with all versions of System 7), whose icon is shown in Figure 10-2. The Thread Manager is a system extension that allows for multithreading within a single application. This is still lightweight, concurrent processing, but it's another step along the way toward a fully multitasked system.

Figure 10-2: The Thread Manager extension.

With the Thread Manager, you can work in your database, word processor, or spreadsheet while calculating other functions in the same application. It's up to application developers to implement the programming necessary to take advantage of the Thread Manager, but the capability is ignored by applications that don't choose to implement it. Therefore, no compatibility problems are expected.

In Mac OS 8, however, the functionality provided through the Thread Manager has been integrated into the operating system itself, so the Thread Manager is no longer present. Some older applications written to take advantage of the Thread Manager may insist upon the Thread Manager being installed, but that's OK because Mac OS 8 will ignore it if it is unnecessarily installed.

One example of multitasking can be found in the OpenDoc compound document architecture. In OpenDoc, the architecture creates a document frame and manages parts within the document. When you add a part, the Part Handler checks to see whether the applet (text, sound, video, and so on) is open, and if not, opens it. As you work in a text part, clocks, animation parts, movie parts, or a live video feed can be running concurrently. It looks like multitasking, but it's really more a form of multithreading within a single application.

Currently, full multitasking is being written into the Macintosh operating system purchased from the NeXT Corporation. It's slated to be unveiled to consumers during 1997 and 1998 with the release of the next-generation operating system code-named Rhapsody. In Rhapsody, Apple is building the core of its operating system into a very small, fast, and portable core of code called the microkernel. The microkernel will allow Apple to run the operating system on a variety of microprocessors.

More importantly for this discussion, the microkernel comes with true memory protection. Memory protection isolates programs' threads in their own "containers" so that one thread cannot call for memory used by any other thread. A thread can crash and burn, but it does not bring your system to a halt. Memory protection is the single most important difference between the Macintosh and the high-price spreads. It will allow real-time multiuser transaction processing to run on a Macintosh, processing of the kind that banks use to run ATM machines and airlines use for reservations.

Working With Multiple Applications

Mac OS 8 allows you to open multiple applications automatically, without any special configuration or initiation. In fact, when you launch your first application from the Finder, you'll immediately notice the effect: the Finder desktop (the volume icons, Trash, and so on) does not disappear as the new application is launched, as was the case in older versions of the system software. The Finder remains visible in Mac OS 8 because both your new application and the Finder now run simultaneously. (See Figure 10-3.)

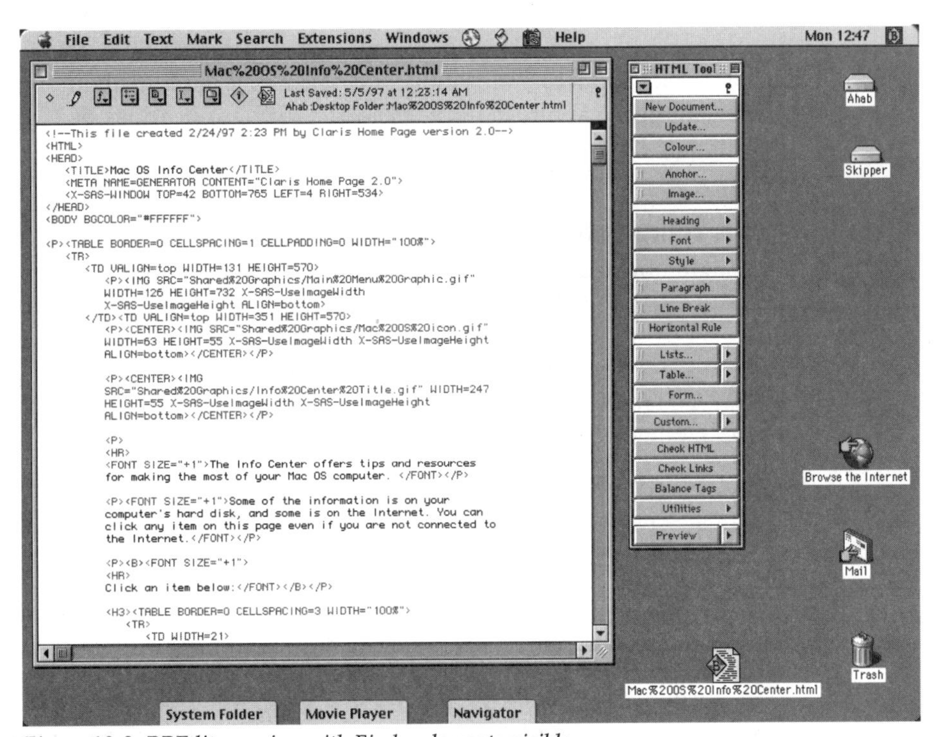

Figure 10-3: BBEdit running with Finder elements visible.

Note that in System 7.0.1P, 7.1P, 7.5, and later, an option allows you to "hide the Finder." In that case, the Finder icons will disappear when you switch to another application. See "Hiding the Finder" later in this chapter for more details.

When you launch additional applications, you continue to see the capabilities of multitasking. As each additional program opens, its menu bar and windows are displayed, and other open applications are unaffected.

When you first start using multiple applications simultaneously, the sight of several windows open at the same time may be a little disconcerting. As you learn to arrange and manipulate these windows and enjoy the benefits of multiple open applications, you'll soon find yourself wondering how you ever got along using just one program at a time.

The number of applications you can launch simultaneously is limited only by the amount of memory you have available. If your launch will exceed available memory, a dialog box will alert you to the problem, and the additional application will not be launched. (You'll learn more about memory and running multiple applications in "The Memory Implications of Multitasking" later in this chapter.)

Foreground & Background Applications

Although more than one program can be open at once, only one program can be active at any one time. The active program is the foreground application, and other open but inactive applications are background applications, even if you can see portions of their windows or if they're simultaneously processing tasks (see Figure 10-4).

You can tell which program is currently active in several ways:

- The menu bar displays the menu commands of the active program only.
- The active program's icon appears at the top of the Application menu.
- The active program name is checked in the Application menu.
- The Apple menu's About This Computer command lists the active program name.
- Active program windows overlap other visible windows or elements.
- Active program windows display a highlighted title bar, which includes horizontal lines, the close box, and the zoom box.

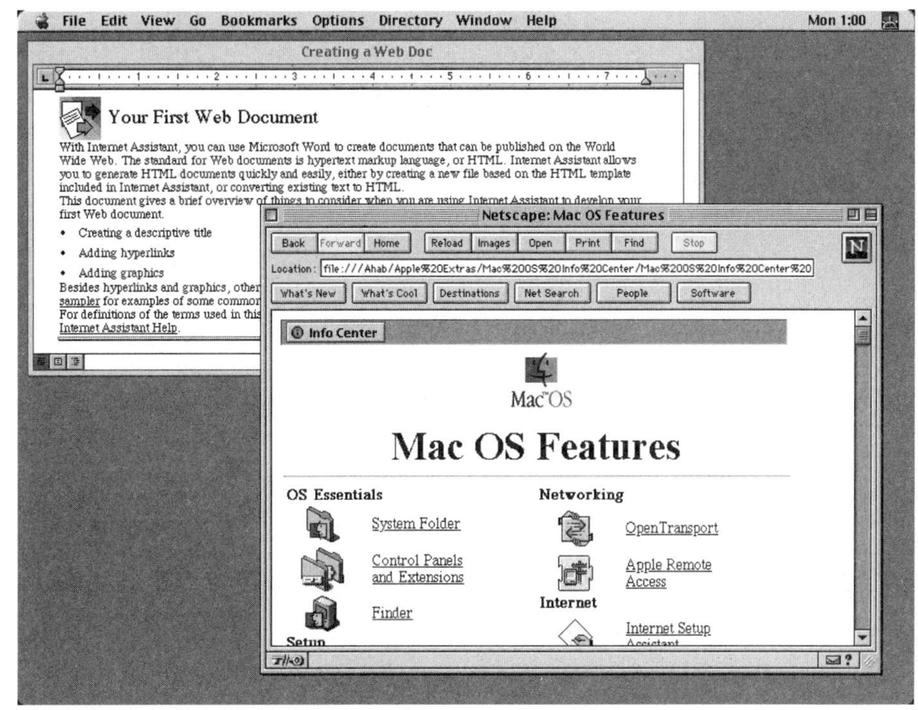

Figure 10-4: Netscape Navigator is the active program in this window; Microsoft Word is in the background.

In contrast, a background application's menu bar does not appear, its icon is not checked in the Application menu, none of its windows are highlighted, and some or all of its windows may be hidden or obscured.

Because only one program can be in the foreground, it's important to be able to switch quickly and easily from one foreground program to another. Switching between applications is commonly referred to as "sending to the back" and "bringing to the front."

You can switch between open applications in two ways:

- **Use the Application menu.** Located in the upper right corner of the menu bar, the Application menu lists the names of all applications currently running. Choose the name of the application you want to switch to, and that program will bring its menu bar and windows to the front.

  For example, to switch from an application to the Finder, choose the word *Finder* from the Application menu. The Finder's menu bar will appear, and any icons and windows on the desktop will become visible. (See Figure 10-5.)

Figure 10-5: The Application menu as it appears with numerous open applications.

- **Click any visible window.** Clicking any visible element on the screen brings the application owning that element to the front. For example, while working in your word processor, if you can still see the icons on the Finder desktop, clicking one of them will bring the Finder to the front, making it the current application. You can then return to the word processor by clicking its window.

Background Processing

You can bring any application to the foreground, which sends any other to the background, at any time except when dialog boxes are open. You can even send most applications to the background while they're processing data—they'll continue to calculate or process in the background. Background processing adds an entirely new dimension to using multiple open applications simultaneously.

If you could use multiple open applications only sequentially, one after the other, the increase in productivity would be limited to the time you saved by avoiding repeated opening and quitting of applications. Background processing, however, lets you print a newsletter, calculate a spreadsheet, and dial up a remote bulletin board at the same time. This capability is the ultimate in computer productivity.

Background processing is easy. Start by doing a lengthy process, such as a spreadsheet calculation or a telecommunication session; then bring another open application to the foreground. The background task continues processing while you use the computer for another task in another application. Because foreground and background applications are sharing the hardware resources (there's only one central processing unit in the Macintosh), you may notice a slowdown or jerky motion in the foreground application. The severity of this effect will depend on your Macintosh's power and the number and requirements of the background tasks being performed, but there should be no detrimental effect on your foreground application.

Periodically, you may need to attend to a task left running in the background, or you may be given notice when the task is completed. If so, an Alert dialog box will be displayed, a diamond will appear before the application's name in the Application menu, or the Application menu icon will flash alternately with the alerting application's icon.

Background Printing

The first background processing most people use is printing. Background printing is not quite the same as using two applications at once, but it's similar.

Without multitasking, you have to wait for the entire file to be printed because of the time it takes for the printer to mechanically do the job. In background printing, files are printed to disk as fast as the application and printer driver can handle them. Then a utility called a print spooler sends the print file from the disk to the printer. The advantage is that the print spooler takes over the task of feeding the pages to the printer while you continue working in your main application or even use another software application.

Background PostScript printing support is built into Mac OS 8, so the Background Printing option has been removed from the Chooser, as shown in Figure 10-6.

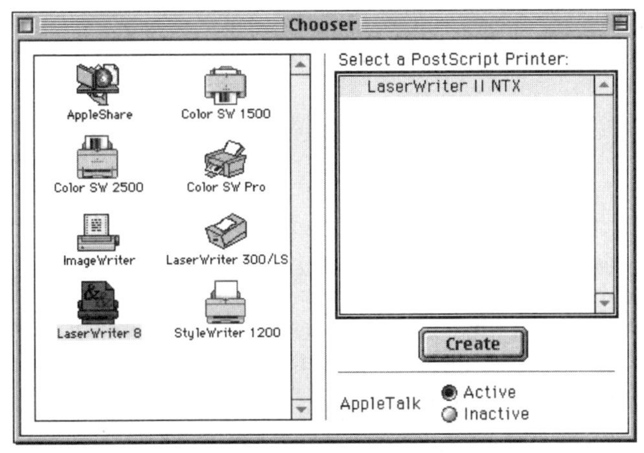

Figure 10-6: The Chooser.

With background printing, files printed using the LaserWriter and other drivers are spooled to your hard drive. At the same time, the Desktop PrintMonitor utility, automatically running in the background, begins printing the spooled file to the selected PostScript printer. While Desktop PrintMonitor is printing, you can bring it to the foreground by selecting its icon from the Desktop. The Desktop PrintMonitor dialog box is shown in Figure 10-7.

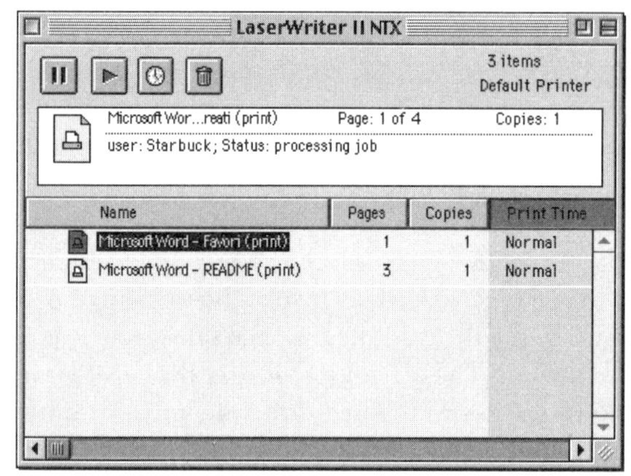

Figure 10-7: The Desktop PrintMonitor dialog box.

Copying Files in the Background

Copying files from one location to another is a basic capability the Finder has always provided, but through successive Finder versions, the activity has continued to evolve.

Early versions of the Finder provided only a simple dialog box during file copying. Later, a counter of files being copied was added. Then names of copied files were added, and finally the progress bar became a part of this dialog box. Despite these improvements, which seemed to make time pass more quickly, you were still forced to wait while files were copied.

In Mac OS 8, the process of copying files takes a huge step forward: you can now work in any open application while the Finder runs multiple copy operations in the background. To use this feature, follow these steps:

1. Open the application you want to use while the Finder is copying.
2. Switch to the Finder by using the Application menu or by clicking the Finder desktop.
3. Start the copy process in the normal way by dragging the desired files from their source location to the icon of the destination folder or volume (or by selecting Command+D). The copying process will begin, and the copying dialog box will appear. You can also select another item to copy while the first item is copying. For example, Figure 10-8 shows a 37.8MB folder being copied three times simultaneously.

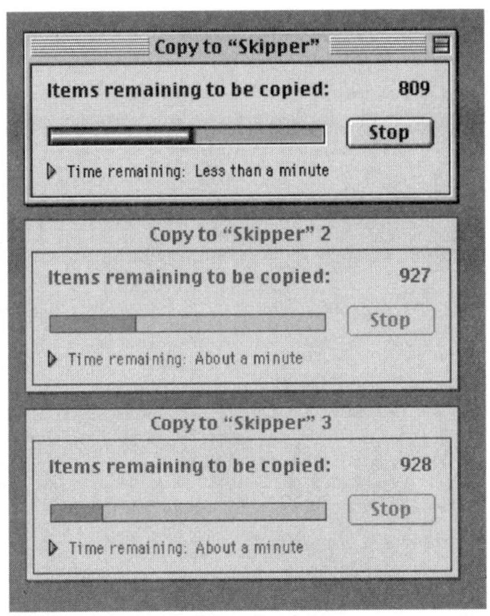

Figure 10-8: Initiating multiple copying tasks while programs continue to function.

4. Then use the stopwatch cursor to select the Application menu and choose the name of the open application you want to use while the file copy is in progress. This application will come to the foreground ready for you to use while the Finder continues its copy operation in the background.
5. Switch back to the Finder any time you like using the Application menu or clicking the Finder desktop.

Hiding Applications

Running several applications concurrently can result in an onscreen clutter of windows displayed by open applications. To alleviate this problem, Mac OS 8 lets you "hide" open application windows, thus removing them from the screen without changing their status or the background work they're doing. You can hide an application at the time you leave it to switch to another application or while it's running in the background. Figure 10-9 shows how your Desktop can become cluttered when running multiple applications in the foreground simultaneously.

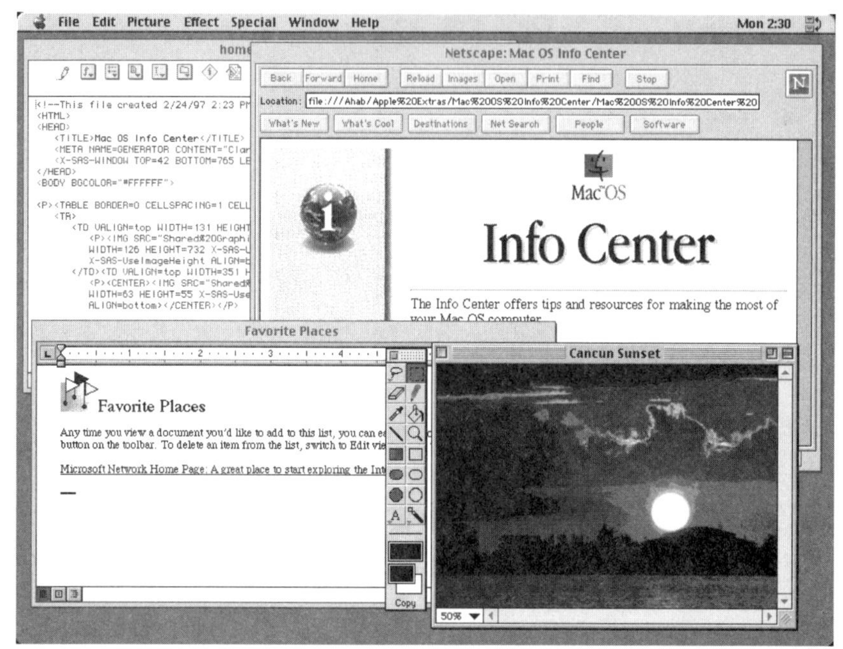

Figure 10-9: Running multiple applications without hiding can result in a crowded display.

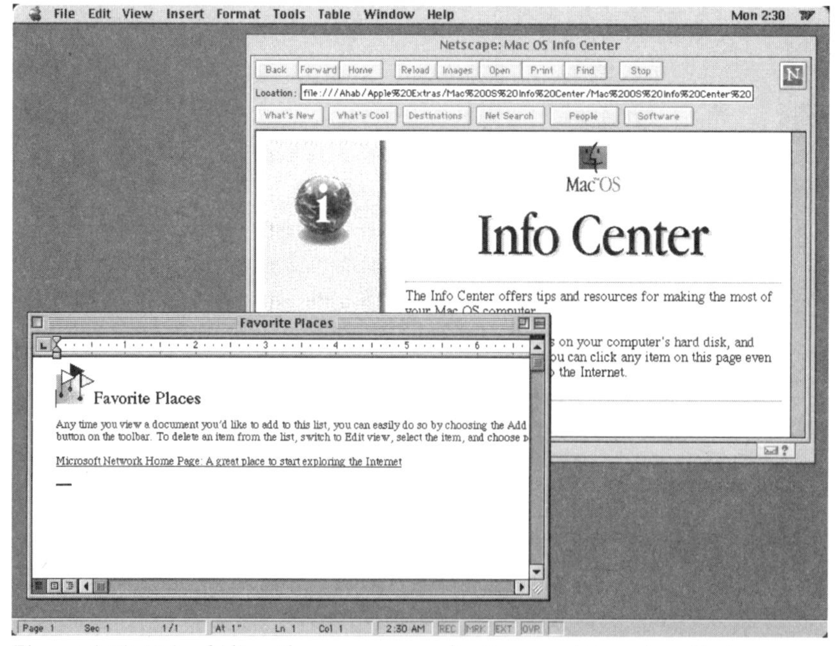

Figure 10-10: Using hiding, the same open applications result in a clear display.

Hiding some programs in the background while continuing to operate other programs in the foreground can help clear things up a bit, as shown in Figure 10-10.

The Application menu provides three Hide commands: Hide Current Application (Current Application being the name of the current foreground application), Hide Others, and Show All:

- **Hide Current Application.** Removes all windows of the current application from the screen and brings another window of an open application to the foreground. Usually, the Finder is brought to the foreground, but if the Finder itself has been hidden, the next application in the Application menu is brought forward instead.

  A hidden application's icon is dimmed in the Application menu to signify that it's hidden. To unhide the application, either select its name from the Application menu, which will bring it to the foreground, or choose the Show All command.

- **Hide Others.** Removes all windows from the screen except those of the current application. This is useful when onscreen clutter is bothersome or if you're accidentally clicking windows of background applications and bringing them forward. After the Hide Others command has been used, all open applications icons, except those of the foreground application, are dimmed in the Application menu as a visual reminder that these applications are hidden.

- **Show All.** Makes all current applications visible (not hidden). You can tell which applications are currently hidden by their dimmed icons in the Application menu. When you choose the Show All command, the current foreground application remains in the foreground, and the windows of hidden background applications become visible but the applications remain in the background.

While an application is hidden, it continues to operate exactly the same as it would if it were running as a background application and not hidden. If an application can normally perform tasks in the background, it will still perform these tasks in the background while it's hidden. In fact, because of the effort saved by not having to upgrade the screen display, some tasks operate faster in the background when their application is hidden.

You can also hide the current foreground application when you send it to the background by holding down the Option key while bringing another application forward (either by choosing its name from the Application menu or by clicking the mouse on its window). You can retrieve applications hidden in this manner by using the Show All command or by selecting their dimmed icons from the Application menu.

Hiding the Finder

There's a potential problem for novices working with multiple applications at the same time. If you inadvertently click the Finder desktop, you switch into the Finder and out of your current program. Suddenly you've lost your place, and the menus have changed. Because the old Performa series was built for the home market (and novices), Apple included a feature called Finder hiding into System 7.0.1P and 7.1P that prevents you from switching to the Finder by inadvertently clicking on the desktop.

Voluntary Finder hiding has appeared in System 7.5 and continues to be a popular option in Mac OS 8. With Finder hiding, when you switch into an application other than the Finder, the desktop disappears (rather like the way things worked before System 7—the difference is that this hiding is by choice). You can't click the background and switch out of your application. You turn on Finder hiding by disabling the Show Desktop When in Background check box in the General Controls Control Panel. So if you're working in an application and you can't see your hard disk, Trash, or file and folder icons where they should appear, Finder hiding is the cause. Figure 10-11 shows an example of Word running with the Finder hidden.

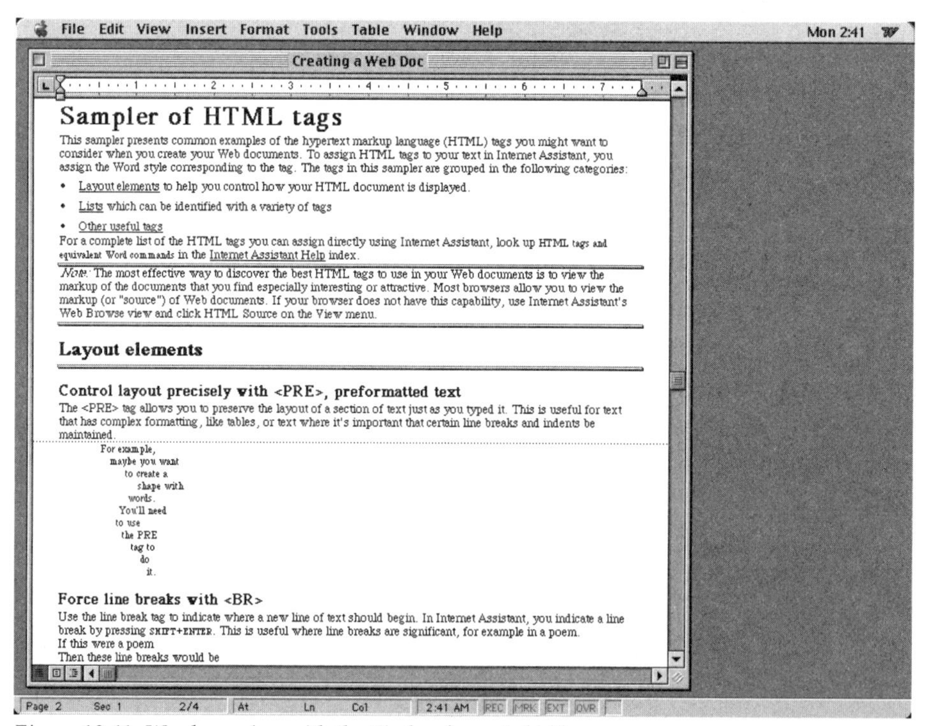

Figure 10-11: Word running with the Finder elements hidden.

Multitasking Tips

Once you start using the Hide commands to reduce screen clutter, you should be comfortable working with multiple open applications. The following tips can help:

- **Saving before switching.** Before bringing another application to the foreground, save your work in the application you're leaving so that if your Mac crashes or is turned off accidentally, you won't lose your work.
- **Resuming after crashing.** If an application crashes in Mac OS 8, you can usually force the Mac to close that application and regain access to your other applications by pressing Command+Option+Escape.

  Note that after resuming after this kind of crash, your system may be unstable and prone to additional crashes. Using this option is a bit like driving a nail with a sledgehammer—it works but is likely to do some damage. You should save any unsaved work in other open applications, and you may want to restart your Macintosh just to be safe.

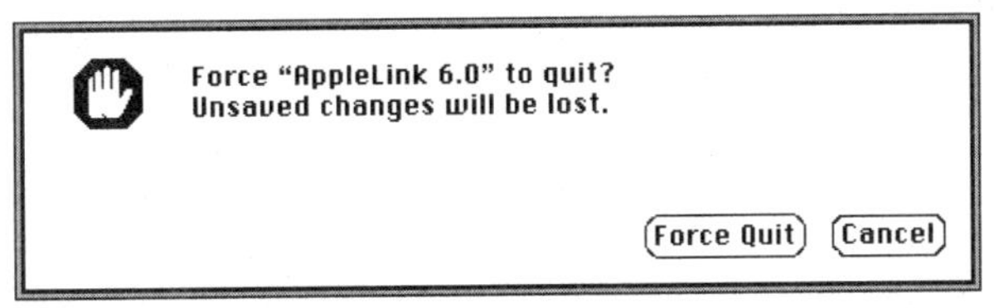

Figure 10-12: The Force Quit dialog box.

- **Shutting down or restarting.** Selecting the Shut Down or Restart commands from the Finder's Special menu while multiple applications are open will cause all open applications to quit (if those applications have been properly programmed to accept the "quit" command using Apple Events). If any open documents contain changes that haven't been saved, the application containing the document will be brought to the foreground, and you'll be asked whether you want to save those changes (see Figure 10-13). Click Yes to save, No to discard the changes, or Cancel to abort the Shut Down or Restart operation.

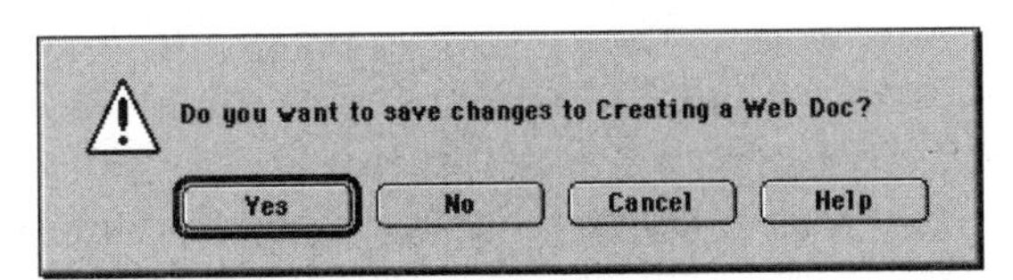

Figure 10-13: Save Changes dialog box.

- **Choosing Shut Down.** In Mac OS 8, the Shut Down command has been added to the bottom of the Apple menu (see Figure 10-14). You can now shut down without switching to the Finder by choosing this option—a minor convenience.

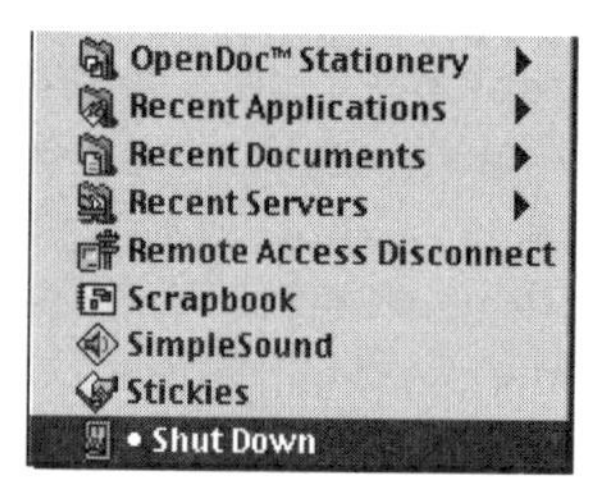

Figure 10-14: The Apple menu Shut Down command.

- **Maintaining efficiency for background applications.** Applications in the background often run more efficiently if hidden with one of the Hide commands from the Application menu. This is true because often the onscreen display can't keep up with the application's processing rate; as a result, the application has to wait for the screen to be drawn. The extent of this delay depends on your computer system and video display. Using the Hide command eliminates all video-related delay.
- **Switching and hiding.** To hide an application while switching to another open application, hold down the Option key while clicking the open application's window or while selecting the name of another open application from the Application menu.

The Memory Implications of Multitasking

Everything has its price. Macintosh users know this well (especially experienced Macintosh users). Multitasking is no exception—its price is memory.

Put simply, you can run only as many applications at once as your available Macintosh memory can handle. A predefined amount of memory must be dedicated to the application while it's open. Running multiple applications simultaneously requires enough memory to satisfy the cumulative amounts those applications require. Your total amount of available memory includes what's supplied by the RAM chips installed on your computer's logic board or on an expansion card (for PowerBooks) plus any virtual memory created with the Memory Control Panel. (See Chapter 9, "Applications & Memory Management," for more information about virtual memory.)

When you first turn on a Macintosh running Mac OS 8, some of your memory is taken up immediately by the system software and the Finder. This amount varies depending on how many fonts and sounds you've installed, your disk cache setting, the extensions you're using, and whether you're using File Sharing. As much as 25 to 33 percent of your Mac's available memory can be consumed by the system software itself in some circumstances. Your Macintosh's memory usage is documented in the About This Computer dialog box, shown in Figure 10-15. If you would like to reduce the amount of memory your system software consumes, remove unused fonts or sounds, reduce the size of your RAM disk, and turn off File Sharing.

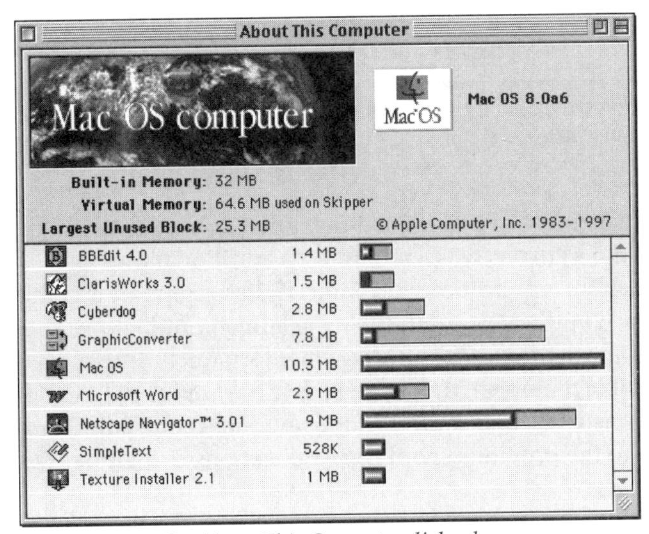

Figure 10-15: The About This Computer dialog box.

Each time you launch an application, it requests the amount of memory that it needs in order to run. If enough memory is available, the application is launched. If enough memory isn't available, one of several dialog boxes will appear warning you of the situation or offering a solution on how to make more memory available. The first, shown in Figure 10-16, informs you there's not enough memory available to launch the selected application. The second, shown in Figure 10-17, tells you the same thing but it also gives you the option of launching the application in the amount of RAM that is available. Lastly, a dialog box appears that tells you that an application with no open windows is open in memory and asks if you'd like to close it. Normally, launching the application under these circumstances will allow you to use the application without incident.

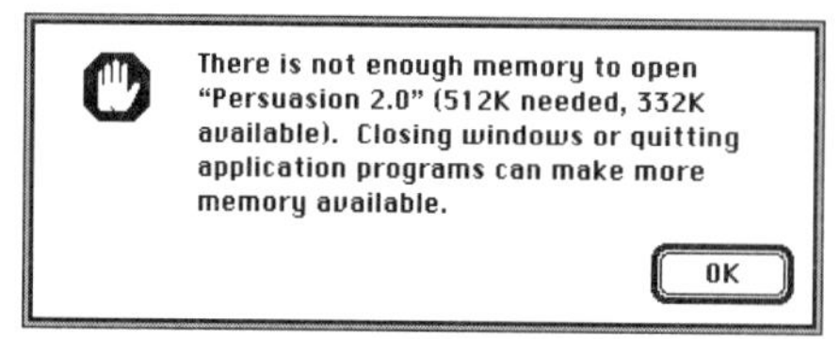

Figure 10-16: This dialog box appears when you're launching an application with limited memory available.

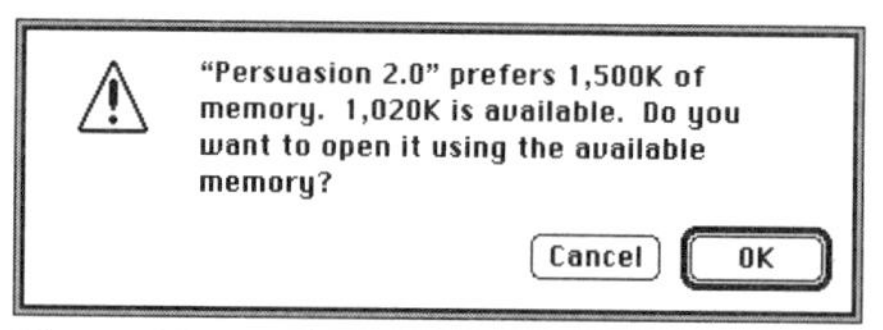

Figure 10-17: This dialog box appears when you're launching an application with almost enough memory available.

If available memory is insufficient to launch an application, quit one or more applications currently open to free up additional memory. Then try again to launch the application you want. If these steps aren't enough, quit additional open applications and retry the launch until you're successful.

For more information on your Mac's memory (including ways you can expand available memory), tips on reducing the amount of memory each application consumes, and more about using the About This Computer dialog box, go back to the previous chapter, "Applications & Memory Management."

Moving On

Working with several applications at once takes some getting used to, but it's the best way to make the most of your time and computing resources. As we've seen in this chapter, Mac OS 8's multitasking support is impressive:

- You can launch as many different applications as your available memory permits.
- Many applications can continue to process data while they're running in the background.
- Hiding open applications reduces onscreen clutter without affecting the operation of the applications.

Like many other Mac OS 8 features, multitasking is available to every program that is compatible with Mac OS 8. Next, Chapter 11 introduces you to how the built-in font and printing capabilities of Mac OS 8 can help you unlock the world of desktop publishing.

CHAPTER 11

Fonts & Printing

Mac OS 8 uses the best font and printing technologies that can be found in a personal computer, drawing on years of experience and technological advances. It is safe to say that a great measure of the success that the Macintosh has achieved has been due to its capabilities in the graphics and publishing arena. Desktop publishing is the Macintosh's heritage. System 7 made major changes in this technology, introducing sophisticated graphics, outline fonts, advanced typography, color matching, a new print architecture, a portable document format, and improved localization for international software. Many of these new changes are due to the release of QuickDraw GX in System 7.5. QuickDraw and the optional QuickDraw GX are Apple's extensions to its graphics programming routines and page description language, which continue to be refined in Mac OS 8.

Fonts are both the blessing and curse of the Macintosh, however. No other computer offers such a variety of fonts or typographic capabilities; but because of technical problems and corporate politics, no other aspect of the Mac has caused so many headaches for so many people.

System 7 extended Macintosh font technology, simplified font installation, improved the appearance of fonts onscreen, and introduced two new font formats called TrueType and TrueType GX. Mac OS 8 offers some relief from "font hell" and some additional complexity.

In this chapter, we'll look at each of the technologies supported by QuickDraw GX, paying special attention to fonts and type issues. Here you'll find out what's practical and what's possible.

What Is QuickDraw?

Of all the sets of routines or managers in the Macintosh toolbox, few are as recognized and recognizable as QuickDraw. QuickDraw was there in 1984 when the first Macintosh shipped. MacPaint and MacDraw, and a generation of Macintosh programs that followed, use QuickDraw for most of their capabilities. Anything you see drawn within a window on your Macintosh screen is due to QuickDraw.

Your Mac uses QuickDraw to create images. Put another way, QuickDraw is an imaging model. These images are then sent to your monitor, to your printer, and to any other output device whose device driver supports QuickDraw. As such, QuickDraw is really a page description language (or PDL) in the same way that PostScript is also a PDL.

QuickDraw is responsible for the lines and shapes you draw; their patterns and fills; properties such as transparency or opacity; colors, color models, and color selection; fonts; and even less intuitively, what you see in a print dialog box.

Printers are QuickDraw printers when they take QuickDraw output and rasterize it to print its image. Similarly, PostScript printers rasterize PostScript output. QuickDraw can be printed on PostScript printers because QuickDraw is translated to PostScript in your Macintosh when it is output to a PostScript device.

QuickDraw was never designed to meet the demands of high-quality output. Apple created QuickDraw to simplify and codify screen display at 72 dots per inch (dpi) in black and white (which were the screen characteristics of the classic Macintosh series) and to draw to simple printers such as the ImageWriter. For higher quality printing needs, Apple cut a comarketing deal in 1985 with a small graphics programming company called Adobe and licensed the sophisticated PostScript language. Apple would sell Cannon's laser printing xerographic engine run by a PostScript controller, and QuickDraw would be converted to PostScript in the operating system of the Macintosh. The rest is, as they say, history.

One of the first QuickDraw upgrades came in 1988 when the Macintosh II was introduced. In its original release, only eight QuickDraw colors were supported. Color QuickDraw was added to system software with the addition of System 5, adding a 32-bit color modeling capability. Soon thereafter, with the introduction of the Mac IIx, Color QuickDraw was written into the new ROMs.

By 1989, high-quality type and graphics had become big business and a central technology on the personal computer. PostScript fonts were encrypted and proprietary, although the rest of the language was published. Therefore, Adobe had created a lock on the type business for the Macintosh, and had control over essential system software and applications.

Responding to the needs of their customers, Adobe created an advanced version of PostScript called PostScript Level 2. PostScript had problems with complexity, file size, and particularly, performance. These problems could be solved by adding a new memory model, new compression technology, and new methods for drawing (rasterizing) a page. Other needed improvements would include better color support for printed (CYMK) color, color matching, advanced printing support, and several other technologies. QuickDraw always suffered in comparison to PostScript; PostScript Level 2 threatened to make QuickDraw an anachronism.

With System 7, Apple decided to make the break. Along with Microsoft, which was developing Windows 3.1, Apple decided to introduce an open outline font type standard called TrueType and a page description language called TrueImage. Apple set about addressing the other deficiencies in QuickDraw by revising it and adding new technologies through an Extension.

Because the TrueType font technology was ready to go in 1991, it was released with System 7.0. Some other components in the original System 7 list—the LineLayout Manager and the New Print Architecture—were not. Those two new features became part of a larger package, QuickDraw GX, meant to support the needs of color publishing. QuickDraw GX would fix problems handling color, text layout, typography, printing, and so on. Because these problems are industry-wide, it's not surprising that both QuickDraw GX and PostScript Level 2 address similar issues.

After nearly four years in development and testing, QuickDraw GX finally shipped in 1994 but will receive limited support in Mac OS 8 due to Apple's purchase of NeXT and the decision to move to Display Postscript. Applications that utilize both QuickDraw and QuickDraw 3D will work just fine under Mac OS 8, however, so you probably won't experience any problems.

About QuickDraw GX

QuickDraw GX is a system extension that supplements the capabilities of QuickDraw, which is now present in your system. If an application is QuickDraw GX aware or savvy, it can use the new capabilities. If not, they are ignored. As you upgrade your applications, fonts, and printer drivers, you will begin to notice the new capabilities that QuickDraw GX provides. Until then, you can continue to work in the way you've become accustomed to. (See the QuickDraw GX icon in Figure 11-1.)

Figure 11-1: The QuickDraw GX icon.

QuickDraw GX has the following important capabilities:

- **Higher level graphics routines.** More complex shapes and transformations are supported. Applications that are QuickDraw savvy can use these system routines; they require less memory to operate and less storage space. The following section, "Sophisticated Graphics Primitives," describes these changes.
- **New print architecture.** You will first notice QuickDraw GX's effect in printing because current applications and hardware can take advantage of it. A new, more powerful, and simplified print dialog box also appears in Mac OS 8. You can create virtual printers on your desktop as icons, drag and drop files to them, and have better control over your printers and spooled documents anywhere on a network.

  All printer types that you now use are supported. For example, Mac OS 8 ships with a new set of Apple PostScript printer drivers. Other vendors are expected to provide timely upgrades. For more information on this topic, see "QuickDraw GX & Printing" later in this chapter.
- **Advanced typography.** QuickDraw GX uses special TrueType GX fonts to create advanced type effects such as automatic kerning, justification, and special-character support based on context. You can continue to use your current font collection, bitmaps or outline fonts, and converted PostScript Type 1 fonts (with a Mac OS 8 utility), or you can upgrade to TrueType GX to take advantage of the new capabilities.
- **Advanced layout.** The LineLayout Manager provides support for international text such as Kanji, Hindi, Hebrew, Arabic, or any character set. You can mix right-to-left, left-to-right, or vertical arrangements of letterforms within a document, a paragraph, or a line. To use these capabilities, an application must be QuickDraw savvy, and you must install QuickDraw GX fonts. TrueType GX fonts are aware of their relative character positioning and can change shapes appropriately. See "Advanced Typography" later in this chapter for a description of both the new type effects and the LineLayout Manager.
- **Improved localization.** WorldScript provides a system for Macintosh developers to transform applications from one language and character set to another. QuickDraw GX performs the display and handling of fonts and supports character sets based on the Unicode standard. See "Unicode, WorldScript & Localization" later in this chapter for a description of these new capabilities.

- **Portable digital documents.** QuickDraw GX supports a new "universal" file format known as a portable digital document (PDD). A PDD created by an application can be opened, viewed, and printed by any other user who has QuickDraw GX on his or her computer whether or not the user has the creator application and typefaces.
- **Custom print functions.** Because fonts, printing, and other objects can be controlled by QuickDraw GX, developers can more easily create custom printer drivers, printer extensions, and solutions for specific markets.
- **Color matching.** QuickDraw GX incorporates ColorSync, Apple's color management technology. Because QuickDraw can profile device characteristics, colors can be reproduced as closely and as accurately as the device allows. ColorSync was released about the time System 7.1 appeared. See "ColorSync & Color Matching" later in this chapter for further discussion.

QuickDraw GX comes as part of Mac OS 8, but it is not installed as part of the default installation process. To install it, you'll need to launch the Mac OS 8 installer, select the Add/Remove option, and select QuickDraw GX. It requires a minimum of 5MB of RAM, and any Macintosh running System 7.1 or later can use QuickDraw GX. Other than the disk storage space required, no other additional hardware demands are made.

Sophisticated Graphics Primitives

QuickDraw GX greatly extends the range of graphics primitives, or shapes, in QuickDraw. Beyond simple line movements that produce the basic shapes—lines, curves, rectangles, polygons, paths, and so on—QuickDraw GX adds more advanced attributes. In this regard, outline type is a just another shape, with both the same attributes and range of possibilities. Drawn or vector shapes are resolution independent and scale to any size correctly.

QuickDraw GX recognizes three different attributes:

- **Style.** Style describes the pen thickness (line or stroke), line end cap (pointed, rounded, or flat), whether the line is drawn inside or outside a shape, line dashes and patterns, and line joins and corners. Text style includes font, size, and other attributes such as bold, italic, and so on.
- **Transform.** A range of shape transformations are supported, including scaling, rotation, perspective, skew, and clipping.

- **Ink.** The ink attributes are the descriptions of the color properties of a shape: data on the selection in a color space, transfer information (opacity, transparency, or mixing), and the description of how to view and display a selected color on a device.

These three words— *style*, *transform*, and *ink*—will enter the vocabulary of any application that uses QuickDraw GX to draw, manipulate type, work with color, and so on. Seasoned Macintosh users have worked with these concepts in their applications for years, but these capabilities were part of an application, not the system software. These capabilities are also part of the PostScript vocabulary. Adding them to QuickDraw makes them available to all QuickDraw applications, resulting in a wider range of possibilities in Macintosh applications with less development time.

Fonts on the Macintosh

The introduction of the Macintosh in 1984 brought with it many innovations, but one of the most important was the way Macintosh enhanced the appearance of text. Whereas earlier personal computers reduced all communication to the drab, mechanical, and impersonal look of pica-12 (the original dot-matrix font), the Macintosh produced text in a wide range of typefaces, both onscreen and on the printed page. Typography—long an important part of printed communication—became a part of personal computing.

The original Macintosh fonts (New York, Monaco, Geneva, and Chicago) were bitmapped fonts, which means that each character in each font was predefined by the series of dots necessary to create that character at a specific point size. Most bitmapped fonts were produced at sizes of 11-, 10-, 12-, and 14-point. In Mac OS 8, Charcoal 12-point is the system font.

These original bitmapped fonts, and the many bitmapped fonts that soon joined them, were optimized for display on the Macintosh screen and for printing on the Apple ImageWriter (which was the only printer available at the time). There were, however, limitations to working with these bitmapped fonts:

- **Dot-matrix bitmapped quality was unacceptable for most business uses.** Although typeface variety was certainly a welcome improvement, most people still considered ImageWriter output quality unacceptable for business use regardless of the fonts.
- **Font variety was limited.** Although bitmapped fonts proliferated, almost all were "novelty" faces with little value beyond advertisements, invitations, and entertainment.

- **The 400K system disks could hold only a limited selection of fonts.** Because hard drives were not generally available at that time, it was necessary to boot the Macintosh from a 400K floppy disk. After you squeezed the System folder plus an application or two onto a floppy, only a small amount of room was left for font styles and sizes.
- **Macintosh applications could support only a limited number of fonts at one time.** When too many fonts were installed in the System file, applications acted strangely, often providing only a random subset of the installed fonts.

These problems were solved, after some time, with new releases of system software, application software, and third-party utility programs. The next big change in the Macintosh font world was not based on software but on the introduction of the Apple LaserWriter printer with its built-in support for the PostScript page description language.

PostScript Fonts

The introduction of the Apple LaserWriter printer brought a new type of font to the Macintosh: the PostScript font. These fonts were required in documents created for output to the LaserWriter (and all later PostScript printers) in order for type to be printed at high resolution. Bitmapped fonts were inadequate for these new printers. Eventually, PostScript fonts came to be known by a variety of names, including laser fonts, outline fonts, and Type 1 fonts.

Each PostScript font consists of two files: a screen font file and a printer font file (see Figure 11-2). The screen font file for a PostScript font is nearly identical to the font file of bitmapped fonts, providing bitmapped versions of the font at specific sizes optimized for onscreen use. There are other similarities too:

- Both appear with a suitcase icon.
- Both are provided in different styles and sizes.
- Both were installed with the Font/DA Mover until the release of System 7.
- Both appear in the font menu or dialog box in all applications.

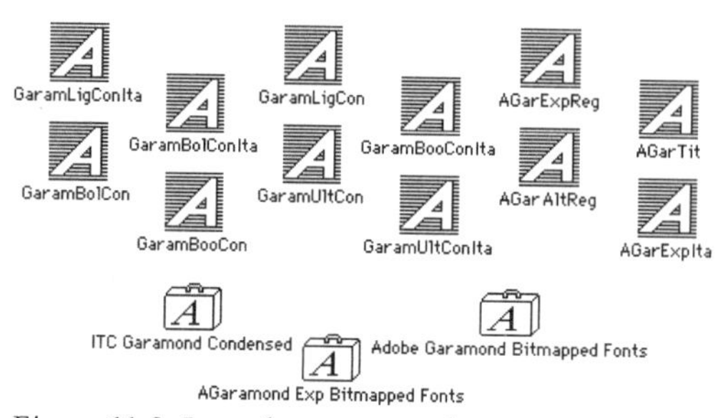

Figure 11-2: Icons for some popular screen font files (below) and printer font files (above).

The difference between PostScript screen fonts and bitmapped screen fonts is that each PostScript screen font has a corresponding PostScript printer font (see Figure 11-3). This printer font provides the PostScript printer with a mathematical description of each character in the font as well as other information it needs to create and produce high-resolution output. When you're printing PostScript fonts, the screen font is used only as a pointer to the printer fonts. Your Macintosh works with the printer font descriptions to create text output.

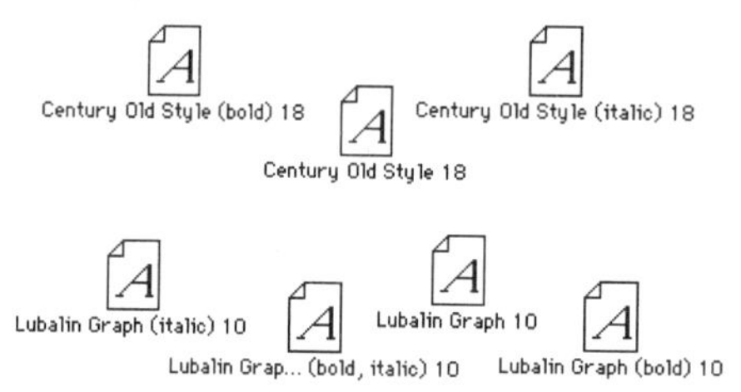

Figure 11-3: Each PostScript screen font represents a single font, size, and style.

Printer font files often display an icon that looks like the LaserWriter, but depending on the way the printer font was created, another icon may appear. Each printer font is usually around 50K in size but can range from a minimum of 10K to a maximum of 75K. In most cases, there is a one-to-one correspondence between screen fonts and printer fonts (there's a unique printer font file for each unique screen font name). In some cases, however, printer fonts outnumber screen fonts and vice versa.

Regardless of whether all screen fonts and printer fonts are matched, you don't always have to use all the available screen fonts, but you must always use all printer fonts. In other words, you can create Helvetica Bold without installing the Helvetica Bold screen font (by using the Helvetica font and the Bold type style), but you cannot print Helvetica Bold without the Helvetica Bold printer font.

For a PostScript font to be printed correctly, the printer font file must be "available" to the PostScript printer when it appears in a file being printed. A font is available when it is built into the printer's ROM chips, stored on a printer's hard disk, or kept on the Macintosh hard disk and manually or automatically downloaded to the printer.

When you install QuickDraw GX, the PostScript Type 1 fonts in your Fonts folder are no longer converted to a form that works with QuickDraw GX. To convert them, you'll need to install a program called Type 1 Enabler and manually convert them.

To install the Type 1 Enabler on your hard drive, do a custom installation of QuickDraw GX and select the QuickDraw GX Utilities option. Several utility applications will be installed. To modify PostScript Type 1 fonts, open the Type 1 Enabler located in the Utilities folder by double-clicking its icon. In the standard dialog box, shown in Figure 11-4, select the font or folder containing fonts that you wish to modify; then select the fonts you want to convert (you may also select Search All Volumes to search for any Type 1 font on you hard drive). The fonts are then converted.

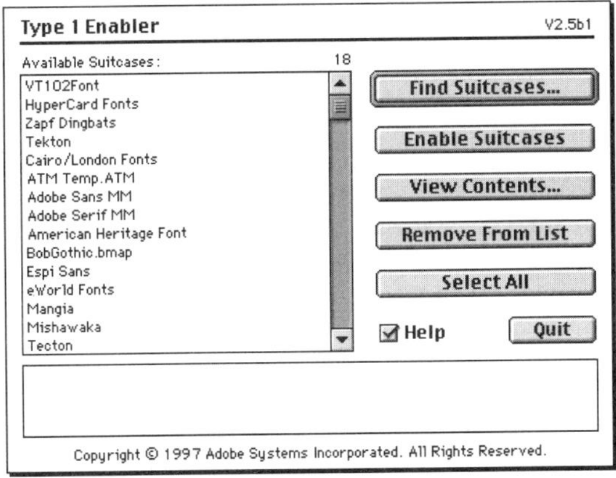

Figure 11-4: Using the Type 1 Enabler application to convert fonts for use with QuickDraw GX.

PostScript Font Challenges

For a variety of reasons, using PostScript fonts in the real-world Macintosh environment has never been easy. The main problem is that the software and hardware environment in which PostScript fonts are used and the PostScript fonts themselves have been in a constant state of evolution. Most of these problems have been overcome through system software upgrades, new font management utilities, or "workaround" methods that have become well known and commonly accepted as necessary for font survival.

The following list describes many of the challenges PostScript font users have faced, along with the corresponding solutions, resolutions, or workarounds:

- **PostScript fonts versus non-PostScript fonts.** Because PostScript screen fonts are not noticeably different from non-PostScript screen fonts, it is difficult for inexperienced users to distinguish between them when creating documents that will be output on high-resolution PostScript printers.
  This problem has been solved, at least partially, by PostScript's dominance in the Macintosh world; most Macintosh users now have access to PostScript printers. And PostScript fonts are now the rule rather than the exception. Apple and Adobe should have provided a better solution, forcing PostScript screen fonts to indicate their PostScript status—perhaps a symbol character displayed before or after their font names. This solution would simplify determining which fonts can be used to prepare documents to be output on PostScript printers.
- **Screen font availability.** After a document is created, there's generally no easy way to determine which fonts it contains in order to be sure all necessary screen and printer fonts are available at print time—especially if the person printing the file is not the one who created it.
  Over time, individual software vendors have developed schemes to help identify screen fonts used in a document. PageMaker displays the dimmed names of used but not currently available fonts in its font menu, and both PageMaker and QuarkXPress produce a list of fonts used, for example. Only Adobe has addressed the problem of screen font availability, allowing Illustrator to print files correctly even if the screen fonts used to create the file aren't available at the time the file is printed. Unfortunately, this solution hasn't caught on with other vendors. (It's possible that Adobe's proprietary font knowledge allows them this advantage.)
  Some applications have a font-substitution capability. PageMaker 4.2 and 5.0 use Checklist. Both also have a Display Pub Info addition that checks for font availability. FreeHand 4.0 checks for and substitutes fonts. Quark has a font-missing alert and can substitute fonts with a built-in utility.
- **Printer font availability.** The most fundamental requirement of PostScript fonts is that for each screen font used in a document, a corresponding printer font must be available at print time. This requirement has caused tremendous difficulty for Mac users because there's no automated way to track the screen font/printer font correspondence.
  The advent of large font-storage printer hard drives, the Suitcase II and MasterJuggler font management utilities, the ability to download screen

fonts, and the NFNT font resource have made the "Font Not Found: Substituting Courier" messages less common. But unfortunately, the only real solution to this problem lies with users and service bureau operators.

- **Too many font names in the font menus.** For non-PostScript screen fonts, a single font is provided in several different sizes, but you must create bold and italic versions using the Style command. PostScript fonts, on the other hand, provide a separate screen font for each size and style. As a result, font menus are very long. For example, Helvetica includes four entries (B Helvetica Bold, I Helvetica Italic, Helvetica, and BI Helvetica Bold Italic). Times has four as well, and so do many other fonts.
- **Font ID conflicts.** The original Macintosh system was designed to handle only a small number of fonts. With the font explosion that followed PostScript's introduction, there were soon more fonts than available Font ID numbers. The Apple Font/DA Mover resolved Font ID conflicts as new fonts were added to the System file, but unfortunately, the Font/DA Mover did so by randomly renumbering the fonts. Renumbering fonts caused problems because some applications tracked fonts by Font ID number, and as a result, the same font would have different ID numbers on different Macintoshes.

  Because many applications used the Font ID numbers to keep track of font assignments within documents, Font ID instability caused documents to "forget" which fonts were used to create them when they were transferred from one Macintosh to another. Working with a wide range of fonts on the Macintosh became like playing a low-stakes game of Russian roulette.

  This problem was partially solved with the release of system software 6.0, which added more complete support for a Macintosh resource called NFNT (pronounced N-Font). NFNT offered a font-numbering scheme capable of handling over 32,000 different fonts. Of course, implementing the new system meant that millions of non-NFNT fonts already in use had to be replaced with new NFNT versions and that a master set of new NFNT fonts had to be distributed for use in this replacement.

  To make matters worse, Apple and Adobe used the same uneven, unplanned, and unprofessional distribution methods for the new font ID system that they used for Apple system software and shareware updates—user groups, bulletin boards, and friendly file sharing. Therefore, the problem was only partially solved.

  To further complicate the introduction of NFNT fonts, Apple and Adobe chose not to "harmonize" the NFNT fonts by allowing only a single font menu entry to appear for each font (as discussed previously).

So it was left to users to perform this harmonization with their own utilities, which results in a nonuniversal set of fonts.

- **Different fonts with the same names.** As more vendors produced more PostScript fonts, another problem appeared: different versions of the same fonts released by different vendors.

  This proliferation of fonts not only caused Macintoshes to become "confused" about which screen fonts and printer fonts were used in documents, but it also made it hard for service bureaus to know if the Garamond specified in a document was the Adobe, Bitstream, or other font vendor version of the typeface. This point was crucial because font substitutions wouldn't work. And, even if they did, character width differences would play havoc with the output.

- **The Type 1 font secret.** Because Adobe Systems had developed PostScript, they kept the specifics of the optimized format known as Type 1 for themselves. The Type 1 font format provided fonts with "hints" embedded in the font outline that made them look better when output in small type sizes on 300 dpi laser printers.

  The Type 1 format was also the only format compatible with Adobe's TypeAlign and Adobe Type Manager (ATM) utilities. This restriction excluded all other vendors' PostScript fonts from using these utilities because all non-Adobe PostScript fonts were in the Type 3 format.

  Because Adobe fonts were compressed and encrypted, other vendors had to reverse-engineer the Type 1 font hinting scheme to optimize their type. Bitstream and others were successful in "cloning" PostScript. So, after the political turmoil surrounding the announcement of TrueType and successful cloning of PostScript Type 1 fonts, Adobe released the specification for the Type 1 font format. There was little reason left for them not to do so. Today most other font vendors have upgraded their fonts to the Type 1 format.

Printing PostScript Fonts

When a document containing PostScript fonts is printed to a PostScript printer, the LaserWriter printer driver queries the PostScript printer to determine whether the printer fonts that the document requires are resident in the printer. These fonts may be built into a printer's ROM chips, or they may have been previously downloaded into the printer's RAM or onto the printer's hard disk. If the fonts are resident, the document is sent to the printer for output. If the fonts are not resident, the printer driver checks to see whether the printer font files are available on the Macintosh hard disk. If they are, they're downloaded into the printer's RAM temporarily. If they aren't, an error message in the Print Status dialog box alerts you that specific fonts are unavailable (this message usually states that Courier is being substituted for the missing font, and your document is then printed with that substitution).

When the document is printed, the PostScript printer uses the printer font information to create each character. The information from the PostScript screen font is translated into new printer font characters. Screen fonts are only placeholders onscreen. The process of creating the printed characters is called rasterization—the most complex part of the PostScript printing process. During rasterization, PostScript uses the PostScript printer font file's mathematical character descriptions to select the output device pixels necessary to produce the requested character at the highest possible resolution.

When a document containing PostScript fonts is printed to a non-PostScript printer, such as a QuickDraw or dot-matrix printer, screen font information is transferred directly to the printer and is the only source used to produce the printed characters. None of the advantages of PostScript are used. On a QuickDraw or dot-matrix printer, there is no difference between the use of a PostScript font and a non-PostScript font (except when ATM is being used, in which case PostScript fonts are superior).

Adobe Type Manager

Not long after Apple's announcement of System 7 and TrueType, Adobe Systems released Adobe Type Manager (ATM), a utility (rasterizer) that allows PostScript fonts to be drawn more smoothly at any resolution onscreen or on any non-PostScript output device. ATM incorporates the elements of display PostScript that Apple chose not to license. This development eliminated the biggest advantages that TrueType fonts initially had over PostScript fonts. It also proved that competition is often good for the consumer.

Adobe Type Manager 4.0 is a Control Panel installed by the Mac OS that allows you to view PostScript printer font data onscreen. When ATM is installed, PostScript fonts display at the best possible resolution onscreen at any point size for any font whose screen and printer fonts are installed. ATM also improves the output quality of PostScript fonts on non-PostScript printers. With ATM, almost any PostScript font can be printed successfully at any size on any dot-matrix, ink-jet, or QuickDraw laser printer. The effect of ATM on PostScript Type 1 type is shown in Figure 11-5.

Figure 11-5: Without ATM (left), fonts appear jagged onscreen at most point sizes. With ATM (right), the same fonts are smooth at any size.

ATM quickly became a huge success, and most people who worked with more than a few PostScript fonts either purchased the utility or received it in a bundle with some other software application or application upgrade. It was estimated that by the time System 7 shipped, over 80 percent of the installed base of Macintosh users were using ATM.

Some time after the initial shipment of System 7, Apple began offering ATM to anyone who purchased System 7 or a System 7 upgrade package. But Apple did not add ATM to the System 7 install disks, making it necessary to order the "free" copy of ATM from a toll-free number for a shipping and handling charge. This practice stops with Mac OS 8, where ATM version 4.0.2 is installed into the Internet/Internet Utilities/Adobe/Fonts folder. Although a Control Panel, the ATM Control Panel may reside practically anywhere on your hard drive.

The primary drawback of ATM is that you must keep a printer font that corresponds to each installed screen font on your hard drive. Doing so requires more space and increases the cost of working with lots of fonts. You can obtain screen fonts without charge from service bureaus or online sources, but you must purchase most printer fonts at costs ranging from a few dollars to a few hundred dollars per type family.

To use ATM, you must also have the printer font files for any PostScript files you want ATM to work with. Several of the fonts provided with System 7 are PostScript screen fonts, but the printer font portions are missing; Times, Helvetica, Courier, and Symbol, for example. You must obtain or purchase these printer fonts separately. Open the ATM Control Panel, shown in Figure 11-6, to configure ATM for you Mac.

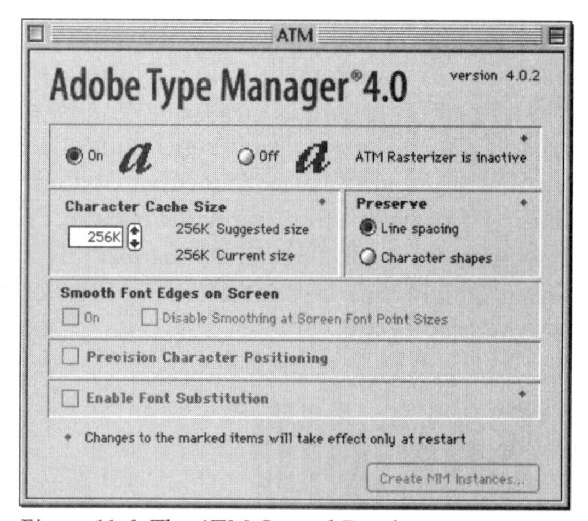

Figure 11-6: The ATM Control Panel.

Several versions of ATM are in circulation, and each has different System 7 considerations:

- **ATM version 2.0.** This version is System 7 compatible but not 32-bit clean (it will cause crashes if 32-bit addressing is turned on). Printer fonts must reside in the System folder itself, even though printer fonts dragged to the System Folder icon will be automatically placed in the Extensions folder (if this happens, you need to manually drag them back into the System folder). It is not recommended that you use this version with Mac OS 8.
- **ATM version 2.02.** This version is Mac OS 8 compatible and 32-bit clean, but it does not recognize printer fonts in the Extensions folder or Fonts folder—they must reside in the System folder itself.
- **ATM version 2.03.** This version is Mac OS 8 compatible, 32-bit clean, and it recognizes the printer fonts in the Extensions folder but not in the Fonts folder. It is a safe version to use with System 7 or version 7.01, but it's not recommended for version 7.1.
- **ATM version 3.0.** This version is fully compatible with—and recommended for—System 7 versions 7.0, 7.01, or 7.1. In addition to adding support for System 7.1's Fonts folder, ATM 3.0 supports Adobe's Multiple Master font technology.
- **Super ATM version 3.5.** This version of ATM not only supports Multiple Master fonts, but it also takes advantage of them to construct fonts when you open or print documents containing missing fonts. It is fully compatible with System 7 versions 7.0, 7.01, and 7.1.
- **Super ATM version 3.6.** Version 3.6 adds support for the Power Macintosh. It is fully compatible with System 7 versions 7.0, 7.01, and 7.1.
- **ATM GX version 3.7.** Version 3.7 adds support for TrueType GX fonts, Type 1 PostScript fonts that have been converted to GX format, and type effects native to the QuickDraw GX language.
- **ATM GX version 3.8.** This version fixes the "fat traps" (see the discussion in Chapter 6, "PowerBook System Software") that result from crossover between 68K emulation and native PowerPC code in the Mixed Mode Manager. Fat traps lead to poor performance when you're using ATM on a Power Macintosh. You can use Versions 3.7 and 3.8 with System 7.1, 7.5, 7.6, and 8.
- **ATM GX version 4.0.** This version of ATM 4.0 has a new feature that will allow these enabled PostScript fonts to print correctly even if QuickDraw GX is disabled. You can use version 4.0 with Mac OS 8.

Installing Fonts

Before the release of System 7, you installed screen fonts using the Font/DA Mover, which transferred them between their font suitcases and the System file. Over the years, however, the Font/DA Mover became a scapegoat for many of the larger problems of how the Mac managed fonts. Because of this, and due to the fact that the Font/DA Mover's interface was seen as inconsistent with the drag-and-drop method by which other files were moved from one location to another, a new method of installing screen fonts was introduced in System 7.

This method requires no utility program—you simply drag fonts onto the System Folder icon or the icon of the System file. They are then placed into the System file automatically. This method works with all kinds of fonts (TrueType fonts, bitmapped fonts, and PostScript screen fonts), and the only limitation is that fonts cannot be installed while any application other than the Finder is open. If you try to drag fonts into the System file or the System Folder while applications are open, the dialog box shown in Figure 11-7 appears.

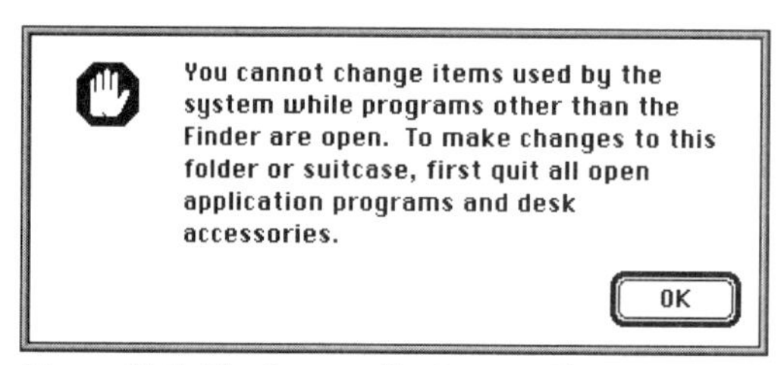

Figure 11-7: The System file Cannot Change Items dialog box.

Another change in System 7 is that you can open screen font suitcases directly from the Finder by double-clicking them as if they were folders. This action opens a suitcase window, displaying individual icons for each screen font in the folder. You can distinguish PostScript screen fonts or bitmapped fonts from ones in the new TrueType format by the icon they display. TrueType fonts use an icon with three *A*s, and PostScript screen fonts or bitmapped fonts use an icon with a single *A*, as shown in Figure 11-8.

Double-clicking an individual screen font icon opens a window showing a brief sample of the font. For TrueType fonts, this sample shows the font at 11-, 12-, and 18-point sizes. Non-TrueType fonts display only a single sample. Figure 11-9 shows two examples.

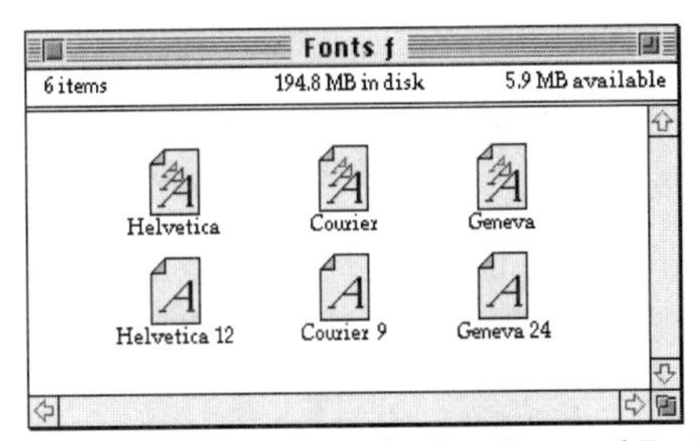

Figure 11-8: Font icons for TrueType and PostScript.

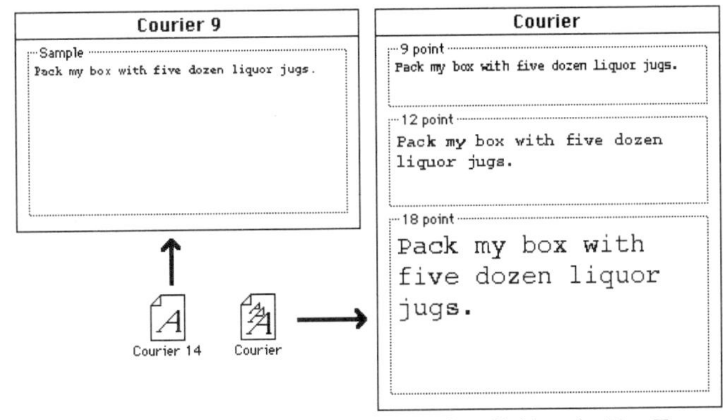

Figure 11-9: A non-TrueType sample window (left) and a TrueType sample window (right).

When screen fonts are installed into the System file in System 7, the suitcase is discarded and only the individual font file icons are added. If you install fonts by dragging the suitcase to the System Folder icon or onto the System file, the suitcase itself will be discarded automatically. You can also drag individual font icons from an open suitcase window to the System Folder icon, to the System File icon, to an open System file window, or to another suitcase icon or open suitcase window.

In System 7.0, individual font icons must always be stored in a font suitcase or in the System file; they cannot be stored as files in any other folder. System 7 provides no easy way to create new empty font suitcases, so if you need a new suitcase to store your fonts, you'll have to duplicate an existing suitcase file and then discard the fonts contained in that duplicate. You can then copy any fonts you want into that suitcase and rename it as necessary. Shareware and commercial font-management utilities that can create empty suitcases are also available.

Changes in Fonts

Although System 7 eliminated the Font/DA Mover, it did little to correct the more fundamental problems of Macintosh font management. One of these fundamental problems was that installing fonts into the System file—when done by the system software or by some utility—resulted in large System files that tended to cause crashes. Sometimes these crashes were so severe that they required a complete system software reinstallation.

The release of System 7.1 corrected this problem by adding a Fonts subfolder to the System folder; all screen fonts and printer fonts now reside in this folder—they are no longer stored in the System file. Up to 128 screen font files or font suitcases (each containing any number of fonts) stored in the Fonts folder will be loaded at start-up and become available in the font menu or dialog box of your applications. Mac OS 8 continues the use of a Fonts folder within the System folder.

You can add font suitcases or individual font files to the Fonts folder by dragging them there just as with any other folder. Or you can drag fonts onto the System Folder icon, and they will be placed into the Fonts folder automatically. If you open the Fonts folder window, you can merge the fonts from one font suitcase with another by dragging one suitcase onto another (see Figure 11-10).

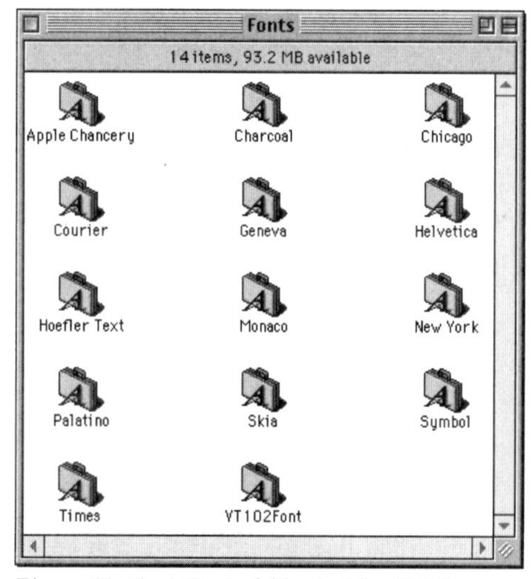

Figure 11-10: A Fonts folder in Mac OS 8.

When you add fonts to the Fonts folder, they do not become available to any applications that are already open until you quit and relaunch those programs. Fonts or suitcases with the same names as existing fonts or suitcases cannot be added to the Fonts folder; you must first move the previously installed font to another folder or into the Trash.

Removing Fonts

In System 7 through Mac OS 8, you remove fonts by a drag-and-drop method. In version 7.0, double-click the System file to open a System file window and then drag the icons of any fonts you want to remove to another location or into the Trash. In versions 7.1, 7.5, and 8, simply open the Fonts folder and drag the icons of any fonts you want to remove to another location or into the Trash. In neither case can you remove fonts while applications other than the Finder are open.

TrueType

In addition to supporting the same bitmapped and PostScript fonts that Macintosh users have worked with for years, Mac OS 8 uses a font format introduced in System 7. TrueType fonts were designed to appear on the Macintosh screen at high resolution at any point size and to print at high resolution on virtually any output device.

TrueType is a fundamental shift from bitmapped fonts and PostScript fonts. Each TrueType font exists as a single file that does the work of both the screen font and the printer font. And when used along with Mac OS 8, TrueType fonts appear onscreen without "jaggies" at any point size and without the use of any extensions such as ATM. TrueType fonts can be printed at full resolution on any dot-matrix, QuickDraw, TrueType, or PostScript printer.

TrueType is an open type format whose font specifications have been published for use by a wide variety of type vendors. It is supported by AGFA Compugraphic, Bitstream, International Typeface Corporation, Monotype, and others. Future versions of Windows and OS/2 will continue to support the TrueType standard, providing for strong cross-platform compatibility. You can buy TrueType font packages from most vendors, with the notable exception of Adobe—at least to this point. Both Apple and Microsoft now sell repackaged typeface packages.

TrueType GX

TrueType GX is an extension of the TrueType specification. It takes advantage of the capabilities found in QuickDraw GX. You buy QuickDraw GX fonts—as you would any other font format—as software bundles. For example, Bitstream and the International Typeface Corporation have announced a set of 26 GX fonts, and Linotype-Hell has also announced their intention to sell GX fonts. Although TrueType and converted PostScript Type 1 fonts are compatible with QuickDraw GX, they are not upgradeable.

QuickDraw GX will be notable for its handling of complex character sets and pictographic languages, and it should help make the Macintosh more attractive to users of non-Roman languages. It also introduces advanced typographical capabilities for fine control over letterforms and intelligent handling of characters in a layout. Apple describes GX fonts as "smart fonts" for their added intelligence.

TrueType GX and PostScript Type 1 fonts that follow the QuickDraw GX data structure can store information about justification, optical alignment, optical scaling, hanging punctuation, tracking, and kerning. Additional intelligence can add fractions based on the context of the character. Just like Adobe's Multiple Master technology, TrueType GX can create precise styling: bold, italic, and expanded or condensed along two, three, or four variation axes. Apple defines these axes as weight, width, slant, and optical size (optimal shape at a size).

Because you can adjust letter size and spacing, you can use one TrueType GX font in place of another without changing line and page breaks. QuickDraw GX supplies the conversion that lets you make this substitution. TrueType GX fonts are the "ink" that Apple's new portable document format uses. See "Portable Digital Documents" later in this chapter.

TrueType & PostScript

TrueType is an alternative to PostScript, not a replacement for it; PostScript is fully supported in Mac OS 8, as described previously in this chapter. Neither is necessarily better than the other; they're just different. Later in this chapter, we'll examine the realities of working in a world of mixed PostScript and TrueType fonts and offer some suggestions on the best ways to organize and utilize these font technologies on your system.

Although TrueType is in many ways a competitor for PostScript fonts, it's not a competitor for the complete PostScript language. TrueType printers use TrueType for fonts but QuickDraw descriptions for all other page elements. QuickDraw has proven itself on the Macintosh screen, but its use in QuickDraw GX as a high-resolution printing model is new. It's unlikely that the PostScript standard will be replaced in the near future; it has firm support from developers of high-end software, hardware developers, service bureaus, and end users. The PostScript language will likely continue to dominate personal computer printing.

TrueType Technology

TrueType fonts, like PostScript printer fonts, are outline fonts, which means that each character is described mathematically as opposed to the bit-by-bit description used by existing screen fonts. TrueType mathematical descriptions are based on quadratic Bézier curve equations rather than PostScript's standard Bézier curve equations. The difference between these equations is in the number of points used to determine the position of the lines and curves that make up each character. Apple claims TrueType's method creates better-looking characters at a wider range of output and display resolutions.

Because TrueType uses mathematical descriptions for onscreen and printer font versions, a single file can serve both the display and any output devices. As mentioned previously in this chapter, PostScript requires two files, a screen font file and a printer font file, to print or display at full resolution. Although it's easier to manage one font file than two, Adobe claims that putting its screen fonts and printer fonts in separate files is an asset because either can be updated or enhanced independently at any time without affecting existing documents or printer configurations.

When a document containing TrueType fonts is printed, the sequence of events depends on the type of printer used:

- **Dot-matrix printers.** When a document containing TrueType fonts is printed to a dot-matrix printer, the characters are reproduced in their natural contours, just as they appear on the screen. The output images are the results of the onscreen rasterization process, not the TrueType outlines. Therefore, dot-matrix output can only provide a more exact representation of the Mac's onscreen display.
- **QuickDraw printers.** When a document containing TrueType fonts is printed to a QuickDraw printer such as the LaserWriter II SC, the same process described for dot-matrix printers occurs—information from the onscreen rasterization process is sent to the printer.
- **68000-based PostScript printers with 2MB of RAM.** When a document containing TrueType fonts is sent to a PostScript printer or output device using a Motorola 68000 CPU and at least 2MB of RAM (such as the LaserWriter IINT and most of today's imagesetters), the printer driver queries the device to see whether the TrueType font scaler is available.

The TrueType font scaler may be built into the printer's ROM, or it may have been previously downloaded onto the printer's hard disk or into printer RAM (using the LaserWriter Font Utility). If the TrueType font scaler is not available, it is automatically downloaded into the printer's RAM where it will reside until the printer is reset. This font scaler will consume approximately 80K of printer memory.

With the font scaler in place, the page is sent normally. Mathematical descriptions of any included TrueType fonts are sent to the printer and processed by the TrueType font scaler. The page is then output at full resolution using any TrueType fonts rasterized by the font scaler software.

- **68000-based PostScript printers with less than 2MB of RAM, or RISC-based Adobe PostScript printers.** When a document containing TrueType fonts is printed to a PostScript printer or output device using a Motorola 68000 CPU and less than 2MB of RAM (such as the LaserWriter Plus) or to a RISC-based Adobe PostScript printer, TrueType fonts are encoded into PostScript Type 1 font format and sent to the printer where they're processed just like all other PostScript fonts. The encoded Type 1 fonts do not contain PostScript "hints."
- **Printers with built-in TrueType scaling.** When a document containing TrueType fonts is sent to a printer with a built-in TrueType (TrueImage) font scaler, such as the LaserMaster 400XL or MicroTek TrueLaser, the TrueType outline information is sent directly to the printer where the font is rasterized and imaged.

A Mixed World

In a laboratory environment, where some Macintoshes used only PostScript fonts and some used only TrueType fonts, where all documents using PostScript fonts were created only on the PostScript machines and those using TrueType fonts were created only on the TrueType machines, the daily use of these systems from a font-technology perspective would be very straightforward.

Unfortunately, none of us live or work in such a laboratory. Most Macintosh computers are more likely to be configured with PostScript fonts, TrueType fonts, and non-PostScript, non-TrueType bitmapped fonts. And most people will have some documents created with only PostScript fonts, some with only bitmapped fonts, some with only TrueType fonts, and many with mixes of TrueType, PostScript, and bitmapped fonts. So how can all this jumble work in the real world?

Picking Your Font Standard

When you install Mac OS 8, the Installer adds both the PostScript and TrueType versions of many default fonts, including Courier, Times, and Geneva. Over time, you will add additional fonts to your system—some PostScript, some TrueType—and sometimes you will add both PostScript and TrueType versions of the same fonts. Figure 11-11 shows two types of Courier fonts installed by Mac OS 8.

Courier

8 items, 88.8 MB available

Name	Kind	Size
Courier	font	58K
Courier 9	font	5K
Courier (bold)	font	56K
Courier 10	font	5K
Courier 12	font	6K
Courier 14	font	6K
Courier 18	font	7K
Courier 24	font	10K

Figure 11-11: Different types of fonts can coexist in the same folder.

Once you've installed these fonts, their names will appear in the font menus or dialog boxes of all applications, but you will have no easy way to distinguish the TrueType fonts from the PostScript fonts or to distinguish those for which both versions have been installed: you cannot tell which formats are installed by looking at a name in a font menu. (Again, it's a shame Apple didn't make these distinctions visible.)

As you use fonts in your documents, when you choose a font that is installed in both PostScript and TrueType formats, the Macintosh will decide whether to use the PostScript screen font or a scaled TrueType font for each occurrence depending on the point size at which the font is used. Assume, for example, that you have the PostScript screen fonts for Helvetica, Helvetica Bold, Helvetica Italic, and Helvetica Bold Italic installed in your System file, each in 10-, 12-, and 14-point sizes. Also assume that the TrueType Helvetica,

Helvetica Bold, Helvetica Italic, and Helvetica Bold Italic files are installed. In this case, most applications would use the PostScript versions of Helvetica for any instances of 10-, 12-, or 14-point type and the TrueType version in all other cases. In other words, PostScript screen fonts are used when they're available at the size specified, and TrueType fonts are used for all other sizes.

Of course, when no TrueType font has been installed, PostScript versions are used at all sizes just as they were before TrueType. If ATM is installed, ATM will scale the onscreen font display to provide smooth character representations. PostScript outlines will be used at print time to produce smooth type at the resolution of the output device (assuming the output device is equipped with a PostScript interpreter).

This process of alternating PostScript screen fonts and TrueType fonts is controlled by each application. Some software developers choose to use TrueType fonts even when PostScript screen fonts of the exact size requested are available. There's no way to tell whether TrueType or PostScript fonts are being used until the document is printed, so consult your application manuals for more information.

This situation is clearly confusing. It gets worse if you consider the possibility that some older documents on your hard drive were created using only PostScript fonts, and when you now open them, you may be instead using TrueType versions of those same fonts. These old documents will then be forced to use TrueType fonts, and extensive text repositioning may occur as a result. The same thing will happen if you're using an application that ignores PostScript screen fonts and uses the TrueType fonts in all situations.

Text repositioning occurs because character widths for TrueType fonts will not always exactly match PostScript font character widths, even in the same font and family. The width of a 14-point Helvetica Bold **H** may be slightly different in TrueType than it was in PostScript. The cumulative result of the character width accommodations in your document will be text repositioning.

Because using both PostScript and TrueType versions of the same font makes it impossible to determine which version is being used at any one time, it is best not to install both PostScript and TrueType versions of the same fonts. This is especially true for fonts you'll use in documents being prepared for high-resolution output that will be printed at a remote site such as a service bureau.

If you use the default Mac OS 8 fonts (Times, Helvetica, and so on) for high-resolution output, you may want to remove either the PostScript or the TrueType versions of them from your Fonts folder so both are not installed. If you just use these fonts onscreen and from your local laser printer, however, it is probably not worth the trouble of removing one of them.

Advanced Typography

The development of computer-aided design tools has led to both an explosion in type design and a typographical revival. There have never been as many high-quality typefaces available as there are now, in almost any format you choose to buy. Several technical challenges remain to be overcome in typography: contextual use of letterforms, international character sets, and more flexible type handling. Using QuickDraw GX along with TrueType GX fonts may provide some solutions to these problems.

The contextual use of characters is a style issue. Characters are language elements that include letters, numbers, punctuation marks, and other linguistic symbols that have a value or meaning in a certain language. QuickDraw GX introduces the concept of a glyph. A *glyph* is a representation of a character. Glyphs are what the characters looks like in that particular instance, but they don't contain any meaning beyond the characters they represent. An application specifies a character, and QuickDraw GX automatically draws the appropriate glyph of the right size, style, and so on.

A TrueType GX font follows the Unicode specification for an international character set. It can contain up to 65,000 glyphs (called characters in other systems). This expansion of the character set and the LineLayout Manager's line layout capabilities makes it easier to support digital type in non-Roman languages. Roman language users will benefit by additional characters being added to character sets: small caps, fractions, superior/inferior characters, ligatures, swashes, fleurons, and borders are included in a single font. The LineLayout Manager creates these special characters in context based upon the intelligence built into the font.

In Roman languages, glyph substitution places ligatures where two or three characters make the text more readable and attractive. For example, _ is substituted for the letters *f* and *l*, and _ for *f* and *i*. Because these glyphs retain the original two character definitions, they spell check, search and replace, and substitute correctly. Ligatures can be made to appear inside or at the end of words.

Whereas glyph substitution is a nice type style feature in Roman languages, it assumes added importance in text systems such as Arabic or Hindi in which characters change their shape based upon their positions in a word. QuickDraw GX makes the appropriate placement of glyphs, cutting down on data entry and character selection.

Glyph substitution also lets developers create animated fonts. The animation occurs between different glyphs of the same characters in the same manner that cursors can be animated in Macintosh system software.

In Mac OS 8, as applications become QuickDraw GX savvy, use glyphs, and apply glyph substitution, you will find that much of the work you do styling a document is now done for you automatically. You may also find that applications come with menus or dialog boxes that allow you to select which of these typographical features you wish to apply in a document. Figure 11-12 shows an example of one such menu.

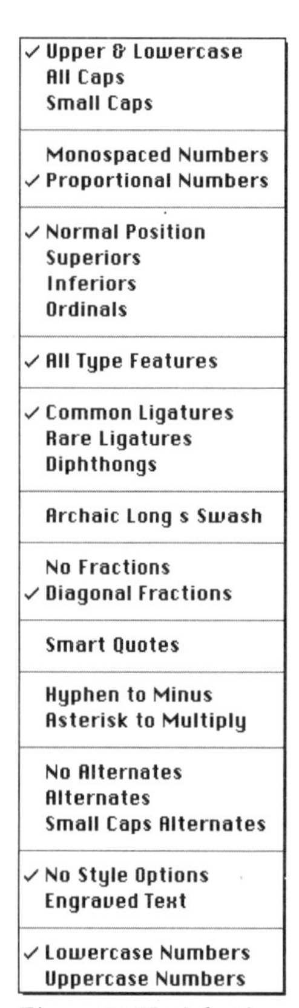

Figure 11-12: Selecting advanced type effects in a QuickDraw GX-savvy application.

Text Effects

Because QuickDraw GX treats text as a shape, designers have the same latitude in applying special effects that illustrators do in creating artwork. Certain of the more tedious tasks that designers require have already been automated inside TrueType GX fonts, including optical scaling and alignment, glyphs, automatic kerning, and tracking.

You can expect to see a proliferation of text effects. Some effects include applying transformations such as skew, rotation, mirroring, and perspective to a line of text. The results of such transformations rival programs such as Adobe's TypeAlign, BroderBund's TypeStyler, or other illustrators' tools. However, since these effects are now part of system software, they will appear in many other (often smaller) programs. Other effects, such as ductile type, may be new to you. In ductile type, a character can expand or contract to provide script continuity.

Because written languages can be like English (read left to right), Hebrew (read right to left), and Japanese (read top to bottom), QuickDraw GX can mix a variety of scripts together—even on the same line.

For anyone who has traveled abroad—say to Japan, where Japanese and English are mixed on the same page—this capability is a boon. With ideographic languages (those using pictures for characters, such as Japanese, Chinese, or Korean), QuickDraw GX can apply proportional vertical writing and automatic alignment to centered baselines. That line can be rotated to any angle or transformed like any shape. You also can mix different lines of text, such as Kanji and Roman type, and apply the baseline of your choice.

Typography is not the subject of this book, however; Mac OS 8 is. The typographical capabilities that QuickDraw GX gives Macintosh users are unique for any computer system—probably a landmark in the type and computer industries.

Unicode, WorldScript & Localization

Computer vendors have long struggled with the task of translating software between languages and cultures. A version of software for another language or culture is called a *localized version*, and the process is called *localization*. The problem is compounded by several issues. Different languages use different character sets. Even when the languages are the same, as is the case for American and British English, the character sets may differ. Character sets can even be based on different alphabets, with different numbers and characters. Ideographic languages—Japanese Kanji, Chinese Han, and Korean—have thousands of characters. These differences make translation difficult, affect sort orders, and slow down the spread of new innovative software worldwide.

Many standard character sets have been used locally throughout the years. The ACSII standard for American text is one such standard. A consortium of industry vendors has created and codified a system of 65,000 characters incorporating all the modern languages in the world and some of the ancient languages as well. That system is called Unicode, and it has been adopted by Apple in Mac OS 8. Now there is a standard complete character set that localized versions can refer to.

Apple has developed a technology called WorldScript that manages a variety of localization issues such as date and time formats, sort orders, and input methods. To change the text features for the script system on your Macintosh, open the Text Control Panel and choose the feature you want from the pop-up menu. The Text Control Panel was discussed briefly in Chapter 5, "Managing Your Hard Drive." Similarly, you can choose dates, times, and numbers from the Date & Time and Numbers Control Panels.

Input methods are important in non-Roman languages such as Japanese or Chinese. For these languages, users enter phonetic values used in speech and the input method translates to a character. This way, with an ideographic language, you can use a standard keyboard for data entry. For example, Japanese users type Roman characters until the Kanji characters are recognized and substituted. WorldScript works by using a user-installed script or onscreen instructions that make the appropriate character translations.

QuickDraw GX expands WorldScript's capabilities by providing the advanced typographical capabilities for text and characters that have been described previously. Now WorldScript can provide sophisticated scripting of text handling in any language. With these new tools, developers have a method for localizing software quickly.

QuickDraw GX & Printing

QuickDraw GX introduced a new print architecture that was supposed to ship with the original version of System 7.0. A panoply of changes introduced in System 7.5 and continued in Mac OS 8 make printing easier, more intuitive, and more convenient. Among the most important features, you will find the following:

- **Desktop printers.** Printers can appear on your desktop, virtual printers that output files to real printing devices. You can drag and drop files to a printer, manage its print queue, and print to several printers without visiting the Chooser. Printers can be shared across a network via File Sharing.

- **New Print dialog boxes.** The new print architecture provides a redesigned Print dialog box. You can now select a printer within the Print dialog box of any application.
- **Better print spooling.** Each individual printer manages its own print queue. You can reorder and delete print jobs and drag and drop print jobs from one printer to another.
- **Improved background printing.** You'll notice less drag on your foreground application when you print in the background; this is due to the redesigned print architecture.
- **Expanded print options.** You can mix page formats in a document. You could, for example, print a document with both landscape and portrait pages. Also, you could print a letter, envelope, and post card in a single print job. Multiple tray, double-sided, and other options are supported. You can also print a document to any printer; QuickDraw GX makes the needed conversions so that the page prints correctly even if the page size or printable area changes.
- **Printer extensions.** Developers can create specialized printer drivers, called printer extensions, that provide your printer with special capabilities. Writing printer drivers has also become easier because QuickDraw GX provides a ready-to-use toolbox for developers.
- **Portable digital documents.** You can print PDD files on any Macintosh with QuickDraw GX installed—whether or not you have the creator application and fonts. A PDD file can be created by any Macintosh application, whether it's QuickDraw GX savvy or not.

These changes are major—more changes to the way you do printing than in any other system software version. Although a lot is new here, most of it will seem intuitive and much easier than what came before.

Desktop Printing

As you learned in Chapter 2, "The System Folder," you select printers using the Chooser, specifying a serial port or network connection for the printer. When you want to change printers, you must go back to the Chooser to make another selection. You can check the status of print jobs, delete print jobs from the queue, and suspend or resume printing using the Print Monitor. But that's about it.

With QuickDraw GX installed, you still need to select printers from the Chooser. Now, however, when you select a printer, you simply click the Create button and the printer's icon appears on your desktop as a virtual printing device. You can select several printers of different types and in different locations and then place them on your desktop. Figure 11-13 shows some examples. You only go to the Chooser once to mount your printers, a process that can be automated using AppleScripts or any other macro utility.

Figure 11-13: QuickDraw GX printer icons.

You can mount any output device, either a network printer or personal printer, on your desktop. Connections to shared devices are controlled through the standard File Sharing Users and Groups Setup dialog box and passwords schemes, which are described in Chapter 16, "File Sharing." Not only can you mount printers, but you can also mount film recorders, fax modems, or any device that can currently be selected in the Chooser. With appropriate controls, only selected individuals can use only the devices you want them to, saving on wasted materials or inappropriate usage.

The Print Dialog Box

In Mac OS 8, printing from within an application has been enhanced with a new Print dialog box, shown in Figure 11-14. Although many of the options in the Print dialog box will be familiar, over time you will see many new print options. Some of these, such as document formatting, are software specific; others, such as automatic printer functions, will be added as hardware and printer drivers are updated.

When you click the Print button in the Print dialog box, the document is spooled and sent to the printer of your choice. It's placed in a print queue, as discussed in the next section. If the printer is connected, the document is printed. If not, it prints when you connect to that printer again.

The Mac OS enables device-independent printing. You can format a document to print on a specific printer. Page formatting is preserved even when the size of the page or printable area changes. For extreme changes in size, in which the text would be unreadable or the quality of the page compromised, QuickDraw GX will apply user-selected defaults to tile, scale, or clip the printed image. You can also select to format a print job for any printer. You do so when sending a document to an unknown printer. In that case, the document's line and page breaks are preserved.

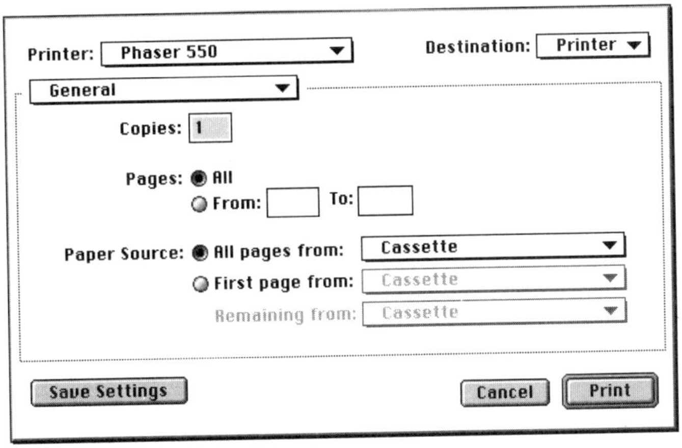

Figure 11-14: The Print dialog box.

As it stands now, applications provide their own page definitions. QuickDraw GX provides standard definitions for page formatting that lets one application copy and paste pages to another without having to reformat the document. Because pages have uniform definitions, you can also break documents into separate pages, each with its own format and page setup. These options will appear as standard Print and Page Setup dialog box options across all Macintosh applications.

You could mix letters, mailing labels, envelopes, or anything within a document that you print appropriately. Because you will have control over tray selection and other features, these capabilities will be practical in the near future. As you print to a standard printer with just one tray, you will be signaled when you need to feed odd-sized paper or envelopes manually into the printer for a print job. When you have multiple trays, the new print architecture automatically routes pages to the correct tray. You do not have to select a bin number; just feed your printer print stock.

The Print Spooler

Desktop printers work like actual printers, and you can drag and drop files to them. When a printer has a queued document in its queue, you see a desktop printer icon with a document on your desktop, as shown in Figure 11-15.

Figure 11-15: A Desktop printer icon with several documents in the print queue.

Each printer manages its own print queue, an example of which is shown in Figure 11-16.. In this regard, QuickDraw GX printers are print servers in the same sense that you have network file servers. To manipulate the print queue, do the following:

- To open a print queue, double-click the printer icon.
- To reorder the queue, drag the document icon to a new position.
- To move a print job to another printer, drag the document icon to that printer icon.
- To delete a job, select a document icon and click the Trash icon.

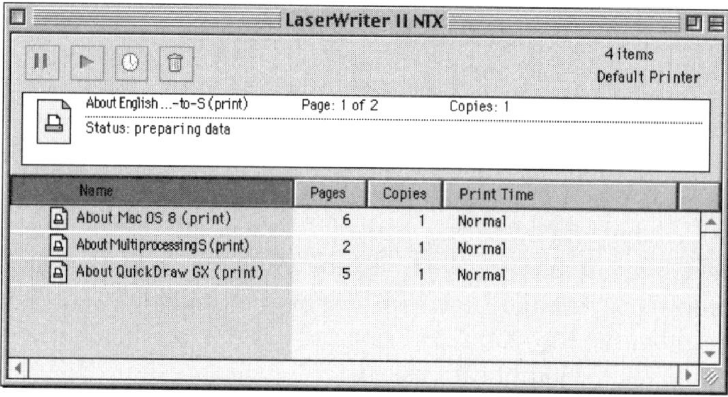

Figure 11-16: A print queue with several documents waiting to be printed.

You'll notice several other changes that are apparent when you print using a print queue. Because of the new background printing architecture, there's less of a performance hit when you are working in the foreground. You'll notice this benefit more on slower, older Macintosh computers, but it's a welcome change. QuickDraw GX monitors the needs of the foreground application and allocates more resources to printing when that application is idle. Resources are returned to the foreground when activity increases.

The print queue is smarter, too. If your Macintosh crashes, you'll find after rebooting that your print job resumes from the point where it stopped, even if that point was in the middle of a job. Therefore, for a multipage print job, the last page prints again, followed by the next one. You no longer have to reprint the entire job or respecify the print job when you crash.

Printing Extensions

Creating printer drivers has been a major chore for developers. The slow start that IBM's OS/2 had in the marketplace was attributed to just this reason. QuickDraw GX provides over 100 standard functions that developers can use to create their own printer drivers and custom printer extensions. This toolbox eliminates 95 percent of the code that developers have to write to create a printer driver.

Among these programmed calls are print components; standard dialog boxes; font, color, and resolution selectors—nearly every standard print function. Even difficult PostScript font management is provided with a program call. Having system calls to work with not only makes it easier to create printer drivers, it makes them more consistent and more capable. QuickDraw GX device drivers can output to PostScript Level 1 and 2 printers, raster impact printers, and even vector devices like plotters, doing any necessary data conversions between formats.

What you, the user, will see is a new class of printer, or driver, extensions that can create a custom solution base on the device you use. Printer extensions appear in a scrolling window at the left side of the Chooser. These driver extensions can add the following capabilities:

- Overprinting letters with marks such as confidential, top secret, or shred.
- Printing watermarks.
- Activating printer functions through responses to dialog boxes.
- Securing access to devices through password protection.
- Creating and managing print jobs based on job numbers.
- Counting users' pages printed.

ColorSync & Color Matching

The Mac's proficiency and popularity as a publishing computer is well known. And in the past few years, advances in processing power, storage capacities, scanning, and output technology have earned the Mac OS the leading role in even the most demanding high-quality color publishing situations. Publications from the *New Yorker* to *People* to *Playboy* are now produced fully or partially on the Macintosh. In fact, many reports indicate that some 80 percent of all desktop publishing is done on the Mac OS.

Despite this acceptance, and the overall improvements in color publishing technology, one aspect of color publishing has remained a challenge: matching colors that appear onscreen to those that are printed on color proofing devices and, finally, to the colors of the finished product, which are usually based on film output. Keeping colors consistent as they move from an onscreen display to different output devices has been difficult for two basic reasons.

First, computer monitors produce colors by adding together differing percentages of red, green, and blue light. This method of mixing light from original sources is called *additive color*. Output devices, on the other hand, work by applying color to a page that will selectively absorb light waves when the document is illuminated via an external white light (such as light bulbs or the sun). This method of creating colors is called *subtractive color*. There are fundamental differences in the ranges of colors that additive and subtractive color can produce. For this reason, onscreen color (additive) offers bright, highly saturated colors that invariably appear darker when printed (subtractive) on paper or other materials.

Second, variations between different printers, monitors, and presses make it impossible for them all to produce the exact same range and quality of colors. An inexpensive ink-jet printer is going to have one set of printable colors, a color laser printer another, a dye sublimation printer yet another, a web press another, and a high-quality sheet-fed press another still.

Differences in the color models and technical characteristics of color devices result in each having its own specific gamut, or range of colors. The trick to achieving consistent color across different devices is to map colors from one device to another so that when a file is displayed or produced on each device, the differences between the devices' gamuts are accounted and compensated for and the color remains as consistent as possible.

Apple's ColorSync System Profile performs this task exactly. When ColorSync is installed, colors are converted from their original definitions into a device-independent definition based on the international CIE XYZ color standard or color space. (A color space is the range of colors that are possible shown in a three-dimensional mapping.) This conversion is done using a device profile, which is a small file that tells ColorSync about the color characteristics and capabilities of the input device or monitor. Once a color is defined in CIE XYZ, it can then be translated using a set of color matching method (CMM) algorithms for output using the device profile of the output device. Figure 11-17 shows the ColorSync System Profile Control Panel and the selection dialog window that you'll use to select the display that is attached to your Mac or Mac clone.

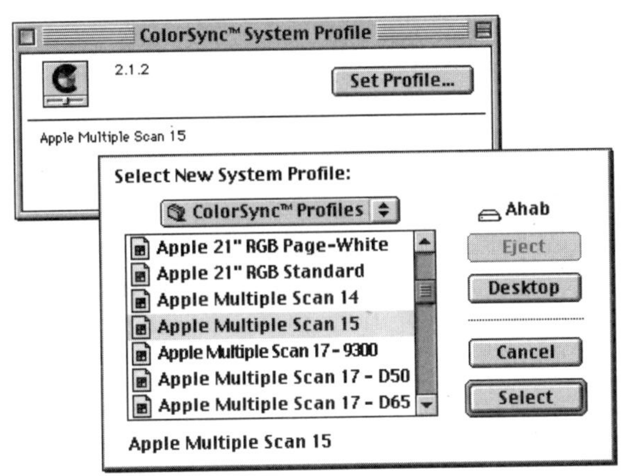

Figure 11-17: The ColorSync System Profile.

Apple will provide device profiles for its own monitors, scanners, and color printers, but the success of ColorSync will be dependent upon third-party developers producing and distributing their own device profiles for their scanners, monitors, and printers. In order for you to use ColorSync effectively, you must have device profiles for the exact scanners, monitors, and printers you are using (or intend to use) for any given project.

When ColorSync translates colors into or out of the CIE XYZ color model, it does so with the goal of providing the best possible match between the original color and the final color. Differences in devices do not always make an exact match possible, as explained earlier. The algorithm ColorSync uses to perform this translation was designed for optimum results, but it was also designed to use a small amount of memory and provide good performance. Other companies, such as EFI and Kodak, have developed other conversion methods—based on lookup tables rather than algorithms—which will produce superior results but require much more memory, information, and expertise about each input and output device. These methods are compatible with ColorSync, however, and can be taken advantage of by anyone working in high-quality color who desires improved results.

ColorSync was released as a separate extension when System 7.1 appeared. It became part of the system software in version 7.5 (as part of the QuickDraw GX package) and is now installed as part of the default Mac OS 8 installation. You may find ColorSync distributed with color peripherals that you buy—scanners, printers, cameras, and so on—along with the device's color profile file.

QuickDraw GX can also control the way two or more colors are mixed, which is called the transfer mode. A range of behavior is possible, from one color being opaque to various percentages of mixing to having transparent colors. When two colored shapes are overlaid, you can have any range of transfer, from opacity to equal mixing to replacement of one color by another in any degree.

By providing an automated color-matching system, Apple has taken the uncertainty out of using color. What was once tedious work is now handled for you by hardware vendors and solutions providers. The quality of this translation will no doubt improve over time.

Moving On

QuickDraw and QuickDraw GX bring to the Macintosh imaging capabilities that equal, and in some areas exceed, that of the Adobe PostScript page description language. You will see more powerful graphics, type descriptions, color handling, and printing functions in your applications. These innovations should further the Macintosh's presence as the preeminent personal computer in the publishing and graphics market and Apple's role as a leader on the cutting edge.

Fonts continue to be an exciting part of the Macintosh, and as shown in this chapter, font technology remains a source of innovation and controversy. Mac OS 8 supports four different font formats: bitmapped, PostScript, TrueType, and TrueType GX. It supports five if you count Adobe's Multiple Masters font technology.

In this chapter, you learned about the following:

- **QuickDraw and QuickDraw GX.** Apple's system-level graphics and type page description language allow for easy development of sophisticated applications.
- **Fonts.** How to select, install, and work with fonts on the Macintosh. You also learned about TrueType GX fonts and their effect on foreign language applications.
- **The print architecture.** System 7.5 introduced a new way of working with printers, print spoolers, and printer extensions.
- **Color matching.** ColorSync can help your images look their best on your Mac, someone else's Mac, or even in print.

In Chapter 12, "Interapplication Communication & OpenDoc," you'll learn about Apple's compound document standard that allows pieces of applications to be easily reused among different applications.

CHAPTER 12

Interapplication Communication & OpenDoc

As you saw in Chapter 10, launching several applications simultaneously can dramatically improve your productivity on the Macintosh. But Mac OS 8 makes it possible to integrate your applications more closely: text and graphic elements can be shared between documents, and messages and commands can be passed from one application to another. These capabilities are made possible by the Edition Manager and Inter-Application Communication (IAC), respectively.

Although the power of the Edition Manager and IAC is provided by Mac OS 8, neither feature is automatically available to applications. Each capability must be specifically added by software developers, and since the ability was offered in System 7, only a handful have done so. Basic support for IAC is also a part of being System 7 savvy, but as you'll see, full support for IAC is much more complex and is therefore appearing in applications more slowly.

Taken to the extreme, the best way to mix different data types and application capabilities is to use a compound document architecture. With this model, a document is the central construct, not an application. When you add data to a compound document or try to modify it, a small application capable of handling that part is called.

This architecture is what OpenDoc is about. OpenDoc provides a document framework using AppleEvents and the Open Scripting Architecture (to which AppleScript subscribes) to enable a new class of application and a new style of computing. Best yet, when you use OpenDoc, you are using concepts you already know (such as cut and paste) in a familiar way. Your Macintosh still feels like a Macintosh.

However, OpenDoc's future is uncertain. OpenDoc is no longer under active development at Apple; instead, it is in "maintenance mode," meaning bug fixes will continue to be made. However, the OpenDoc engineering team is busily working on Rhapsody, Apple's new operating system. But OpenDoc is built into every copy of Mac OS 8, and as long as developers create applications for it, it will continue to be a more natural way to work. Chances are that, over time, OpenDoc—or something very much like OpenDoc but built on the Rhapsody framework—will bring about profound changes in the way Macintosh users buy applications and do their work. Since it is still a part of Mac OS 8, we'll look at how OpenDoc works, its components, and what it can do for you.

The Edition Manager

Creating text and graphic elements within one application and using them in other applications has always been a hallmark of the Mac OS. Its legendary Cut and Paste commands are even being offered by other graphical operating systems. But while others were matching the 1984 Macintosh's capabilities, the Mac OS raised the ante considerably for this type of feature way back in System 7 with the introduction of the Edition Manager's Publish and Subscribe commands.

By using Publish and Subscribe in your applications, you can move elements between applications, and those elements can be manually or automatically updated as you modify them. In other words, when text, graphic, sound, or video elements are moved from one document to another, original and duplicate elements remain linked. When the originals are changed, so are the duplicates.

The benefits are obvious:

- Charts created in spreadsheets or databases and used in word processors or page layout applications can be automatically updated any time the data changes.
- Legal disclaimers and other boilerplate text commonly used in documents can be automatically updated (such as dates on a copyright notice, for example).
- Illustrated publications can be created using preliminary versions of graphic images that are automatically updated as these graphics are completed.

And you can use Publish and Subscribe commands for more than simple "live copy and paste" between two applications on your own Macintosh.

These commands support Macintosh networks (using System 7's File Sharing feature or other networking systems), so your documents can include components created, manipulated, and stored by many people on many network file servers.

Note: Although the term Edition Manager is the technical programming term for this set of capabilities, we'll use the term Publish/Subscribe for the remainder of this chapter to refer to the entire set of Edition Manager capabilities.

How Publish/Subscribe Works

Although Publish/Subscribe is a powerful feature, its basic premise is simple: any elements—text, graphics, sound, or video—or combinations of elements can be transferred from one document to another using Publish/Subscribe:

1. The transfer begins when elements to be shared are selected and then published to a new edition file (see Figure 12-1). This process is similar to the Cut or Copy process except that instead of being transferred into memory, the selected elements are saved to the edition file on disk. At the time you publish these elements, you name the edition file and specify where on your hard drive it will be stored.

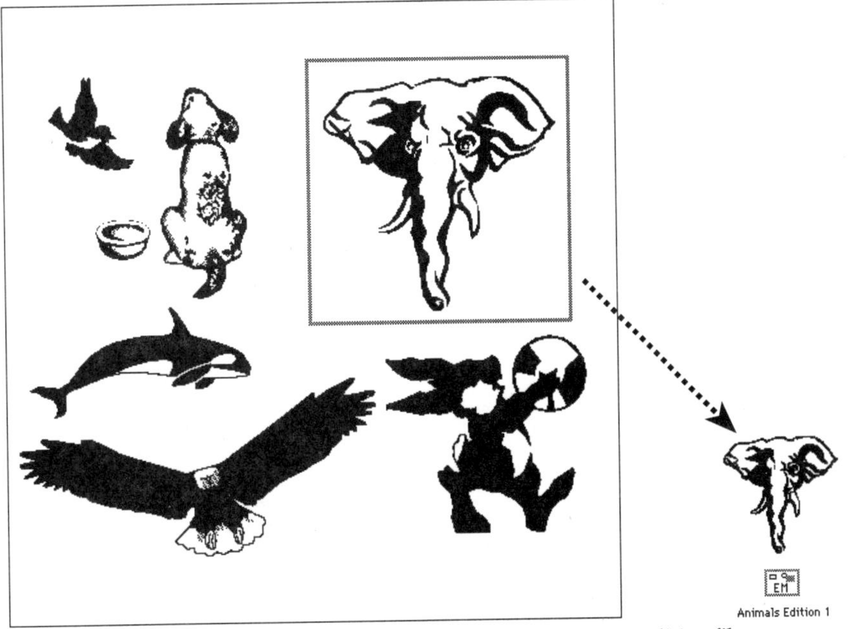

Figure 12-1: An element published from a document is stored in an edition file.

2. The section of your document used to create an edition is called the Publisher. A link is automatically maintained between an edition file and the document that created it. When changes are made in the Publisher, the edition file is updated to reflect these changes (see Figure 12-2). Updates can be made any time the original document is changed or at any other time you initiate them.

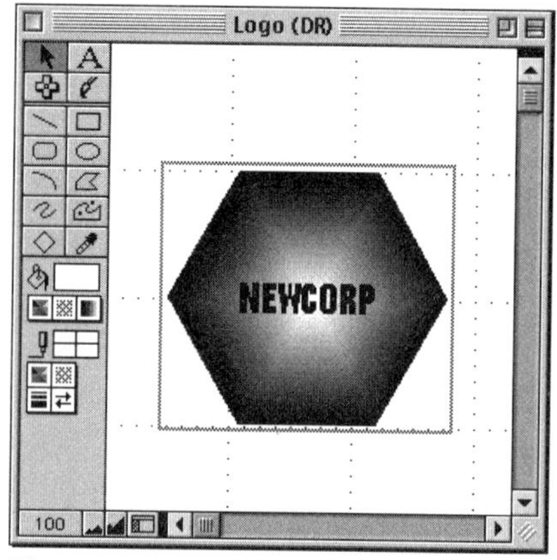

Figure 12-2: The edition file is automatically updated when the document changes.

3. To complete the transfer of elements between documents, the receiving document subscribes to the edition file by importing the edition file elements and establishing a link between the edition and the subscribing document. The document section imported from an edition becomes a Subscriber (to the edition). Figure 12-3 illustrates this process.

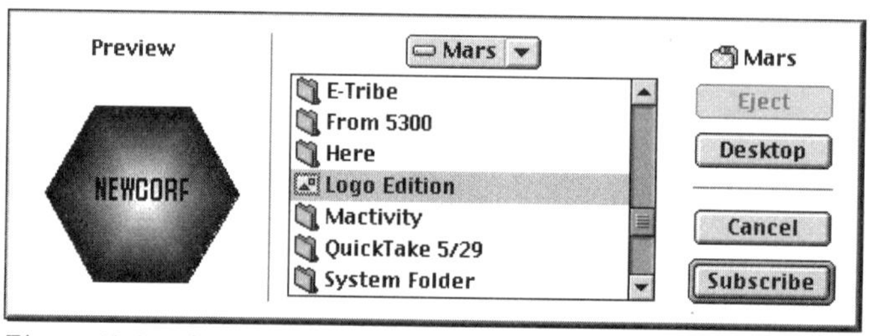

Figure 12-3: Edition files can be subscribed to by any number of other documents.

At this point, the edition file is an independent disk file, linked to the document that published it and any documents subscribing to it (any number of documents can subscribe to a single edition). As elements in the publisher document change, the edition file is updated according to options set in that original document. As the edition file is updated, the edition data used by subscribers is also updated according to options set in the subscribing document. This entire process is shown in Figure 12-4.

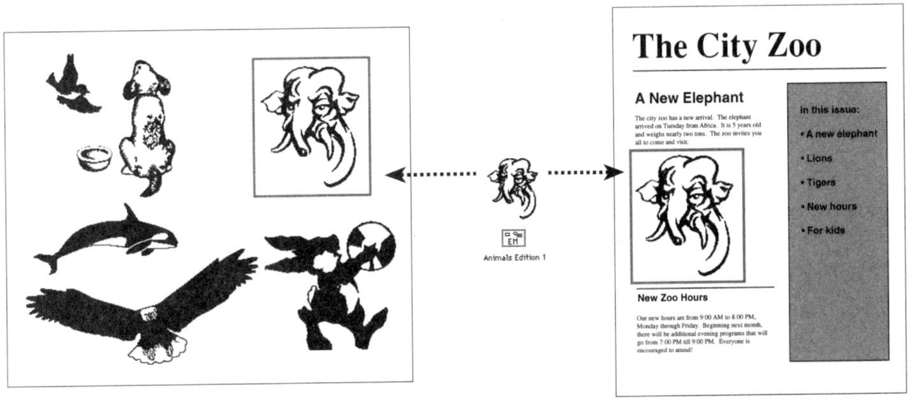

Figure 12-4: Both the publishing document and the subscribing document are linked to the edition file.

Publish/Subscribe Commands

In applications that support Publish/Subscribe, four new commands usually appear in the Edit menu: Create Publisher, Subscribe To, Publisher Options/Subscriber Options, and Show Borders. Some applications use other command names for these functions, but they should work essentially the same as those described in the following sections.

The Create Publisher Command

Create Publisher creates a new edition file, which you name and store in any desired location on any available volume. The edition file contains the text and graphic elements selected when you choose the command. To publish any elements, select the areas of the current document that you wish to share and choose the Create Publisher command from the Edit menu. The Create Publisher dialog box, shown in Figure 12-5, then appears.

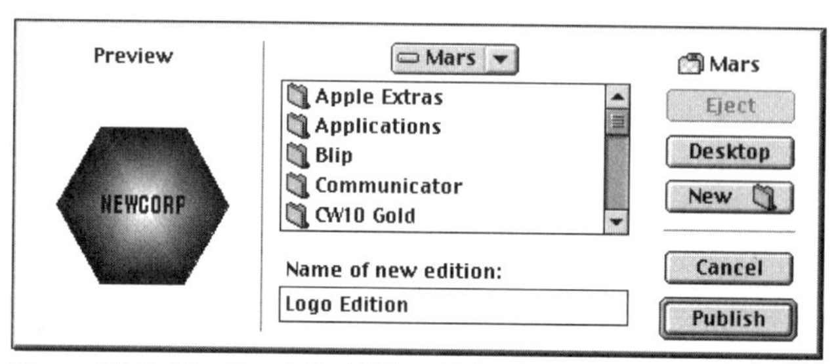

Figure 12-5: The Create Publisher dialog box.

The left side of this dialog box previews the elements that will be included in the edition. The edition contents depend not only on which elements were selected with the Create Publisher command, but also on the Select How Publisher Decides What to Publish option setting. This option is described in the section on the Publisher Options dialog box.

To complete the creation of the edition, enter a name in the Name of New Edition option box and select a destination to which the file will be saved. Then click the Publish button, which saves your new edition to disk.

There's now a new file on disk (separate from the document you're currently working in) that contains a copy of the elements you selected to publish. This file—this edition—will be placed into other documents and applications using the Subscribe To command. According to the options set in the Publisher Options dialog box, the edition will be updated to include any changes made to the elements it contains.

The Subscribe To Command

The Subscribe To command, the Publish/Subscribe equivalent of the Paste command, imports a copy of an edition file into the current document. When you choose this command, the Subscribe To dialog box appears (see Figure 12-6). The names of edition files appear in the scrolling list, and a preview of an edition appears when you select its filename. Select the edition you want, click the Subscribe button, and the chosen edition appears in your document.

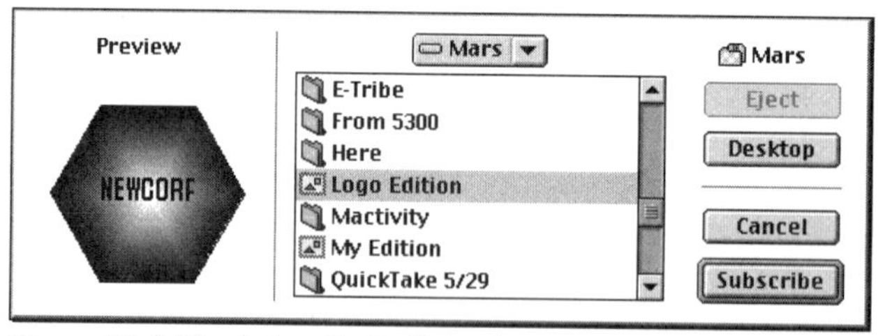

Figure 12-6: The Subscribe To dialog box.

When you're working in text-based applications, the edition appears at the place where the cursor was positioned when you chose the Subscribe To command. In graphics applications, the edition file usually appears in the current screen display area. Details on how to use these included editions follow.

The Publisher Options Command

The third Edition Manager command is either Publisher Options or Subscriber Options, depending on the current selection. The Publisher Options command, available only when you select the rectangle surrounding published elements, presents the dialog box shown in Figure 12-7.

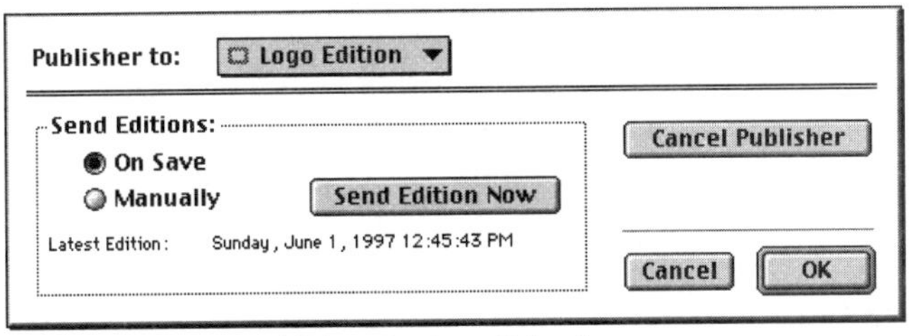

Figure 12-7: The Publisher Options dialog box.

You also can access the Publisher Options dialog box by double-clicking the border of any published elements.

This dialog box presents five important options:

- **Publisher To.** This menu is not really an option because it offers no alternatives; it simply shows you where the edition is stored and the path to that location. To see the storage location, click the Publisher To pop-up menu.
- **Send Editions.** This option lets you choose when the file associated with the selected edition will be updated. If you choose On Save, the edition file is updated each time the current document is saved; if you choose Manually, you must click the Send Edition Now button to update the edition file.

  This option also displays the date and time the edition file was last updated. If On Save is selected, this information probably indicates the date and time the creating file was last saved. If Manually is selected, the time the elements included in the edition were last changed is also listed, letting you know how up-to-date the edition is in relation to the file's current status.

- **Send Edition Now.** Clicking this button updates the edition file to reflect the current status of the published elements. This button is normally used only when Send Editions Manually is selected.
- **Select How Publisher Decides What to Publish.** As mentioned earlier, the light rectangle that appears after a Publisher has been created defines the portions of the current document to be included in the edition. With this option, you decide if the edition will include only objects completely inside the box or all elements (those partially enclosed as well as those fully enclosed).

  Select Clip if you want the edition to include all elements you select or partially select. Select Snap to include only fully enclosed elements (see Figure 12-8).

  Because the content of an edition is defined by a rectangle, you may notice some elements in the preview that were not selected when the Create Publisher command was selected. There's no way to exclude these elements, other than by altering the Select How Publisher Decides option.

Figure 12-8: Using the Snap option would exclude the whale from the edition created by the top example and the eagle from the edition file created by the bottom example. The Clip option would include both animals in both examples.

- **Cancel Publisher.** The Cancel Publisher button removes the link between the published elements in the current application and the edition file. Canceling the publisher does not delete the edition file, so it doesn't directly affect any documents that subscribe to that edition.

  You can't reestablish the link to an edition once it's been canceled (although you can use the Create Publisher command to create a new edition with the same name, saved in the same location), so you should use the Cancel Publisher button only in certain circumstances. It would be better to use the Send Editions Manually option to temporarily prevent editions from being updated.

  If you accidentally use the Cancel Publisher button, you may be able to undo it by exiting your document with the Close command, clicking the Don't Save button to avoid saving your changes, and then reopening the document with the Open command. (Of course, doing so means you lose any changes you've made.) The Revert command offered by some applications may also return your document to the state it was in before you canceled the Publisher.

The Subscriber Options Command

The Subscriber Options command can be selected only when a subscribed edition is selected, as shown by the dark rectangle around the edition. When you select an edition, the Subscriber Options dialog box, shown in Figure 12-9, appears.

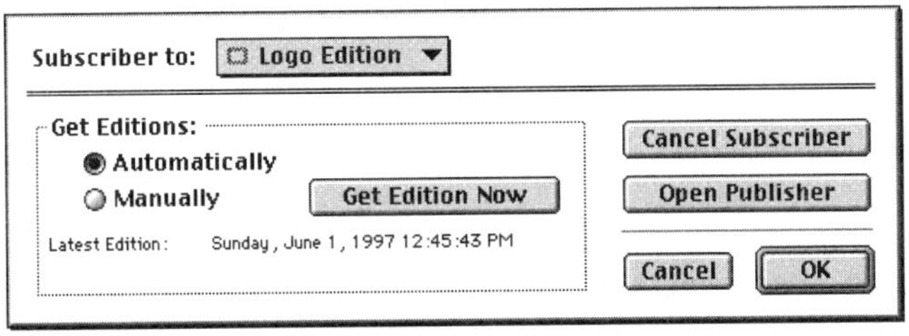

Figure 12-9: The Subscriber Options dialog box.

You also can access the Subscriber Options dialog box by double-clicking the subscribed elements.

This dialog box presents five options:

- **Subscriber To.** This menu offers no alternatives; it simply lets you see where the edition is stored and the path to that location. To see the storage location, click the Subscriber To pop-up menu.

- **Get Editions.** This option lets you choose when the edition elements will be updated to reflect any changes made to the edition file. The Automatically option causes any changes to the edition file to be imported each time you open the document or whenever the edition file changes; the Manually option requires you to click the Get Edition Now button in order for changes to the edition to be reflected in your document.

  If you choose Automatically, your document will always have the latest version of the text or graphic elements contained in the edition file. If you choose Manually, your document may not always reflect updates to the edition file, but you can choose when those updates are made.

  The date and time the current edition was last changed by the application that created it are displayed below the Get Editions option. If you selected Manually, the date and time the edition was imported into the current document are also listed. If these dates and times are not the same, the edition data contained in the current document is not up-to-date with the current edition file.

  If the dates and times are dimmed, the edition file can't be located; it's been deleted or moved to another volume. The link between the current document and the edition file has been broken.

- **Get Edition Now.** Clicking this button imports the current edition file contents into your document. It's normally used only when the Manually option is selected.

- **Cancel Subscriber.** The Cancel Subscriber button removes the link between the imported elements and the edition file. The imported elements remain in the current application, but future changes to the edition will not be reflected in the current publication.

  You cannot reestablish the link to an edition once it's been canceled (although you can use the Subscribe To command to create a new link to that same edition), so you should limit using the Cancel Subscriber button to particular circumstances. A better strategy would be to use the Get Editions Manually option to temporarily prevent editions from being updated in the subscribing document.

  If you accidentally use the Cancel Subscriber button, you may be able to undo it by exiting your document with the Close command, clicking the Don't Save button to avoid saving your changes, and then reopening the document with the Open command. (Of course, following these steps means you lose any changes you've made.) The Revert command offered by some applications may also return your document to the state it was in before you canceled the subscriber.

- **Open Publisher.** The Open Publisher button performs an impressive task indeed, launching the application that created the selected edition and opening the document from which the edition was published. This way, you can edit the contents of the edition using all the tools and capabilities of the application that originally created it.

There is no difference between using the Open Publisher button to both launch an application and open a document that created an edition and performing these same tasks using the Finder. The Open Publisher button just makes the process convenient. Changes you make to the open document will be reflected in the disk file and related edition files, depending on the settings you use in the Publisher Options dialog box and whether you use the Save command.

You also can modify the edition file without changing the original document, using the following steps after launching the application with the Open Publisher button: (1) set the Publisher options for the edition to Send Editions Manually; (2) make the necessary changes to the text or graphic elements; (3) click the Send Edition Now button in the Publisher Options dialog box; (4) close the document or quit the application without saving your changes. The edition file will now be updated, but the original document and any other editions will remain unchanged.

The Show Borders Command

Rectangular borders distinguish elements in your document that have been published in an edition file from elements that are part of another edition file that's been subscribed to. The border around published elements is light (about a 50 percent screen); the border around subscribed elements is dark (about a 75 percent screen), as shown in Figure 12-10.

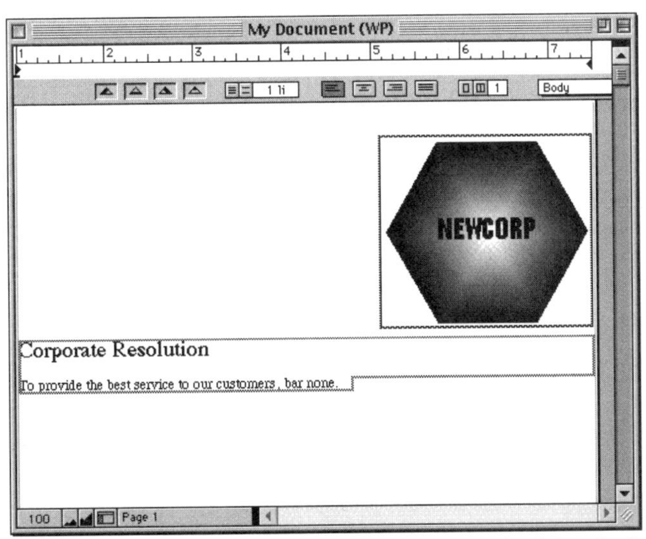

Figure 12-10: Borders surround published elements (right) and subscribed elements (left).

The Show Borders command toggles the display of these borders, allowing you to hide or display them as necessary. Regardless of the Show Borders command setting, borders always appear when a publisher or subscriber is selected. Borders never appear on printed versions of your documents—they're for onscreen use only.

Editing Subscribers

Because the contents of a subscriber are provided by an edition file and are usually updated periodically (according to the setting in the Subscriber Options dialog box), there are limits to manipulating a subscriber within any document. In general, you can't make any changes that would be lost when a new version of the edition becomes available.

The following are some of the limitations in editing subscribers:

- **Text subscribers.** With subscribers that include only text, you can't edit the text when subscribing to the edition. The only exception is that you can set the font, type size, or type style of the text as long as the change applies to the entire subscriber text. You can't make one word in the edition bold or set one sentence in a different font.
- **Graphic subscribers.** When using subscribers that include graphics, you can reposition the editions you've subscribed to, but in most cases you can't resize them. (If you are permitted to resize the subscriber, graphic handles appear on the corners of the subscriber border.)
- **Text in graphic subscribers.** The text in a graphic subscriber cannot be modified in any way. In the subscriber, the text is considered a part of the graphic element.

The correct way to edit a subscriber is to reopen the document that published the edition, make changes in that document, and then save those changes or use the Send Edition Now button to update the edition. You can quickly access the original document for any edition by clicking the Open Publisher button in the Subscriber Options dialog box.

Edition Files at the Finder

The edition files created with the Create Publisher command look just like any other files on your disks. They use a small shaded rectangle icon like the one surrounding editions in publishing or subscribing applications; you can add comments to them using the Get Info command.

Double-clicking an edition file in the Finder opens a window (shown in Figure 12-11) that contains the edition contents, the edition type (PICT and so on), and the Open Publisher button. The Open Publisher button launches the application that created the document from which the edition file was created and opens that document.

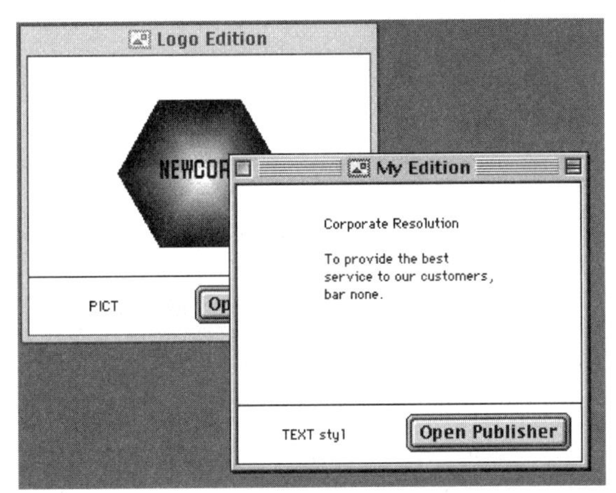

Figure 12-11: These windows are opened by clicking edition files.

You work only on the document that created the edition, not on the edition file. Any changes made to the edition elements are then updated to the edition file (based on the options in the Publisher Options dialog box). Therefore, deleting a file that has published editions makes it impossible to modify or update those editions again—the data in the editions cannot be accessed from either the edition file or the subscriber document.

Edition File Links

The link between edition files and their publishers and subscribers is automatically maintained even if you rename or move these documents to new locations on the current volume. If you move an edition file, publishing document, or subscribing document to a new volume and delete the copy on the original volume, the links to and from the file will be broken.

When links to or from an edition file are broken, it's impossible to automatically or manually update the edition file or the version of that edition file used in any subscribing documents. You can tell that a link is broken by the notification "Edition cannot be found" in the Subscriber To dialog box, as shown in Figure 12-12.

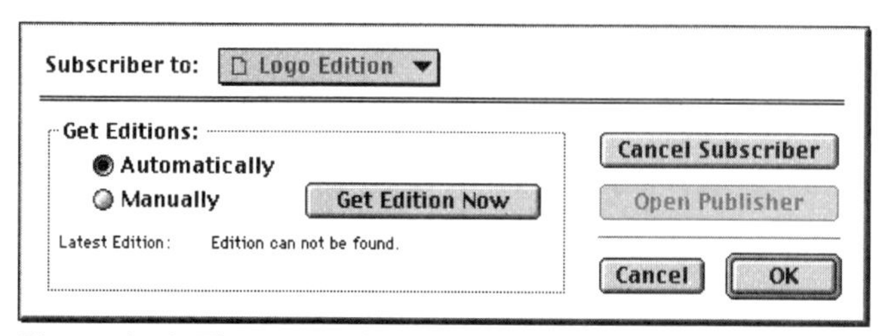

Figure 12-12: The Latest Edition line changes when the edition has been deleted or moved to another volume.

Although there's no direct way to "reconnect" a broken Publisher or Subscriber link, you can recreate a link between an application and an edition published from it:

1. Open the application and select the border surrounding the previously created edition. Even though the link has been broken, the border will still be visible.
2. Select the Create Publisher command and save the edition with the same name as the previous edition to the same location as the previous edition, overwriting the unlinked copy that remains.
3. Any Subscribers using this edition will now update according to their option settings, using the information in this new version of the edition.

To re-create a link between an edition and a subscribing application:

1. Open the subscribing application and select the element that was imported as a subscribed edition.
2. Select the Subscribe To command and locate the edition file to which you want to re-create a link. Then click the Subscribe button.
3. The data from the edition file as it now exists will appear in your document, replacing the older version that was selected. This edition is now linked to the edition file on disk and will update according to the settings of the Publisher and Subscriber options.

Unavailable Edition Files

When you open a document containing subscribers, the Macintosh attempts to locate edition files linked to each subscriber. If any of these edition files reside on unmounted floppy disks or removable volumes, you'll be prompted to insert the disks or volumes. Then the document will open normally, and the links between the subscribers and their edition files will be maintained.

Edition Files & Your Network

Edition files can be published to or subscribed from any available network or File Sharing volume. There's no real difference in the way they operate on network/File Sharing volumes except that documents containing publishers and subscribers must access the editions over the network in order to keep all files updated properly.

To expedite sharing editions via a network, you can create aliases of editions stored on network volumes that you access frequently. You can then browse these aliases on your local hard drive (from the Subscribe To dialog box), and when the editions are used, the aliases will automatically connect to the appropriate network volumes and access the edition files.

To subscribe directly to editions on network volumes, aliases will also mount automatically when you open documents subscribing to the editions.

Figure 12-13 shows one sample network. In this case, edition files could be stored on the AppleShare file server or on either File Sharing Mac to be used either directly or through aliases by any network user.

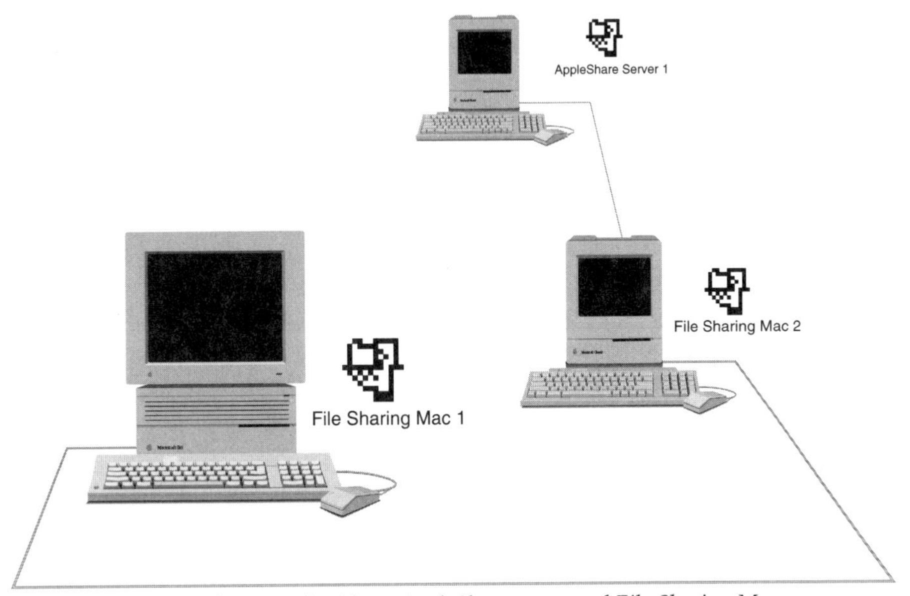

Figure 12-13: A sample network with an AppleShare server and File Sharing Macs.

Edition Manager Tips

The following are several tips you can use when working with the Edition Manager:

- **Republishing an edition.** If you overwrite an edition (by creating a new edition with the same name in the same location as an existing edition), the new edition will be linked to all documents that subscribed to the old edition.

  For example, if you wanted to replace an existing edition file named Corporate Logo with a new graphic, you could use the Create Publisher command to create a new edition named Corporate Logo and save it in the same volume and folder as the old Corporate Logo edition. (When you're asked to confirm that you want to overwrite the old file, click the Yes button.) At this point, all documents that subscribed to the old Corporate Logo edition file will begin using the new Corporate Logo edition file the next time they're updated.

- **Using nested editions.** You can create editions that contain text or graphics subscribed to from other editions (see Figure 12-14). After you set appropriate updating options in all associated Publish To and Subscribe To dialog boxes, changes you make to elements in original documents will be correctly updated everywhere they occur.

  For example, if your page layout program subscribed to your Corporate Logo document for the purpose of using it, along with some text and ornamental graphics, to create a corporate insignia, you could use the Create Publisher command to save an edition file named Corporate Insignia. This edition could then be subscribed to for use on the first page of all corporate reports created in your word processing programs. If the Corporate Logo edition was updated, this update would appear in the page layout file (where the insignia was created) and extend to the Corporate Insignia edition when the page layout document was opened (assuming the Publisher options and Subscriber options were set correctly). The updated Corporate Insignia edition would then be updated in all documents in which it was used (if you set the appropriate Subscriber option).

- **Double-clicking edition borders to open option dialogs.** Double-clicking a subscriber in a document will open the Subscriber To dialog box. Double-clicking the border around any publisher will open the Publisher To dialog box. This is Apple's recommended behavior, but some vendors implement this feature and others do not.

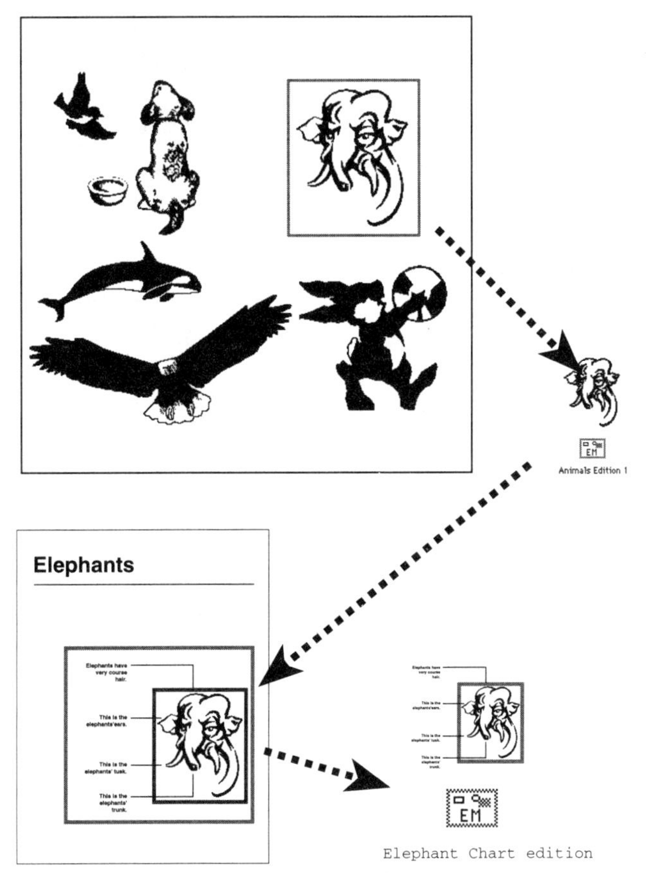

Figure 12-14: Edition files can contain other editions.

- **Saving Publisher documents.** When an edition is created, the edition file appears on disk and can be subscribed to immediately. If the document that published the edition is closed without being saved, however, the edition file will be deleted, and all subscriber links will be broken.

  For example, you open a drawing application and quickly create an illustration of a cow jumping over the moon. Using the Create Publisher command, you create an edition named Cow Over Moon and then switch to your word processor where you subscribe to the Cow Over Moon edition and continue to work on your text document. Later, when you're ready to quit for the day, you choose the Shut Down command from the Finder's Special menu, and your drawing application asks whether you want to save the untitled file you used to create Cow Over Moon. At this point, if you don't name and save this file, the Cow Over Moon edition will be deleted from your disk. The image will remain in the word processing document that subscribed to it, but the link between the word processing document and the deleted edition file will be broken. It will be impossible to edit the graphic in the future without re-creating it.

- **Using edition aliases.** You can subscribe to edition file aliases just like you subscribe to standard edition files. As always, the alias file will maintain a link to the original file even if you move or rename the alias or the original. If the alias's original document is on a network server or File Sharing volume, the volume is mounted automatically.

Publish and Subscribe has been available now for many years, but it gets very little press in Macintosh literature. Apparently, few users make good use of this powerful feature. Perhaps having the data and publisher application available remotely is difficult for people to conceptualize. That's too bad because Publish and Subscribe is powerful—and it's easy to use.

A similar concept in Microsoft Windows is the linking in Object Linking & Embedding, or OLE. You can link data automatically (hot link) or manually (warm link). When you open a linked document, Windows posts a dialog box asking whether you want the data updated. OLE uses Dynamic Data Exchange, or DDE (introduced in Windows 3.0), as its messaging system. DDE is similar to AppleEvents, which is described in the next section. DDE lets one application pass data to and from another through the Windows clipboard with a reference to the source of the data. DDE is just one layer of OLE's functioning. OLE is similar to OpenDoc; both are discussed in more detail later in the chapter.

Interapplication Communication

Publish and Subscribe, like the Cut, Copy, and Paste commands, are examples of how the Macintosh system software lets applications share data and communicate indirectly with each other. System 7 also provides even broader application-to-application communication, known as Interapplication Communication (IAC). Mac OS 8 continues upgrading the capabilities of IAC.

IAC provides a structural framework within which software applications can send messages and data to other software applications. These capabilities make the Macintosh more powerful in many ways. They reduce the pressure on any one application to "do it all," allowing each application to specialize in what it does best.

Spell-checking is a good example. Almost every Macintosh application allows text to be created, and over the last few years, many have added built-in spelling checkers, each with its own version and its own dictionary files. You have to learn and remember how each one works and make room for each data file on your hard drive. And the developers of each program have to spend time and money developing and testing utilities.

Suppose, instead, that one independent spelling checker was the best of them all, offering the biggest dictionaries, the most features, and the best user interface. Using IAC, all your software applications could access this one spelling checker, saving you the hassle of learning multiple commands, customizing multiple dictionaries, and wasting hard drive space on duplicate files. And your software developers could spend their time and money on other things, such as improving their applications' features.

Understanding AppleEvents

The mechanics of IAC are quite technical, but fortunately you don't need to know anything about them unless you intend to write your own Macintosh programs. You'll be aware of IAC when your software takes advantage of its features; but even then, the entire IAC operation will be translated into friendly Macintosh commands and dialog boxes you're already familiar with (so you can skip the rest of this section, if you'd like). However, if you have an interest in AppleScript, Apple's systemwide macro programming language (the subject of the next chapter), this subject will interest you because AppleEvents is the fundamental messaging system upon which AppleScript is based.

IAC is a protocol that defines a type of communication between applications and provides a mechanism for the delivery and implementation of that communication. You can think of IAC as a set of grammatical rules that make up an acceptable format for messages sent between applications. A message in this format is an AppleEvent.

For example, an application issues an AppleEvent to another application. The AppleEvent is normally a command like "Open filename and Copy Data record #, fieldname," followed by the sending application pasting the data somewhere. Using this kind of mechanism, it is possible to link a directory with a to-do list with a calendar. In fact, some of the first and best implementations of AppleEvents have been in the personal information manager (PIMs) category.

In addition to the AppleEvents format, IAC provides a messenger service to transmit the properly formatted message from one application to another.

Although IAC defines the communication format, it doesn't specify the message content. The "language" of AppleEvents is being defined by Apple and by the Macintosh software developer community in cooperation with

Apple. This cooperation is very important; a computer language designed to communicate between a variety of software applications developed by different companies must be carefully constructed in order to accomplish its goal of facilitating precise communication.

For an application to send an AppleEvent or to understand an AppleEvent it receives, the program must be specifically programmed to handle it properly. This interoperability is why it's impossible for non-System 7-savvy applications to use IAC. Only when the AppleEvents language is clearly defined can software developers update their programs to engage in an AppleEvents dialog properly.

AppleEvents are described by commands and actions that act on objects. You can think of these constructs as being roughly equivalent to verbs and nouns in the programming language, as you will see in the next chapter. AppleEvents include nouns and verbs in their definition descriptors, as you can see when you open an application's AppleEvent dictionary. To help software developers implement program support, Apple classified AppleEvents into categories called suites. The suites are as follow:

- **Required suite.** Open Application, Open Document, Print Document, Run Application, and Quit Application are the four basic AppleEvents and the only ones required for applications. Think of them as the Hello, Please, Thank You, Start, and Good-bye of AppleEvents. This suite is the smallest of the standard suites.
- **Core suite.** These AppleEvents are not as universal or fundamental as those in the Required suite, but they're general enough that almost every Macintosh application should support them. The list of Core AppleEvents, quite large already, is growing as Apple and its software developers work to make sure every type of communication that may be needed is provided for. Using the Core suite applications, you can perform a wide range of tasks.
- **Text suite.** The Text suite supports AppleEvents used by word processors, page layout applications, and other applications that use text editing functions. The Core suite contains minimal text functions, so the Text suite is for a higher level of support than simple text functions used in dialog boxes.
- **QuickDraw Graphics suite.** QuickDraw events define actions required to draw simple graphics to your monitor, printers, or other devices. Most graphics programs adopt this suite. The QuickDraw Graphics Supplemental suite contains additions and extensions to the original suite, such as the ability to rotate objects, and it is yet another level of graphics messaging support.

- **Table suite.** Tables are a fundamental property of spreadsheets, databases, and other systems that use two-dimensional data arrays. This suite provides data addressing, retrieval, and modification capabilities. Other suites, like the Database suite and Spreadsheet suites, provide complementary functions.
- **Finder suite.** Starting with System 7.5, a set of 13 Finder commands and actions was added to the Finder. Actions such as copy, trashing, and other Finder events are supported. See "The Scriptable Finder" in the next chapter for more information.

  The Finder suite contains the following items: open about box, copy to, duplicate, empty trash, make aliases for, move to, sleep, shut down, open, print, put away, restart, and select.
- **Miscellaneous suite.** Apple groups events that don't quite fit into other suites into this grab bag of miscellaneous events. Utilizing this suite allows Apple to extend Inter-Application Communication without having to define large numbers of small suites. There are now many specialized suites in the AppleEvent Registry. Some examples are the Mail, the Personal Information, and the Telephony suites.
- **Custom suites.** A Macintosh software developer might have a need for AppleEvents designed for proprietary or cooperative use by its own applications. If a developer's word processor included a unique feature not controllable with any existing Core- or Functional-area AppleEvents, the company could define its own Custom AppleEvent. This AppleEvent could be kept secret and used only by the software developer's applications, or it could be shared with other software developers. Some examples of custom suites are Aladdin System's StuffIt suite, Apple's HyperCard suite, and CE Software's QuicKeys suite.

  You can see in FileMaker Pro 2.0 a custom suite that is a subset of Core, Table, and Database suites. That suite also contains some FileMaker-specific commands. FileMaker Pro also contains a FileMaker suite with two classes: menu and menu items. You can view supported suites using the Open Dictionary command in the File menu of the Script Editor, a standard part of the AppleScript package. Figure 12-15 shows the FileMaker suite in the FileMaker dictionary. Refer to the discussion in the next chapter on application dictionaries.

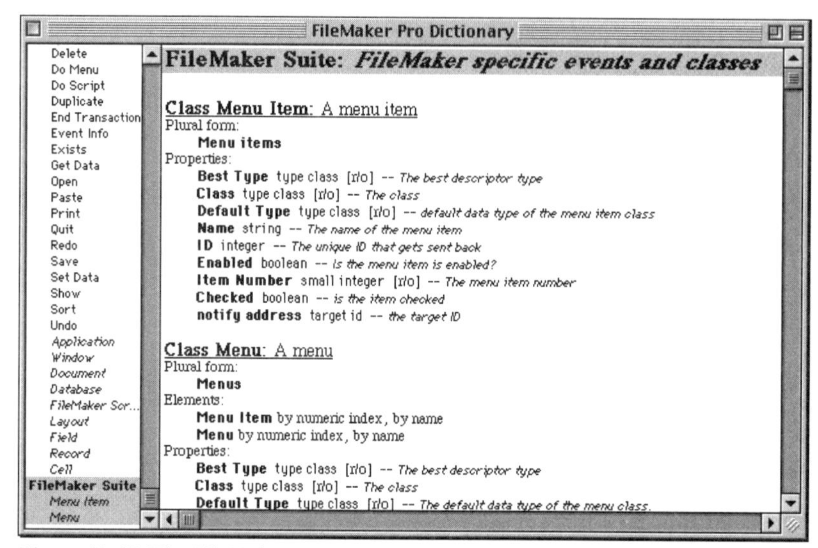

Figure 12-15: The FileMaker suite viewed in the FileMaker Pro dictionary.

The entire current list of AppleEvents, along with detailed descriptions of each, is regularly sent to all Macintosh software developers so they can incorporate these events into their software updates. Apple compiles a standard AppleEvent Registry to which developers can refer.

You can obtain a copy of the current support levels of your favorite applications in a more readable form (and for free) by obtaining the brochure, *AppleScript Guide to Scriptable Applications*, published by Apple. Request this guide by contacting Apple at the Internet address, applescript@applelink.com, or by calling 408-996-1010. You can get the AppleEvent Registry: Standard Suites ($85) and the AppleEvent Education Suite v. 1.0 ($25) from the APDA by calling 716-871-6555. AppleEvents have been largely a developer's tool, and end users typically don't even know they exist.

AppleEvents & Program Linking

When an application sends an AppleEvent to another program, the receiving program is usually launched and then asked to perform a task. Of course, this process assumes that the receiving program is available. In addition to being able to communicate with programs that exist on the same hard drive, AppleShare events, through IAC, can communicate with programs that reside on other parts of a network as well.

AppleEvents have found their first important use linking small related programs together into a more capable system. Several Personal Information Managers use AppleEvents to achieve data exchanges between modules and to make them more powerful and seamless. Other candidates for AppleEvents projects are flat-file databases that require relational capabilities and application or system macros. In the next chapter, you will learn how to use the Script Editor to record AppleEvent scripts.

Chapter 16, "File Sharing," introduces the System 7 capability that lets any user on the network share data with any other user on the network.

In Chapter 17, "Working on a Network," you'll learn about the Program Linking option, which allows you to access software from other Macintoshes on the network via IAC commands. If you use this option, applications on one Macintosh can use AppleEvents to communicate with applications on other Macs across the network. As with other aspects of IAC, it remains to be seen how this capability will be translated into new Macintosh software features.

OpenDoc

As computers get more powerful and the industry matures, you would expect them to get easier to use. That has not been the case. There's been a trend in the industry to release ever more feature-filled software packages, as if the quality of a program is measured by the number of check-offs it can achieve on a feature list. Word processors now contain spell checkers, grammar checkers, thesauruses, page layout modules, graphics, charting, outlining, idea processing, table of contents and index generation, databases and mail merges, envelope label printers, telephone and fax machines, and e-mail message centers.

What's a user to do? You can hardly find these "features," let alone learn about them. Only "get-a-lifers" can love the current state of the software industry. If there were no penalty to pay, you could safely ignore the stuff you weren't interested in. However, extra features burn up processing power and disk space. Checked your hard drive lately? There are probably half a dozen spell checkers lurking about in there. This trend has probably reached its peak with the release of huge, everything-including-the-kitchen-sink packages such as Microsoft Office, Lotus SmartSuite, and Novell's WordPerfect office package.

Vendors have long noted the problem. It's both a resource management opportunity and an industry barrier. Large programs from large software houses crowd out innovative small products from small companies. One solution is to link small programs into a compound document architecture with an object-oriented framework and Interapplication Communication. Then you can buy and learn just the functions you need—one text editor, one spell checker, one paint module, and so on.

With this goal, Apple and a consortium of partners, including IBM, pursued an industry-wide standard called OpenDoc. OpenDoc is an architecture under which documents are built. OpenDoc is the result of the "Amber" project at Apple, with other technologies added to the mix by the other vendors in the program.

What Is OpenDoc?

Users viewing demonstrations of OpenDoc have described it as a "bug fix" because it fits into a natural way of working with data objects as parts in a compound document. A compound document is much more natural than an application-centered document: you don't have to do context switching between applications to get the capabilities you need. Just click a part and the menu changes. You don't even notice it. But when you go to the menu, the command you expect to use for that part is there. Need a part? Just add it. OpenDoc supplies the reference to the appropriate part handler.

OpenDoc offers the following user benefits:

- **Easy creation of compound documents.** You use the same Cut and Paste, Drag and Drop, Publish and Subscribe, and other metaphorical commands that you are used to. It looks and feels like a Macintosh. OpenDoc uses the Open Scripting Architecture (OSA), of which AppleEvents and AppleScript are a part, as its messaging medium.
- **In-place editing.** Point at and click what you want to change. Cut and Paste, Drag and Drop, and most other aspects of data handling you've come to know are also supported.
- **Improved multitasking.** You can have several parts "playing" at the same time in the same document. For example, you could have a clock and a video running while you work in a text file. OpenDoc provides multithreaded, multitasked system time-slicing among all three parts.
- **Central data storage and unified document management.** All your data pieces are in your document; only the services needed to use them are referenced. Therefore, data can't be lost or inaccessible as it can be in the Publish and Subscribe model. You also can track the revision history of your document.
- **Cross-platform support.** OpenDoc is a vendor-neutral, platform-neutral specification supported by major industry players. As yet, Microsoft doesn't directly support OpenDoc. They sell a competing compound document architecture called Object Linking & Embedding (OLE 2.0).

In order to promote OpenDoc and make it an open standard, a non-profit association called the Component Integration Laboratories (or CI Labs) was formed. CI Labs published the OpenDoc standard. It was not only responsible for making OpenDoc available to everybody, it also provided rigorous testing and evaluation procedures to approve software under the program. Apple pulled out of CI Labs in early 1997, and the organization was dissolved soon thereafter.

OpenDoc can work with other compound document architectures such as Microsoft's OLE 2.0 and Taligent's forthcoming operating system, so you can open a document created in those architectures and have access to the services referenced within them.

- **Consistency of operation and uniformity of interface.** Use one part editor for each data type. When your needs grow, you can upgrade to a more powerful editor. OpenDoc defines a consistent user interface for documents, parts, and part handlers.

OpenDoc has the potential to profoundly impact the way you use your Macintosh. It will make it much easier for you to customize your environment or for vendors to provide quality vertical market packages (software written for a niche audience) suitable for your line of work.

Documents & Parts

OpenDoc adds a few additional words to the vocabulary of the Macintosh user. But these words are based on common ones you use in your everyday speech, so they shouldn't be much of a burden. Documents are the central framework in OpenDoc. A document is no longer tied to a single application but is composed of small pieces of content called parts.

Parts are the fundamental building blocks in OpenDoc. They have the same relationship to documents that atoms have to molecules. Parts come in flavors, which are content containers. Text parts contain characters; graphics parts contain lines and shapes; spreadsheet parts contain cells, formulas, and a spreadsheet engine; video parts contain digitized video sequences and a player; and so on. OpenDoc makes its best effort to compartmentalize capabilities within part types, although some mixing occurs. The type of data in each part is known as the part's intrinsic content.

Parts can contain other parts (embedding), so a document has a part hierarchy. That is, at its root level, a document has a single part in which other parts are embedded. Developers must decide whether their parts can embed other parts, but if the parts can be embedded, they can accept any type of part.

Parts are created and modified by part editors. These editors are small programs that are called upon by an OpenDoc document—system routines really. Some part editors will ship with the OpenDoc package so that in system software you will have basic capability right out of the box. This capability is similar to current functions of system software such as TextEdit, QuickDraw, the Communications Toolbox, and other routines that let you work with parts of the Macintosh interface in standard ways.

Part handlers are more complex editors that third parties create for OpenDoc. You buy them shrink-wrapped in stores. Part handlers are the equivalent of applications; they are responsible for the following functions under the OpenDoc architecture:

- **Displaying the part onscreen and rendering it to a printer.**
- **Editing the part.**
- **Storage and management.** The part handler reads and writes the part to and from memory and disk. For this reason, part handlers can be of two types: editors and viewers. Many will be both.
- **Acting as an interface modifier.** The editor part handler is responsible for switching menu commands, adjusting dialog boxes, and changing the interface to make available whatever tools a part requires. A viewer part handler is a subset of an editor; it allows users to display and print a part but not edit it. You use viewers to provide security lockout features for parts in documents.

Another important concept in OpenDoc is that of frames. Whereas parts are areas of one kind of content, frames are the boundaries separating the collection of objects and operations supported by one part from those supported by another. You can embed a button in a part, and that compound construct is a frame that can be manipulated. Frames have properties such as layering (front to back), transparency, and so on that will be familiar to users of draw graphics programs. In Figure 12-16, you see a frame with a clock. Other parts in the document—the button, the text, and the molecule graphic—are not part of the clock frame. It may be helpful to think of frames as grouped collections of objects; each grouped collection has its own identity.

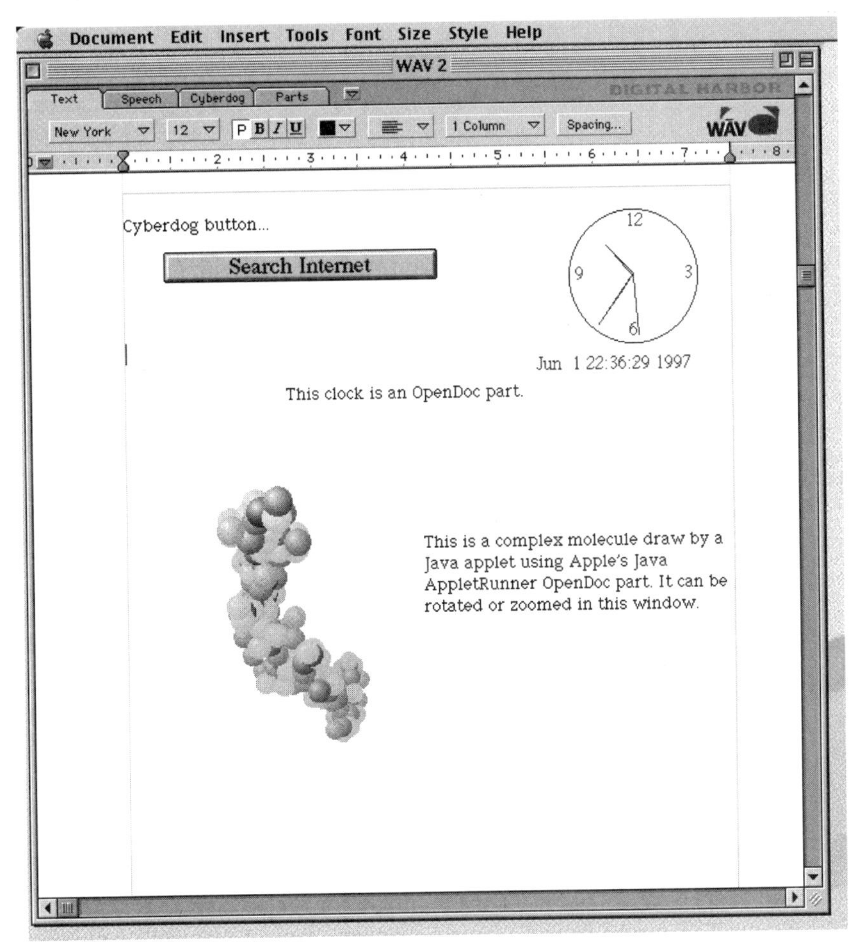

Figure 12-16: An OpenDoc document with a frame and several parts.

Thankfully, it's much harder to explain what a frame is than it is to use one. The notion is almost entirely transparent to the user. Frames are not simply windows that appear or disappear from view; they are persistent. When you open a frame in a window, you see the frame. When you close that window, the part returns to the condition it was in before you opened the window. A frame can show however much of its contents is displayed. That is, if a frame contains a graphic larger than the frame, you would see the cropped part of that graphic within the frame.

Storage of compound documents requires a system of saving the document to disk with each part referenced to its part handler. OpenDoc uses an object-oriented storage model based on Apple's Bento standard. Storing a document to disk compartmentalizes each part as a data object and provides references to appropriate part handlers. Opening that document begins a process of calling appropriate part handlers one after another to "build" the document in memory. When you move an OpenDoc document to another computer or type of computer, these part handler references let the OpenDoc document be opened by other appropriate handlers when the creator part handler isn't available. This system ensures cross-platform capabilities and also provides a mechanism for collaborative access. You can write part handlers that are both multiuser and version-history sensitive.

OpenDoc Menus

OpenDoc applications have a slightly different menu bar than the usual Mac program. The File menu is replaced with a new menu, the Document menu. Since the basic idea behind OpenDoc is that users will work on "documents" instead of individual files, this makes more sense. However, it is a bit disconcerting to see the good old File menu replaced. Other menus work, act, and look the same as with non-OpenDoc apps.

Take a look at Figure 12-17, the Document menu from Digital Harbor's WAV word processor. All of the things you'd expect from the File menu are there. Here are the items you can expect from any OpenDoc Document menu:

- **New.** Opens a new, empty document.
- **Open document.** Opens a previously created document from the disk drive.
- **Insert.** Inserts the contents of the file you select into the current document.
- **Close.** Closes the current document.
- **Save.** Saves the current document.
- **Page Setup and Print.** These items work as you'd expect.

Figure 12-17: The OpenDoc Document menu isn't too different from the old-fashioned File menu.

OpenDoc Control Panels

Since OpenDoc is completely modular, you might have more than one editor that can work on a particular piece of data. For instance, you might have a text frame in a document. If you want to edit that text, any text editing part will do. But what if you have more than one? Luckily, you can choose which editor you want to use on a particular kind of data.

The Editor Setup Control Panel (in Figure 12-18) lets you do so. To choose an editor, simply open the Control Panel, find the part type, select it, and click the Choose Editor button. It will display all editors you have installed that can work with that kind of data. In Figure 12-19, I've chosen to use a Cyberdog editor.

Editor Setup

Kind	Category	Editor
Other Outline	Outline	Cyberdog Notebook Manager 2.0
Other Page Layout	Page Layout	WAV
Other Painting	Painting	Cyberdog Picture Viewer 2.0
Other Plain Text	Plain Text	Cyberdog Text Viewer 2.0
Text	Plain Text	Cyberdog Text Viewer 2.0
Text	Plain Text	WAV
application/text	Plain Text	Cyberdog Text Viewer 2.0
text/plain	Plain Text	WAV
Other Query	Query	Cyberdog News Search 2.0
Other Sampled Sound	Sampled Sound	Cyberdog QuickTime Viewer 2.0

Note: Changes take effect for the next document that is opened.

Show All   Choose Editor...

Figure 12-18: The Editor Setup Control Panel lets you match parts to editors.

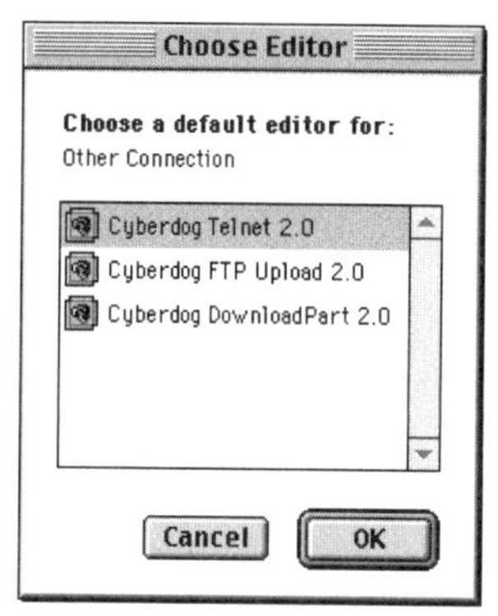

Figure 12-19: The Choose Editor dialog shows you all parts that can edit the data type you've selected.

One more Control Panel to know about is OpenDoc Setup (Figure 12-20). This Control Panel lets you set two things: the amount of RAM allocated to new OpenDoc documents and whether and when OpenDoc is on (loaded into RAM) or off (unloaded).

If you use OpenDoc all the time, you might decide to leave it on from system start-up to system shutdown. To do this, simply click the radio buttons for Start OpenDoc at System Startup and Stop OpenDoc at System Shutdown. However, the default settings start and stop OpenDoc so that it's not loaded when it's not being used. This is probably the best setting for most people.

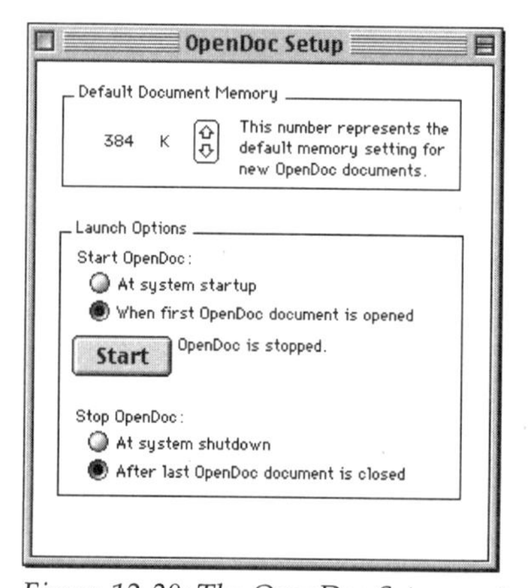

Figure 12-20: The OpenDoc Setup controls RAM settings for OpenDoc.

Moving On

Edition Manager allows you to transfer text and graphics between applications, while maintaining a "live link" to the original data, using just a few simple commands:

- **Create Publisher.** This command saves the selected data to a new edition file on disk.
- **Subscribe To.** This command imports an edition file from disk into the current document.
- **Publish/Subscribe options.** These commands control the way changes to original documents are updated to the edition file and documents subscribing to the edition file.

The OpenDoc architecture provides a framework for creating compound documents using small applications. While OpenDoc provides a glimpse of the possible future of software and is included in System 8, Apple has put the project into maintenance mode and no further updates other than bug fixes are expected. Apple is concentrating its component programming efforts on the forthcoming Rhapsody operating system.

AppleEvents provides a rich object-oriented messaging language that IAC uses to let applications talk to one another. As you will see in Chapter 13, "AppleScript," this system software programming tool uses AppleEvents and a natural programming language to let you automate many actions into easy-to-use programs.

CHAPTER 13

AppleScript

When the first version of MS-DOS shipped with the IBM PC in 1983, it came bundled with a version of the Basic programming language. PC users could control their computers and operating systems. With programs called batch files, they could start programs automatically, repeat actions, do timed backups, set the operating environment, and more. Over the years, Macintosh owners have gazed longingly upon those capabilities—one of the few areas in which the PC was more gifted, out of the box, than the Macintosh.

Although several third-party developers provide systemwide macro programming tools—most notably UserLand's Frontier, Affinity Microsystems's Tempo II Plus, WestCode Software's One Click, and CE Software's QuicKeys—none of them were officially blessed by Apple, nor have they achieved broad enough support in the Macintosh community to become a standard. Either they were too hard to learn, or they were too easy to learn but not powerful enough. Apple finally released its own programming language, AppleScript, to provide these much needed capabilities as part of an overall strategy meant to provide automation tools across Macintosh applications and beyond.

AppleScript has many different kinds of applications:

- Users can use AppleScript to tailor applications and their desktops to their needs.
- AppleScript simplifies the work of developers, systems integrators, and Value Added Resellers (VARs), providing custom solutions based upon standard Macintosh applications.

- AppleScript allows you to seamlessly integrate small components into larger solutions. You could write an *applet*, an *intelligent agent*, or *a smart document* using AppleScript. This capability is part of Apple's strategy for downsizing applications, of which Inter-Application Communication, AppleEvents, and OpenDoc (described in the preceding chapter) are part.
- New product opportunities are created using AppleScript. You'll see some of these possibilities in Apple Guide and PlainTalk, which incorporate, can be controlled by, and in turn can use AppleScript to control other applications.

AppleScript is a pervasive part of the Macintosh operating system—even if you don't use it for programming, at least you will use it routinely.

What Is AppleScript?

AppleScript is a high-level, object-oriented, natural-language type of programming language. It is a real programming language: it can store variables and lists (records or arrays); repeat through looping; make decisions based on cases; do IF branching; compare; do Boolean logic; and manipulate text, numbers, dates, times, and other values. AppleScript can also declare variables, create user-defined commands or subroutines, and store and manipulate data to return values.

AppleScript is an object-oriented programming language because it imposes actions on objects that are defined as part of its programming model: objects can be applications (Finder, Scriptable Text Editor, FileMaker, and so on), files, resources, interface elements (buttons, windows, and so on) and data. In the Finder, objects can be a variety of named Macintoshes, printers, and even AppleTalk zones on a network. Objects you can see on your desktop can be manipulated with AppleScript, a capability made even easier with the Scriptable Finder introduced in System 7.5 (described later in this chapter).

Objects have two additional characteristics that are programmatic: *inheritance* and *encapsulation*. Objects, like applications, can contain other objects (encapsulation); objects derived from other objects share common characteristics (inheritance). Third-party applications behave as if they are object-oriented databases to AppleScript because they contain a group of objects. These features impose regularity to objects, making them behave in ways you expect and have come to learn intuitively.

AppleScript uses words and statements to form scripts. Words are nouns (objects), verbs, and modifiers. Verbs are common action commands such as open, close, print, or delete. Often verbs are derived from standard menu commands. Statements are commands that can be communicated in the form of messages to objects in other applications. Applications themselves are objects because they can be commanded to do actions.

As an example of an AppleScript statement, consider the following:

```
tell application "Scriptable Text Editor" to activate the window name
"Untitled."
```

This one-line statement is a complete script that instructs the Scriptable Text Editor to search its list of opened windows, and if an "Untitled" window is open, it makes that the frontmost active window. The formatting of this statement with bolded verbs, plain nouns, and italicized variables is traditional but not required. Often you will see AppleScripts written in clegic logic (or display) format, with indentations for each command structure. You can see an example of this formatting in the Add Alias to Apple Menu AppleScript, which is shipped with the collection of Useful Scripts of System 7.5. It is shown in the Script Editor window in Figure 13-1.

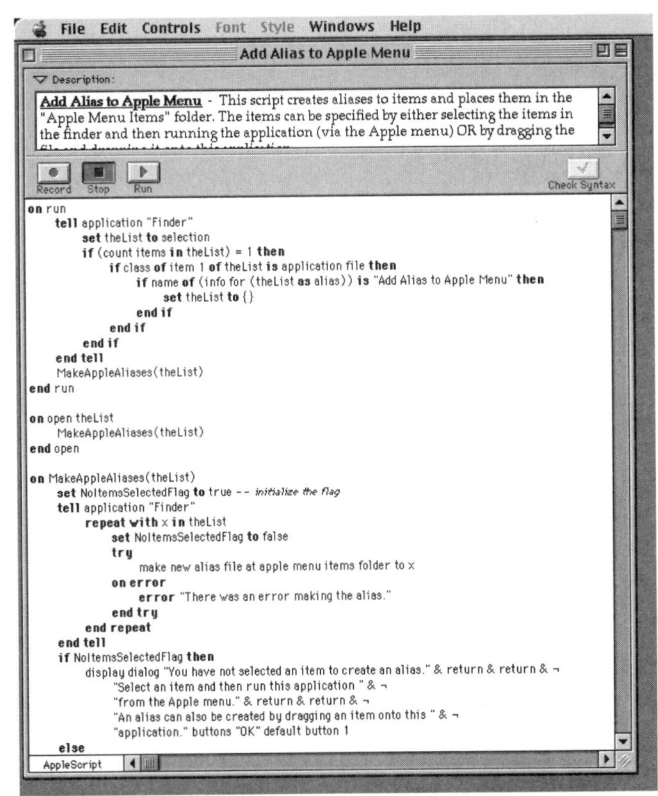

Figure 13-1: The Add Alias to Apple Menu AppleScript shown in the Script Editor window.

As much as possible, AppleScript is written in a manner similar to the way you write and speak. The syntax is much more precise and demanding, to be sure. But the intent is to lower the learning curve for AppleScript by using words, expressions, and modifiers that you use in your everyday life in the English language. Other dialects of AppleScript exist for other languages: French, German, Japanese Kanji, and so on.

The programs you write in AppleScript, called *scripts*, are like those you write for all other high-level programming languages. Scripts must be interpreted and compiled to run on your Macintosh. You can store scripts for interpretation at run time, or you can transform your script into interpreted read-only programs that you can distribute freely to other users. When you compile an AppleScript, it is transformed into a dialect-independent format called *Universal AppleScript*. If you open an AppleScript, you will see the script displayed in the default language of the Macintosh you're working on, not necessarily the language in which the script was originally written. A translation from Universal AppleScript has been done.

AppleScript also supports dialects similar to more traditional programming languages such as C. When a programmer writes a script in the C dialect and sends it to you, you would view that script in your own language dialect, such as English. Having that capability makes it easy for programmers to write a driver to retrieve a file on an optical jukebox, for example, but have you call that procedure by using syntax like this:

```
get filename optical jukebox
```

If you have used the HyperTalk programming language in HyperCard, AppleScript will seem familiar. Unlike HyperCard, AppleScript is extensible by other applications within the language. AppleScript uses a dictionary of commands (verbs), objects (nouns), and modifiers that are defined within each program that has chosen to implement AppleScript. Applications codify their data and functions by defining dictionaries of objects and commands. You can see an application's dictionary by using the Open Dictionary command of the Script Editor. Figure 13-2 shows you FileMaker Pro's dictionary.

When AppleScript loads an application's dictionary, external data become objects and external functions become commands, and the language of that application becomes part of AppleScript's syntax.

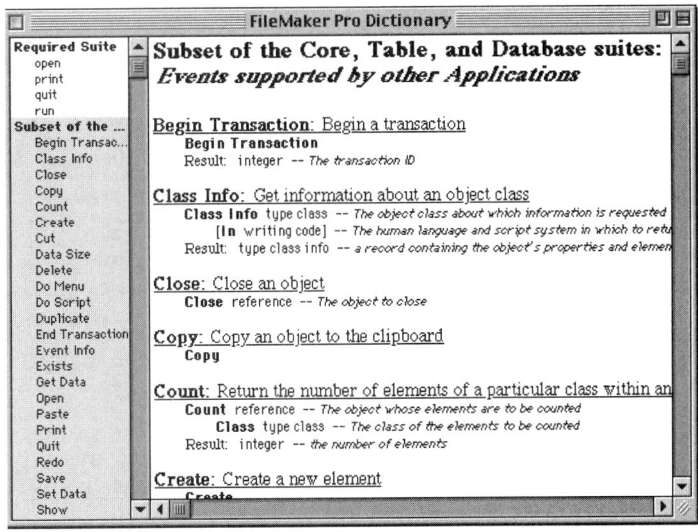

Figure 13-2: The FileMaker Pro AppleScript dictionary.

The AppleScript Architecture

The problem with most programming languages is that they require that you learn a new language, if not a new programming model. To minimize this problem, Apple introduced the Open Scripting Architecture (OSA) as a language standard that others could adopt.

The standards definition phase of OSA began in 1989 and is ongoing. OSA and Apple Event Registry were released concurrent with System 7.0 in 1991. Some key applications that supported AppleScript (such as Excel 4.0, FileMaker Pro 2.0, PageMaker 4.2, and others) were released in 1992. AppleScript 1.0 followed in 1993 as a separate product. It was bundled with System 7 Pro. Version 1.1 and the Scriptable Finder appeared in System 7.5. Finally, Apple plans to release a cross-platform version of AppleScript at some as yet unspecified time.

AppleScript is one expression of OSA, but other developers can provide their own applications. OSA includes AppleEvents (which you learned about in the previous chapter), the Object model, and a reference library of objects and events that are codified by third parties through Apple. These components form the basis for an open standard that Apple hopes others will build upon in the years to come.

As you may remember from the preceding chapter, AppleEvents is a messaging language that makes Inter-Application Communication (IAC) possible in System 7. With AppleEvents, programs communicate with one another, performing interapplication operations. One expression of the power of IAC is Publish and Subscribe. AppleEvents works between applications that are either on the same computer or connected through a network.

AppleScript uses AppleEvents as the messaging medium through which commands are passed and results returned. Scripts are sent to the AppleScript Extension, which interprets the statements in a script and sends AppleEvents to the appropriate application. The Apple Event Manager Extension serves as the traffic cop that interprets these messages and routes them appropriately. You see the Event Manager in System 7.1; in later systems its function is incorporated into the System file.

To prevent AppleScript from growing in nonstandard ways, Apple imposes a standard language. Objects in AppleScript are identified by compound names, called *references*. The overall naming scheme is called the *Object Model*. With this "dictionary," the language allows you to refer to individual objects in one of several alternate ways without worrying about how each application prefers to describe an object. Some commands have alternate expressions and so do some objects. It would be a burden to have to learn which application supports which variant, so AppleScript validates both kinds in any application.

A standard syntax is imposed on developers only for common language tasks. Apple has organized events and objects into event suites. These suites are common ways to do tasks based on application categories: text processing, databases and spreadsheets, communications, page layout, and so on. These suites extend the concept of common menu-command language elements such as *copy* and *paste* to scripting commands such as *delete, contain, get,* and *set* across the programming language. Event suites were covered in detail in the preceding chapter.

Event suites are evolving, and developers can register their commands, objects, and suites in the AppleEvent Registry (available from the Apple Professional Developers Association, or APDA). The event suites in this registry are the standard language for Inter-Application Communication implemented at the machine level and a standard reference to developers on implementing AppleScript support within their own applications.

Scripting Basics

Upon installation of AppleScript, you will notice that three files are added to your Extensions folder: AppleScript, Record Button, and the Apple Event Manager. In System 7.1 you see all three; in System 7.5 only the first two files appear. Under Mac OS 8, you'll only see the AppleScript Extension. You may see additional modules depending on your installation:

- **AppleScript Extension.** This Extension contains the language and the code necessary to interpret the language to your Macintosh. It also passes messages between applications and the Apple Event Manager. AppleScript Extension loads at boot-up as a 2K handler in system memory when no scripts are running. When scripts are running, the full 330K of the Extension is loaded. The icon for AppleScript is shown in Figure 13-3.

Figure 13-3: The AppleScript Extension icon.

- **Record Button.** The Record Button enables the "watch me" recorder feature you see in the Script Editor (described later in this section).
- **Apple Event Manager.** The Apple Event Manager provides the necessary communications between AppleEvents and AppleScript. The Apple Event Manager is used by other programs for Publish and Subscribe and other features, but it was designed to work hand in hand with AppleScript.
- **Scripting additions.** These language Extensions can be written in another programming language and added to AppleScript. They are often referred to as user-definable programs. In AppleScript, these scripts are called using simple syntax with the named command or filename.

  As AppleScript develops, you will find scripting additions in third-party books and as shareware or freeware on online services. A scripting addition file icon is shown in Figure 13-4. You can find some sample scripting additions in your Useful Scripts folder in the AppleScript folder (located in the Apple Extras folder on your drive).

Figure 13-4: An AppleScript Addition file icon.

- **Alternate Scripting components.** OSA provides the capability to exchange messages between OSA-compliant scripting systems, also called *components*. A program's scripting system can send and receive messages from AppleScript, making integration between the two seamless. Each script is tagged with a *creator code* that defines the scripting system from which it originated. Any scripting component required is loaded at the time the script is executed.

In the Apple Extras folder that is part of the System 7.5 installation, you will also notice an AppleScript folder. Additional, nonsystem components of AppleScript are contained there: the Script Editor, a Scriptable Text Editor, AppleScript Guide, and a folder of Useful Scripts. The following list describes what these components do:

- **Script Editor.** You use this application to write or record, edit, check the syntax of, compile, and run scripts. The icon for the Script Editor is shown in Figure 13-5.

Figure 13-5: The Script Editor Application icon.

- **Scriptable Text Editor.** This feature is a completely AppleScript-aware and recordable word processor. As such, it is often used as a teaching aid in AppleScript books and presentations. Figure 13-6 shows the icon for the Scriptable Text Editor.

  The Scriptable Text Editor is *not* part of a standard Mac OS 8 installation. Depending on how you obtained AppleScript, you may or may not have this application installed in the AppleScript folder.

Figure 13-6: The Scriptable Text Editor Application icon.

- **AppleScript Guide.** This feature is a SimpleText file of the Apple Guide manual that shipped with System 7 Pro.

- **Automated Tasks folder.** Automated Tasks are a series of prerecorded AppleScripts that you can use in your daily work. An alias of this folder is included in the Apple Menu Items folder. You can initiate the script by choosing its menu command from the Automated Tasks submenu. You will look at some of these scripts later in the chapter. There are even more scripts in the More Automated Tasks folder; you can drag one of these into the Automated Tasks folder so that it's available from the menu.

AppleScript support is added by an application's developer. You should note that three different levels of AppleScript support are recognized:

- **Scriptable.** A scriptable application represents the highest level of AppleScript support. These applications can understand and respond to AppleEvents generated by scripts. A scriptable application can be *controlled* by an AppleScript script.
- **Recordable.** A recordable application is capable of sending itself AppleEvents and reporting user actions to the Apple Event Manager so that a script summarizing these actions can be recorded. When you use the Record button of the Script Editor, recordable applications let you create and compile scripts as applications.
- **Attachable.** This type of application can trigger a script as a response to a user action (such as clicking a button or entering a text string). Apple describes an attachable application as "tinkerable." Attachable applications are useful as a front end to other applications.

Any combination of support is possible, so you can have an application that is scriptable and recordable, recordable and attachable, scriptable and attachable, or all three. Apple publishes a booklet entitled *AppleScript Guide to Scriptable Applications* with a listing of each application's capabilities. To get this brochure or add an application to the list, you can contact Apple by calling 408-996-1010; you can also contact them at their AppleLink address APPLESCRIPT or through the Internet at Applescript@apple.com.

The Script Editor

The Script Editor is the application that Apple provides with AppleScript to open and run scripts, record or write scripts, and save scripts in various forms. The Script Editor illustrates many of the basic principles used in creating and working with AppleScripts, so let's look at this application first.

Recording a Script

The Script Editor comes with a recorder feature that lets you create scripts based on your actions. Other macro programs call this a "watch me" kind of macro programming. As described previously, applications can only be scripted in this way if they are recordable. TeachText is neither scriptable nor recordable, but SimpleText is. The Finder, for example, is only scriptable and recordable in System 7.5 and later.

Start the Script Editor, and in the script window, enter the script name. Click the Record button to turn on the recorder. The Script Editor window is shown in Figure 13-7. You will notice that the Apple menu icon flashes as a script is being recorded. Go about switching to the program of your choice and performing other actions as desired. You complete your recorded script by switching back to the Script Editor window and clicking the Stop button. Clicking the Stop button in the Script Editor lets you run that script by name whenever the Script Editor is open. You can also use the commands in the Control menu of the Script Editor in place of the buttons you see in the window.

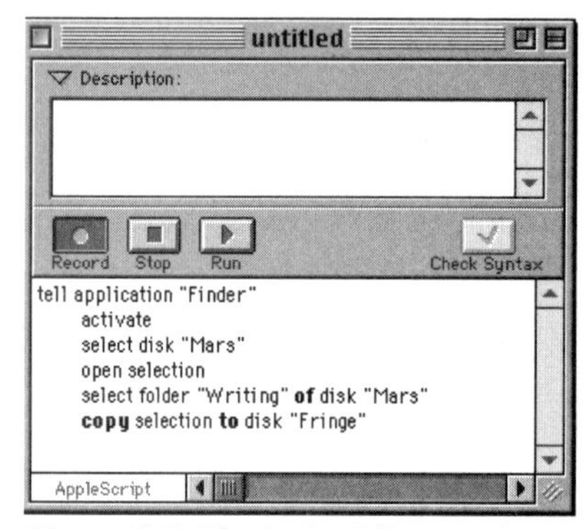

Figure 13-7: The Script Editor window with a sample recorded script.

You will notice that the Script Editor has entered all the commands in stylized clegic logic that correspond to your actions. As with other keystroke macro recorders, only certain actions can be captured by the Script Editor: using menu commands, pressing keys, saving files, opening and closing windows and files, and clicking the mouse. Drags and clicks are not normally captured because they don't result in any actions or changes. When a click does result in an action, such as activating a button, that action is recorded.

Because the actions were recorded to a script, there is no chance that the syntax requires checking. Therefore, the Check Syntax option (described later) is not available to you using the Check Syntax button in the Script Editor window.

Saving a Script

When you stop the recording of a script in the Script Editor, you save it within the Script Editor. It's more useful to save the script as a document that you can call up from the Finder. Use the Save command in the Script Editor to bring up the standard Save dialog box shown in Figure 13-8. Scripts are normally compiled when saved. To save a script without compiling it first, choose the Save As command from the File menu and save the script as Text. The following list describes the three formats to which you can save scripts in the Script Editor:

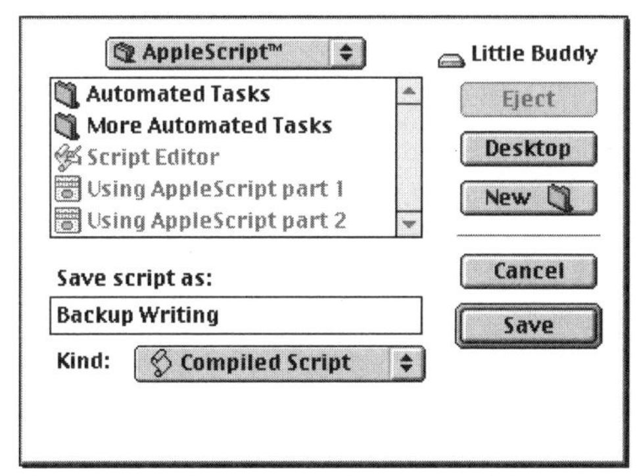

Figure 13-8: The Script Editor Save dialog box.

- **Application.** When you double-click the application icon shown in Figure 13-9, the application runs by itself without the Script Editor open.
  When you select the Application option, you can choose check boxes to keep applications open after the script is run (Stay Open) or to close the Script Editor (Never Show Startup Screen) when the script starts up.

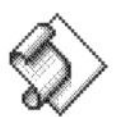

Figure 13-9: An AppleScript Application icon.

- **Compiled Script.** You can use compiled scripts directly or as commands within other scripts. Because run-time and compile engines are separate, scripts execute quickly and with few memory requirements. The icon for a compiled script is shown in Figure 13-10.
  Compiling a script changes the script from the dialect you can read into Universal AppleScript, a pseudocode that your Macintosh can read. A compiled script requires additional translation, but is much more easily executed by the OS than a script written in a dialect.

Figure 13-10: An AppleScript Compiled Script icon.

- **Text.** You can open text files from within other programs and reuse them. It's best to save a script as a text file when you wish to use it in the Scriptable Text Editor. The icon for an AppleScript Text file is shown in Figure 13-11.

Figure 13-11: An AppleScript Text file icon.

You can save an application or compiled script as a *run-time*—or as AppleScript calls it, *run-only*—version of your script. You cannot save text files as run-only. To save a run-only version of a script, choose the Save as Run-Only command from the File menu. The dialog box that appears will ask you to specify its location, name, and the format.

As noted previously, you can use the Script Editor to write scripts in other scripting systems or other dialects. If you are using a Macintosh with other scripting systems installed, you can choose from between them in the dialect pop-up menu that appears at the bottom right corner of the Script Editor window. You can also choose a dialect with the same pop-up menu from within the AppleScript Formatting dialog box shown in Figure 13-14.

Running a Script

There are several ways to run a script depending on how it was saved. You can select scripts recorded in the Script Editor by double-clicking them or choosing File | Open and then run them using the Run button. You can also double-click a name to run it. You can stop scripts running from within the Script Editor by using the Stop button.

If the script is a Finder file, either an application or a compiled script, you can run it by opening the file. Double-click an application or select that application and give the Open command (as you would any other application) to start the script running. When you launch an AppleScript application, a start-up screen (see Figure 13-12) may appear if you chose that option from within the Save dialog box. Click the Run button or press the Return key to run the script; click the Quit button or press the Command+Period keystroke to abort the script.

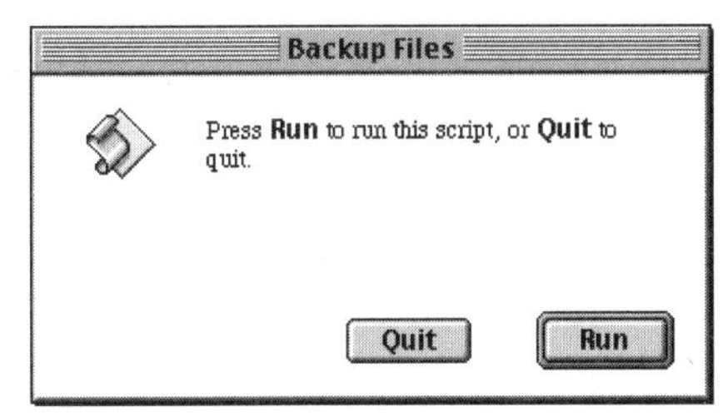

Figure 13-12: An AppleScript application start-up dialog box.

Scripts that are run result in an action. Some scripts return a value or expression based on their results. If you expect an outcome that you wish to see displayed in a window, choose the Show Result command from the Script Editor Control menu. The Result window will appear with the result. If there is an error in your script, you may see an error message in the Result window.

Scripts also can be saved in the form of a *droplet*, that is, a drag-and-drop enabled application. Droplets are indicated with a down-pointing arrow on their icons, as shown in Figure 13-13. To initiate the action supported by an AppleScript droplet, you simply drag the object you wish the action to take place with over the icon or alias of the droplet. This process is similar to dragging a file icon over a Desktop Printer icon to print the file. If the object is supported by the droplet, the action takes place immediately; otherwise, an error message is posted. To make a script a droplet, the object acted upon has to be scripted into the AppleScript program.

Figure 13-13: An AppleScript droplet icon.

Scripts can, of course, be embedded inside other applications or files. In this form, as an attached script, there can be many ways to call it up. Some will be under your control; others will not. You will often see scripts attached to buttons. When you click the button, the script runs. Other scripts will look for a text string in a field, check a condition, or do other tasks that may not be obvious to you, such as when an action automatically triggers the script. These scripts can often run in the background and escape your detection.

Modifying a Script

Scripts recorded in the Script Editor are fully editable in the script window, as is any text document. To begin modifying a script, you must launch the Script Editor and use the Open Script command from the File menu to open the script by name.

Most of the text editing actions in the Script Editor should be familiar to you from your word processor. Just type in your changes and save the results. In addition to simple clicks and drags, you can use the following shortcuts in the Script Editor window:

- Double-click to select a word; triple-click to select a line.
- Use the arrow keys to move the insertion point.
- Use the Command+Left arrow or Command+Right arrow keystrokes to move to the beginning or end of a line, respectively.
- Use the Command+Up arrow or Command+Down arrow keystroke to move to the beginning or end of the script, respectively.
- Use the Tab key at the beginning of a line to indent it. Tabs typed in the middle of a line are converted to space characters when you apply syntax formatting.
- Use the Return keys at the end of an indented line to apply indenting automatically to the next line.
- Use the Option+Return keystroke to insert a continuation character (¬) and move to the beginning of the next line. This shortcut lets you work with a line that is too long to fit in the view of the active window. AppleScript ignores the continuation character and treats the lines on either side as one line.
- Use the Shift+Return keystroke to move the insertion point from the end of an indented line to the beginning of a new, unindented line.

Notice that the Script Editor has a Check Syntax button for written or modified scripts. This feature will run through a script to check that the syntax of programming steps is correct. Syntax is the collection of grammar rules for a programming language. That is, if you have a command that requires a certain command step (an end to an IF command, for example), that step is in the syntax—if you forgot to put it in, you will get an error when you click on the Check Syntax button. The Check Syntax button will not correct errors in programming logic, only errors in construction.

When applied, the Check Syntax feature returns the first error as selected text. If there is an error in the text, no formatting is applied to the text in the Script Editor window. When the error is corrected, the Script Editor compiles the script, showing it with clegic (indented) formatting and other formatting options.

Some Script Editor features let you set the formatting of the script to make it easier to read. Some programs call this *beautifying* the program. You can change fonts, styles, sizes, and colors that are used in your scripts. These formatting styles make it easier to read the script and understand it, but they have no effect on the operation of the script. To set formatting options, choose the AppleScript Formatting command from the Edit menu. The dialog box shown in Figure 13-14 appears. Changes you make in this dialog box appear in any script you open from the Script Editor. Other programs that work with scripts, such as the Scriptable Text Editor, have similar features.

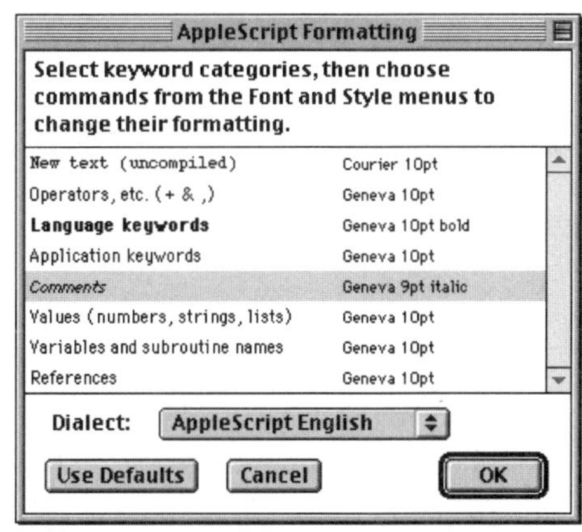

Figure 13-14: The AppleScript Formatting dialog box.

The elements of formatting you can apply based on the AppleScript formatting dialog box are as follow:

- **New text.** Any modifications you make to a script before you check its syntax, run it, or save the results. These modifications let you view your changes easily from a "wall of text."
- **Operators.** Actions (verbs) applied to objects in AppleScript.
- **Language keywords.** Commands available as part of the AppleScript language. They are often also actions and verbs.
- **Application keywords.** Language Extensions added to AppleScript by an application called within a script.
- **Operators.** Actions (verbs) applied to objects in AppleScript.
- **Comments.** Explanatory text that you add to a script to make its purpose understandable. Some people add comments to the beginning of a script as a header, to the beginning of a procedure, or even after important lines.

  Comments in AppleScript are preceded by a double hyphen. Anything on a line to the right of the double-hyphen is set in italics when compiled and then ignored at execution time or during a syntax check.

For multiline comments, use an asterisk at the start and end of the comments. Good commenting is the sign of a good programmer. Supplying cogent commenting without overdoing it is an art. For beginners, it is better to over-comment script than under-comment it.

- **Values.** Data or information that AppleScript uses, such as names, words, and numbers.
- **Variables.** Containers you name that can contain values. Values can change based on conditions.
- **References.** A pointer to an object is a reference. When you describe "window 1 of application Scriptable Text Editor," AppleScript knows you are referring to the topmost window open in the application. You see reference formatting in the Result window, not in the script window.

Scripting Applications

Every application has its own set of terms that it can add to the AppleScript vocabulary. Those terms are described in the dictionary within the application. At a script's run time, a called application's vocabulary is added to AppleScript for its use. To view an application's dictionary, choose the Open Dictionary command from the File menu of the Script Editor. Then select the application in the standard Open dialog box. Items, commands, and other verbs are described in the left scroll panel. These items are organized in event suites that the program supports.

When you click on an item, you will see the definition of the command in the right panel. Figure 13-15 shows you the dictionary for the Scriptable Text Editor. You will see information about the item such as the kinds of objects it acts on, the information or values it requires, and the results that are returned. Nearly every AppleScript-aware application supports the required suite and the standard suite of AppleEvents. Refer to Chapter 12, "Interapplication Communication & OpenDoc," for more information on this topic.

For applications that support AppleScript, you may find that you can select an object in the application and paste that object's reference into an AppleScript that you are building in the Script Editor. This system is still in its infancy, so this important feature is likely to be extended in the future. For now, you'll have to try out objects based on what you see in an application's dictionary to see what works. An object can be scriptable and recordable without allowing the pasting of object references.

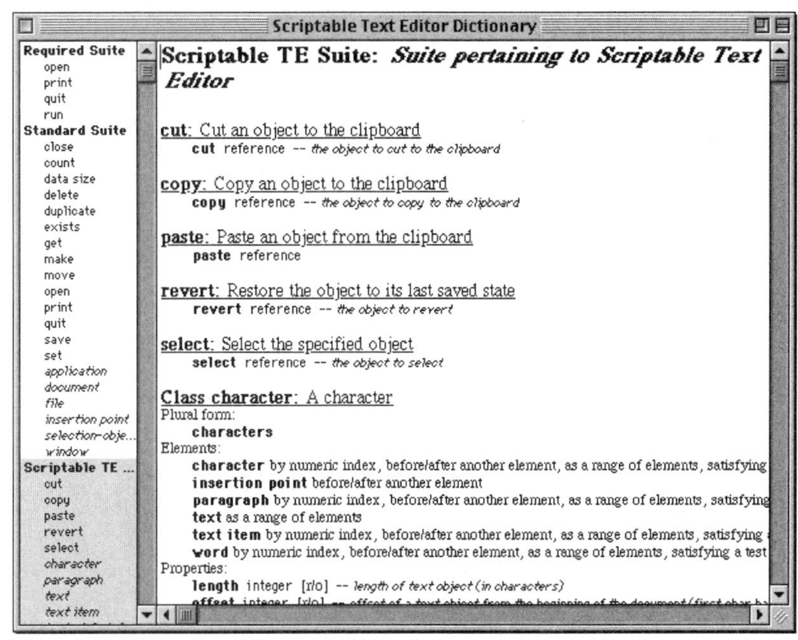

Figure 13-15: The Scriptable Text Editor dictionary.

When you can paste an object, the procedure is simple. Select the object in your application, and use the Copy command from the Edit menu. Then switch to the Script Editor and place the insertion point where you desire. Issue the Paste Reference command from the Edit menu. That reference then appears; for example:

```
"word 2 of document 'Untitled'"
```

The Scriptable Finder

To use AppleScript to automate tasks of the 7.0 and 7.1 Finder, you needed to use an external library of functions called the finderLib, which was distributed by Apple. These 13 Finder routines, 5 input-checking and utility routines, and 2 properties-checking routines form the basis for the Finder suite that was incorporated into System 7.5's Finder. Now when you open the Finder's dictionary from within the Script Editor, you will see the Finder suite, as shown in Figure 13-16.

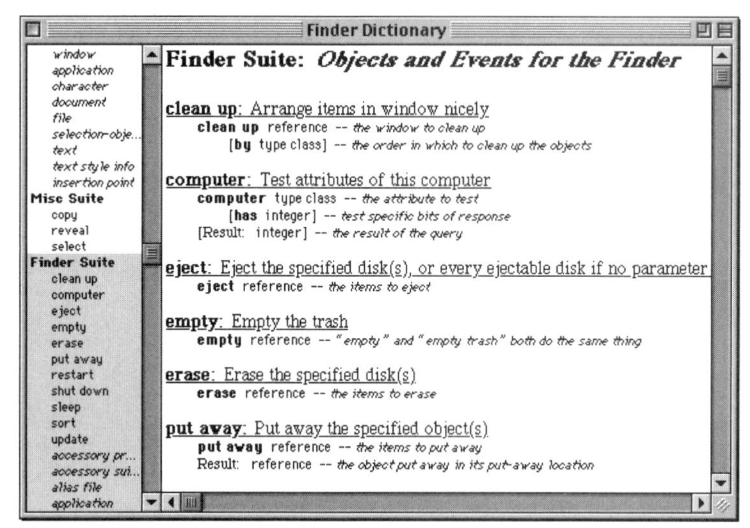

Figure 13-16: The Finder suite.

Scripting the Finder means that these commands can be used directly in scripts that use the Finder without having to call scripts from this external library. As a matter of convenience, you can record scripts using the recorder function of the Script Editor and using the Finder as one of your applications.

The Useful Scripts Folder

Mac OS 8 includes a set of preprogrammed AppleScripts that users can access from a hierarchical submenu of the Apple menu. An alias in the Apple Menu Items folder points to the Automated Tasks folder found in the AppleScript folder.

These scripts are, in fact, very useful because they add additional compound functionality to the Finder. A short SimpleText file, "About Automated Tasks," is included in the Automated Tasks folder describing its contents.

There is a folder called More Automated Tasks that includes additional AppleScripts. You may wish to add these to the Automated Tasks folder so that you can access them from the Apple menu. Over time you may find many other AppleScripts that you can add to the Automated Tasks folder. Figure 13-17 shows the Automated Tasks folder window in list view.

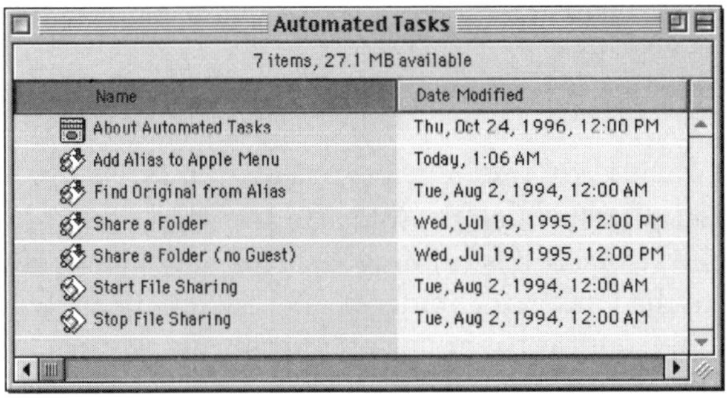

Figure 13-17: TheAutomated Tasks folder window.

When Mac OS 8 was released, the initial set of Useful Scripts included the following:

- **Add Alias to Apple Menu.** To create an alias to an item in the Apple menu, select this script. Because the Add Alias to Apple Menu is a drop-let script, you can also drag the item over the AppleScript icon.
- **Find Original From Alias.** Select an alias and run this script to find the original file. Using this script is equivalent to using the Find Original button in the Get Info dialog box or the Show Original menu item in the Finder's File menu. It is another droplet AppleScript.
- **Close Finder Windows.** This script is the equivalent of a Close All Windows command or holding the Option key and clicking a window close box.
- **Start File Sharing/Stop File Sharing.** These two scripts turn File Sharing on and off without your having to open the Sharing Setup Control Panel. You can also use the Control Strip of a PowerBook for this function.
- **Share a Folder/Share a Folder (No Guest).** A shared folder is one that is available to other users on the network (as described in Chapter 16, "File Sharing"). Files put in a shared folder can be copied by another user using File Sharing; others can copy files into it. This script makes the folder you drop onto it a shared folder and turns on File Sharing. Use the No Guest script if you don't want guest users to access the folder. If you restart your Macintosh, reapply this command to reactivate the shared folder.

The scripts in the More Automated Tasks folder are:

- **Hide/Show Folder Sizes.** This script turns on and off the Calculate Folder Sizes option in the Views Control Panel.
- **Alert When Folder Changes.** When you select a folder and apply this script, AppleScript will watch the folder to see what new items are added to it while the script is running. When a new item is added, you are switched to the Finder, the folder is opened, and the new item is highlighted. This script is useful for monitoring a download or communications folder.
- **Synchronize Folders.** With this script, two folders are compared and the contents of both are synchronized. That is, both folders are made identical by having missing files added to and files with recent modifications replace older versions. To use this script, select two folders and apply the command.

Learning More About AppleScript

The best beginning introduction to AppleScript is *The Tao of AppleScript* by Derrick Schneider (Hayden Press, 1993). This book gives you a feeling for some of the power of the language by scripting some interesting examples. It is also useful for examining the programming processes. You may also want to read *Complete AppleScript*, by Danny Goodman (Random House, 1993). This book is more complete and authoritative but less approachable than the one by Derrick Schneider.

For serious "script-heads," there are more powerful applications available for writing scripts. Apple sells the AppleScript Software Kit for $199; it is a complete package with an interface processor for building projects in AppleScript. You can purchase the AppleScript Scripter's Toolkit, a subset of this product, through stores. This toolkit comes with the FaceSpan Interface Processor from Software Designs Unlimited, a Data Access Language scripting addition, development tools, sample code, Finder scripting code, and electronic documentation. APDA also sells the Developers's University AppleEvents/AppleScript Tutorial, a $150 course with floppy-based instructions. Call APDA at 716-871-6555 for information.

Moving On

AppleScript fulfills a long-standing promise to provide automation capabilities within the Macintosh operating system. Although the subject is still developing, AppleScript is thorough and rigorous in its implementation, laying the groundwork for more important and convenient expressions to come.

In this chapter, you've seen how to use AppleScript to:

- Record actions with the Script Editor.
- Save scripts as programs that you can run.
- Work with applications that are AppleScript aware; that is, recordable, scriptable, and attachable.

In the next chapter, you'll look at one of the most important features of Mac OS 8: the Mac Runtime for Java. Java is a powerful, cross-platform language that is used to enhance Web pages or create full double-clickable applications.

CHAPTER 14

Java

It seems that anyone who knows anything about computers these days has heard about Java. Java has been hailed as the greatest advance in computer programming since the one and the zero. Java's hype greatly precedes it, but to some extent, Java has yet to live up to its hype.

Java was developed by Sun Microsystems as a platform-independent language for the Internet. Originally, Java was designed as a language for embedded systems (the tiny computers in your car, or VCR, or what have you), but before long Sun realized how Java fits the needs of the Internet perfectly. Since most users access the Internet over modems and phone lines, Internet-based software needs to be small and able to download quickly. And since the Internet is based on TCP/IP, Internet-based software needs to understand TCP/IP as well as the higher level things that use it, like Web servers and FTP servers.

Java, in fact, isn't all that new, claims to its breakthrough status notwithstanding. Many of the concepts it uses come from other languages; its syntax is very close to C++, and its object orientation is very much like Smalltalk. But Java's networking ability is fairly unique, and that's important in today's interconnected world.

Java has a great future, and Apple has embraced the technology in a big way. Mac OS 8 ships with Java, and so will Rhapsody, Apple's future operating system. In fact, Apple expects programmers to move to Java and is making sure their new system software can be accessed by Java programs. That's a pretty big endorsement! So, we should spend some time getting to know Java. This chapter will tell you what Java is and how you can run Java on your Macintosh.

Java on the Macintosh

Apple began supporting Java with the Macintosh Runtime for Java in late 1996. Now, support is bundled into the Mac OS 8 so that all Macs can run Java programs without users needing to install any new software.

A Java program is often called an *applet*, which refers to the fact that most Java programs are tiny in size and focused on providing a small set of features. However, there's no reason why a full-featured application couldn't be written in Java. In fact, Corel has released a beta of a Java-only version of its well-known Corel Office suite of applications. Over time, more developers may use Java to create the programs we use every day. Why? Well, Java offers many unique benefits:

- **Cross-platform.** Java applets use what's called *byte code*, which any computer can read using a Java Virtual Machine (commonly abbreviated VM). All an operating system needs to run Java applets is a Virtual Machine. In this way, a single Java applet can be run on a Mac, a Windows computer, or a Sun workstation.
- **Apple-supported.** Apple has, in its infinite wisdom, provided the Mac Runtime for Java (often abbreviated MRJ) in Mac OS 8. Owners of earlier OSes need to install MRJ separately.
- **Small.** Since Java is an object-oriented language, applets "inherit" features of the language that reside on the users' computer and hence don't need to be downloaded. Java also features built-in compression features, so things like bitmaps and sounds can be as small as possible.
- **Secure.** Java applets are restricted in many ways so that your computer can't be harmed by applets written by malicious (or inept) programmers.
- **Network-ready.** Java includes a rich feature set for connection over the Internet. Java applets can connect to Web servers, FTP servers, chat servers, or just about anything else that uses TCP/IP.

All of these features make Java a great language for any computer, but especially for the Mac. Over the years, we've seen a lot of software get developed for Windows-running PCs, and often Mac users would get left out in the cold waiting for developers to make Mac versions. With Java, there's no waiting: an applet that runs under Windows will run under the Mac OS. As more and more software is created for Java, the Mac will benefit greatly.

For example, look at Figure 14-1, which is Marimba's Castanet Tuner. This Java program, which works on all Java-enabled computers, offers a unique TV-like metaphor for viewing Internet-based content known as push media. This new technology is capable of broadcasting, or pushing, data to your computer instead requiring users like yourself to request the information page by page. Take a look at the Netscape home page at http://home.netscape.com for information on the latest version of the Navigator Web browser, which takes advantage of push technology through a Navigator component called Netcaster.

Since the Tuner is written in Java, one single version runs on all computers without any modifications.

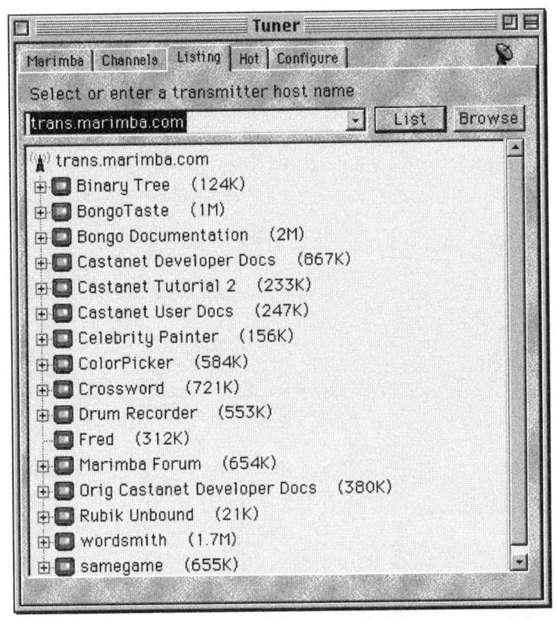

Figure 14-1: The Castanet Tuner works the same on Macs, Windows, and UNIX computers.

Mac Runtime for Java

When you install Mac OS 8, Java is installed for you automatically. Apple's Java is called the Macintosh Runtime for Java, or MRJ, for short. There isn't a whole lot to the installation. The pieces are actually very simple:

- **Library files.** The MRJ Libraries folder is installed inside your Extensions folder, but it's not an Extension; rather, it's a shared code library. Unlike many other things in your Extensions folder, the Java libraries aren't loaded unless you're actually running a Java applet. The Java libraries can't conflict with other Extensions at boot time, so you don't have to worry about Extension conflicts.

- **Apple Applet Runner.** This very simple program lets you run Java applets. Other than applet-running, this program is pretty sparse; there are a few features for troubleshooting (such as the Java console).
- **Applets**. The standard MRJ install comes with a whole host of Java applets created by the folks at Sun to test your Java installation out. They're neat and fun to play with, but not very useful.

That's all there is to the installation. Since Java runs inside another application, it doesn't consume RAM from your System partition. If you have a particularly large applet, you can change the memory allocation of the Applet Runner program. However, its default size should be plenty for any applet. Figure 14-2 shows the Get Info dialog box for the Apple Applet Runner, where you'll need to go to change the memory requirements.

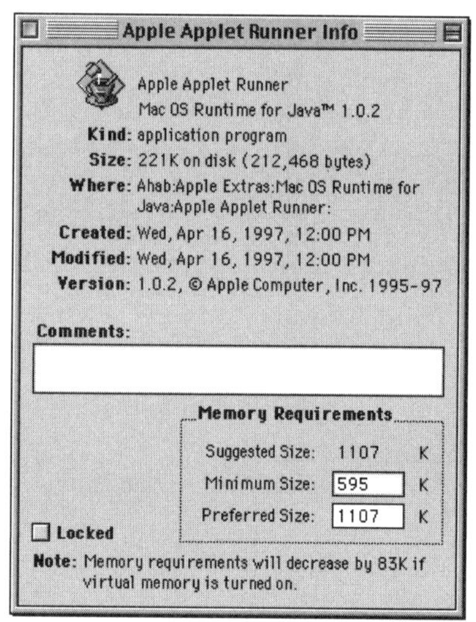

Figure 14-2: Use the Get Info dialog box to give more memory to the Applet runner to allow it to execute large Java applications.

The rest of the Java installation consists of an Extension and the class libraries Java requires to run (shown in Figure 14-3), which are located in your Extensions folder.

Figure 14-3: There isn't much to the MRJ installation. These are the files that are in your Extensions folder.

Running Java Applets

To run one of the many example Java applets that is installed by Mac OS 8, just drag and drop an applet's HTML file onto the Applet Runner. The program will launch and the Java applet will start. That's all it takes! Running Java on the Macintosh is incredibly simple. The Applet Runner application has a menu of Java applets you can try out. To try an applet, navigate through the hierarchical menu to the applet HTML file you want to try. Figure 14-4 shows some of the applets that come with Mac OS 8.

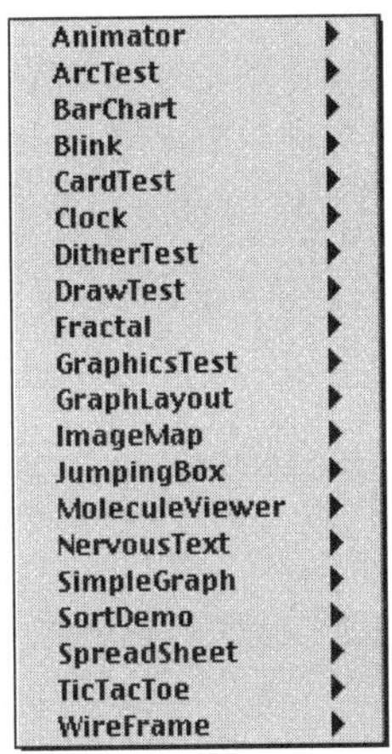

Figure 14-4: The Applet Runner has a menu of sample applets for you to try.

The Applet Runner has a File menu with the usual items:

- **Open URL.** Opens an HTML file from the Internet using the Uniform Resource Locator (URL) you specify.
- **Open Local HTML File.** Opens an HTML file from your local hard disk.
- **Properties.** Shows a dialog box that displays the attributes for that applet.

You can also use the File menu to run an applet, or you can just drag an HTML file onto the Applet Runner to make it run (although this won't work for a network-based HTML file). An applet's Properties specify the security settings for an applet. Applets are usually restricted in what they can do. For instance, applets usually can't write files to the user's hard disk. That way, applets can't overwrite important files (like the Finder and System, or your precious data). However, this can be a pain, especially if you're using a Java-based productivity application and really *want* to save files to the hard drive.

That's why the Applet Runner lets you change the properties of an applet. When you open the Properties dialog box, you have seven options, as you'll see in Figure 14-5:

- **Network Access.** This controls how your applet connects to the Internet. There are three options:
  - **No Access.** The applet can't use the network at all.
  - **Applet Host.** The applet can use the restricted network access provided for applets.
  - **Unrestricted.** The applet can use the network in any way it wishes.
- **Filesystem Access.** This controls how your applet uses your hard drive. There are three options here as well:
  - **No File System.** The applet can't use the hard drive at all.
  - **Local Applet Access.** The applet can read and write files into the local directory it's stored in, but nowhere else.
  - **Unrestricted.** The applet can access and modify any file anywhere on the drive.
- **Package Access and Package Definition.** These control how the applet interacts with the Java VM system and whether or not the applet can change your Java's built-in classes. These settings are either restricted or unrestricted.

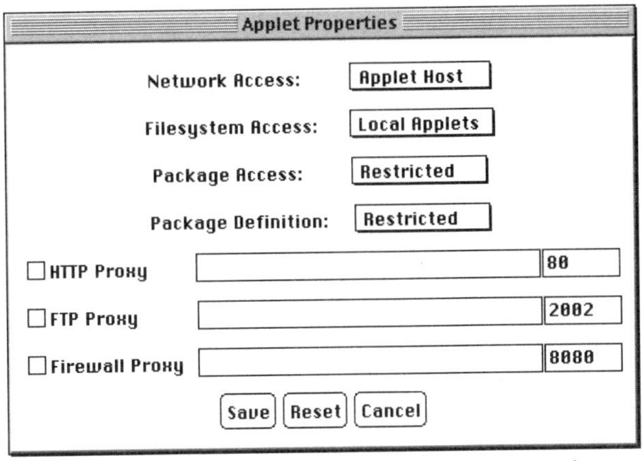

Figure 14-5: The Applet Properties dialog lets you restrict an applet's abilities.

If you're at a company that uses a firewall, the next three controls are for you. They control how the applet connects to the Internet through a proxy server:

- **HTTP Proxy.** Enter the address and TCP/IP port of the Web proxy server.
- **FTP Proxy.** Enter the address and TCP/IP port of the FTP proxy server.
- **Firewall Proxy.** Enter the address and TCP/IP port of the firewall proxy server.

In the above case, you can set your applet to have permission to use the file system and hence write files. If you do this, however, you should be very sure that the applet comes from a reputable source and isn't a "Trojan horse," or a program that looks angelic but is actually destructive.

Note that unless you make changes, the default settings make sure a Java applet cannot cause harm on your system. You don't need to do anything to be safe.

In addition to the File menu, the Applet Runner has an Applet menu that affects the currently running Java applet:

- **Reload Applet.** Dumps the applet from RAM and loads it freshly from the disk.
- **Restart Applet.** Forces the applet to start again from the beginning.
- **Suspend.** Pauses the applet.

- **Resume.** Continues a paused applet.
- **Show Applet Tag.** Shows the HTML tag used to specify the applet (applets are run from HTML files). Usually, this tag includes some special initialization commands for the applet. If you wish to see this, use this option.

These options only affect the frontmost applet. To affect another applet, click on its window to bring it to the front.

Other Java VMs

Apple isn't the only maker of a Java VM for the Mac OS, however. Since Java is an open standard, any company is welcome—in fact, encouraged—to try its hand at producing Java software. There are at least three other companies that make Java Virtual Machines that you can easily get for your Mac:

- **Metrowerks.** The makers of CodeWarrior, the premiere programming environment for the Mac, have created a fast VM that Microsoft includes with its Internet Explorer. I've had some problems with applets crashing when using this VM.
- **Symantec.** Another maker of compilers and developments tools, Symantec, makes a VM for the Mac for use with its Cafe Java visual programming environment. However, it's not widely used on the Mac.
- **Roaster.** The first Java for the Mac just might be the best. Roaster, Inc., produced the first VM for the Mac, which Apple licensed for its first release of the MRJ. The Roaster VM was the first to provide a Just-In-Time (JIT) compiler for the Mac, and its speeds make the Mac equal to any other platform for running Java.
- **Apple.** Apple now uses its own Java VM for the MRJ, so if you're a Java junkie, it may be worth your while to check out the Roaster version.

While there are these other Java VMs, they aren't integrated into the OS like the MRJ is. Each Java applet uses its own applet-running program. Apple's MRJ, however, is available to all programs (such as Web browsers) as an application-level service, so it's easy for programmers to add applet-running ability to their own programs. At some future point, Apple may offer the ability to add plug-in Java Virtual Machines, so you could switch to the VM of your choice. In fact, Internet Explorer lets you do this to some extent right now; you can choose between the Metrowerks and Apple VM. However, this isn't the case yet. Until then, you'll have to drag and drop applets onto an Applet Runner for each VM you want to use.

Java & OpenDoc

OpenDoc and Java complement each other very nicely. OpenDoc provides an architecture for using small components; Java provides small components. Was it any wonder they got together? Of course, there's more to OpenDoc than that, but it's a good way to look at their relationship. Apple has made it clear, however, that future support for OpenDoc is limited to maintenance releases, whereas with Java, it's full steam ahead.

When you install OpenDoc, a special version of the Applet Runner program is installed. This special version is an OpenDoc "part" (see Chapter 12 for more information on OpenDoc). When you're in any OpenDoc document, you can embed any Java applet simply by dragging and dropping its HTML file onto the document. When this happens, the AppletRunner part is automatically used to run the Java applet inside the document.

Yes, it's weird to think about, but you can have Java applets running inside your word processing documents, spreadsheets, and e-mail programs. Try it yourself:

1. Go to the OpenDoc Stationery folder in the Apple menu and double-click on the AppletRunner Stationery file. You'll get an empty AppletRunner document.
2. Select an HTML file from the Java Applets folder and drag it into the document you just opened. It will load and run! Look at Figure 14-6 for an example.

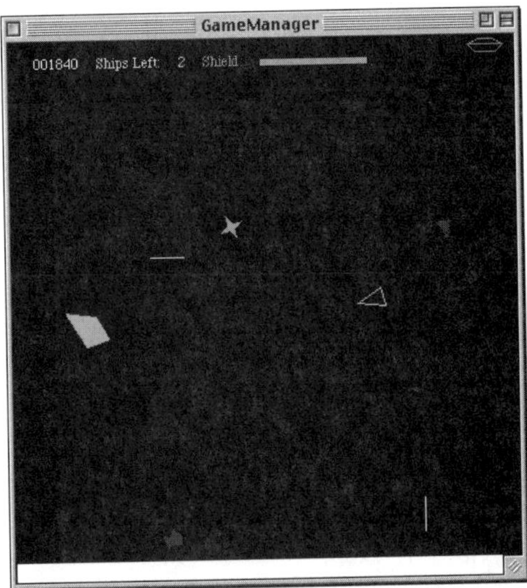

Figure 14-6: Java applets running in the WAV OpenDoc container.

That's all there is to it. If you're using a document shell like WAV, you can create complex word processing documents that include Java applets. Think of it as a totally customizable version of ClarisWorks, where if you find Java applets you like, you can include them!

Moving On

Java is the newest element to the Mac OS, as well as the one with the most promise. The key to remember about Java and the Mac OS is that Java allows computer programmers to write one version of a program, such as a word processor, which can then be run on many different types of computers without modification. Programmers refer to this powerful ability as "write once, run anywhere." As we've seen earlier, the Mac OS is just about the most friendly operating system around, and if Java developers can write some of the unique features found in the Mac OS into Java applets for use on all computers, then the world will have a better computing environment. In the next chapter, we'll look at one of the oldest elements of the Mac OS, support for multimedia applications.

CHAPTER 15

Multimedia Applications

The way the word *multimedia* is bandied about in the computer press, it seems to refer to the progress we've made toward making computers like we see on *Star Trek: The Next Generation*—you know, a computer that you can talk to, does flashy things with sounds and animations, charts space in 3D, and can talk back when it needs to. That's multimedia, as far as the average user is concerned. However, in our corner of space-time, computers aren't quite powerful enough to make a convincing holodeck.

These days, multimedia refers to the combination of sounds and images on a computer. But not just that: the definition of multimedia has grown to encompass animation files, QuickTime movies, MIDI, virtual reality, and 3D rendering.

Ironically, as its definition grows it seems to specify less: what exactly is a "multimedia-ready computer" ready for? In the case of a Macintosh running Mac OS 8, we know exactly what this means. In the standard installation of Mac OS 8, you'll get these components:

- QuickTime and QuickTime VR
- QuickDraw 3D
- Text-to-Speech

Together, these components give you a high performance multimedia computer that can play movies and animations, sounds and MIDI files, and even speak back to you using a variety of voices. Captain Picard would be proud of our progress, don't you think?

QuickTime

The Macintosh has led the way for personal computers in typography, graphics, sound, and high-resolution color. With the QuickTime, the Macintosh continues this tradition by leading the way in video and multimedia.

QuickTime is an extension that gives your Macintosh the ability to play and record moving video images, animation, and sound in ways never before possible. It makes moving images and sounds a basic type of Macintosh data. All types of applications—word processors, databases, presentation graphics packages, page-layout programs—can now incorporate these moving images as easily as they now use standard graphics.

Any Macintosh model containing a 68020 or later processor that uses System 6.07 or later (including System 7.0 and above) can use QuickTime—all you need is the QuickTime extension. QuickTime version 1.0 has been available since January 1992, and an improved version, QuickTime 1.5, was released in November 1992. The current version of QuickTime is 2.5, which shipped with Mac OS 8. A full version of QuickTime for Microsoft Windows, which has all of the features the Macintosh version has, was also released by Apple.

There is no charge for the QuickTime extension, although in typical Apple fashion that doesn't mean you will be able to get it easily or without cost. QuickTime is being distributed in a number of different formats and channels:

- QuickTime is included as part of Mac OS 8.
- The QuickTime Starter Kit features the QuickTime extension, a player utility, a few sample movies, and more, and can be purchased from any Apple reseller or most mail-order software dealers.
- QuickTime can be downloaded from Apple's QuickTime Web site (http://quicktime.apple.com). It can also be downloaded from online services or obtained from most Macintosh user groups.
- You can legally copy QuickTime from another Macintosh user who has it.
- Many QuickTime-dependent applications include the QuickTime extension on their distribution disks.

QuickTime Movies

The QuickTime extension adds support to your Macintosh for a file format called Movie (the file type is MooV). Like other file formats, such as PICT, EPS, or TIFF, the Movie file format saves a certain kind of data—in this case moving video, animation, or sound (or all of these)—in a way that can be viewed at a specified rate and quality. By defining this file format at the system-software level, Apple makes it easy for application developers to support this kind of data, which encourages them to develop sophisticated ways to create and use data that changes or reacts over time (such as moving images or sounds) on the Macintosh.

A QuickTime movie acts much like any other text or graphic element—you can select, cut, copy, or paste it either within or between QuickTime-savvy applications and store it in the latest version of the Scrapbook. In some cases, you can't even tell that an object is a movie until you select it; before that, it looks just like any other graphic element. When you select a movie, however, it displays an identifying set of controls that allow you to adjust the volume (if it has sound) and play the movie as well as fast-forward, reverse, or randomly adjust the movie, as shown in Figure 15-1.

Figure 15-1: A QuickTime movie with its controls.

The image you see in a movie element when the movie isn't playing is called its *poster*. The poster is a selected image from the movie. Because it's often not the first frame of the movie, you'll see the image of the poster jump to another image when the movie begins.

A *preview* is a moving representative of the movie. Not all movies have previews, but most longer ones do. A preview gives you a quick look at the movie highlights. Many standard file dialog boxes let you choose whether to see the poster or a preview before you open a movie.

QuickTime & Data Compression

One of QuickTime's most important technological breakthroughs is the real-time compression and decompression it provides to video, animation, photographs, and other graphics. QuickTime supports several built-in compression schemes and can easily support others as necessary. The built-in compression is a software-only solution, capable of achieving ratios as great as 25:1 without any visible loss in image quality. With specialized hardware, compression ratios as high as 160:1 are possible.

Compression is particularly important because of all the data needed to generate moving images and accompanying sounds. A good rule of thumb for estimating movie size is that every minute of motion consumes 10MB of disk space. As another example, a seven-minute, full-size, full-resolution video movie could consume 200MB in its uncompressed form. Compressed, that same movie might need only 45MB. Of course, most movies are significantly shorter (lasting between 5 and 30 seconds), so files in the 200K to 1MB range are common.

The actual size of a QuickTime movie depends on the following:

- **Image size.** Measured in horizontal and vertical pixels, the image size determines how large the movie will appear onscreen. The larger the image, the larger the movie file. Movies defaulted to 160 X 120 pixels in QuickTime 1.0, but version 1.5 expands this default to 240 X 180 pixels. Version 2.5 takes it all the way to 640 X 480.
- **Resolution.** QuickTime supports all the Mac's resolutions—or depths of color—including 1-, 2-, 4-, 8-, 16-, 24-, and 32-bit. The higher the resolution, the larger the movie file.
- **Frames per second.** Most QuickTime movies are recorded using 10, 12, 15, or 30 frames per second (fps). Without additional hardware, 15 fps is the QuickTime standard, although 30 fps, which is the standard for commercial-quality video, is supported by QuickTime 1.5. Version 2.5 supports 29.97 fps (which matches the frame rate of professional video equipment). The higher the frame rate, the larger the resulting movie file.
- **Audio sampling rate.** This rate can be thought of as the "resolution" of the sound. The Macintosh supports 8, 11, 22, or 44 KHz audio sampling, although anything higher than 22 KHz requires additional hardware. The higher the sampling rate, the larger the sound portion of a movie file.
- **Compression.** As mentioned earlier, QuickTime supports a number of compression schemes, and for each you can select the degree of compression used. Increasing compression reduces movie size but sometimes affects playback quality. New compression schemes introduced with QuickTime 2.5 should reduce or eliminate these kinds of problems.
- **Content.** Beyond the previously mentioned technical factors, the actual set of sounds and images contained in a movie is what will finally determine its size. This factor makes it difficult to estimate the size of a QuickTime movie solely based on its length or technical characteristics.

Using QuickTime

You can use QuickTime to watch movies (which may be included on CD-ROM disks, obtained from user groups or online services, or come embedded in documents you get from other Mac users), or you can create your own QuickTime movies. It's easy for almost anyone with a Mac to view a QuickTime movie, but creating one requires a fairly substantial investment in hardware, software, and the development of what may be brand-new skills.

Most QuickTime movies now being delivered are part of CD-ROM-based information discs, providing education or information on music, history, sports, news, entertainment, or computer-related topics. CD-ROM is the perfect media for QuickTime because it has huge storage capabilities (650MB), can be inexpensively reproduced, and has access times sufficient to deliver good-quality playback. CD-ROM support for QuickTime has recently been enhanced by faster CD drives (such as the 12x drives that come standard on most new Macs and Mac clones) and performance improvements included in QuickTime 2.5.

Most movies delivered as part of these CD-ROM discs are viewed using some controlling application, such as MacroMedia Director player, that is included on the CD. Movies included as part of other documents can be viewed from within their applications; Microsoft Word, Aldus Persuasion, and others have this capability. To watch movies that exist only as stand-alone Movie files, you'll need a player application.

Several movie-player applications are available as shareware or freeware. One from Apple is called Simple Player, and another is called Movie Player. Aladdin Systems, makers of the StuffIt line of compression utilities, offers a player called Popcorn (the perfect movie companion), which is available online and from most user groups. If you ever need to view a movie but you don't have one of these movie-player utilities handy, try SimpleText—the version that comes with Mac OS 8 knows how to play QuickTime movies.

What's New With QuickTime?

About the time Mac OS 8 is released, QuickTime 3.0 will appear. QuickTime 3.0 has many new features, most of which are performance related. You will notice improved performance, especially on Power Macintosh computers. Movies can now vary from 240 x 180 pixels at 1 fps to up to 320 x 240 pixels at 30 fps, depending on your Macintosh type. The MoviePlayer 2.0 application replaces the SimplePlayer application that shipped previously with QuickTime.

The following aspects of QuickTime have undergone improvement in versions 2.0 and 2.5:

- **QuickTime DataPipe.** The DataPipe improves performance on all types of CD-ROM drives. Tracks can be preloaded into memory prior to playback.
- **Music.** Movies can now contain music tracks. Data is stored as a series of note commands like music is stored in MIDI files.
- **MPEG.** MPEG is an international standard for digital video. QuickTime 2.5 can play MPEG if you have an MPEG board installed in your computer or if you have a PowerMac and the MPEG playback extension.
- **Timecode.** QuickTime 2.0 can store a timecode (SMPTE or otherwise) in a movie. Timecodes point to the source tape.
- **Burnt text.** QuickTime 1.6 introduced anti-aliasing text. Version 2.0 adds the capability to store prerendered text in a compressed image for faster redraw.
- **Drag and Drop.** With version 2.0, you can drag one movie to another to perform a paste operation. You can also pull a movie from the Finder when you are in MoviePlayer to drag it into a sequence. When you drag a text movie into a SimpleText document, the text is extracted into the document.
- **Power Macintosh.** All compressors and decompressors are now native on the PowerPC. Cinepak compression is two and a half to three times faster on a model 8100 than on a Quadra 950.
- **Copyright dialog.** You can now add copyright information directly to a movie. You use the Set Movie Information command in the MoviePlayer 2.0 application to add the information in the authoring mode. View the information with the Show Copyright command.
- **Sprites.** A sprite is a graphic that can be animated using commands that tell how the sprite moves (as opposed to storing a full frame for each step of the animation). It's like MIDI for image files: you don't need to store the digital video for an animation.
- **Improved Web support.** When you download QuickTime movies over the World Wide Web, the movie will begin to play as soon as enough data has arrived.
- **Miscellaneous.** A number of other small changes have been added. They include the ability to play AIFF, MU-LAW, and WAV sound files directly, a standard export dialog box, and an improved grayscale slider bar.

QuickTime 3.0 promises further performance improvements as well as eye-catching features like live digital effects and vector graphics. You can follow its progress at http:// quicktime.apple.com.

QuickTime VR

QuickTime VR (abbreviated QTVR) is a powerful extension to QuickTime. It allows you to actually walk through a movie, spin around, and look up and down as well as manipulate objects within a movie. QTVR takes digital images, stitches them together, and makes them look as if they were taken with a movie camera. Pretty neat stuff. If you have Netscape Navigator, you can download a QTVR plug-in so you can even view QTVR movies within a browser window. For more information on this, see the QTVR home page at http://quicktimevr.apple.com/.

There are two basic types of QTVR movies, one in which you move through or around inside a movie and another in which an object, such as a book, car, or planet, is manipulated. The difference is whether it is you or the object that is moving. A really complex QTVR movie can contain both. For example, Figure 15-2 shows a sample QTVR movie of the flight bridge of the USS *Intrepid*.

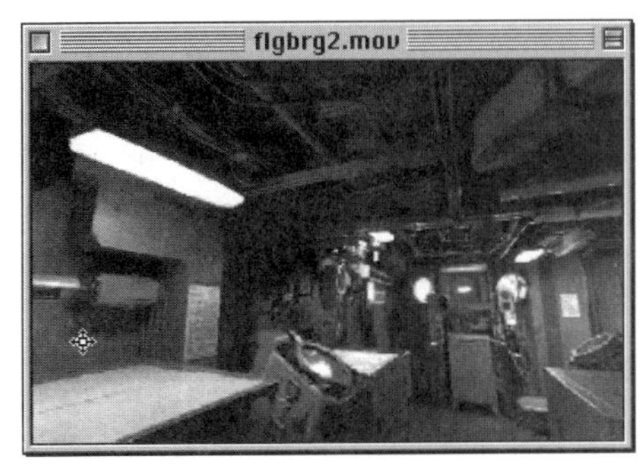

Figure 15-2: Tour an aircraft carrier through a QTVR movie.

You can see this and other QTVR movies on the Organa home page at http://www.organa.com/ and on Apple's QTVR Web site.

QuickDraw 3D

The final frontier in multimedia must be 3D. Ever since *Jurassic Park* and the stunningly popular game Doom, there's been an explosion of interest in creating 3D worlds on a Desktop computer. Over the years, a variety of companies created many different Mac applications to allow a user to create objects in 3D and render (that is, draw) them realistically. However, these programs could not interoperate in any significant way. Each of these programs had their own data file format; each had the ability to use plug-ins, but only their own special kind of plug-in.

Why is this? Well, it's difficult to write a 3D program. There's so much a programmer must learn just to get a basic image on the screen. Although it would be neat, it wouldn't be very cost-effective to have the folks that created ClarisWorks add true 3D support to their program.

Apple created QuickDraw 3D in a bold attempt to cut this Gordian knot. QuickDraw 3D lets different programs share files, 3D models, textures, and camera positions. QuickDraw 3D adds standard renderers and a standard way of adding new renderers. And QuickDraw 3D makes it simple for programmers without any 3D experience to support it.

Installation

The Mac OS 8 installer has a check box for QuickDraw 3D. Just check this off and it will be installed. Once this is done, you'll find that QuickDraw 3D adds a few more extensions to your System folder:

- **QuickDraw™ 3D.**
- **QuickDraw™ 3D IR.**
- **QuickDraw™ 3D RAVE.** This file allows programmers to access the low-level portions of QuickDraw 3D and thus gain rendering speed. This is mostly used by 3D games that don't need the user-interface features of QuickDraw 3D but do need to be able to render models. One program that uses RAVE is AMBrosia Software's Avara.
- **QuickDraw™ 3D Viewer.** These extensions provide basic 3D support for all applications. An application can use QuickDraw 3D to load a model, position it in space, light it, and render it.
- **Apple QD3D HW Driver and Apple QD3D HW Plug-In**. These extensions let you use hardware 3D accelerators to speed the rendering and display of images. For instance, Apple sells a low-cost PCI card that will make QuickDraw 3D 10 times faster at displaying complex images.

If you're low on hard disk space, you can remove extensions that you're not using. For example, if you don't have a hardware accelerator, you don't need the HW Driver and HW Plug-In files.

The standard installation also includes new versions of the Scrapbook and SimpleText, which extend these programs to open and manipulate model files. Also, a set of sample models is included so you can play around with them in SimpleText.

3D MetaFile Format

Apple created a special file format, the 3D MetaFile format, for use with QuickDraw 3D. Although there's already a plethora of formats for 3D files (including DXF and 3DS), none includes all of the features found in the 3DMF format. A 3DMF file stores:

- The geometrics that make up an object.
- Saved camera views.
- Textures, shading, and coloring information for all objects.

Unlike the DXF file format, 3DMF files can store complex geometrics like splines and NURBS (Non Uniform Rational B-Splines). These allow the designer to specify things like smooth curves and cut-out surfaces. In the DXF file format, you'd have to specify a curve as a series of short straight line segments; if you make the model larger, these straight lines become obvious and the model less life-life.

3DMF files can be saved in one of two ways:

- Text, which you can open with a text editor like BBEdit.
- Binary, which is smaller but not human readable.

Not all applications give you a choice, but when they do, usually binary is the best choice. Text is useful mainly when trying to figure out why a model doesn't work in a particular program or when sending files over the Internet in text (as opposed to binary) mode.

Apple gives away information on the internal structure of the 3DMF file format and even has sample code for reading and writing these files so that developers who want to support these kinds of files from their software can do so. When this is coupled with the fact that no other file format offers so much, you see why 3DMF has become so popular.

In fact, the 3DMF file format has rapidly become a cross-platform standard for 3D model files. All major 3D programs on Macs, Windows, and even UNIX machines provide the ability to read and write 3DMF files. Portions of 3DMF have even been incorporated into the specifications for VRML, the Internet-based 3D "virtual worlds" specification. So it's safe to say that 3DMF will be around for a while.

In your Apple Extras folder you'll find a sampling of models available from different companies, all of which you can buy and use in your own 3D designs. You can also find a rich treasure trove of models to download on the Internet.

User Interface

QuickDraw 3D, like its big brother QuickTime, is more than just a file format. QuickDraw 3D includes a set of tools that let a user manipulate 3D models. The user can move, rotate, and zoom a 3D model. The user can reposition the camera (the point in 3D space from which you are seeing the model) and save camera positions. As they can with the standard QuickTime window, applications can use these built-in user interface tools or implement their own.

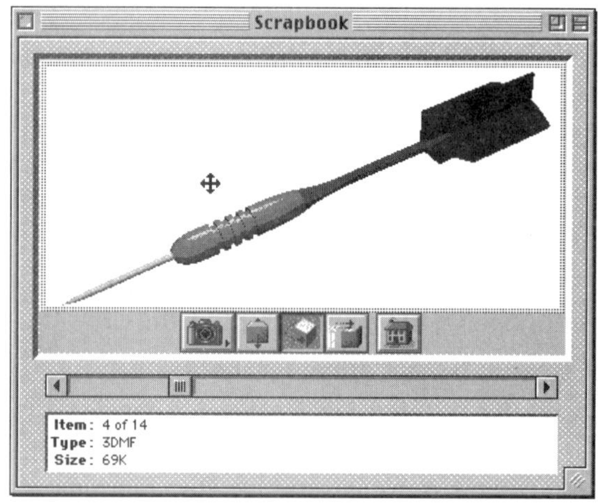

Figure 15-3: A QuickDraw 3D model in the Scrapbook can be rotated, moved, or scaled.

Take a look at Figure 15-3. You can see a 3DMF model in the Scrapbook. There is a bank of controls along the bottom edge of the window:

- **Camera.** This button is actually a pop-up menu that lets you look at the model from the front, back, top, bottom, left, or right.
- **Scale.** This button lets you scale the object up or down, making it bigger or smaller in the window.
- **Rotate.** This button lets you rotate the object in the view. When clicked, the cursor changes to a hand; you can "grab" the model and rotate it about a central point.
- **Move.** This button lets you move the model in the window. When clicked, the cursor changes to a hand; you can "grab" the model and move it left or right.
- **Home.** This button returns you to the "home view," or the original view of the object as was specified in the 3DMF file.

Making Models

One thing QuickDraw 3D doesn't include is a program with which you can create models. If you're serious about 3D, you'll want to purchase a top-notch program like Infini-D, Strata Pro, Macromedia Extreme3D, or ElectricImage Studio. These programs all support QuickDraw 3D's support for hardware acceleration, user interface standards, and the 3DMF file for import and export. In addition, they offer professional features and control, but at a cost: the cheapest is priced at $395 and the most expensive costs $7,995.

If you just want to play around with QuickDraw 3D, an example of which is shown in Figure 15-4, I recommend a cheaper solution: Microspot's 3D World. This low-cost program ($139) offers a good basic set of tools and features. You can create simple shapes, shade them, group them, and apply textures to them. You can also create 2D or 3D text using whatever TrueType fonts you have installed. You can even create simple animations that you can export as QuickTime movies.

Figure 15-4: It's easy to create 3D text in 3D World. Notice the globe; it was created by making a sphere and then dragging the world map picture from the Scrapbook and dropping it onto the sphere.

A demo of 3D World is available from Microspot's Web page at http://www.microspot.com. This demo won't let you save, export models, or print. However, it's a great way to play around with QuickDraw 3D and learn the basics of 3D modeling.

Drag & Drop

QuickDraw 3D makes great use of Mac OS 8's drag-and-drop features. You can drag a model from one program to another or drop it on the scrapbook (for use later) or the Desktop. Both SimpleText and the Scrapbook implement the standard QuickDraw 3D user interface tools, so you can manipulate images inside them.

You can also drag a QuickDraw 3D model into a program that only accepts pictures. QuickDraw 3D will render the view you're currently looking at and drop it into the application as a PICT clipping. This way you can use all your existing applications with QuickDraw 3D—no upgrades necessary!

Speech

Computer-generated speech has had an interesting history on the Macintosh. The very first program anyone saw running on a Mac in public was Macintalk, a text-to-speech generator that could create fairly realistic-sounding speech. At the introduction of the Macintosh, Steve Jobs pulled a Mac out of a carrying case and the Mac joked, "Thanks, it was hot in there." Ah, progress.

Apple eventually released Macintalk for developers to use, but not too many ever did since it wasn't part of the standard system installation. But Mac OS 8 comes with the Speech Control Panel, which provides much more power than the old Macintalk.

Text-to-Speech

What the Speech Control Panel does is implement a form of Text-to-Speech; any text on the screen can be read aloud by the computer. Of course, programs have to be written to support this feature, but many already do. For instance, SimpleText can speak any portion of a document.

Look at the Control Panel in Figure 15-5. You can choose the voice your computer will use and also set the speed at which the computer speaks. Some of the voices are slow and could use a little speeding up.

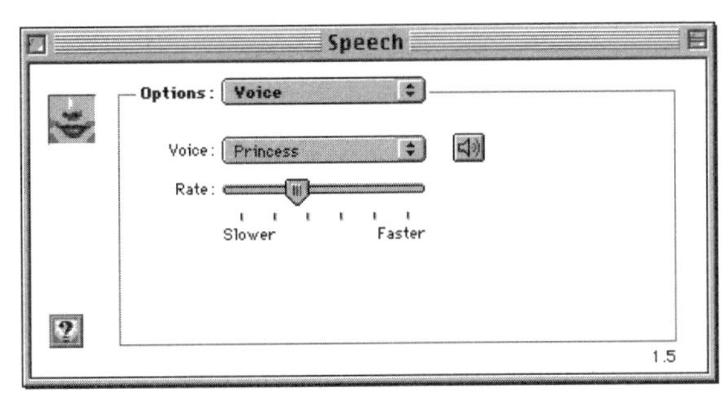

Figure 15-5: The Speech Control Panel lets you pick your computer's voice.

There are a number of different voices available. They run the gamut from pleasant and understandable to difficult and unintelligible. Some are quite amusing—the Deranged voice speaks through a lunatic laugh, and the Good News voice sings your text to the tune of "Pomp and Circumstance."

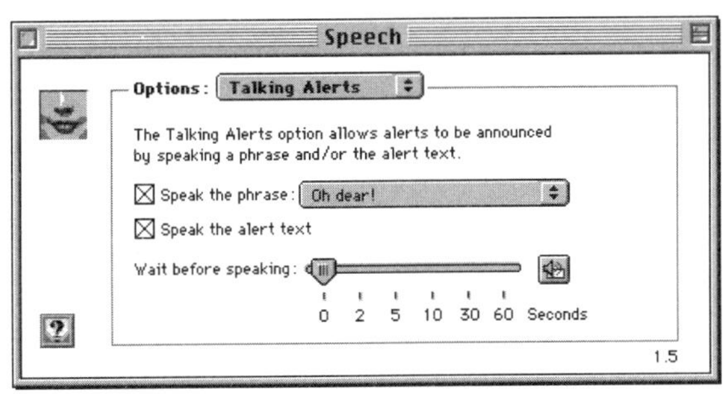

Figure 15-6: The Speech Control Panel can also be set so that any alert dialog box will be read aloud to you.

You can have your computer read any alert dialog boxes that pop up by using the Speech Control Panel (see Figure 15-6). The Speak the Alert Text setting means that the computer will speak whatever text is in the alert dialog box; the Speak the Phrase option will add a prefix of your choice beforehand. I find that any delay before speaking is annoying, so I set that option to zero.

Moving On

In this chapter, you've learned about the multimedia features of Mac OS 8. You've seen how to play digital video and audio with QuickTime and view 3D models with QuickDraw 3D and how to use the text-to-speech features of Mac OS 8.

Next, in Section III, you'll see how Mac OS 8 interacts with the world outside via networking. You'll learn how to work on a network, how to connect to the Internet, and even how to set up your own Web page!

PART III

Networking

CHAPTER 16

File Sharing

File Sharing is one of the many areas where the Macintosh was ahead of its time when it was introduced in 1984. The first Macintosh had a built-in AppleTalk port, allowing any number of Macintosh computers to be strung together with inexpensive phone cable to form a network. Back then, however, there was no compelling reason to create a Macintosh network.

Today, an AppleTalk port remains standard equipment on every Macintosh, and there are many good reasons for putting a Mac on a network. But AppleTalk is no longer the only network available for the Mac; Ethernet and Token Ring networks are available as well.

There are three main reasons why you might want to put your Macintosh on a network:

- **Computer-to-computer communications.** Networked Macintoshes can use electronic mail and messaging systems, and can transfer files directly from one computer to another.
- **Shared peripherals.** Laser printers, color printers, slide recorders, high-speed modems, fax/modems, and scanners are all expensive peripheral devices that can be shared among networked Macintoshes.
- **Centralized or distributed file servers.** Storing large amounts of data on file servers provides an easy way to share information, allows a number of people to participate in workgroup projects, and reduces the data storage requirements of individual users. Apple's AppleShare is the dominant file-serving software, but other servers compliant with the AppleShare Filing Protocol (AFP) can also be used.

It's in this last category that earlier versions of the Mac OS first provided greatly expanded abilities that continue into Mac OS 8. In Mac OS 8, Macintosh users can share files from their hard drives and other storage devices, such as Zip or Syquest drives, with other computers on the network and access files being shared by these other computers. This feature is called File Sharing under the Mac OS. In this chapter, you'll learn the basics of File Sharing and how to use it to allow others to access your files. Chapter 17, "Working on a Network," discusses additional File Sharing features, including accessing the data shared by other Macs and ways you can connect to your own Macintosh from another computer on your network.

What Is File Sharing?

File Sharing is a Mac OS 8 feature that lets you designate up to 10 folders and volumes on your computer to be shared with other computers on your network. For each shared folder or volume, you can assign access privileges, which can limit the use of your shared data to only the computers you specify.

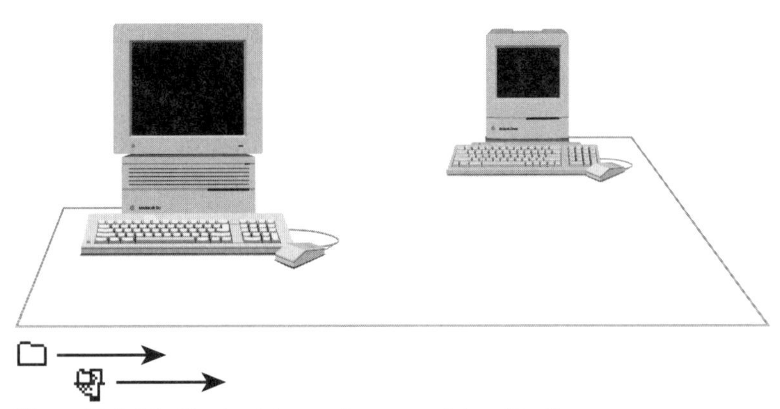

Figure 16-1: File Sharing lets you share your data with others.

File Sharing also lets you access folders and volumes other Macintoshes are sharing, provided you've been granted access privileges. Once accessed, folders and volumes from other Macs appear on your desktop and can be used as if they were your own.

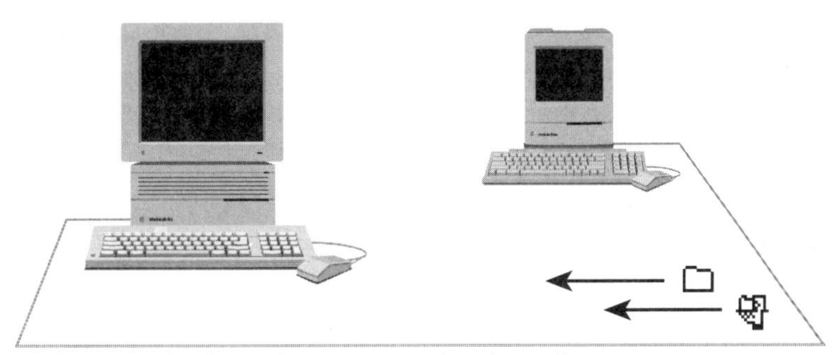

Figure 16-2: File Sharing lets you access data from other computers.

In networking parlance, when your computer is sharing files, it's acting as a server; when it's accessing files from another computer, it's acting as a client. File Sharing allows every user on a Macintosh network to become a server, a client, or both.

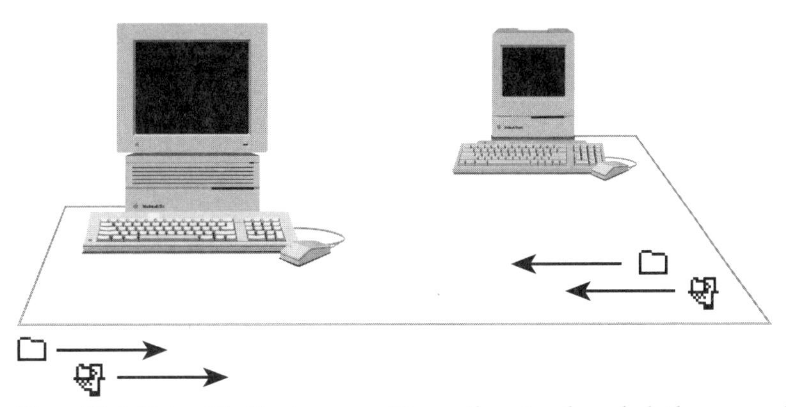

Figure 16-3: Using File Sharing, every Mac on the network can be both server and client.

Sharing data from your Macintosh, and accessing data shared by others on your network, can increase your capabilities and productivity in many ways. Here are some examples of resources that can be shared:

- **Central libraries.** Reference files such as clip art, templates (or Stationery Pads), and historical records can be kept in one location and shared with the entire network.

- **Drop-box folders that send and receive files.** Each network user can define an electronic "Out box" and "In box." By assigning access privileges, you can use an Out box to let everyone add files but not look at the folder's contents, and an In box to let users "pick up" the files they need, but not add any files.
- **Shared edition files that create living "workgroup" documents.** The Edition Manager features (described in Chapter 12, "Interapplication Communication & OpenDoc"), together with File Sharing, give network users access to edition files created by many users and stored on several hard drives.

The Limits of File Sharing

Although the capabilities of File Sharing are impressive, it's important to understand that File Sharing is only a "personal" version of AppleShare, Apple's dedicated file-server software. For a small number of Macs, File Sharing is sufficient, while larger or heavily used networks should use a combination of AppleShare and File Sharing. In these situations, File Sharing will supplement AppleShare, not replace it.

There are several reasons why File Sharing in some cases should be limited in this way:

- **Administration requirements.** As you'll see later, the administrative requirements of sharing files are not incidental. When many users need frequent access to numerous files and folders, centralized File Sharing administration, provided by central file servers such as AppleShare, is usually more efficient than distributed administration.
- **Security risks.** To avoid the burden of administrative requirements, users often neglect security issues, leaving confidential or sensitive data unprotected and available to anyone on the network. This is less likely to occur on centralized, professionally managed file servers.
- **Performance degradation.** Even with a very fast Mac and a very fast hard drive, File Sharing takes a noticeable toll on computer performance. Macintoshes or peripherals that aren't particularly speedy to begin with make the problem even worse. The benefits outweigh the inconveniences for the casual or infrequent user, but continually having to deal with long delays can be annoying and counterproductive. A centralized server with resources dedicated to the burdens of serving network users is the practical alternative in these circumstances.

- **Access limitations.** File Sharing can serve only 10 folders or volumes from one Macintosh at a time, and support only 50 logged-on users at one time (and that would be pushing it) with perhaps 15-20 concurrent users maximum. These constraints are too restrictive in many cases. Also, the sharing Macintoshes must be left on all the time to ensure files are always available on the network (files on a shut-down Mac are not accessible for sharing).

A File Sharing Quick Tour

File Sharing's capabilities are powerful and therefore require more preparation and attention than most other Mac OS 8 features. Here are the steps necessary to use File Sharing:

1. **Prepare your Macintosh.** This includes physically connecting to a network, installing the File Sharing files, and activating AppleTalk.
2. **Start File Sharing.** The File Sharing Control Panel provides configuration information and the master switch. In Mac OS 8 you can start (and stop) File Sharing using one of the AppleScripts found in the Useful Scripts folder under your Apple menu. If you have the Control Strip active on your desktop (for PowerBook users), there is a File Sharing switch there as one of the panels.
3. **Configure Users & Groups.** Users must be defined, and user preferences and access privileges set in the Users & Groups Control Panel. In most situations user groups will also need definition. You must also specify access privileges your Macintosh will enforce when network "guests" log on.
4. **Specify folders/volumes to share.** To share any folder or volume, the Sharing command must be applied, and sharing options set.
5. **Connect with others using File Sharing.** In order to access folders and volumes being shared by others, the Chooser is used to complete a log-on process.
6. **Use the File Sharing Activity Monitor to track access to your shared data.** The Activity Monitor within the File Sharing Control Panel constantly gives you updates on who's accessing what on your computer.

The remainder of this chapter looks in detail at the first four of these steps. The last two are covered in Chapter 17.

Preparing for File Sharing

File Sharing success depends on correctly connecting your Macintosh computers and installing network drivers. The simplest and most common Macintosh networking scheme uses LocalTalk or PhoneNet-style connectors and cabling that plug directly into the AppleTalk port on the back of the Mac.

More sophisticated networks require Ethernet or Token Ring adapters via NuBus or PCI slots (although most newer Macs come equipped with built-in Ethernet ports). When the network is physically connected, network availability and the presence of network software drivers must be verified by opening the AppleTalk Control Panel, which displays the available network drivers (shown in Figure 16-4).

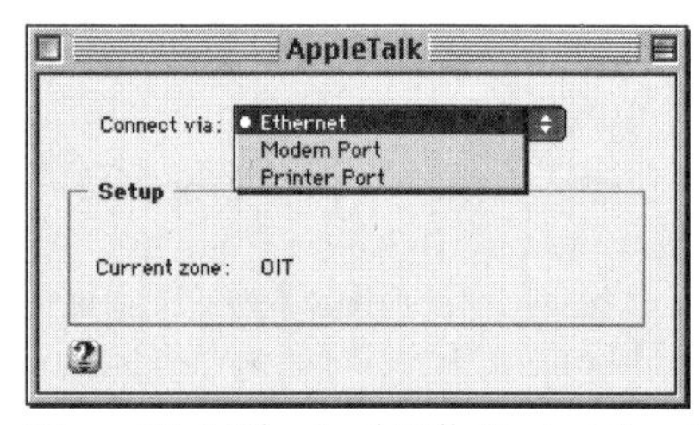

Figure 16-4: The AppleTalk Control Panel displays the available networking systems.

After verifying installation, open the Chooser and call AppleTalk by clicking the Active radio button. If your network is divided into zones, the Chooser also displays a list of available AppleTalk zones, as shown in Figure 16-5.

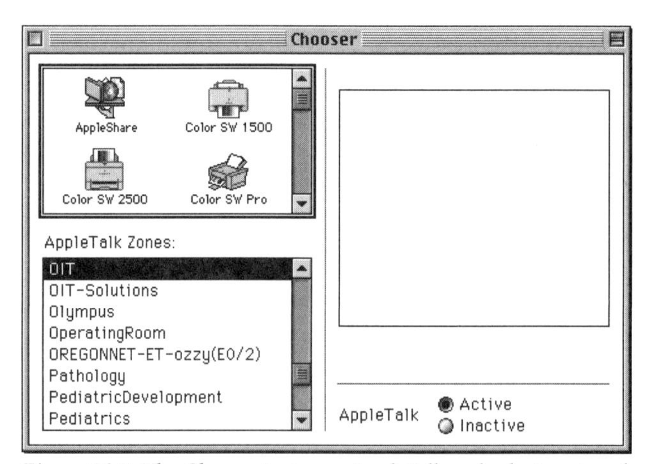

Figure 16-5: The Chooser turns on AppleTalk and selects network zones.

Starting File Sharing

Once your network is ready to be accessed, you can configure and turn on File Sharing with the File Sharing Control Panel located in your Control Panels folder. The File Sharing Control Panel (shown in Figure 16-6) lets you define your "network identity," turn File Sharing on and off, and start and stop Program Linking, using the Network Setup dialog box.

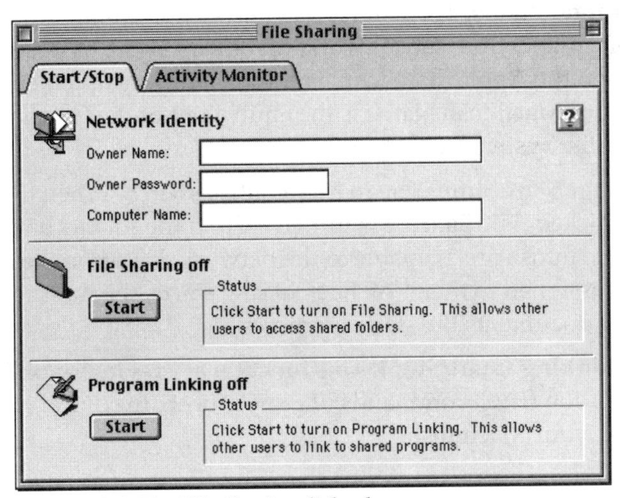

Figure 16-6: The File Sharing dialog box.

The options in this dialog box are:

- **Owner Name.** The name your Macintosh displays to others when you seek access to their computers via File Sharing. It's also the name you use to access your computer from any other on the network. Any name of up to 32 characters is acceptable, and you can change the Owner Name at any time.
- **Owner Password.** A security gate, allowing you as owner to access this Macintosh's entire hard drive from anywhere on the network when File Sharing is turned on. It also allows you, as an assigned owner, to access any shared folders or volumes. (By default, you're assigned ownership of all folders and volumes shared by your Macintosh. You can then assign this ownership to others, if you wish, as described in "Configuring User Preferences" later in this chapter.)

Note that this password can be changed at any time, and it's not necessary to know the old password to define a new one. This means you don't have to worry about forgetting your password—which may seem like a breach of security, and it is. But File Sharing controls only remote-user access to your Macintosh. It doesn't apply to anyone who sits down at your Mac's keyboard. Thus, the ability to change the password at any time is consistent with the Mac's total lack of local security.

- **The Computer Name.** The name other network users see when looking at your Macintosh from the network. It appears in the Chooser when they click on the AppleShare icon, and when they print to network printers. This Macintosh Name is the equivalent of the Chooser name used in earlier system software versions.
- **File Sharing (Start/Stop).** The master control switch. When the Start button is clicked, File Sharing is turned on and the folders and volumes on your Macintosh are available to the network, based on the access privileges assigned to them. As File Sharing starts, the message in the Status area documents the startup process.
- **Program Linking (Start/Stop).** This function allows inter-application communication (IAC) commands of remote users to control programs residing on your Macintosh.

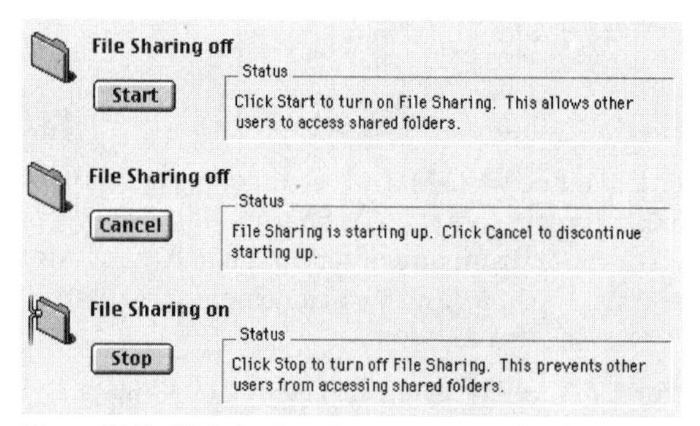

Figure 16-7: Click the Start button to start File Sharing and a status message will document the progress of File Sharing.

Once File Sharing is running, the Start button becomes the Stop button. When the Stop button is clicked, you're asked how many minutes until shutdown. Enter a number between 0 (for immediate shutdown) and 999 (for delayed action). Figure 16-8 illustrates this action.

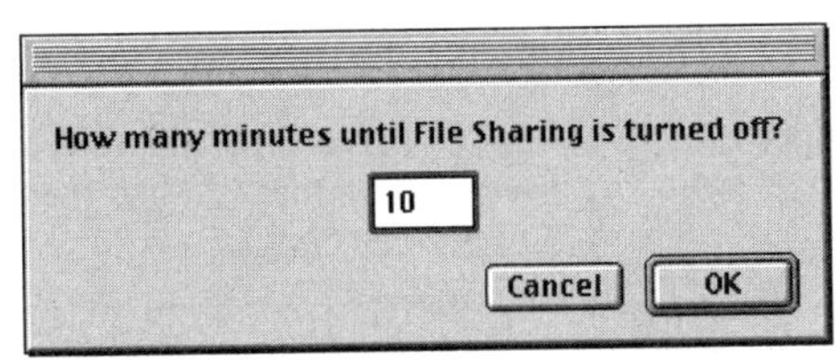

Figure 16-8: The Shut Down dialog box.

After you click OK in this dialog box, the Status message tells you how many minutes remain before File Sharing is turned off. As turn-off time approaches, other users accessing your Macintosh files are warned of impending shutdown, so they can save their work and release any volumes or folders they're using. It's not necessary for users to release your files before the shutdown; contact with your Macintosh is terminated immediately in any case. However, the Mac simply extends the courtesy of warning other users, so they won't lose work or be abruptly interrupted. If you choose the 0 minutes option, cutoff will occur without warning. (To check the number of users connected to your Mac, use the Activity Monitor window in the File Sharing Control Panel, as described in "Monitoring File Sharing" later in this chapter.)

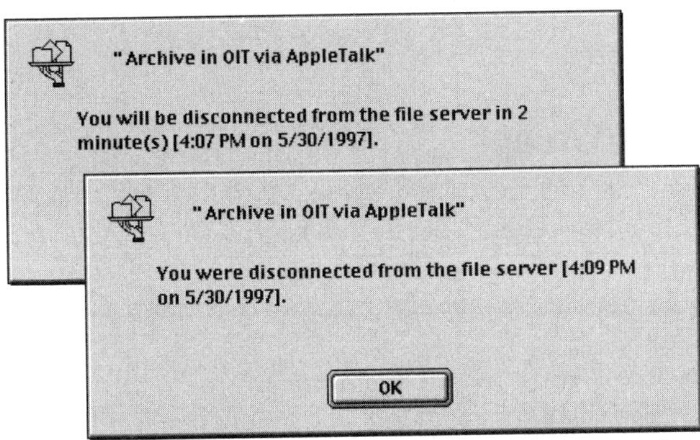

Figure 16-9: Clients are warned before a File Sharing server closes and after it has closed down.

When File Sharing is on and users are connected to your Macintosh, the Shut Down or Restart command brings up the Alert dialog box shown in Figure 16-10. Again, be sure to give your network users enough time to save their work before shutting down. If possible, cancel the Shut Down or Restart and leave your Macintosh running so network use can continue.

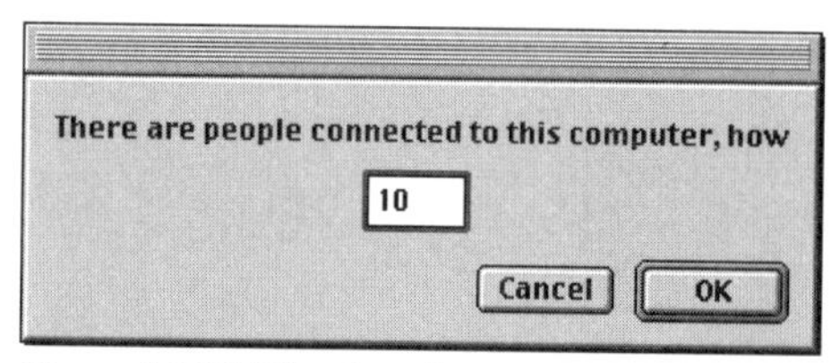

Figure 16-10: The alert that appears at Restart or Shut Down.

As a convenience, Mac OS 8 adds two more places where you can turn File Sharing on and off. In the Useful Scripts submenu of the Apple menu you will find two commands (AppleScripts, really): one called Start File Sharing, the other called Stop File Sharing. They do the same thing as clicking the Start and Stop button in the Sharing Setup dialog box. If you have the Control Strip installed, one of the panels is for controlling File Sharing, as shown in Figure 16-11. It works similarly.

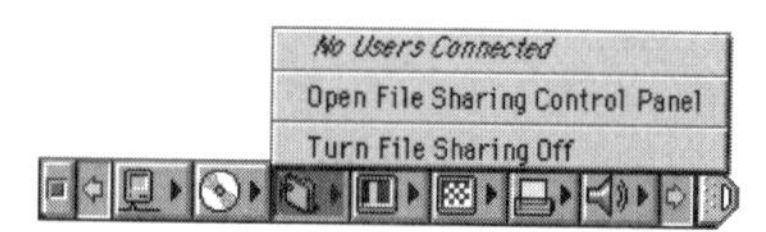

Figure 16-11: The File Sharing section of a Control Strip.

Registering Users & Groups

If you plan to use File Sharing to make your Macintosh folders and/or volumes available to other network users, you must decide who may and may not share your files. You may want to share your files with every user on your network, but it is more likely that you will want to restrict access to some or all of your shared files.

To designate access you open the Users & Groups Control Panel (shown in Figure 16-12), which displays a window containing one icon for each user and one icon for each group registered to access your Macintosh, in addition to a Guest icon and an icon for you, the Macintosh Owner.

Of course, when you open the Users & Groups Control Panel for the first time, no users or groups are yet defined, so only the Guest and Macintosh Owner icons will appear.

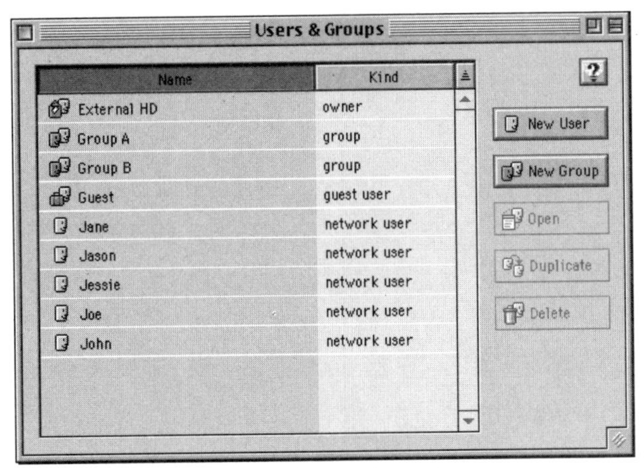

Figure 16-12: The Users & Groups Control Panel.

Via the Users & Groups Control Panel, you can grant access to four user categories:

- **Registered Users.** These are specific people you want to have access to your shared folders or volumes. Registered Users are given access to your data as individuals or as members of a defined Group.
- **Groups.** A Group is a collection of defined Registered Users. Individual Registered Users can be included in any number of groups.
- **Guests.** Any user on your network who has not been defined as a Registered User can attempt to log on to your shared folders or volumes as a Guest. You define whether you want these non-Registered Users to have access to your data.
- **Macintosh Owner.** As the owner, you can give yourself special remote abilities and access privileges to your computer.

In addition to the definitions and privileges mentioned so far, the Sharing dialog box provides additional security safeguards. This dialog box specifies Registered Users and Groups who have access privileges to particular folders and volumes. (More on the Sharing dialog box in "Sharing Folders or Volumes" later in this chapter.)

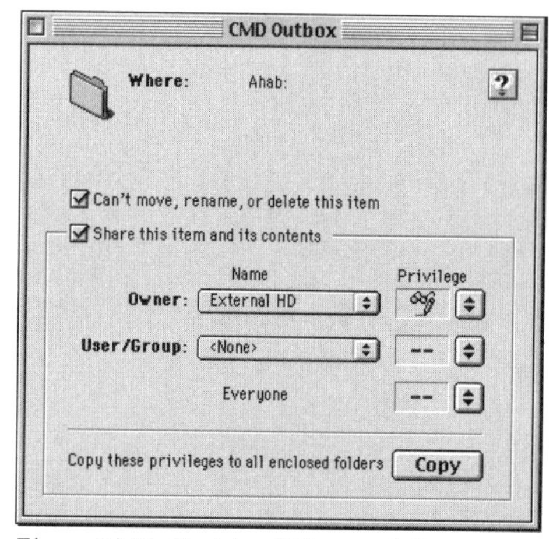

Figure 16-13: Registered Users and Groups are assigned access privileges via the Sharing dialog box.

Creating New Users

To create a new user, open the Users & Groups Control Panel, and choose the New User button. This creates a new "New User" Registered User icon in the Users & Groups window and opens the File Sharing options window which will be discussed in the section "Configuring User Preferences." Enter the name of the user you want this icon to represent.

It's best to enter the person's actual name, rather than a code name. A code name is more likely to be misspelled when the Registered User logs on.

File
New User ⌘N
New Group ⌘G
Open ⌘O
Duplicate ⌘D
Delete
Close Window ⌘W
Quit ⌘Q

Figure 16-14: The File menu provides the New User and New Group commands.

Up to 100 Registered Users can be defined, but Apple recommends staying under 50. If more than 50 people need regular access to certain shared folders or volumes, consider moving that data to a dedicated AppleShare server or allowing all Guests access to that data. (There is no limit to the number of Guests who can access your Macintosh, only to the number of Registered Users.)

You don't need to register users individually unless you want to limit access privileges. If you're going to allow everyone on the network to see and change your data, they can all log on as Guests. If not, you should define Users and Groups.

Configuring User Preferences

After registering a new user, or to alter a user's password or preferences, click on the user's name in the Users & Groups Control Panel to open the File Sharing options window, as shown in Figure 16-15. This dialog box sets the user's password and allows or disallows the user to connect via File Sharing or Program Linking. This dialog box also displays a list of all groups the user is included in (you can't change or modify group memberships in this dialog box).

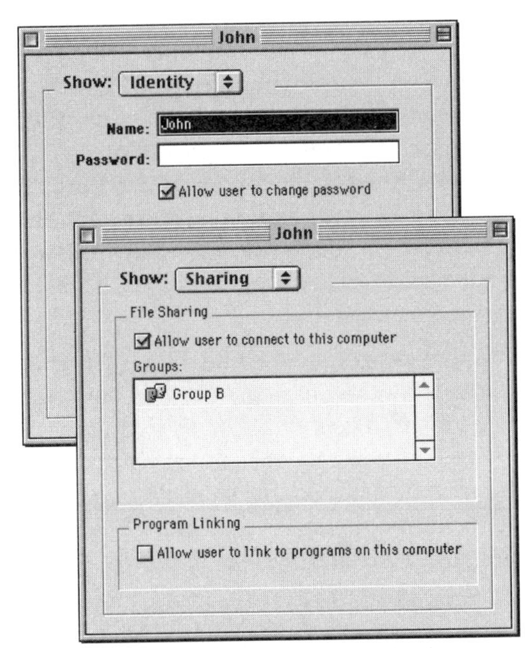

Figure 16-15: The User Preferences dialog box.

Let's look at the options under the pop-up menu "Identity" in this dialog box:

- **User Password.** In order to access your data from another Macintosh on the network, a username and, in most cases, a password must be entered. By default, the user has no password, and logs on by simply entering the username and leaving the password option blank. (More information on the log-in process later.) This obviously doesn't provide much security assurance that the user logging on is supposed to have network access.

  To add a password, type one into the User Password option box. For security, bullets will appear instead of the characters typed.

  When you add or change a user password, you must notify the user, for obvious reasons. Another approach is to leave the user without a password, letting them define their own passwords the first time they log on. They can then change their password periodically after that. This is done with the Allow User to Change Password option, described below. A variation would be to start with an obvious password like the user's first name, then encourage the user to change it at the first opportunity.

  You can change any user password at any time. For example, if a user forgets his or her password, there's no way for you to find it; you must "change" it to resolve this problem. Changing a password also lets you bar a particular user's access until you provide a new password.

  Avoid using obvious passwords like names, zodiac signs, and birthstones, and change passwords regularly.

- **Allow User to Change Password.** This option allows Registered Users to change their passwords using the Change Password button that appears in the Chooser as they log on to your Macintosh. In most cases, this option should be selected, because changing user passwords frequently increases the security of your data. Of course, since you as the Owner can always change passwords directly in this dialog box, you lose no privileges by allowing users this option.

Select the pop-up menu "Identity" and select "Sharing" for these options:

- **Allow User to Connect.** This check box is the "personal" master switch for File Sharing that makes it possible or impossible for a user to connect as a Registered User (they still may be able to connect as a Guest). This option is on by default, but occasionally you may want to turn it off. Using this option to revoke access privileges is less drastic than deleting the user, which makes later reinstatement more difficult.
- **Program Linking.** Users can take advantage of this option if the feature is turned on in the File Sharing Control Panel.

Creating & Working With Groups

Since a network comprises many individual users, assigning access privileges to each individual for each item would be a very tedious job. To avoid this, File Sharing lets you define Groups, add Registered Users to these Groups, then assign access privileges that apply to all Group members.

New Groups are created by selecting the New Group button while the Users & Groups Control Panel is open, which places a new "New Group" Group icon in the Users & Groups window and launches the Group Preferences dialog box. Enter the name of the group you want this icon to represent (descriptive names are best). Registered Users never see the group names you assign, nor do they need to know which groups they're assigned to.

You can't make a Guest icon a member of any group; but you can add yourself as the Macintosh Owner to any group. This isn't as useless as it may seem: if you assign ownership of folders or volumes to another user or group, you won't have access to that folder (over the network) if you're not a member of a group that has access privileges (unless you add yourself to that group) or use the Allow User to See Entire Volume option in your Owner Preferences (described later).

To add Registered Users to the group, drag their icons onto the Group icon and release them. Or you can double-click on the Group icon to open the group's window and then drag user icons directly into this window. You can also combine groups by dragging one group icon over another. Adding a user to a group does not remove the User icon from the main Users & Groups window. You can drag a single user icon into any number of groups. To check which groups a user is part of, double-click the Registered User's icon and see the list in the User Preferences dialog box.

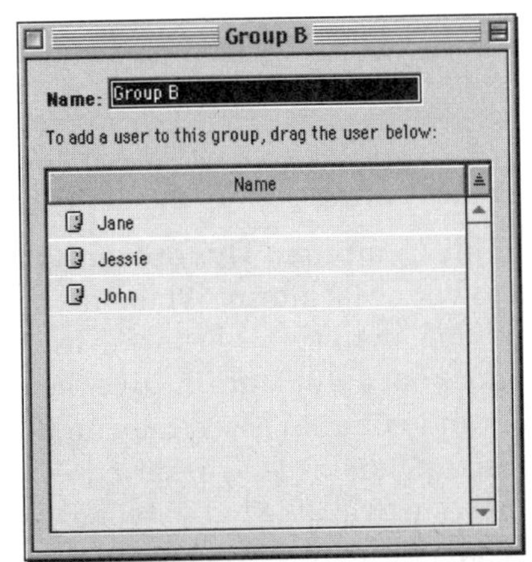

Figure 16-16: A defined Group containing three Registered Users.

To remove a user from a group, open the Group window, select the user's icon, and choose the File menu's Remove command. This deletes the user from the group; it does not remove the user entirely, and it doesn't remove the user from any other groups he or she belongs to. Similarly, you can delete an entire group by selecting the group and choosing the File menu's Remove command, which removes the group but does not affect any group member individually.

Configuring Guest Preferences

You may occasionally want to share files with someone on your network who isn't a Registered User. This is made possible by File Sharing's support of guests. A single Guest icon is automatically included in the Users & Groups Control Panel, and this icon is used to control access to your shared data for all non-Registered Users. The Guest icon cannot be deleted. Double-clicking on the Guest icon brings up the Guest Preferences dialog box.

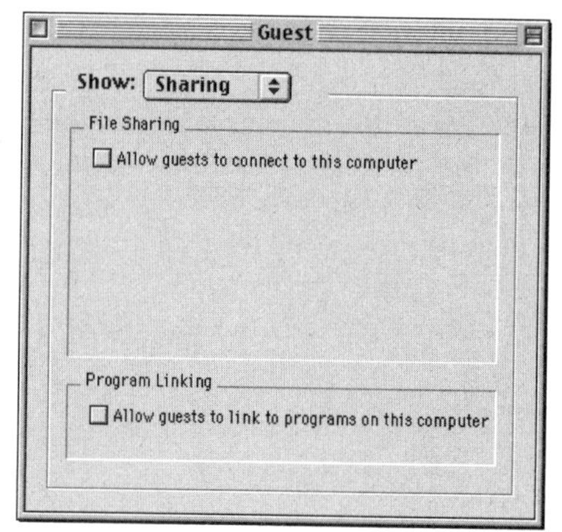

Figure 16-17: The Guest Preferences dialog box.

There are only two options under the Sharing pop-up menu in this window:

- **Allow Guests to Connect to This Computer.** This option is the master switch that lets guests log on to your Macintosh. When this option is deselected, network users can't log on to your Macintosh as guests.

  Allowing guests to log on does not automatically give them access to data. Guests can access folders and volumes based only on the "Everyone" access privileges in the Sharing dialog box, as described later in this chapter. If no folders or volumes are available to Everyone, guests who attempt to log on will find no data available.

- **Allow Guests to Link to Programs on This Computer.** Program is used by the Mac OS's IAC feature. If you select this option, guests can link to your programs; if you deselect it, they can't.

Configuring Owner Preferences

The preferences you set for yourself, the Macintosh Owner, affect the way you can access your Macintosh from elsewhere on the network. They have no affect on what you can do directly from your keyboard (and mouse). The Macintosh Owner icon is created automatically, and named with the Macintosh Owner Name, as set in the Sharing Setup Control Panel. The Owner icon appears with the label "Owner" in the Users & Groups window. Double-clicking on this icon opens the Macintosh Owner Preferences dialog box.

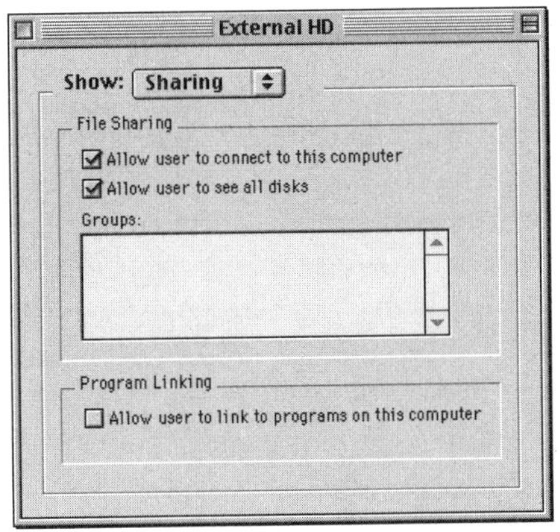

Figure 16-18: The Macintosh Owner Preferences dialog box.

The options in this dialog are the same as those described previously for any Registered User, with the exception of the Allow User to See All Disks option. This option lets you access entire volumes on your Macintosh from anywhere on the network at any time–even when the volumes have not been specifically shared with the Sharing command. When accessing volumes in this way, you have full access privileges to all files, folders, and applications.

This feature is very powerful—and potentially dangerous. It allows you to work on your Macintosh, or access any data stored on your Macintosh, from any Mac on the network just as if you were at your own keyboard. The danger is that anyone else who knows your Owner Name and password could gain the same access.

If you don't need this feature, leave it deselected. If you do use this option, be very discreet with your password, and change it frequently. If you won't need to use this feature over an extended period of time, temporarily deselect it. Of course, there's always the possibility that someone might sit down at your Macintosh keyboard and access your data or change your password, then remotely access your Mac. File Sharing should not lull you into a false sense of security. If you have good reason to believe this could happen, other security measures should be taken.

Sharing Folders or Volumes

For any folder or volume to be shared with others on your network, the Sharing command must initiate sharing and specify access privileges. Any mounted volume, including hard disks, hard disk partitions, removable cartridges, CD-ROMs, and any folder on any mounted volume can be shared. Floppy disks and folders on floppy disks cannot.

To initiate sharing, select the folder or volume and choose the Sharing command from the File menu, which brings up the Sharing dialog box (shown in Figure 16-19). This dialog box is used to turn on Sharing and assign access privileges to this item. Access privileges, as you learned earlier, determine who can see the folders and volumes, who can see the files inside those folders and volumes, and who can make changes to existing files or store new files. (More on access privileges later in this chapter.)

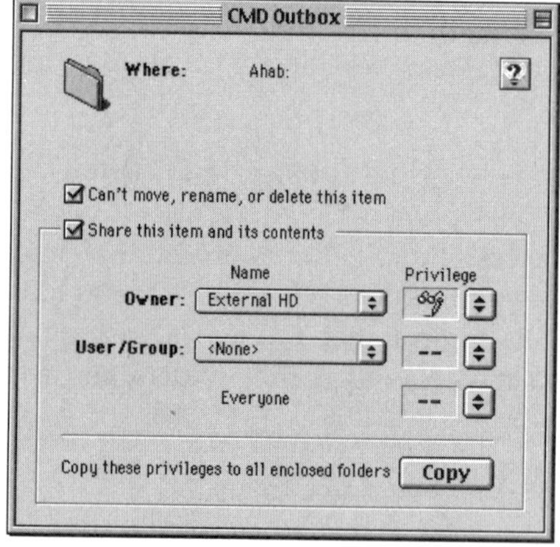

Figure 16-19: A Sharing dialog box.

The Sharing dialog box presents a number of important options:

- **Can't Move, Rename, or Delete.** This option gives you a safety net to ensure that the folder or volume you share is not moved, renamed, or deleted by any network user—including the owner. It's a good idea to select this option in all cases, unless you know that repositioning, renaming, or deleting the item will be necessary. This will prevent accidental changes with unpleasant results.
- **Share This Item and Its Contents.** This check box is the master switch that turns sharing on or off for the selected folder or volume and the contents of that folder or volume. Until this option is selected, all other options in this dialog box are dimmed.
- **Owner.** This option specifies the owner of the selected folder or volume and the owner's access privileges. In most cases, you (as the Macintosh Owner) will remain the owner of shared folders and volumes.

  However, using the pop-up menu, you can designate any other Registered User as the owner of the selected folder or volume. The assignee can then reset access privileges for the item. Your access to the folder or volume from another Macintosh on the network is then dependent on your inclusion in the User/Group option (discussed in the following subsection). Of course, your access to the folder or volume from your own Macintosh will not be affected; these options affect only network access.

  Once an owner has been specified, use the check boxes to assign access privileges. (More on available access privileges and their use in the next section of this chapter.)
- **User/Group.** This option grants one user or one group access to the selected folder or volume (via the pop-up menu), and defines the access privileges available to this user or group. In many ways, this is the most important Sharing option, because it usually designates the person or group of users that will most frequently access the shared data. (See the "Access Privileges" section of this chapter for the ways this feature can be used, including bulletin boards, drop boxes, read-only filing systems, and true workgroup File Sharing and storage systems.)
- **Everyone.** This option specifies access privileges granted to Guest users on your Macintosh. As mentioned before, anyone on your network can log on to your Mac as a Guest, providing you've specified that Guest log-ins are permitted. In that case, the "Everyone" option determines which volumes and folders they can access.

- **Copy These Privileges to All Enclosed Folders.** When you share a folder or volume, all enclosed folders are also automatically accessible to users with access privileges. You cannot "unshare" a folder enclosed in a shared folder or on a shared volume, but you can change the access privileges of an enclosed folder so that they don't match those of the enclosing folder. This option also can reset the access privileges of the enclosed folders so they match those of the currently selected folder or volume.

  For example, a folder called Outbox is shared, with full access privileges by everyone on the network. Inside this folder is a folder called Project A. We want to limit access to Project A so that only members of the Project A group can share it. To do this, after using the Sharing command for the Outbox folder, you'd select the Project A folder and choose the Sharing command again. Now, access privileges are reset, limiting access to group members only. Figure 16-20 displays the Sharing dialog box for the "CMD Outbox" folder and the "Project A" folder.

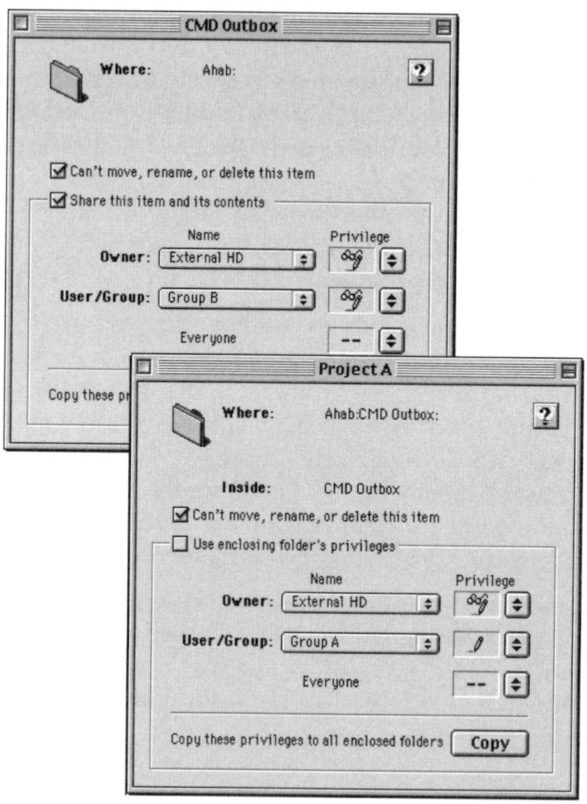

Figure 16-20: The Sharing dialog box for a parent and child folder.

Notice that the Share This Item and Its Contents option has been replaced in the "Project A" folder dialog box with a Use Enclosing Folder's Privileges option. This occurs because the "Project A" folder is inside a folder that is already shared. By default, this new option is selected, and the access privileges match those specified for the enclosing "CMD Outbox" folder. Deselecting this option makes it possible to change the access privileges.

After making any changes to these options, click the close box in the title bar to close the dialog box and apply these options to the selected item. If you've made changes to the ownership, dialog boxes appear asking you to confirm or cancel the changes requested. A dialog box will also appear if you chose the Make All Enclosed Folders Like This One option. Figure 16-21 displays these warning dialogs.

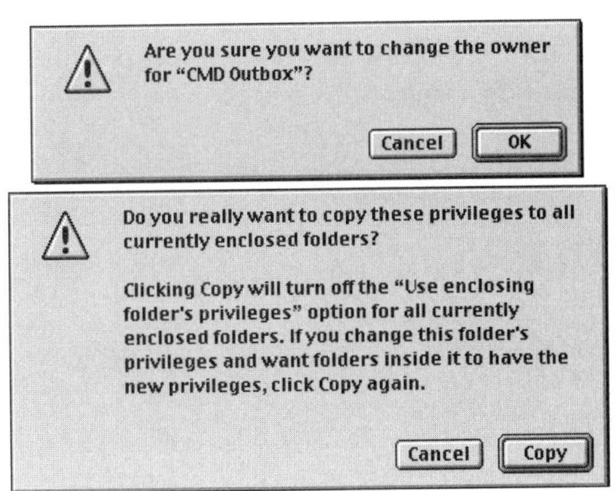

Figure 16-21: Two confirming dialog boxes appear after changing Sharing options.

Icons of Shared Items

Figure 16-22 shows a folder icon and its changes. After you have specified and implemented sharing options, icons of the shared folders will modify, confirming their shared status.

Figure 16-22: A folder as it appears before Sharing (left), after Sharing (center), and when users are connected (right).

Unsharing

There are two ways to make shared items unavailable to network users: you can turn File Sharing off completely, or you can turn File Sharing off for individual folders and volumes.

To turn File Sharing off completely, open the File Sharing Control Panel and click the File Sharing Stop button, as described earlier. When File Sharing is turned off, the settings and access privileges set with the Sharing command are retained for all shared folders and volumes, and will go back into effect when File Sharing is again turned on.

To turn off the sharing of a particular folder or volume only, select the appropriate folder or volume icon, choose the Sharing command, and deselect the Share This Item and Its Contents Option. When you close the Sharing dialog box, the selected folder or volume will become unavailable for network access. (An Alert dialog box will appear if users are currently accessing the shared item, as shown in Figure 16-23.) Note that all access privilege settings are lost when sharing is turned off for a particular folder or volume; you'll have to reset them the next time the item is shared.

Figure 16-23: Unsharing with users.

As an alternative to turning off File Sharing either completely or for particular folders or volumes, you could also change the Allow User to Connect and Allow Guest to Connect options in the user icons found in the Users & Groups Control Panel. This method is not generally recommended, but it does allow access privilege settings to remain in force while temporarily making it impossible for some or all users to connect.

Access Privileges

Shared folders, volumes, and folders enclosed within those shared folders and volumes are provided to other network users according to access privilege settings you apply in the Sharing dialog box. These privileges, along with users and groups designated in the Users & Groups Control Panel, are the key to controlling File Sharing.

As shown in Figure 16-24, the three access privilege options are assigned to three different users or groups. Option settings and combinations you apply determine how network users can access and modify your shared data and storage space. Let's look at these access privileges, the users and groups they can be assigned to, and the results of applying them in different combinations.

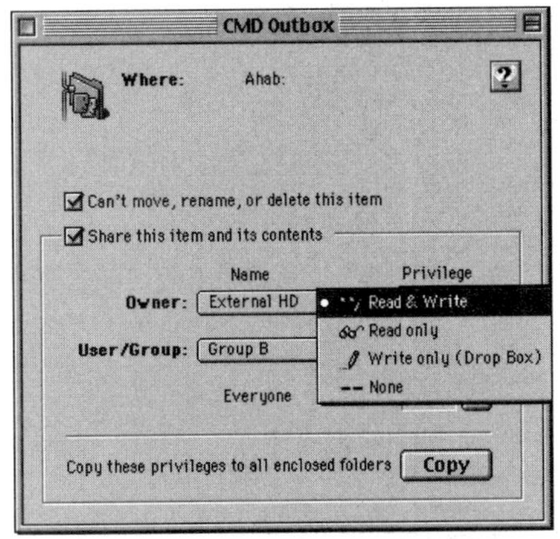

Figure 16-24: The access privilege options.

- **Write Only (Drop Box).** This privilege hides all folders from the specified user or group—users don't even know which folders exist in the selected folder or volume. Users can place files in the shared item but only the owner can see and manage the contents. When the Write Only option is selected, an icon appears in the upper-left corner of the title bars of all windows accessed via File Sharing, letting the user know that folders are not being displayed.

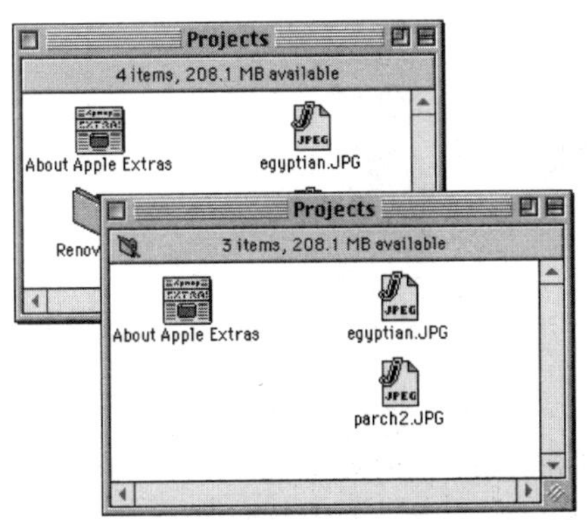

Figure 16-25: A shared folder with and without Write Only privileges.

- **Read Only.** This option limits a user to view the contents of the folders. No changes can be made within the shared item. When the See Files option is deselected, an icon appears in the upper-left corner of the title bars of all windows accessed via File Sharing, letting the user know that the folder or volume is write protected.

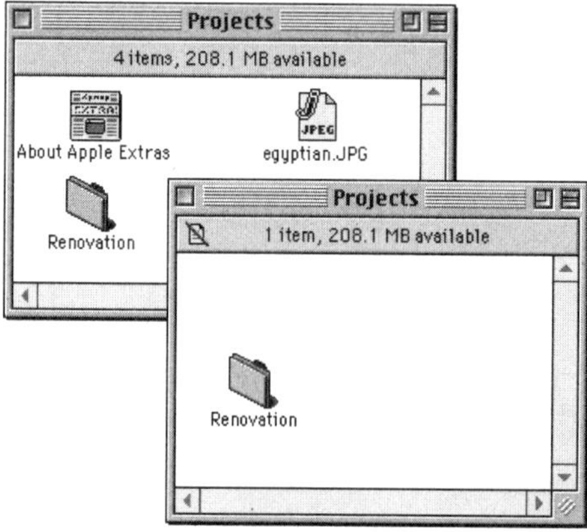

Figure 16-26: A shared folder with and without Read Only privileges.

- **Read & Write.** When the Read & Write privilege is set, the user can save new files, change existing files, and create new folders. The user enjoys almost unlimited access to the folder and it's contents.

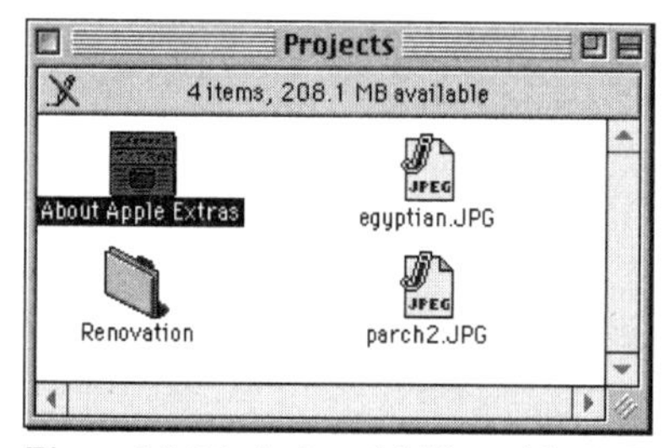

Figure 16-27: A shared folder without Read & Write privileges.

These three options are assigned individually to three user categories:

- **Owner.** The owner of a folder or volume is the person or group who can change the access privileges of that folder or volume while accessing it over the network. The person who creates a folder is automatically the owner of it; therefore, you are default owner of the folders and volumes on your Macintosh. When a user creates new folders in shared folders or volumes, however, that user becomes the owner of the new folders.
  Using the pop-up menu, the owner can be designated as any defined user or group. Or, selecting the <Any User> option gives any guest who accesses the folder or volume full owner privileges (including the right to reassign access privileges). When setting access privileges on remote volumes, the Owner pop-up menu does not appear and the Owner Name must be entered manually.
- **User/Group.** The User/Group category assigns access privileges to one specific user or group. When sharing folders or volumes, select the desired User/Group from the pop-up menu listing of all registered users and groups. When setting access privileges on remote volumes, the User/Group pop-up menu does not appear and the Owner Name must be entered manually.
- **Everyone.** The Everyone category grants access privileges to all Guests who connect to the Macintosh that contains the selected folder or volume. Of course, in order for Guests to log on, the Allow Guests to Connect option must be set in the Users & Groups Control Panel.

Access Privilege Strategies

This elaborate matrix of categories and access privilege levels allows precise control over the way shared files can be used. Several common ways of using access privileges are described below:

- **Create an In Box folder.** The key aspect of an In Box is that those who pick up the files can see them but not make changes to them. This is accomplished by granting "Read only" privileges as shown in Figure 16-28. Of course, those who should not have access to the files in the In Box should not even see files or folders.

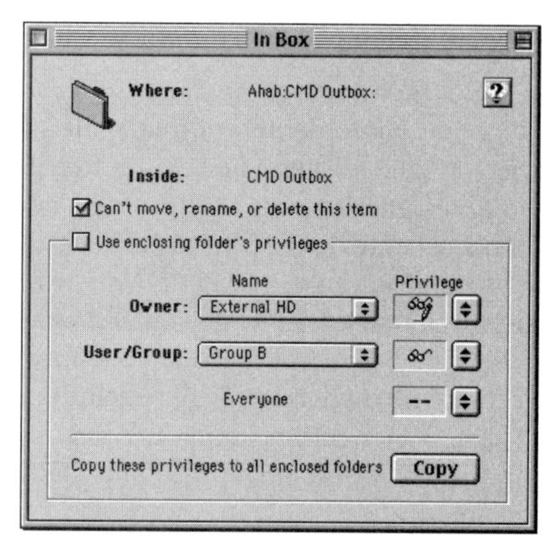

Figure 16-28: A set of access privileges that defines an In Box.

- **Create an Out Box folder.** The opposite of an In Box, an Out Box allows users to add files, but not to see anything that's already there—it's like a mail slot. This is defined by granting "Write only" access privileges as shown in Figure 16-29.

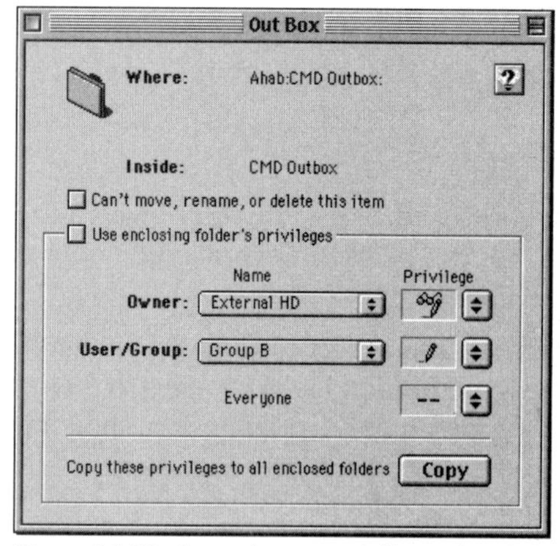

Figure 16-29: A set of access privileges that defines an Out Box.

- **Create a Bulletin Board.** Combining the attributes of Out Boxes and In Boxes in various folders and enclosed folders, you can create a place where people can read and retrieve some files and add and modify others, depending on who they are and which folder they're accessing. Figure 16-30 shows a set of enclosed folders and the privileges that provide such an arrangement.

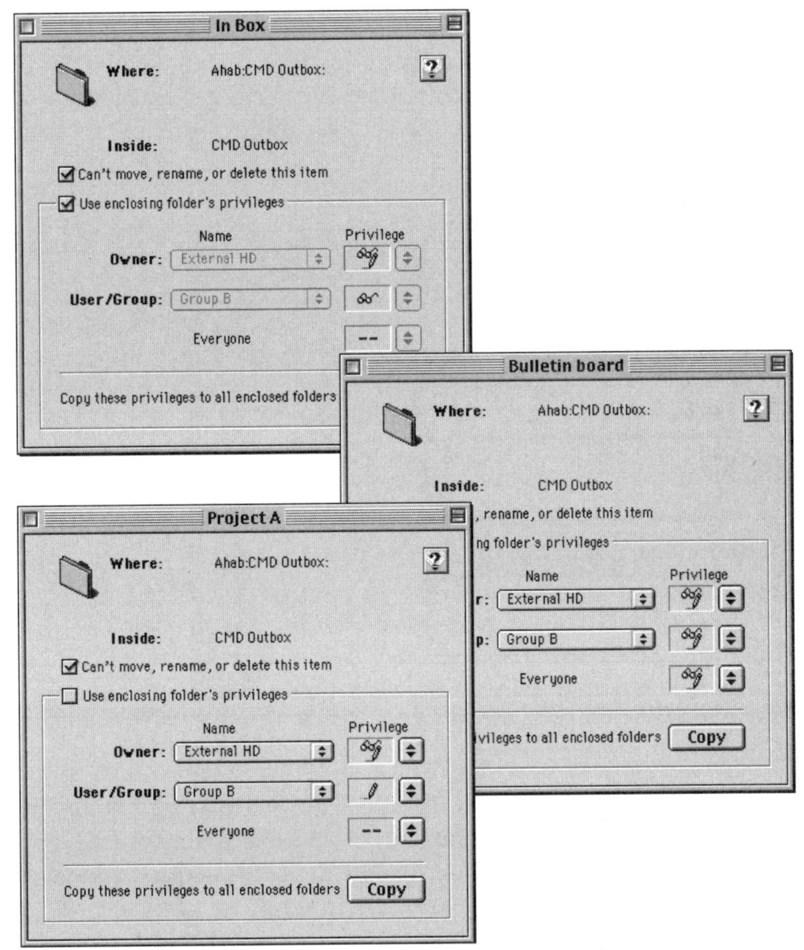

Figure 16-30: Privileges for several folders in a Bulletin Board.

- **Provide a group work area.** A simpler but more common way to use access privileges is to make a set of files available to specific users and groups. For example, you may have a folder to which the members of the "Engineers" Group have full privileges, while members of the "Sales Reps" team can see the files but not modify them.

Monitoring File Sharing

The File Sharing Control Panel gives you information about the items shared, the users connected to your computer, and the activities of these users. Open the File Sharing Control Panel, select the Activity Monitor tab, and the dialog box in Figure 16-31 appears.

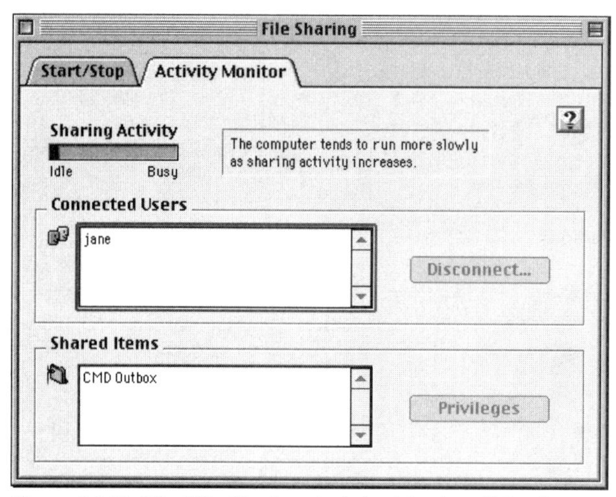

Figure 16-31: The File Sharing Activity Monitor dialog box.

The first item in this Control Panel is the File Sharing Activity Monitor. This gauge fluctuates with the demands on your computer system as connected users access your Macintosh. When the demand is high, the local operation of your Macintosh slows. If slowdowns caused by remote users are a persistent problem, you may need to limit the access of Registered Users and Guests by reducing the amount of shared data you make available. Or you can shift some shared data to dedicated AppleShare file servers.

The window labeled Connected Users lists network users currently connected to your Macintosh. You can disconnect any user by selecting the user's name from this list and clicking the Disconnect button. A dialog box lets you give the selected user warning by delaying disconnection for the number of minutes you select, or you can use the default 0 minutes and disconnect immediately.

The last window of this dialog box presents a list of the folders and volumes you've shared. To see the access privileges for an item, select I and click the Privileges button and the Sharing dialog box will appear.

Moving On

The power and flexibility File Sharing offers will undoubtedly change the way you work on a Macintosh network. File Sharing removes almost all the barriers—physical and psychological—that previously inhibited the flow of data between computers. With File Sharing, you can:

- Make any folder or volume on your computer available to anyone connected to your Macintosh network.
- Designate who can access the files and folders you share.
- Specify privileges extended to each regular user and network guest.

In Chapter 17, you'll see the other side of the File Sharing coin—accessing data shared by other Macs and by centralized file servers. You'll also look at other aspects of network life, such as printing over a network.

CHAPTER 17

Working on a Network

Mac OS users have long known the benefits of computer networking. Shared printers, and other peripheral Mac-to-Mac communications, and remote access to network file servers are commonplace on almost every Mac network. This chapter focuses on using your Macintosh network to access AppleShare and File Sharing volumes, the effects of access privileges, and how you control files stored on remote volumes. We'll also look at using Program Linking to allow applications to talk to each other over a network.

Accessing Network Volumes

As described in Chapter 16, "File Sharing," every Mac on your network can share up to 10 folders or volumes with other network users; this ability is based on User and Groups access privilege designations for each Mac that shares network data. In addition, dedicated AppleShare file servers can make any number of complete volumes available to all network users according to specified access privileges.

Connecting to other computers running the Mac OS for File Sharing and AppleShare file server access is easy. This section describes how to do it and how to manage shared data.

Before connecting to your file server, check that you have the appropriate network services selected. Open the AppleTalk Control Panel and click on the Ethernet, Modem Port, Printer Port, or an alternate means of connectivity. Then, proceed with the instructions that follow. If you don't understand the options as they are presented, you may wish to talk to a network administrator if one is available.

Connecting With the Chooser

The first step in accessing network data is to open the Chooser (in the Apple menu) and click on the AppleShare icon, which is shown in the upper left corner of Figure 17-1.

The available network file servers appear on the right side of the window, and if your network is divided into zones, those zones are listed in the lower left corner of the Chooser. If a zone list appears in your Chooser, select the zone in which your Macintosh is registered; available server volumes in that zone will appear.

The list of file server names that appears includes both dedicated AppleShare file servers and Macs on your network using File Sharing. There's no easy way to tell from the listing which are AppleShare servers and which are File Sharing Macintoshes. In any case, as a client accessing data over the network, it makes no difference to you whether you're accessing data from a dedicated AppleShare file server or from a File Sharing Macintosh.

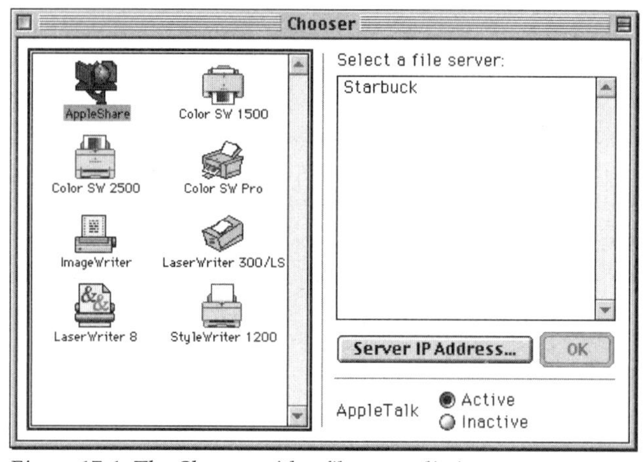

Figure 17-1: The Chooser with a file server listing.

When you've located the name of the file server you wish to access, double-click on the filename or click the OK button below the file server list. The Connect dialog box appears (shown in Figure 17-2). This dialog box gives you the option of connecting to the selected file server as a guest or as a registered user.

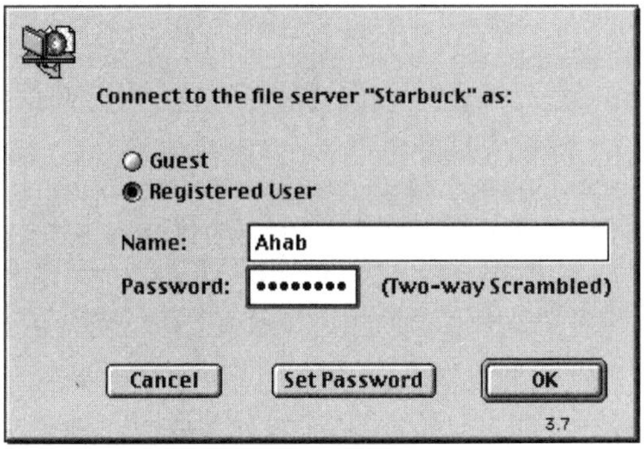

Figure 17-2: The Connect dialog box.

In order to connect as a registered user, a user icon with your name and password must exist on the AppleShare server or File Sharing Macintosh. This shows that the systems administrator or Macintosh owner has created and defined your Macintosh as a registered user, as described in Chapter 16.

You can now click the Registered User option. The owner name specified in your Sharing Setup Control Panel will appear as the default in the Name option box. If this is not the name under which you're registered, make the required changes to the Name option. If a password has been assigned, enter it in the Password option. If none is needed, leave the option blank. Then click the OK button.

Connecting as a guest is simpler but may restrict your access privileges. Of course, this is your only option if you're not a registered user. To connect as a guest, click the Guest option and then click the OK button. If the selected file server does not allow guests to connect, the Guest option will be dimmed. In this case, the only way to connect is to contact the Macintosh owner or server administrator and ask to become a registered user.

The final option in the Connect dialog box is the Set Password button, which allows registered users with appropriate access privileges to reset their passwords for a particular file server. Changing your password affects only the currently selected file server, not all servers on which you're a registered user.

Selecting Specific Volumes

After you identify yourself as either Registered User or Guest (and clicking the OK button), a list of available volumes on the selected server appears, as shown in Figure 17-3. If an incorrect name or password was entered, an Alert dialog box appears, and you'll be returned to the Connect dialog box.

This dialog box lists all volumes that the selected server is sharing with the network. When accessing File Sharing volumes, it's not possible to differentiate between shared folders and shared volumes, so I'll use the term volumes generically. Refer to the previous chapter for more information.

The names of any volumes you're not allowed to access will be dimmed. You can mount any one non-dimmed volume by double-clicking on the volume name or selecting the volume name and clicking the OK button. To mount more than one volume, hold down the Shift key while selecting volume names and then click the OK button.

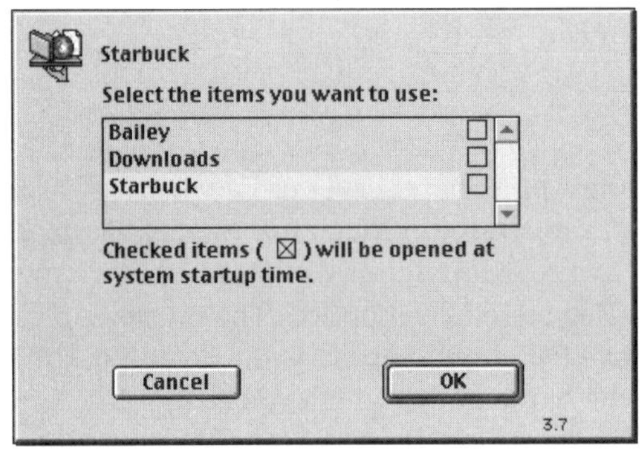

Figure 17-3: Available Server listing.

You can also configure the volume to mount automatically each time you start up your Macintosh by clicking on the check box next to a volume name. You'll have to enter your password manually each time you start your Macintosh, and the volume is mounted since by default your password is not stored as part of this automatic-mount process. To simplify the automatic mount (but at the same time reduce security), click the Save My Name and Password option and then double-click the volume name or click the OK button.

After mounting a volume, you're returned to the Connect dialog box. To mount additional volumes from the selected file server, click the OK button again to return to the volume list and repeat the mounting process for another volume.

Remote Volumes & Access Privileges

Any remote volumes you've mounted appear on your Desktop as AppleShare Volume icons (see Figure 17-4) unless they have a custom icon associated with the folder or hard drive (in which case the custom icon will be displayed instead). The AppleShare Volume icon also accompanies these volumes in

Open or Save As dialog boxes. These volumes are used just like local volumes (those physically connected to your Mac) except that any restrictions imposed by your access privileges apply. When your Macintosh is communicating with remote volumes, arrows flash just to the left of your Apple menu.

Figure 17-4: A volume icon on the Desktop (left), and the activity arrows that flash while remote volumes are accessed (right).

As described in Chapter 16, access privileges determine whether you can see folders, see files, and make changes to available volumes. The Finder windows for remotely accessed volumes indicate your access privileges by displaying small icons in the upper left corner just below the title bar (shown in Figure 17-5). To see your assigned access privileges, choose the Sharing command from the File menu while the folder is selected or open.

Figure 17-5: The Cannot Write, Cannot See Folders, and Cannot See Files icons.

When you don't have Make Changes privileges, you can't save or copy a file to a volume. In Save dialog boxes, the Save button is dimmed when the selected volume is write-protected in this way; and at the Finder, any attempt to copy or create files will bring up the dialog box shown in Figure 17-6.

This same dialog box will appear if you attempt to create a new folder on a volume for which you don't have See Folders privileges.

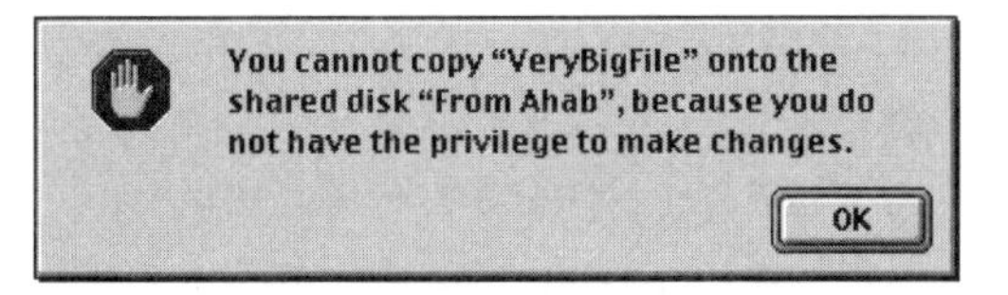

Figure 17-6: Not Enough Access Privileges dialog box.

Use the Sharing command to see the complete access privileges for any volume you can mount. Select the volume icon and choose the Sharing command from the File menu. If you own the volume, you can change these access privileges. If you create a folder on a shared volume, you're automatically assigned as the folder's owner and allowed to use the File menu's Sharing command to reset the access privileges.

A Volume Access Shortcut

To avoid this lengthy process every time you mount a networked volume, you can create an alias of the volume icon that appears on your Desktop and store that alias in a convenient spot on your hard drive, perhaps in your Apple Menu Items folder for easy access. In fact, you can create a folder full of network volume aliases, as shown in Figure 17-7.

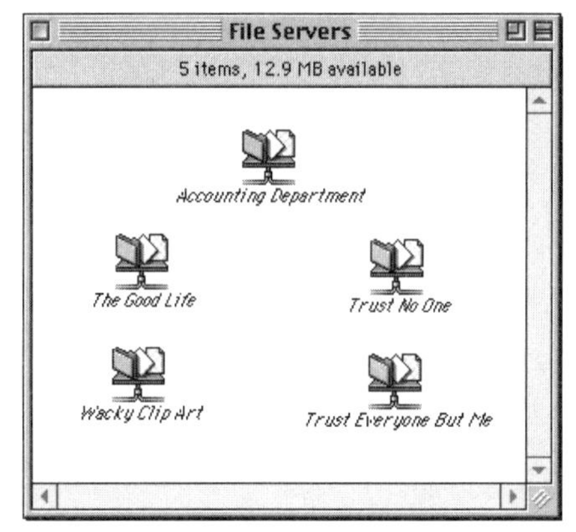

Figure 17-7: Folder of volume aliases.

Double-clicking on the network volume alias icon mounts the volume after you supply any necessary passwords. This shortcut can save lots of time and effort.

Disconnecting From Remote Volumes

There are three ways to disconnect a mounted network volume:

- **Trash the volume.** Simply drag the volume icon into the Trash. Just as this action ejects removable disks, it releases mounted file server volumes.

- **Shut Down or Restart.** All mounted volumes are also released when you use the Shut Down or Restart command.
- **Put Away.** The File menu's Put Away command, or its keyboard equivalent, Command+Y, dismounts any selected volumes.

Accessing Your Hard Drive Remotely

When File Sharing is on, you can access your entire hard drive and all volumes currently mounted from anywhere on your network—unless you've deselected the Allow User to See Entire Volume option in the Owner Preferences window of the Users & Groups Control Panel. This option is accessed by double-clicking on the user icon that displays your Owner Name.

To reach your hard drive from another Mac on your network, select the Chooser just as you would to log on to any network volume. Locate the name of your Macintosh in the scrolling file server list and double-click on it. A new dialog box appears, listing the name of each hard drive connected to your Macintosh. These are not volumes you've shared with the Sharing command; they're complete hard drives as they appear on the Macintosh Desktop. To mount your drive, double-click on the drive name or select the drive name and click the OK button.

Your hard drive then appears with AppleShare volume icons on the Desktop of the Macintosh you're using. You now have complete access to your drive, including all files and folders, with no limitations based on access privileges. You can create files and folders, delete files, redefine Users & Groups, set File Sharing access privileges, or do anything else you could do if you were sitting at your own Mac keyboard.

When you're finished using a remotely mounted hard drive, you can release it just like you would any other volume, by dragging it to the Trash, using the Put Away command, shutting down, or restarting.

Program Linking

As mentioned in Chapter 12, "Interapplication Communication & OpenDoc," applications specifically programmed to support AppleEvents can communicate with application programs residing on any AppleShare server or File Sharing volume on the network. If you want programs that can take advantage of Program Linking, to communicate with each other across your network, you must specifically enable Program Linking.

The master control for Program Linking is found in the File Sharing Control Panel, as shown in Figure 17-8. The message in the Status area will document the Program Linking start-up process. Once Program Linking is running, the Start button becomes the Stop button.

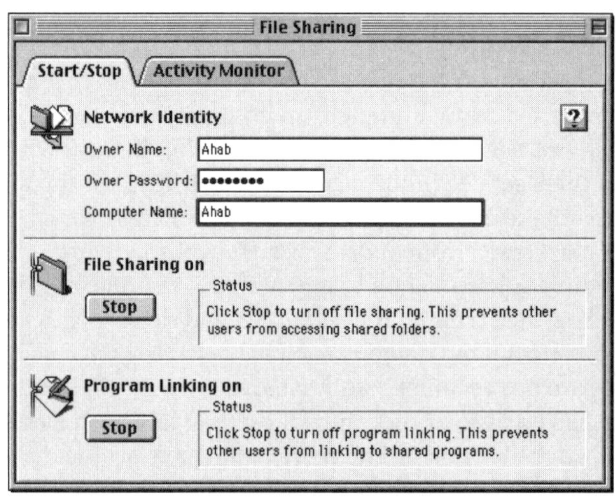

Figure 17-8: The Sharing Setup dialog box provides the master control for Program Linking.

Program Linking must also be enabled in the Macintosh Owner icon found in the Users & Groups Control Panel (the Macintosh Owner icon has a dark border around it and displays the name entered in the Sharing Setup dialog box). Double-clicking on this icon displays the dialog box shown in Figure 17-9. The Program Linking option, in the lower portion of the dialog box, enables Program Linking.

Even when Program Linking has been turned on and enabled in the File Sharing dialog box, it is only available to applications that support it. To initiate Program Linking for an application that supports it, highlight the application you wish to use and then choose the Sharing command from the File menu. Figure 17-10 shows an example of an application that can be shared.

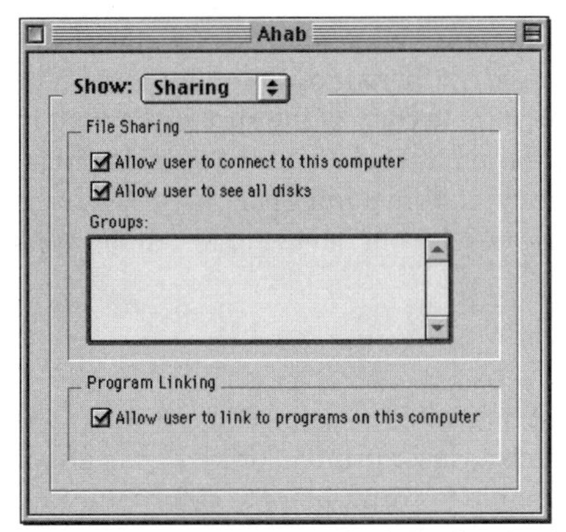

Figure 17-9: The User Options dialog box for the Macintosh owner.

Figure 17-10: An application's Sharing dialog box.

If the application you selected supports Program Linking, the Allow Remote Program Linking check box is displayed. Otherwise, this option will be dimmed. To make the application available for Program Linking, click the check box and then close the Sharing dialog.

Program Linking is a nice feature, but few people use it today—even most "power users" haven't worked with it much, if at all. There are two main benefits of Program Linking that you should think about:

- If you have a computationally intensive task, say 3D rendering or visualization studies, you can off-load the assignment to a more powerful computer on your network. The result can then be returned back to you over the network much more quickly.

- Through AppleEvents, Program Linking provides you with additional capabilities that are not resident in your own application. Using Program Linking, you can access a remote copy of the application that has the capabilities you need without having to load the outside program on your own computer. This saves you from additional purchases and reduces the time it takes you to do the task by not having to install the application.

Moving On

Most Macintosh users are first interested in connecting to a network in order to share peripheral devices such as laser printers or perhaps network modems. But networks also make it possible for computers to communicate with each other and for data to be shared either between computers or by accessing centralized file servers.

In this chapter you've seen how to make the most of these abilities:

- Using the Chooser to select an available File Sharing Macintosh or AppleShare server.
- Mounting volumes and setting up automatic mounting connections.
- Working with assigned access privileges.
- Setting up and using Program Linking.

Next, in Chapter 18, we will look at how Mac OS 8 prepares you to connect to the biggest network in the world, the Internet.

CHAPTER 18

Internet Connectivity

If the big story of the '80s was the advent of affordable personal computers, then the big story of the '90s is the Internet and the World Wide Web. The Net is *the* hot news topic of today, and in just a few years the World Wide Web has grown from a handful of university pages to a massive conglomeration of commercial, personal, governmental, and educational sites. The interconnectivity the Internet provides is a powerful solution for many business, educational, and entertainment needs, and the Web provides an easy-to-use interface to the Internet much in the same way the Mac OS serves as an interface to powerful and complex computer hardware.

If you've ever worked on the Web with other computers, you know that there's no better way to get online than with a Mac. Combining text, sound, images, and movies, the Net is actually a form of multimedia itself, and the Mac OS is a superior multimedia platform. The people at Apple realized this, and have integrated Internet connectivity into the operating system itself. In addition, they included everything you'll need to connect to the Net as part of the basic installation of Mac OS 8.

All of the major applications and utilities you'll need to master the Internet and the Web are installed on your machine, and your home or office Mac can even become a Web server. We'll discuss these new applications and server abilities in the next two chapters; for now, let's talk about how the Mac OS can help you get online in just a few minutes.

Getting Connected: ISP vs. LAN

There are two basic ways people connect to the Internet: through an account with an Internet Service Provider (ISP), or by connecting through a local area network (LAN). Most people connecting to an ISP from home use a modem, while most business and educational users connect via a corporate or educational LAN. In fact, manES | arge colleges and universities use their LANs to provide Internet access for their faculty, staff, and students.

Modem connections make use of two sets of rules, called *protocols*: Transmission Control Protocol and Internet Protocol, commonly referred to as TCP/IP. The first determines how information is split into smaller parts and then reassembled at the destination, while the latter determines the best path for the information to travel.

ISP/Modem Access

Most people who access the Internet from home use a modem and special software to connect to their ISP. Once the account is set up correctly, there's little need to change the settings.

Under old versions of the Mac OS, it was sometimes tricky to get all the settings tweaked, all the software working together, and the modem talking to the ISP. Previous versions of the Mac OS also didn't ship with the proper software to connect your Mac to the Internet unless commercial software such as America Online was added by a value-added reseller (VAR). This was because, for the most part, Internet connectivity software was written by third-party developers uninterested in corralling a lot of disparate programs together.

Thankfully, this won't be much of a problem in the future. Mac OS 8 allows you to bypass much of this hassle by automating the process of registering with a new ISP or updating your old account.

LAN Access

Many businesses now have networks that connect the various computers throughout an office or group of offices. These networks are called local area networks (LANs). A group of LANs makes up a wide area network (WAN), and when several WANs are connected, they are referred to as an intranet. What LANs, WANs, and intranets often have in common is the use of communications software such as e-mail clients, Web browsers, and collaboration software that use the same protocols the Internet uses.

Connecting to the Internet through a LAN is generally less confusing for novice users than connecting through a modem because the steps necessary to get connected are ridiculously easy and because most large networks also have full-time computer and networking professionals on staff to take care of all the nasty configuration details. However, the Mac OS 8 has automated the process to such a point that most people will be able to set themselves up on a LAN with little effort. The automation takes the form of three Internet Assistants.

Internet Assistants

Mac OS 8 comes with a suite of helper applications that enable you to get up and running on the Web with a minimum of work. Whether you're accessing the Web from home via a modem or from work via a LAN, these helpers will have you surfing in no time. Figure 18-1 shows the programs you are most likely to use to get connected to the Internet.

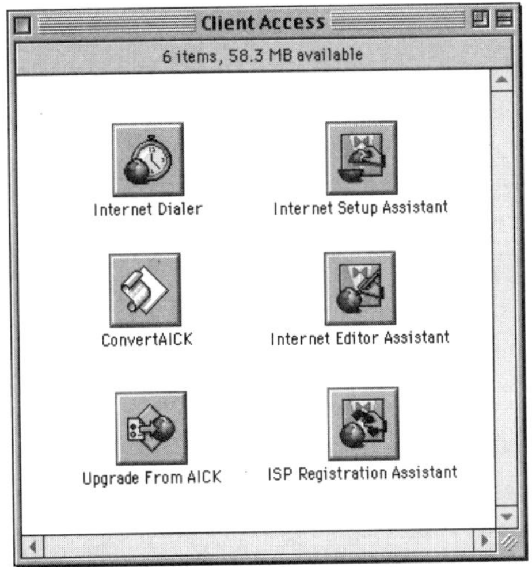

Figure 18-1: The Client Access folder contains everything you'll need to connect to the Internet.

The applications you'll use most are:

- Internet Setup Assistant
- Internet Editor Assistant
- ISP Registration Assistant

These assistants were developed by Apple after years of observing the trials and tribulations of users connecting to the Internet using ISPs and all the major types of modems. What they realized, is that there are just a handful of difficult tasks involved with using the Mac OS for Internet access, and they usually center on configuring your modem hardware to communicate with the Mac OS. The assistants help do this for you and make the whole process just about as easy as possible.

Internet Setup Assistant

This version of the Mac OS doesn't waste time on formalities. At the end of the setup process, the installer asks you if you want to launch the new Internet Setup Assistant (don't worry, if you want to spend a little time playing around with the new OS first, the helper will wait for you inside the Internet Applications folder). The Internet Setup Assistant leads you through the process of setting up access through an ISP or a LAN. Figure 18-2 shows you what the Internet Setup Assistant looks like when it is launched.

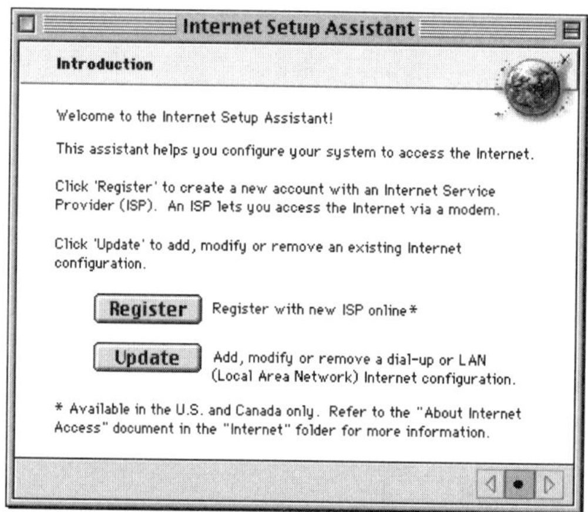

Figure 18-2: The Internet Setup Assistant guides you through the process of setting up Internet connections.

The Internet Setup Assistant links to the other two assistants, so most people will use it primarily to set up new accounts or modify old ones.

Internet Editor Assistant

The Internet Editor Assistant is a component of the Internet Setup Assistant that helps organize the information needed to connect to an ISP. Using this assistant, you can draw together various phone numbers and server addresses into set configurations, as shown in Figure 18-3.

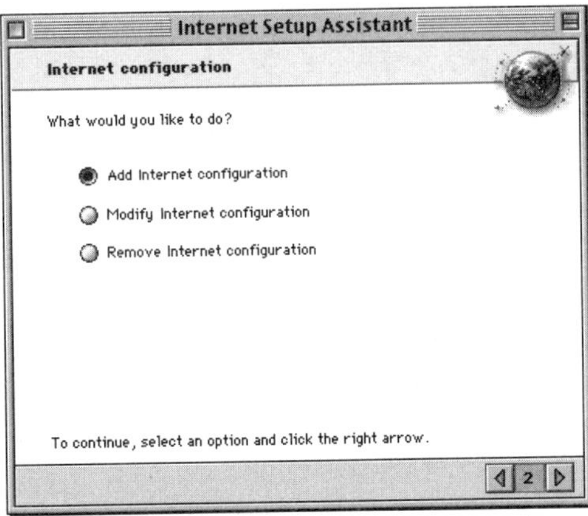

Figure 18-3: The Internet Editor Assistant allows you to set up, modify, or delete settings for ISP and LAN access.

This feature is a godsend for people who have more than one ISP account or who access the Internet with both a modem and a LAN. It allows you to set up a series of settings—one for accessing from home, one for calling into the work LAN—that you can later choose from when connecting. Figure 18-4 shows some of the options available when adding a new Internet configuration.

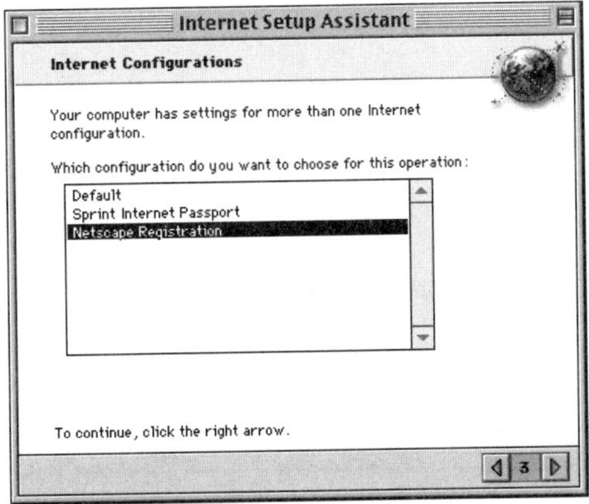

Figure 18-4: A list of the available connections set up through the Internet Editor Assistant.

To create a new settings file, you'll need basic information about the account, including the addresses for the domain name server (DNS), the e-mail server, and the news server. Your LAN administrator or someone at the ISP can provide this information.

You'll need the following information:

- Your username and password.
- The name and type of modem (for modem connections) and the phone number of your ISP.
- Your IP address (if you have one). This is a series of four numbers separated by periods (for example, 122.95.6.789). Most people using modem connections will not have an IP address. If you're on a LAN and you don't have an IP address assigned, you need to know what protocol your server uses to assign these numbers. The most common is MacIP.
- The number of your domain name server (DNS) and the hostname for modem connections. DNS numbers are similar to IP addresses, while the hostname is generally two or more words separated by periods (like apple.com, duke.edu, or ibm.net).
- Your e-mail account and host. The e-mail account is where you receive mail; it is your Post Office Protocol (POP) account. The host is a Simple Mail Transfer Protocol (SMTP) computer that processes outgoing mail. Figure 18-5 shows an example entry for these fields.

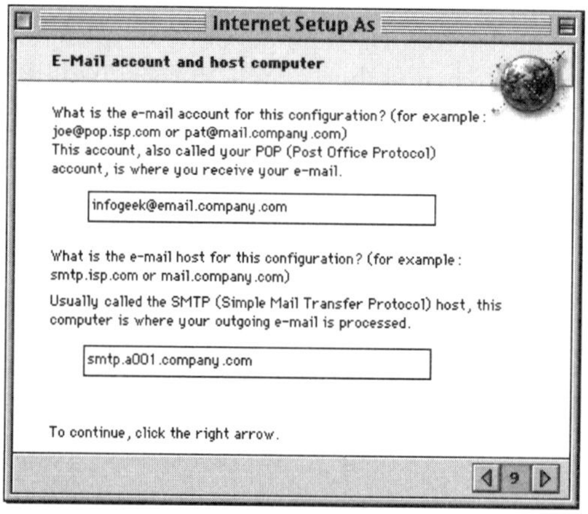

Figure 18-5: The Internet Editor Assistant allows you to enter addresses for your mail, news, and other servers.

If you already have an account with an ISP or if you're set up on a LAN with an older system, make sure to copy down all the information *before* installing Mac OS 8. Otherwise, the new system might overwrite preferences files for your old connection software.

If your existing ISP requires a connect script, you'll need to ask them for an updated version. The utilities that ship with Mac OS 8 don't modify them.

ISP Registration Assistant

All of this is fine and good if you already have access to the Internet, but what if you don't? Never fear; the ISP Registration Assistant automates the process of selecting a new ISP, choosing a payment plan, and calibrating your system to work with the ISP. See Figure 18-6 for an example of what Netscape's Internet Account Server looks like when you connect for the first time using Mac OS 8's ISP Registration Assistant.

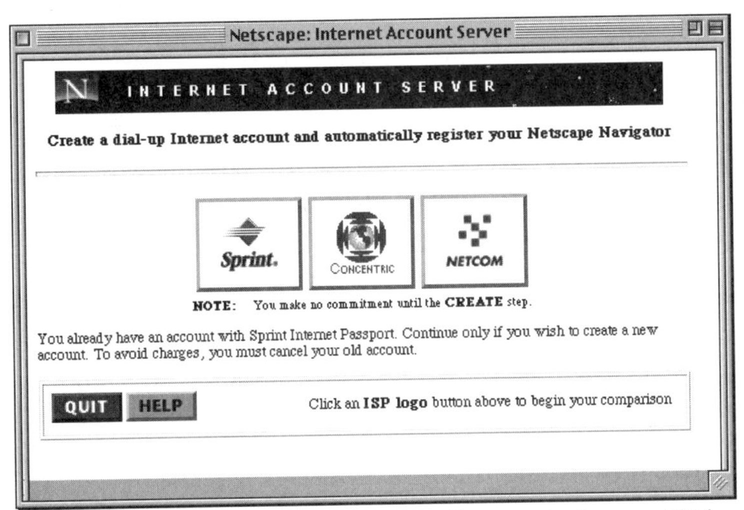

Figure 18-6: The ISP Registration Assistant allows you to choose an ISP from Netscape's registration server.

After asking for some basic information (name, phone number, type of modem), the assistant connects to Netscape's registration server. You can choose among several ISPs, register with the provider, and choose a payment plan. Once you're registered, the assistant automatically sets the appropriate preferences on your machine.

Even though Netscape's registration site is secure, be very wary when you're submitting credit card numbers and passwords to Web sites. Mac OS 8 installs Netscape Navigator 3.01 with international encryption, which is less secure than the North American version of Netscape. Most online commerce sites recommend using the noninternational version.

Now that you're set up, you can just use the Internet Dialer (inside the Internet folder) to connect to the Net, as shown in Figure 18-7.

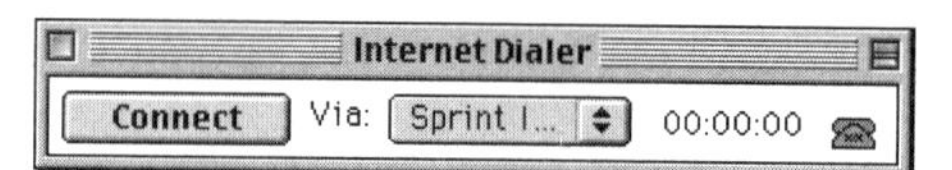

Figure 18-7: After all your settings are in place, you only need open the Internet Dialer to connect.

The assistants help make setup painless, but they aren't the final step. In order to make the whole process as smooth as possible, Mac OS 8 allows you to use the Internet Setup Utility to link certain applications. When these applications are launched, a connection to your ISP is automatically established.

Internet Setup Utility

The Internet Setup Utility serves as a bridge between the Internet Setup Assistant and the Internet Dialer. Using this program, you can tell your Mac to always launch certain applications when you connect to your ISP, as in Figure 18-8.

Suppose the first thing you do when you connect is check e-mail, then, you surf the Web. You can tell this utility to launch your e-mail program and your Web browser every time you go online. If you later decide you want to read newsgroups first, you can add a newsreader program to the mix. To add applications to be launched automatically, just click on the Add button and locate the application. To remove an application, just select it and choose the Remove button. That's it.

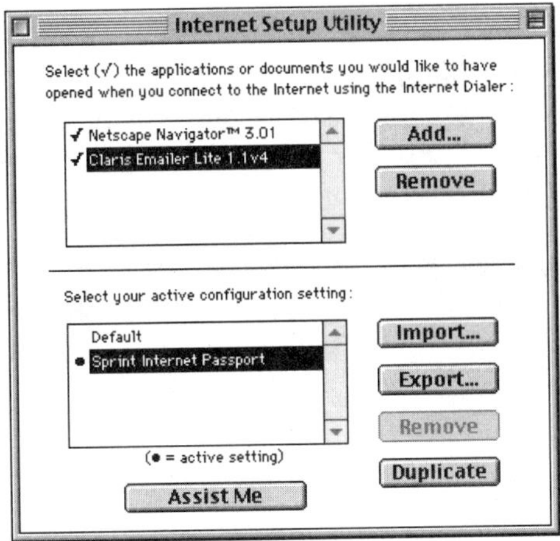

Figure 18-8: With the Internet Setup Utility, you can tell your Mac to open certain programs when you go online.

The Internet Setup Utility also allows you to export connectivity information into a file and copy it to another machine—a nice feature for people sharing one account among several Macs.

Open Transport

Although the assistants make setting up Internet connections much easier, most users will get the biggest benefit from another suite of software: Open Transport and the new Open Transport/PPP.

What Is Open Transport?

Open Transport, the successor to MacTCP, is the part of the Mac OS that handles networking. It's much more flexible than its predecessor, so Macs using Open Transport can easily configure and switch between different types of networks or use more than one type of network at the same time. For example, Open Transport makes it possible to communicate with a network printer while using TCP/IP to connect to the Internet. It's also a lot faster, it's PowerPC native, and when it's used with Macs that are also Internet servers, such as Web, e-mail, and FTP servers, it is capable of hosting more simultaneous connections than MacTCP.

Remember earlier when we discussed the fact that Mac OS 8 allows you to create several sets of connection settings with the Internet Editor Assistant? This is possible because of Open Transport. Open Transport 1.2, which ships with OS 8, also makes better use of online help, so inexperienced users will be able to figure out how to use it with little outside assistance.

Older versions of Open Transport allowed you to turn it off and use MacTCP instead. Mac OS 8 won't allow this; MacTCP is incompatible with the Internet access section of the OS.

Open Transport Components

Open Transport exists in the form of a handful of Extensions and four Control Panels: AppleTalk, TCP/IP, PPP, and Modem. For the most part, if you've used the Internet Setup Assistant to configure your system, you won't need to adjust these Control Panels very often unless your Mac is on a LAN, WAN, or intranet.

AppleTalk Control Panel

The AppleTalk Control Panel, shown in Figure 18-9, allows you to choose which port your AppleTalk connection uses. For the most part, this is the main avenue of communication between Macs and any network devices—printers, network modems, and so on.

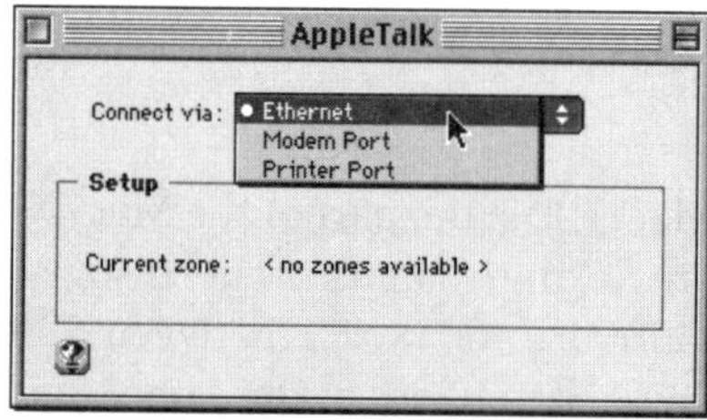

Figure 18-9: Configuring the AppleTalk Control Panel.

This Control Panel also allows you to link to a local Ethernet network and to locally attached printers, which communicate with the Mac OS using AppleTalk through a serial cable. Both the AppleTalk and the TCP/IP Control Panels allow you to set one of three levels of user configuration:

- Basic, for novice users.
- Advanced, for more sophisticated users.
- Administration, for network supervisors or parents who want to keep Junior from tampering with the settings.

A good rule of thumb is to use the lowest user mode possible unless you really understand what you're doing. Figure 18-10 shows the User Mode dialog box.

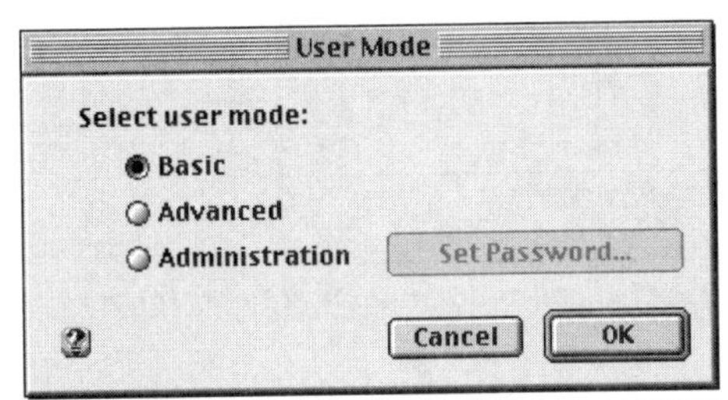

Figure 18-10: Change the AppleTalk or TCP/IP User Mode only if necessary.

TCP/IP Control Panel

The TCP/IP Control Panel controls how your Mac connects to the Internet when you use the TCP/IP protocol. Most Macs use one of two basic ways to connect: a direct connection over an Ethernet network or one of two dial-up networking protocols—Standard Line Interface Protocol (SLIP) or Point-to-Point Protocol (PPP). SLIP was dominant up until a couple of years ago, but PPP offers better throughput when small amounts of information are going back and forth between two computers. It's also a recognized Internet standard, while SLIP never achieved full recognition.

With TCP/IP, users can choose to connect using AppleTalk, Ethernet, or PPP; these options are available with the standard Mac OS 8 installation. You can add additional networking hardware or software that will add additional options to the TCP/IP Control Panel. AppleTalk and Ethernet are for people connecting through a dedicated network using an Ethernet adapter, while PPP is mainly used for one computer to connect via a modem. Figure 18-11 shows the TCP/IP Control Panel.

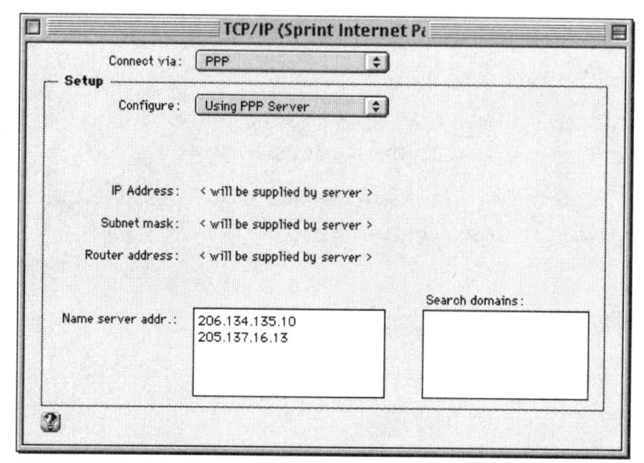

Figure 18-11: The TCP/IP Control Panel allows users to connect to the Internet via Ethernet, AppleTalk, or PPP.

If you connect via PPP, you can either choose to enter the IP address yourself or to get it automatically from a server (which method you choose depends on your ISP). If the IP address comes from the server, it's important to find out if it's a Boot Protocol (BootP), a Dynamic Host Configuration Protocol (DHCP), or a Reverse Address Resolution Protocol (RARP) server. Again, someone at the ISP can answer this question; the default is the simple PPP server.

Modem Control Panel

The Modem Control Panel, shown in Figure 18-12, is a simple interface for choosing the modem brand, model, and port. Presently, Mac OS 8 supports most of the major brands and models of modems. If yours isn't on the list, don't panic; the Apple Modem Script Generator, a tool to add new modem scripts, is available at http://devworld.apple.com/dev/opentransport/ppp.html. A good rule of thumb is to try the Hayes-compatible modem script first, though, because many modems are Hayes-compatible.

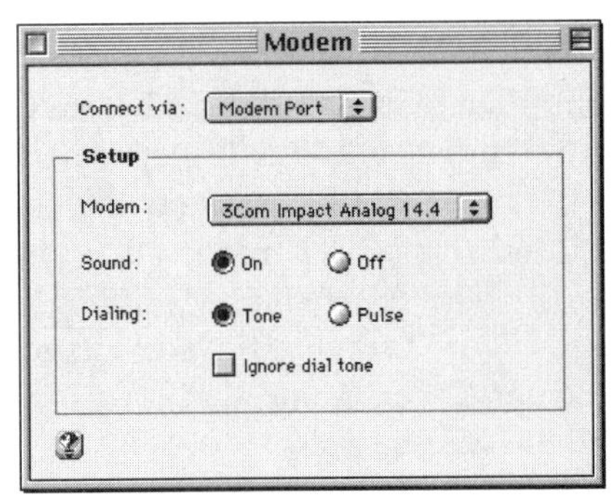

Figure 18-12: The Modem Control Panel allows users to make changes to their modem configuration easily.

The choices presented in the Modem Control Panel are very easy to use (you're using a Mac, after all). To get started, take a look at the back of your computer to see where the modem is plugged in—the modem port or the printer port. If you have a PowerBook, you may have only one choice, a combination modem/printer port. Next, make the appropriate selection in the Connect Via portion of the Modem Control Panel, then choose a modem type, whether you want the modem's sound on or off, and whether your phone line uses touch-tone or pulse. You should probably leave the Ignore Dial Tone option unchecked, as most modems need to detect the dial tone in order to function properly.

PPP Control Panel

PPP, the final Control Panel related to Open Transport, controls a number of settings that determine how the Macintosh interacts with a remote PPP server. The PPP Control Panel is shown in Figure 18-13 below. With this Control Panel, users can connect to an ISP, turn error correction and compression on and off, view and export the activity log, and set up a connect script. This Control Panel—the main component of Open Transport/PPP, Apple's new connectivity software—also allows you to set PPP to connect every time you open a TCP/IP application like Navigator, Emailer, or Cyberdog.

Open Transport/PPP

Open Transport/PPP, which is controlled by the PPP and Modem Control Panels, is one of the most powerful elements of Open Transport. Using this software, users can both determine how they will connect to the outside world and set up shortcuts to work faster and smarter. There are other implementations of PPP that you could use on the Mac OS, such as MacPPP, FreePPP, and MacSLIP (which allows you to use PPP or SLIP), but the advantage of using Open Transport/PPP is that it is PowerPC native and that it was created by Apple, so you know it will be both fast and reliable.

See the instructions and documentation provided by your ISP for details on what settings need to be entered to establish a connection.

For the most part, users will go to this Control Panel to connect to their ISP. However, the Control Panel's Options menu allows more advanced users to change the computer's settings and write timesaving connect scripts for ISPs or networks that require a complicated login process.

Connecting Automatically

People with direct connections to the Internet don't have to worry about logging in to their servers, but those of us who surf via modem are all too familiar with the procedure. Pull down the Apple menu, go to Control Panels, open PPP, click Connect—it's a lot of wasted effort.

Open Transport/PPP avoids all of this rigmarole by allowing the user to set PPP to automatically connect every time a TCP/IP program (like Netscape, Fetch, Cyberdog, or Emailer) is launched. When the Connect Automatically When Starting TCP/IP Applications box is selected on PPP's Connections tab, shown in Figure 18-13, the computer will attempt to connect to whatever server you've chosen as your active configuration.

However, if you do a lot of offline work with Internet applications such as Navigator, you might want to uncheck this option. If it's checked, your Mac will attempt to dial in to your ISP every time you launch Navigator, causing both unwanted delays while you cancel the login attempt and possible charges from your phone company or ISP.

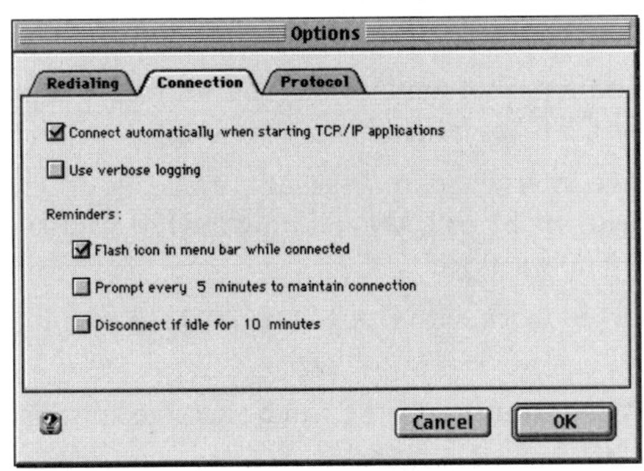

Figure 18-13: Choosing Connect Automatically When Starting TCP/IP Applications tells the computer to connect via PPP whenever Netscape, Fetch, or other Internet programs are launched.

Creating a Connect Script

If your network connection or ISP requires that you log in each time, you can avoid the repetitive typing by writing a connect script. Though it sounds complicated, it's actually quite simple; once you connect successfully, the script can be ready to go.

To write a script, first make sure the PPP Control Panel is set to connect to a command-line host (see Figure 18-14); then, connect to the server and type all the information requested. Before completing the login, though, click the Settings button and click the Prompt to Save Connect Script button on Close. Name the script, save it, and then select it with the Import button on the PPP Control Panel.

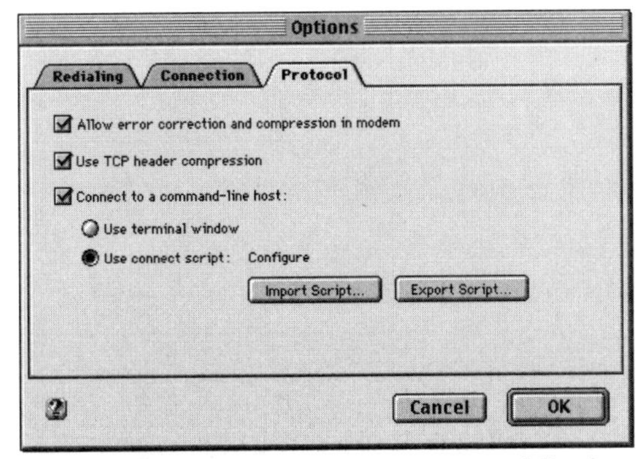

Figure 18-14: After connecting to a command-line host, users can write a script that automates the login process.

Moving On

The Internet is an important part of modern-day life, and this chapter has shown you how the Mac OS 8 has taken this into account:

- You've seen how the Internet Setup Assistant can be used to modify an existing account with an ISP or LAN and how the ISP Registration Assistant can help set up new service.
- You've learned how to work with Open Transport through its four Control Panels.
- You've seen how Open Transport/PPP can be used to speed your connection to the Net.

Of course, there's more to life than Web surfing—eventually it's time to start publishing online. One of the most powerful aspects of the Macintosh is its ability to serve as a sturdy, secure Web server. Until now, third-party developers provided most of the server software. The new Mac OS changes that, bundling fast, efficient Web server software as part of the basic install. As we'll see in the next chapter, "Personal Web Server," any Mac can now be a Web server, and anyone who can use the Mac OS can be a Webmaster.

CHAPTER 19

Personal Web Server

You've seen how easy it is to connect your Mac to the Internet, and now it's time to see just how easy it is to publish on an intranet or the World Wide Web using the Mac OS. New to the Mac OS is Apple's Personal Web Server, a fully-functional Web server designed to be used by individuals who want to share information over the Web without having to install, configure, and manage a commercial Web server. You can use the Web server to share just about anything on your Mac, including HTML documents, images, word processing documents, spreadsheets, and much more. If you can point and click a mouse, then you can be a Webmaster using the Mac OS! Take a look at Figure 19-1, which shows an example of a document that comes with the Web server; it took only one click of the mouse to publish the document using the Web server.

Figure 19-1: With Mac OS 8, you can publish on the Web with just one click of the mouse.

The Web & HTML

The Web is a collection of Web servers that are accessed by Web browsers such as Netscape Navigator, Cyberdog, and many others. There are Web browsers for virtually every computer hardware and software platform and for computers as small as Apple's handheld personal digital assistant, the Newton, and as big as a mainframe. The HyperText Markup Language (HTML) is what makes it possible for one document to be read by so many different types of computers. HTML is a low-level programming language called a markup language; it is very unsophisticated and easily implemented into existing applications and operating systems. HTML uses formatting instructions like this to make certain words appear in boldface type, for example:

```
This is an example of a <B> bold </B> word in the middle of a sentence.
```

HTML is really just a collection of commands written in easy-to-understand ASCII text that instructs Web browsers how to display formatted text, insert images, and link to other pages on the Web. You'll need a good text editor if you plan to get serious about HTML, and a demo version of a great text editor called BBEdit is included on this book's Companion CD-ROM. I think you'll like it, and if you want to get the full version, you'll can visit the Bare Bones home page (http://www.barebones.com) for more information. It will be a worthwhile investment.

The availability of Web servers and ease of HTML programming are two reasons the Web is so popular, but the real reason is the Mac OS. More than 60 percent of all Web sites are created and maintained using the Mac OS. Now, consider that about 10 percent of the computing population uses the Mac OS, and you can only come to one conclusion: it must be much easier to create and maintain Web sites using the Mac OS than any other platform. By including Personal Web Server with Mac OS 8, Apple has made that task even easier.

Web Server Configuration

Everything you need to get started publishing on the Web is available with Mac OS 8, including the following:

- A Web server
- Sample HTML documents
- Documentation
- Resources for further reading

Using a Loopback Interface

And just in case you're wondering if you need a network connection to get some experience running your Web server, the answer is No. The Mac OS is able to do a really nifty networking trick called a loopback, which enables your Mac, Web server, and Web browser to think they are on the Internet. This will allow you to run the Web server and use any Web browser to test it just as if it were on the Internet or an intranet. Also, if you have another Mac and can connect it to the Web server Mac using an Ethernet connection, the other Mac can also access your Web server.

To set your Mac up to use the loopback interface, just follow these easy steps:

1. Open the TCP/IP Control Panel.
2. Choose Connect via Ethernet.
3. Choose Configure Manually.
4. Enter 1.1.1.2 in the IP Address field (see Figure 19-2).

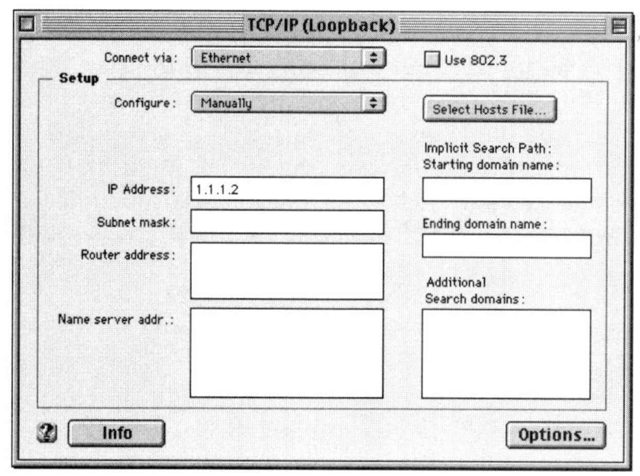

Figure 19-2: Create a loopback interface setup to test your Web server without connecting to a network.

5. Choose File | Quit (or Command+Q), and if warned, "You have not provided a subnet mask value. TCP/IP will use a default subnet mask that corresponds to your IP address class," choose Continue. The networking software is smart enough to take care of the subnet mask value, and it will work like a charm.
6. Finally, if you want to save these settings so you can easily recall them without having to make the changes manually, choose File | Configurations (or Command+K), choose Duplicate, rename it Loopback (or whatever), and then choose Make Active. The next time you want to switch from your ISP to the loopback interface, just choose Command+K, select Loopback, and then Make Active, as in Figure 19-3.

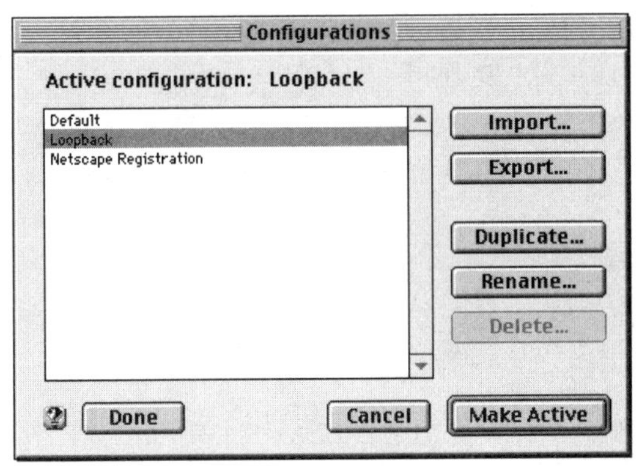

Figure 19-3: Save your loopback interface as an Open Transport configuration so you can easily recall it for future reference.

Starting the Web Server

The Web server isn't active when installed, but starting it up is easy. Once you have either configured your Mac on a network, as outlined in Chapter 17, or configured the loopback interface, you're ready to change a few simple configuration options to start your Web server. Just follow these steps:

1. Open the Web Sharing Control Panel, as shown in Figure 19-4.

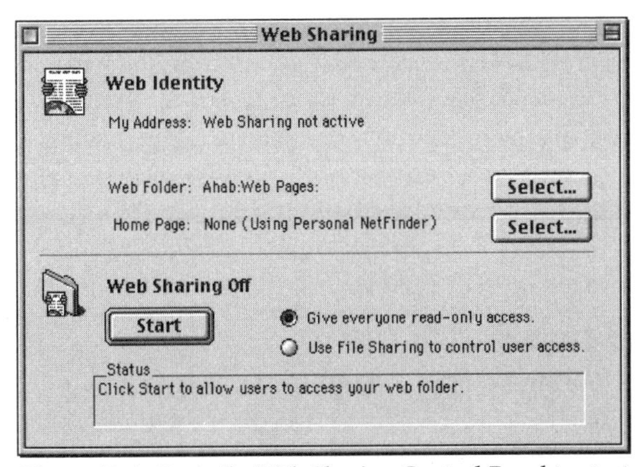

Figure 19-4: Open the Web Sharing Control Panel to start publishing with the Web server.

2. Click the Start button, and the default settings will be applied, including the security settings and the location of the Web folder.
3. The Web server will check to see if a valid network connection can be made and then it will start up, as shown in Figure 19-5.

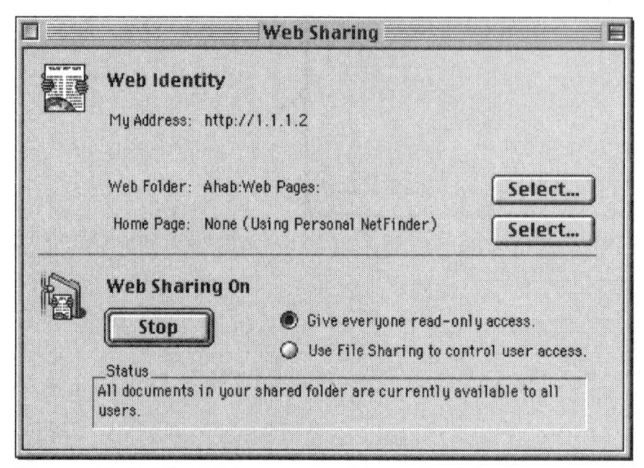

Figure 19-5: The Web server will use the default settings when started for the first time.

Selecting a Web Folder

When Mac OS 8 is installed, the Web server is installed using several defaults, including a folder called Web Pages on the root of the boot volume. This is the folder the Web server uses to store your HTML documents, images, and other content, which is known in Webmasterspeak as the base directory, root folder, or Web folder. Because of a limitation in the Web server program, Apple recommends that if you change the location of this folder or if you choose another folder entirely, that this folder not be located more than five levels deep on the boot volume.

To set or change the location of the Web folder, follow these steps:

1. Open the Web Sharing Control Panel.
2. Click the Select button beside the Web Folder field, shown in Figure 19-6, and select a folder less than five levels deep on the boot volume.
3. Close the Web Sharing Control Panel by clicking the close box or by pressing Command+W.

The Web Pages folder contains many files, including documentation, instructions, and sample HTML documents and images. You should keep these on hand even if you do select another folder as home for your Web pages.

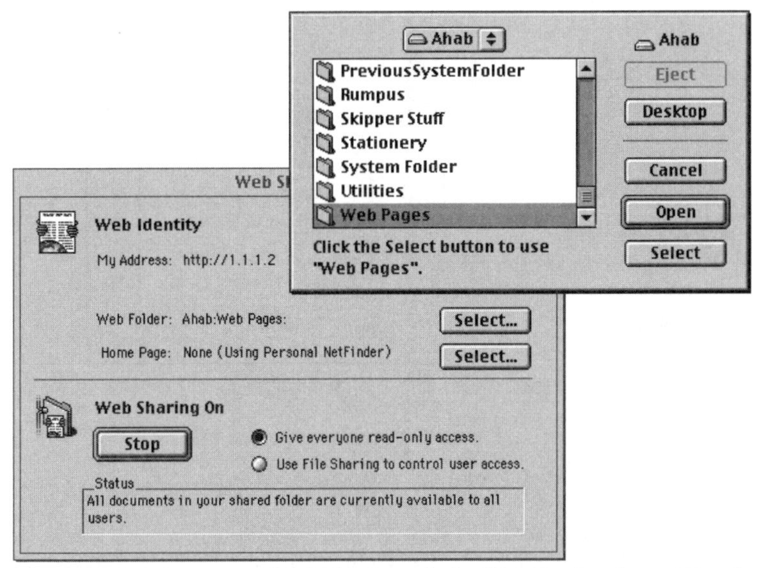

Figure 19-6: Select a new Web folder through the Web Sharing Control Panel.

Selecting a Home Page

All Web servers have what is know as a *default* home page, which means that when you open a Uniform Resource Locator (URL) to that server without specifying a particular HTML document, the Web server gives you a document anyway. For example, when you go to http://www.apple.com (and I hope you do!), the Web server gives you http://www.apple.com/index.html instead because index.html is specified as the default home page. Moreover, when you open a URL to a directory within a Web server without specifying a document, any document in that directory named index.html (or whatever you have selected) will be served by default.

The Mac OS's Personal Web Server allows you to select a home page for your Web site. By default, there is no document selected, which causes the Personal NetFinder to serve as the default (more on this next), so you'll probably want to select a document. To change the default home page for your Web server, follow these steps:

1. Open the Web Sharing Control Panel.
2. Click the Select button beside the Home Page field, as shown in Figure 19-7.

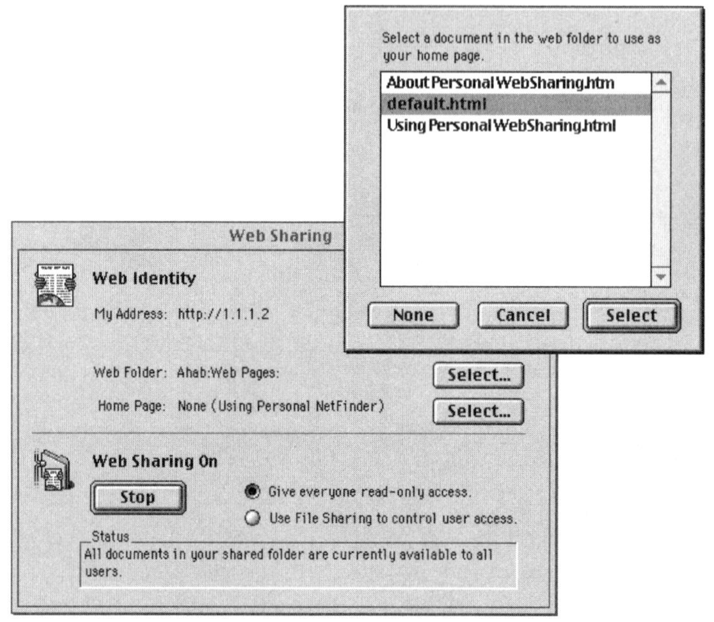

Figure 19-7: Select a default home page to replace the NetFinder.

Personal NetFinder

HTML is a limited language and lacks certain interface features that could make browsing the Web an easier process. Apple has noticed this fact and added a very cool feature to their Web server called the Personal NetFinder, which can replace the default home page to present users with what looks like the Finder in the Mac OS. In Figure 19-8, for example, the Personal NetFinder displays the contents of the base directory of the Web server on my Mac.

The Personal NetFinder gives users a Mac-like experience by presenting the contents of the directory in a list view that lets users view the directory by:

- Name
- Size
- Date Modified

Of course, it doesn't emulate the look and feel of the entire Mac OS. Instead, it mimics the Finder's ability to view the contents of a directory by the three ways people use most. When a user clicks on the Name, Size, and Date Modified hyperlinks at the top of the page, a bunch of funny characters (shown in Figure 19-9) will be sent along with the request, but don't be alarmed. This is just how the Personal NetFinder works.

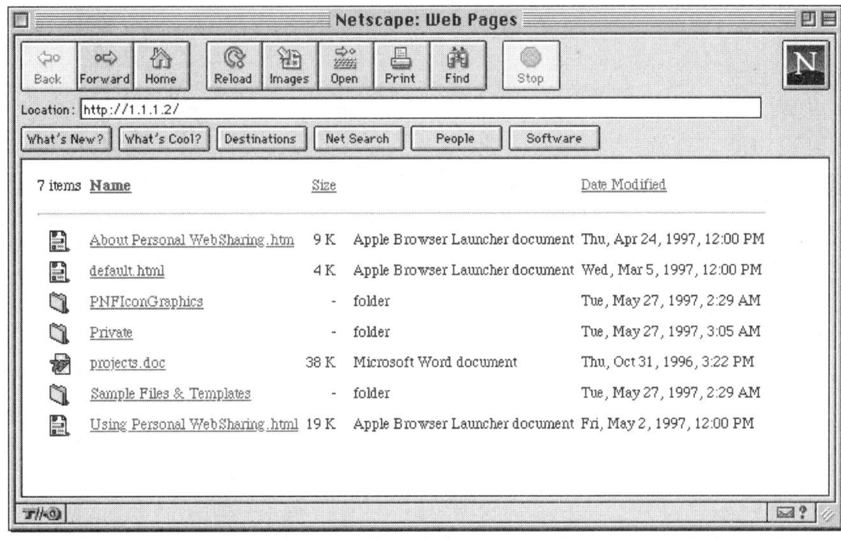

Figure 19-8: Use the Personal NetFinder to help users navigate your Web site.

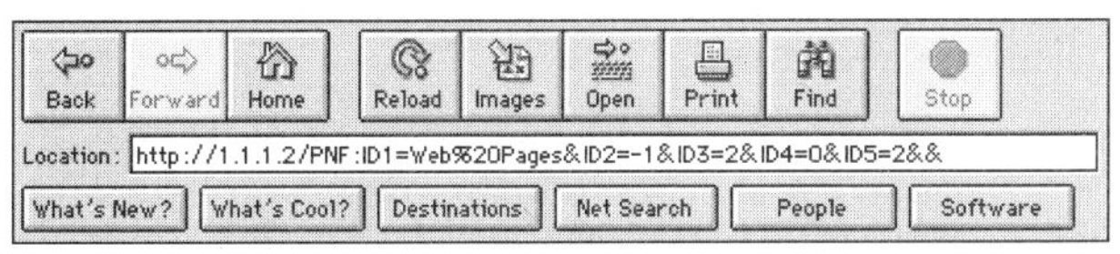

Figure 19-9: The Personal NetFinder works by sending information to the Web server as seemingly nonsensical characters, but don't be alarmed!

The Personal NetFinder takes the place of the default document for a particular directory and is only usable if there is no document entitled index.html in a directory. If index.html isn't available, Personal NetFinder will take over and display the contents of a directory. For example, Figure 19-10 shows the contents of my home directory by Size (top) and Date Modified (bottom), which can make it easier to find things when the directory gets cluttered.

If your Web site slows down, try turning off Personal NetFinder because it sometimes can't handle large folders efficiently.

7 items Name	Size		Date Modified
projects.doc	38 K	Microsoft Word document	Thu, Oct 31, 1996, 3:22 PM
Using Personal WebSharing.html	19 K	Apple Browser Launcher document	Fri, May 2, 1997, 12:00 PM
About Personal WebSharing.htm	9 K	Apple Browser Launcher document	Thu, Apr 24, 1997, 12:00 PM
default.html	4 K	Apple Browser Launcher document	Wed, Mar 5, 1997, 12:00 PM
PNFIconGraphics	-	folder	Tue, May 27, 1997, 2:29 AM
Private	-	folder	Tue, May 27, 1997, 3:05 AM
Sample Files & Templates	-	folder	Tue, May 27, 1997, 2:29 AM

7 items Name	Size		Date Modified
Private	-	folder	Tue, May 27, 1997, 3:05 AM
PNFIconGraphics	-	folder	Tue, May 27, 1997, 2:29 AM
Sample Files & Templates	-	folder	Tue, May 27, 1997, 2:29 AM
Using Personal WebSharing.html	19 K	Apple Browser Launcher document	Fri, May 2, 1997, 12:00 PM
About Personal WebSharing.htm	9 K	Apple Browser Launcher document	Thu, Apr 24, 1997, 12:00 PM
default.html	4 K	Apple Browser Launcher document	Wed, Mar 5, 1997, 12:00 PM
projects.doc	38 K	Microsoft Word document	Thu, Oct 31, 1996, 3:22 PM

Figure 19-10: Two views of the same folder in Personal NetFinder.

Security

Commercial Web servers provide very robust security using several different methods, including realms-based, per-directory, and per-user security and Secure Sockets Layer security, but these types of security take up valuable server resources and can become very complex, which wouldn't be appropriate for a personal Web server. Instead, Apple's Personal Web Server offers two levels of security for your Web server:

- None at all
- File Sharing rights and restrictions

You don't have to worry about Personal Web Server opening up your Mac to attacks by hackers. Apple's File Sharing rights and restrictions are also the basis for security for commercial Web servers such as WebStar. Web servers running on the Mac OS don't suffer from the well-documented security holes other platforms (Unix, Windows NT) do. In fact, properly set-up, they have proven to be unhackable in several well-publicized contests, despite offers of thousands of dollars in prize money and the best attempts of thousands of hackers world-wide.

To change between these two levels of security, follow these steps:

1. Open the Web Sharing Control Panel.
2. In the lower half of the Control Panel, choose one of the radio buttons to change the level of security. The change will take effect immediately.
3. Close the Web Sharing Control Panel.

If you have selected the Give Everyone Read-Only Access radio button in the lower half of the Web Sharing Control Panel, shown in Figure 19-11, then anyone will be able to access any document on your Web server.

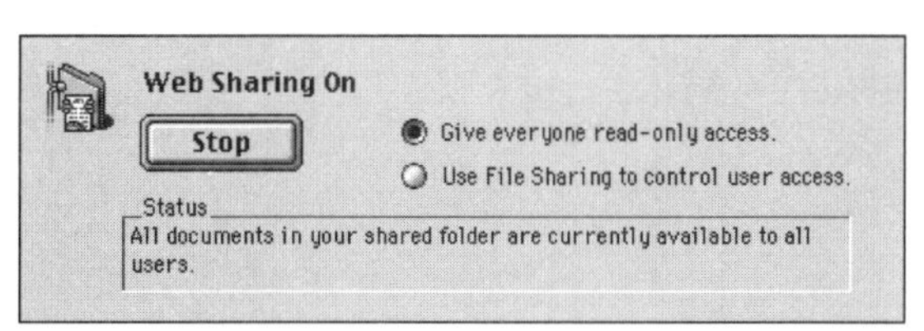

Figure 19-11: Granting everyone access to the Web server.

If you want to share access to your Web server using File Sharing rights and privileges, then select the Use File Sharing to Control User Access radio button, shown in Figure 19-12.

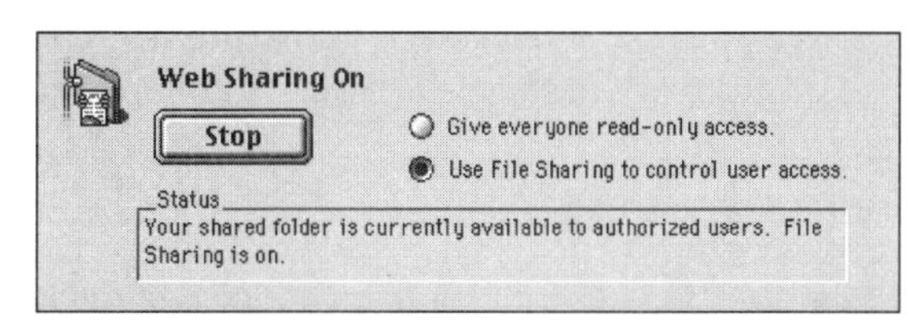

Figure 19-12: Granting access to the Web server using File Sharing.

Finally, to disable the Web server all together, select the Stop button.

Refer back to Chapter 16 for the fine details of File Sharing on the Mac OS. To configure File Sharing for the Web Pages folder, however, follow these steps:

1. Click the Web Pages folder or the alternative folder assigned in the Web Sharing Control Panel.
2. Choose File | Sharing and make any additions, deletions, or modifications to the rights associated with this folder.
3. Close the Sharing window and test access to the server.

You can use the Chooser on another computer on your network to test the access to your Web server; the results will be the same results you would get if you were using a Web browser. To change access rights to my Web folder so members of the group, Web Users, can access its contents, I created a File Sharing group called Web Users, shown in Figure 19-13. I assigned members to that group by dragging and dropping their user icons into the group window.

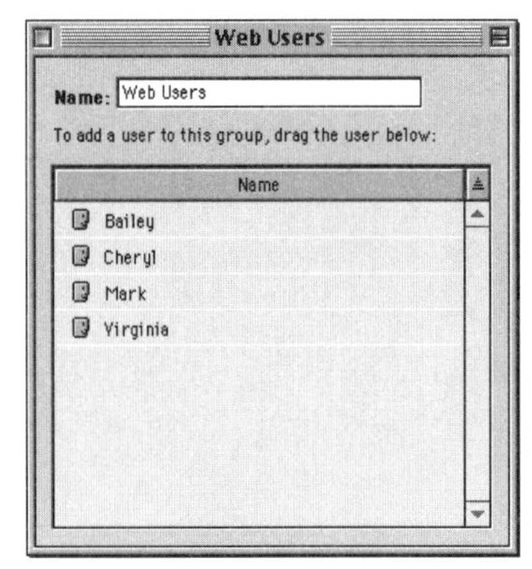

Figure 19-13: Creating a group of users to access my Web site.

Next, I clicked on the Web Pages folder, selected Sharing from the File menu, and assigned the group read and write access, shown in Figure 19-14.

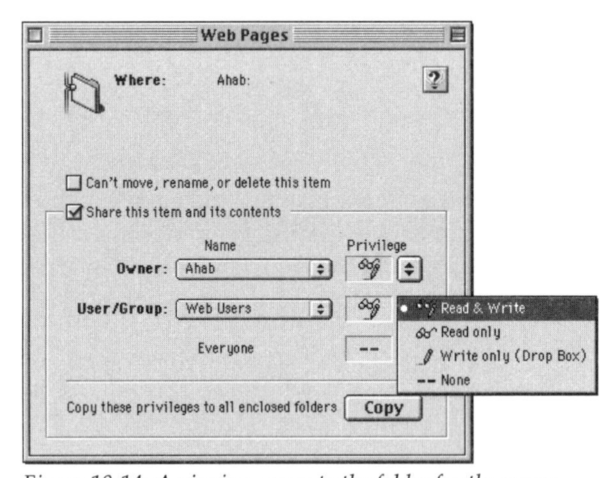

Figure 19-14: Assigning access to the folder for the group.

Next, I tested access by using a Web browser on another computer to access the folder on my Mac by entering the following URL:

```
http://web users@1.1.1.2/
```

Note that I've inserted web users@ into the URL between http:// and the IP address of my server. This tells the Web server, "Hey, I want to access the server as an authenticated user named Web Users." The Web server responds by sending a name and password dialog box for me to enter any of the four usernames in the Web Users group (Bailey, Cheryl, Mark, and Virginia). Figure 19-15 shows what this looks like using Cyberdog.

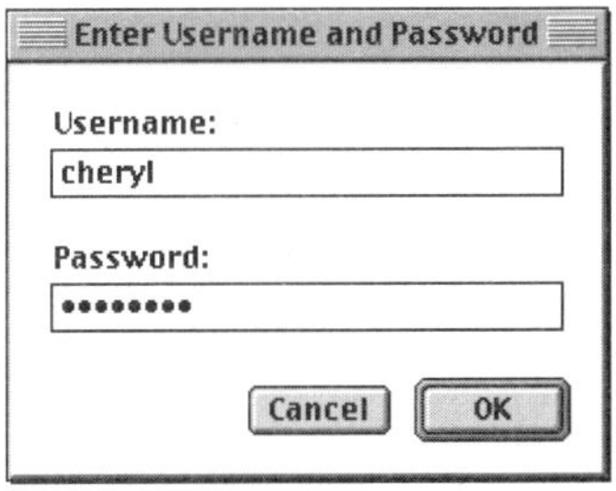

Figure 19-15: A Cyberdog user being authenticated to access my Web site.

Resources

The Web server comes with several resources to help get you started publishing on the Web. The folks at Apple have included everything you'll need to get started learning HTML and using your Web server, including:

- Sample Web pages that include a personal Web page, a calendar, lists created in HTML, and sample hyperlinks.
- Templates for creating your own personal Web page, a calendar, and different types of lists.
- Sample graphics.
- Tips for creating your own Web content.
- Links to resources on the Web for HTML design and tutorials.
- Information on how to run Common Gateway Interface (CGI) programs on your personal Web server.

One resource you may need that isn't provided is detailed information on setting up and maintaining a Mac Web server. There are several books on the market that cover this topic, but let me recommend one in particular: *The Mac Web Server Book*, by Rob Terrell and Mark R. Bell, also from Ventana Press. This book covers everything you need to know to use the Mac OS to set up a commercial or a personal Web server as well as other Internet services. It comes with hundreds of examples, tips, and tricks and several dozen demo and shareware software titles. If you want to keep busy for several months, then check out this book and see how to unleash the power of the Mac OS as a Web server.

Moving On

This chapter introduces personal Web sharing under Mac OS 8, and you should now have a well-grounded understanding of how to configure and maintain a Mac Web server. Of course, the Web server that's included is a very basic server that is capable of meeting the needs of individuals, departments, and small businesses. You can serve any type of HTML document and many types of images, and you can even password-protect your Web site using Apple's personal Web server. In the next chapter, we'll look at the Web browsers and other Internet software that come with the Mac OS. These Internet applications and utilities will enable you to be a power user of the Internet minutes after installing Mac OS 8.

CHAPTER 20

Internet Applications & Utilities

As we've seen in previous chapters, the Mac OS 8 makes it easy to connect to a local area network (LAN), to set up an account with an Internet Service Provider (ISP), and even to set up a simple Web server. These new developments are a continuation of Apple's long tradition of making the Mac OS the easiest and most efficient operating system to use and network with other computers.

So if these innovations are simply a continuation of an old tradition, what's different about the Mac OS 8's relation to the Internet? Well, plenty—and most of it's in your Internet folder. Along with integrating Internet connectivity into the operating system itself, Apple has included as part of the basic installation of Mac OS 8 all of the major applications and utilities you'll need to master the Internet and the Web.

In this chapter, we'll look at some of the applications and utilities that are installed on the machine, find out how they can be used to explore the Net, and examine some other programs that can enhance the online experience. Some of these programs are commercial products, but most are available as inexpensive or reduced-price shareware. We'll discuss these add-ons later in the chapter. First, let's check out what Apple has packaged with this release of the Mac OS.

Mac OS 8 Internet Software

During the basic install of Mac OS 8, the installer leaves a few presents in the Internet folder, like Internet Config 1.3, Netscape Navigator, Cyberdog 2.0, Claris Emailer, Adobe Acrobat Reader, and DropStuff/StuffIt Expander. These programs, which are wildly popular with users of other versions of the Mac OS, can help you make the most of the Internet, the World Wide Web, and—most importantly—your time. Using these applications, you can check e-mail, browse Web pages, read newsgroups, exchange files with other users, and access popular online software libraries. Pretty nice presents, huh? Figure 20-1 shows the Internet folder, where Mac OS 8 installs these programs.

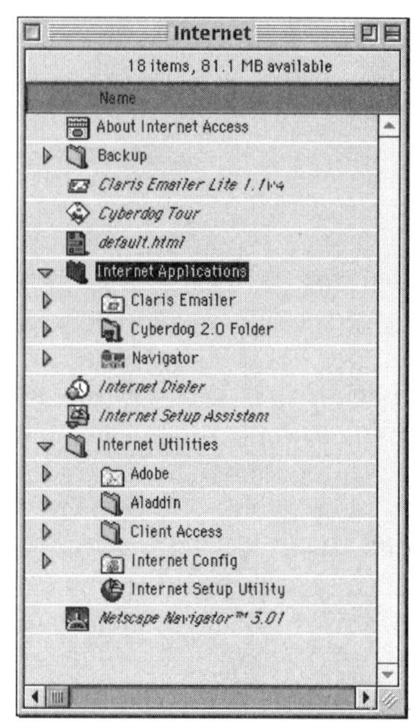

Figure 20-1: The Internet folder of Mac OS 8 includes a variety of popular online applications and utilities.

Let's take a look at some of the items in the folder, beginning with Internet Config 1.3, a utility that expands on OS 8's Internet Setup Assistant (discussed in Chapter 18).

Internet Config 1.3

Internet Config helps overcome the all-too-common hassle of entering the 1.7 million server addresses, passwords, firewall information, and e-mail addresses every Internet program needs to know. Instead of opening each program, entering all this information, saving it, and moving on to the next one, Internet Config allows you to enter the settings once; it then saves them to a system Extension. The individual programs then look into this central file for the preferences information they need.

For example, most applications that do File Transfer Protocol (FTP) transactions—Netscape, Fetch, Anarchie—require that you enter your e-mail address. You could go through and enter all of these by hand, or you could just open Internet Config, as shown in Figure 20-2, make one change, and be done with it. Similarly, you could store your news server's address, an e-mail signature, and a default home page that would be used by all Web browsers on this machine.

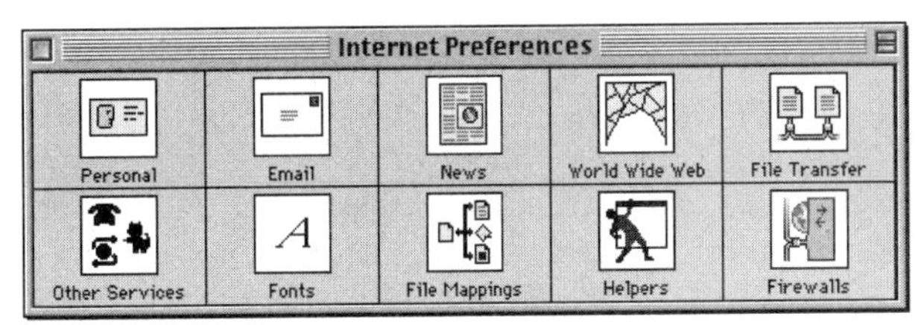

Figure 20-2: Internet Config allows you to create a master preferences file that stores e-mail passwords, FTP server addresses, default home pages, and other online information.

This storage feature is useful, but it's just the tip of the iceberg. With Internet Config, you can add servers for Archie programs, set Finger and WAIS hosts, or choose from a variety of mirror sites for the Info-Mac and UMich shareware archives (we'll discuss shareware later in this chapter).

The program also includes a file-mapping function that allows you to tell the computer to open certain documents with the appropriate application (see Figure 20-3). For example, you can set Internet Config to tell your Mac that all HTML documents should be opened by Netscape Navigator, or you can tell it to open Windows-style .wav sounds with a sound player like SoundApp.

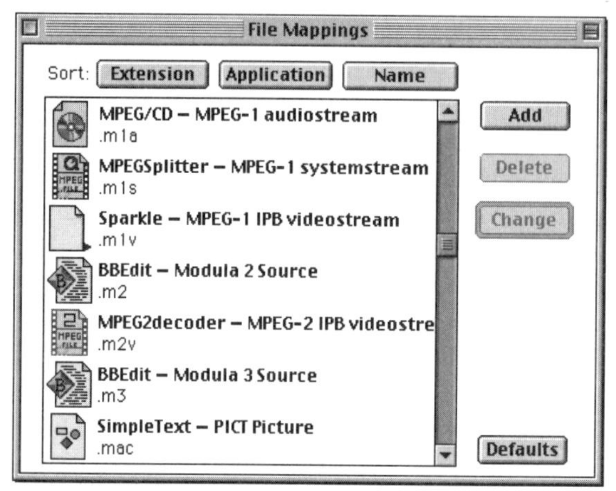

Figure 20-3: Internet Config's file mapping interface allows you to determine which helper applications open certain types of files.

Internet Config's helper applications area works similarly; you can tell the Mac to use Netscape to open Web addresses or Fetch to do FTP transfers. Luckily for newbies, Internet Config comes preset with most of the document types commonly seen on the Net, so you only need to change these settings if you're having problems.

One of the coolest features of Internet Config is its ability to change the fonts and determine the background color for Web browsers. Using the Fonts tool, users can tell their online programs which fonts to use for list views, onscreen type, and printing. Internet Config can also adjust the font size, making windows easier to read for people with visual difficulties.

With the World Wide Web tool, the utility can tell Web browsers which color to use as the background color. To choose a color, select Background Color and then choose either a Red-Green-Blue, Cyan-Magenta-Yellow-Black, or Hue-Saturation-Value amount. Internet Config also features two additional interfaces that are worth exploring: HTML Picker and Crayon Picker. HTML Picker shows you the hexadecimal value for a particular color (which is useful for designing Web pages), while the Crayon Picker allows you to choose from a Crayola-like box of colors (see Figure 20-4). This is truly a cool, fun, and Mac-only feature.

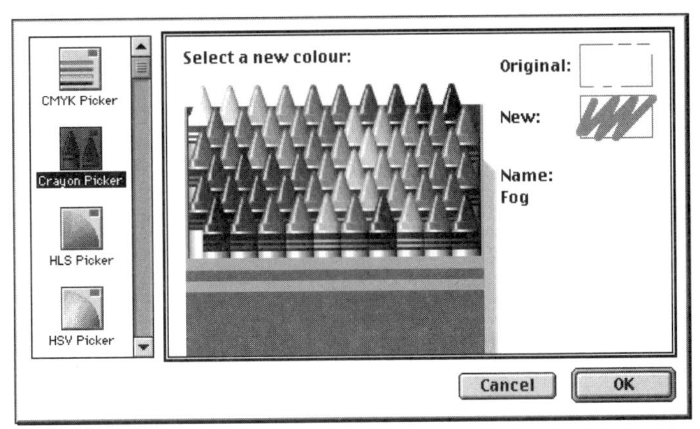

Figure 20-4: Internet Config's fun-for-all-ages Crayon Picker simplifies the process of choosing a background color for Web browsers.

Claris Emailer Lite

OK, so you've got your Internet Config settings in and ready to go. What's next? Well, if you're like most people, a large part of your time on the Internet will be spent sending and receiving e-mail. To do that, you need a fast, easy-to-learn, powerful e-mail program. Like, say, Claris Emailer Lite.

Claris Emailer Lite is a special version of Apple's beloved Claris Emailer program. It's missing some of the features of the original, but it still has the necessary power and flexibility to meet most people's e-mail needs. See the sidebar "Lite vs. Full" later in this chapter for more information about the full version of Claris Emailer.

The Browser

When you launch Emailer, it opens to the main window, the browser. Here, you can link to the Inbox, the Outbox, the Address Book, and the whimsically named Filing Cabinet. The first three are pretty common features of e-mail programs; the last is a place to put special folders that hold themed messages (see Figure 20-5). For example, if you're building a Web site for a local Girl Scout troop, you could sort all the messages pertaining to it into a Girl Scout folder in the filing cabinet.

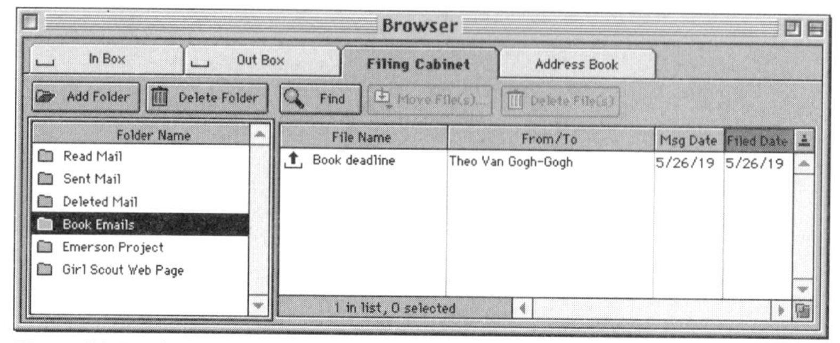

Figure 20-5: Claris Emailer's Filing Cabinet can be used to store e-mails by theme, date, or priority.

If you want to reclassify messages, you can just drag them into the appropriate folder. So if you decide to put all of the Girl Scout Web page information into another folder called Community Work, just select all the messages and drag them over the appropriate folder icon.

The Address Book

Emailer's Address Book, shown in Figure 20-6, uses a similar drag-and-drop interface. Once addresses are created, you can drag them into and out of group entries, which greatly simplifies the e-mailing process. If you regularly send identical e-mails to a group of addresses, you can just create a group entry and send the mail to that group name. Emailer then parcels out the message to the appropriate addresses.

Browser

In Box | Out Box | Filing Cabinet | Address Book

New User | New Group | Delete | Edit | Filter:

Name	Description	Destination	Address
Mom		GEnie	mom
Emma Greenwood	Emma at Work	CitySearch	info
Peter Hoeg	Peter at the office	Internet	phoeg@icelandonline.com
Bill Million	Home	Internet	feelies@rock.com
Richard Nixon		Internet	exprez@whitehouse.gov
		America Online	trickydick
Paul Thompson	Internet Solutions	Internet	paul@solutions.com
Theo Van Gogh-G	Sketch Comedy	Internet	thevggs@ibm.net
		Internet	the vggs@vgg.com
Emerson Project	Contractors		3 addresses in group

10 in list, 1 selected

Figure 20-6: Once an address is set up in Emailer's Address Book, it can be copied into and out of custom group entries.

Emailer's Address Book is also able to track domain names, making it unnecessary to retype @aol.com or @ispnet.net after each address. The program includes settings for popular commercial online service providers like America Online, CompuServe, Prodigy, Delphi, and Fidonet, and setting a new one up takes less than 30 seconds. Simply open the Destinations List (under Setup) and click on Add. This is useful for people who send a lot of mail to one domain or company (see Figure 20-7).

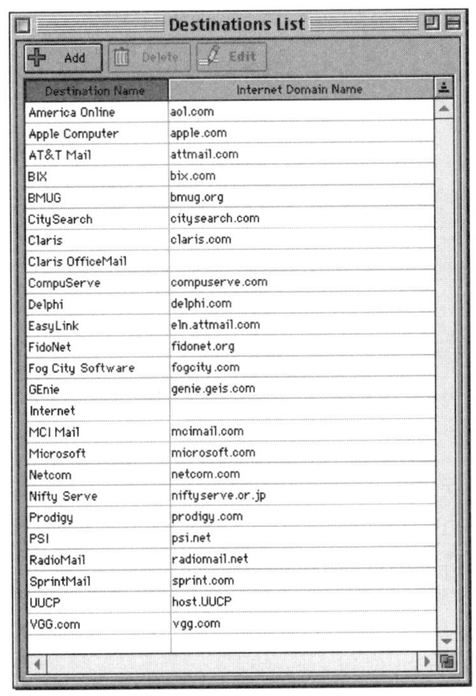

Destination Name	Internet Domain Name
America Online	aol.com
Apple Computer	apple.com
AT&T Mail	attmail.com
BIX	bix.com
BMUG	bmug.org
CitySearch	citysearch.com
Claris	claris.com
Claris OfficeMail	
CompuServe	compuserve.com
Delphi	delphi.com
EasyLink	eln.attmail.com
FidoNet	fidonet.org
Fog City Software	fogcity.com
GEnie	genie.geis.com
Internet	
MCI Mail	mcimail.com
Microsoft	microsoft.com
Netcom	netcom.com
Nifty Serve	niftyserve.or.jp
Prodigy	prodigy.com
PSI	psi.net
RadioMail	radiomail.net
SprintMail	sprint.com
UUCP	host.UUCP
VGG.com	vgg.com

Figure 20-7: The Destinations List includes many popular domains; modifying this list to include domains you mail often is easy.

The Schedules List

One of the great things about America Online's e-mail system is that it can be set to automatically connect to the server, download and send e-mail, and then disconnect. This saves time (and money) and makes it possible to check your account even if you aren't at the computer.

Most ISPs don't have this feature, so Claris added a scheduling feature to Emailer. Thanks to the interconnectivity of Open Transport (see Chapter 18), users can schedule the program to make a remote PPP connection, send and receive e-mail, and disconnect automatically. These automatic sessions are controlled by the Schedules List (see Figure 20-8).

Schedules List

Add | Delete | Edit | Disable all schedules

✓	Schedule Name	Last Conn.	Next Conn.	
✓	Email on Monday	5/26/1997 3:10 P	6/2/1997 3:09:34	Account
✓	Evening Email		5/26/1997 4:09:02	Account
✓	Morning Email		5/27/1997 7:09:43	Account
✓	Noon Email		5/27/1997 12:09:1	Account

Figure 20-8: The Schedules List allows users to tell Emailer to check for e-mail at a certain time and date.

To set up a new schedule item, click Add and then use the simple, button-oriented interface to set up the time and date of the connection (see Figure 20-9). You can also tell Emailer to connect repeatedly (every four hours, every day, or every two days, for example) and you can set it to check for new mail, send mail, or both.

A note of caution: although Emailer performs these remote connections admirably most of the time, it occasionally hangs online for a long period of time. Be sure to test this feature on your ISP before letting the program go online without you there. You might encounter a surprise when you get next month's bill!

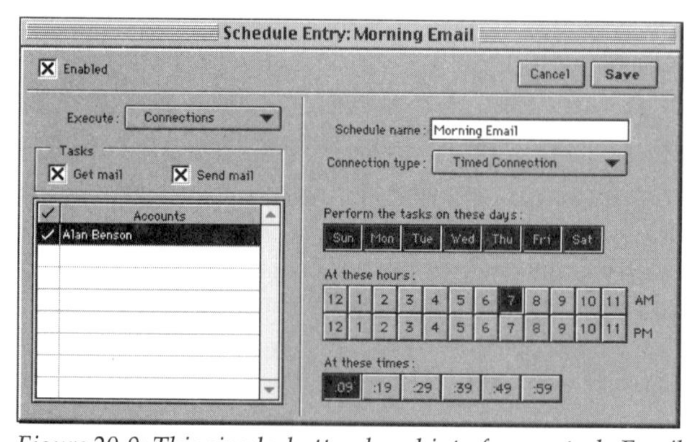

Figure 20-9: This simple, button-based interface controls Emailer's scheduling capabilities.

Claris maintains a home page for e-mailer that includes information about bug fixes, new versions, and answers to common questions at http://www.claris.com/support/products/ClarisEmailer/index.html.

Lite vs. Full

The version of Claris Emailer that comes with Mac OS 8 is not the same version that is sold separately. The full version has a number of added features that make it more powerful and flexible and easier to maintain. It's not necessary to buy the full version—Lite works just fine for most users—but it's worth checking out.

The most notable difference between the two programs is that the full version allows you to have up to five e-mail accounts, while Lite only allows one. Lite can't check mail on AOL, CompuServe, AppleLink, and Radio Mail; you need the full version for that.

The full version of Emailer has more robust mail management capabilities. It can sort and filter incoming messages into custom folders based on the name, subject, date, and other headers. It also supports multiple preferences files, which means that more than one copy of Emailer can run simultaneously on shared machines.

Emailer can also automatically respond to incoming mail. This is useful if you're on vacation or unable to check e-mail for several days; just set Emailer to send an autoresponse of "Sorry, I'm out of the office this week; expect a response sometime next week." You can also set Emailer to forward mail if you're away from your computer but have e-mail access at the other location.

The full version also supports drag-and-drop manipulation of text files in messages. Dragging a text file into the body of a message copies it into the message, allowing you to set up a templated answer for common questions. Instead of retyping or copying and pasting, just drag the whole file into the message and send.

More information about the full version of Emailer is available at http://www.claris.com/support/products/ClarisEmailer/index.html.

Netscape Navigator

If you've used the World Wide Web, odds are you've heard of Netscape Navigator. The program is the dominant browser on the Web, and its logo and name are everywhere. Navigator's influence is so strong that it has been able to drive the development of new Web features like frames, centered text, and background colors and pictures. And now, it's part of the basic install of Mac OS 8.

But what *is* Netscape Navigator, exactly? Well, the short answer is that it's a Web browser, an application people use to view World Wide Web pages. In fact, the comments field of the folder that holds the Navigator installed by Mac OS 8 says it's the "best Web browser for the Mac OS." Figure 20-10 shows an example of a Navigator browser window.

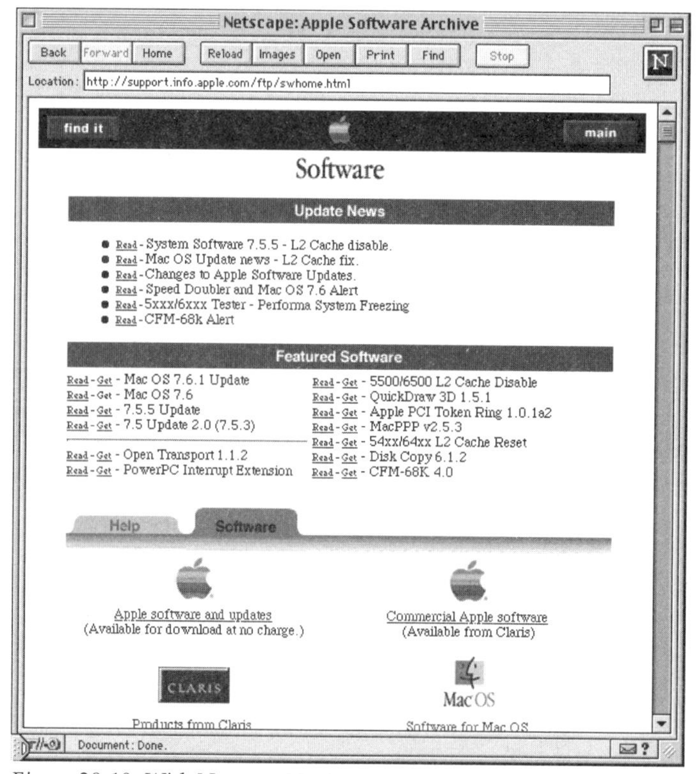

Figure 20-10: With Netscape Navigator, you can easily access both Web pages and FTP sites.

Navigator sports an easy-to-follow interface with well-labeled buttons and loads of help options. The company's home page also has a good number of online resources for both new surfers and Net veterans.

However, Navigator didn't become the single most popular online application simply because it was a good Web browser. The program's strengths lie in its ability to work with non-Web resources like File Transfer Protocol (FTP) and Gopher servers, e-mail, and newsgroups. Navigator can use third-party programs called plug-ins to enhance its multimedia capabilities, and it allows users to build large, organized lists of favorite sites—bookmarks.

Bookmarks

Now that setting up an account with an ISP has been reduced to clicking a button or two (see Chapter 18), the hardest thing about starting new service is building a useful list of bookmarks. Luckily, Apple has done newbies a favor and packed the default list with loads of sites ranging from official Apple sites to publications to software developers and resellers, as shown in Figure 20-11.

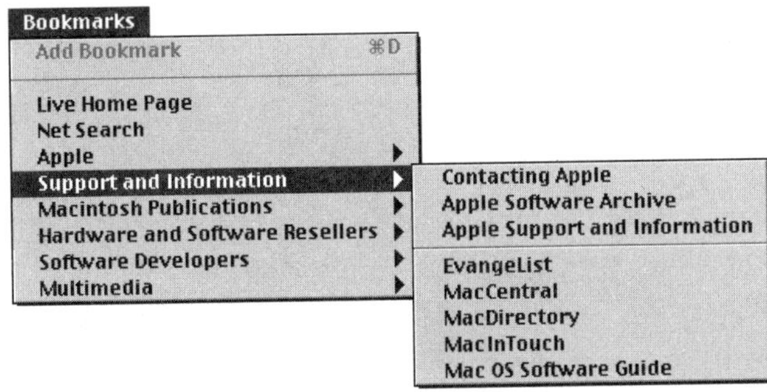

Figure 20-11: Netscape's default bookmarks are chock-full of helpful information sites, computer publications, and software developers.

Plug-Ins

Over the past 10 years, many programmers have moved away from writing huge, monolithic programs that can't be extensively modified. Instead, many popular programs ship with an open architecture that allows third-party developers to write small extensions that enhance the main program's operations.

In the online world, Netscape is the most evident example of this trend. Early versions of the browser relied upon a large number of helper applications that would automatically launch when you downloaded a file of a certain type. For example, if you clicked on a movie, the file would download, and then MoviePlayer or another program would launch and play the file. It was slow, and it made real-time sound and video impossible.

Recent versions of Navigator have taken care of this through plug-ins. With the right additions, the application can now show complex graphics, play movies and sounds in real time, and even display virtual reality environments. With Mac OS 8, you get the following plug-ins for Netscape Navigator, shown in Figure 20-12.

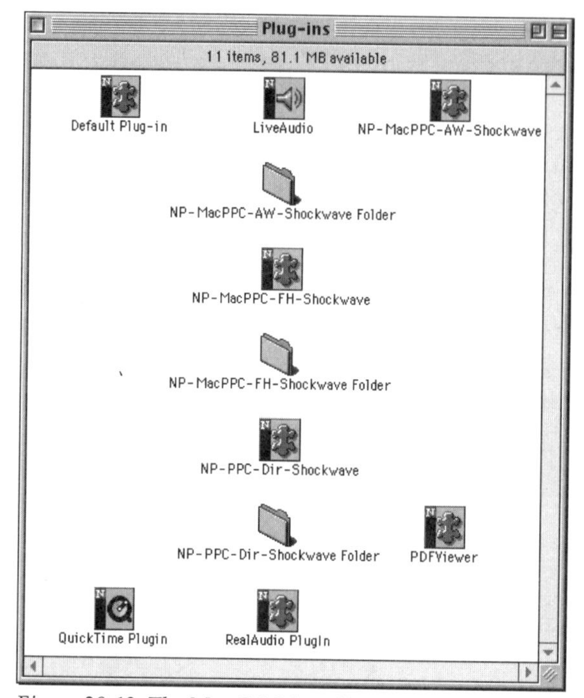

Figure 20-12: The Mac OS 8 installation includes four useful plug-ins for Netscape Navigator.

- **LiveAudio.** The LiveAudio plug-in turns Netscape into a sound-ready multimedia application. Using this plug-in, browsers can play a sound file without launching an external helper, and because you're using the Mac OS, you don't need a sound card or other multimedia hardware.
- **RealAudio.** RealAudio allows you to hear streaming audio—sound files that play while they are downloading. This has allowed sites to broadcast online in real time—a useful feature for radio stations and audio-based Web sites like AudioNet (http://www.audionet.com/).

Progressive Networks' RealAudio and RealVideo page is available at http://www.realaudio.com/.

- **Macromedia Shockwave.** This plug-in is vital for sites that feature games, online animation, interactive interfaces, and other multimedia bells and whistles. Shockwave allows developers to use programs like

Director, Flash, and Authorware to create small, streaming presentations for their Web sites. Since its introduction, the plug-in has become ubiquitous; the player is included with Netscape Navigator, Microsoft Internet Explorer, AOL, and with this release, the Mac OS 8.

More information about Shockwave and how to use it is available at http://www.macromedia.com/, Macromedia's About Shockwave site.

- **PDF Viewer.** PDF Viewer is a plug-in version of Adobe's popular Acrobat software. Acrobat creates Portable Document Format (PDF) files, which can be read on any machine with the Acrobat Reader program installed. This allows them to be transported to a wide variety of machines without worrying about compatibility problems.

  Since Acrobat allows you to include graphics, styled text, and complex information, many developers are moving toward Acrobat and away from SimpleText's limited text file for Read Me files and manuals. (We'll discuss Acrobat Reader in more detail later in this chapter.) PDF Viewer allows you to read these files online without having to download the whole file to your hard drive.

Adobe's home page, http://www.adobe.com/, has a guide to using Acrobat Reader and information about the commercial Adobe Acrobat PDF-creator.

- **QuickTime Plug-In 1.1 for Macintosh.** This plug-in allows you to view QuickTime movies and QuickTime VR documents directly in the browser window. With this plug-in—and the QuickTime Extension installed in your Extensions folder—Navigator can play video, audio, animation, and even virtual reality scenes directly in a Web page. Without the plug-in, you'd have to download the file to your hard drive and play it with MoviePlayer or other software.

More information and updated versions of the QuickTime system extension and the plug-in are available at the QuickTime home page (http://www.quicktime.apple.com).

- **Other Plug-Ins.** There are many more plug-ins out there, but they're best acquired on an as-needed basis. There's no reason to chew up your RAM loading 80 additional files if you only need 1 or 2. If you run into a page that requires a plug-in you don't have, Navigator asks you if you want to get it. It then takes you to Netscape's plug-in finder page, which helps match you up with an appropriate plug-in, as shown in Figure 20-13.

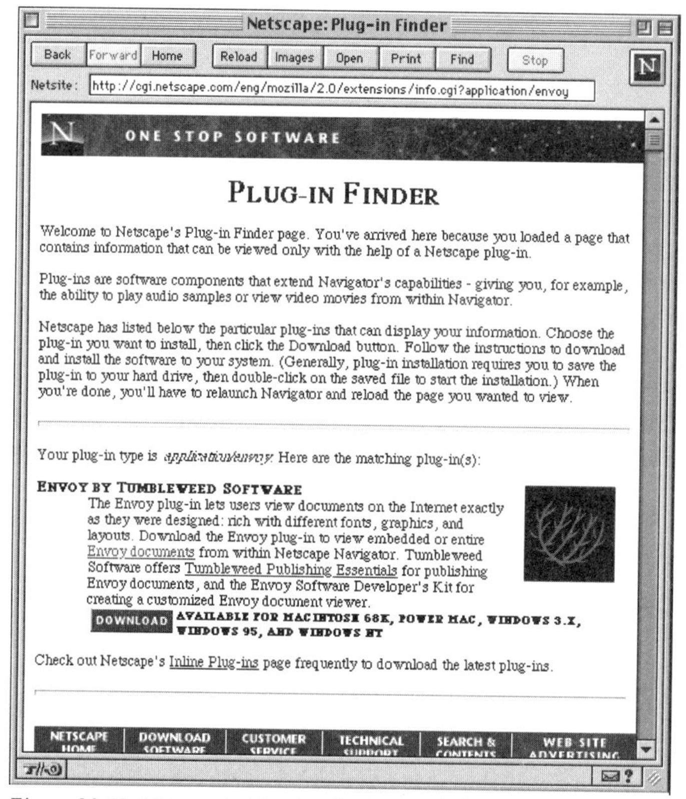

Figure 20-13: Netscape's Plug-In Finder page helps you download the appropriate plug-in for your needs.

Mail & News

Although the browser portion of Navigator is the main draw, the program also includes two other features: Netscape News and Netscape Mail. These two mini-applications allow people to use Navigator as their one and only Internet application.

Netscape News Some of the craziest, silliest, most controversial, and most useful information appears in newsgroups. Newsgroups are automatically updated bulletin boards where people around the world come to learn, debate, swap programs and information, or just chat. Their subjects range from the prosaic (alt.tv.seinfeld) to the profound (soc.religion.bahai), from the technical (comp.lang.fortran) to the tasteless (alt.barney.dinosaur.die.die.die).

Netscape News allows you to burrow through the newsgroups to find subjects that match your interest. Once you find some, you can subscribe by clicking in the column marked by a checkmark (the interface needs a bit of work). Clicking on the name of the newsgroup brings up a list of posts in that group, and clicking on the title of a post brings up a copy of the post (see Figure 20-14).

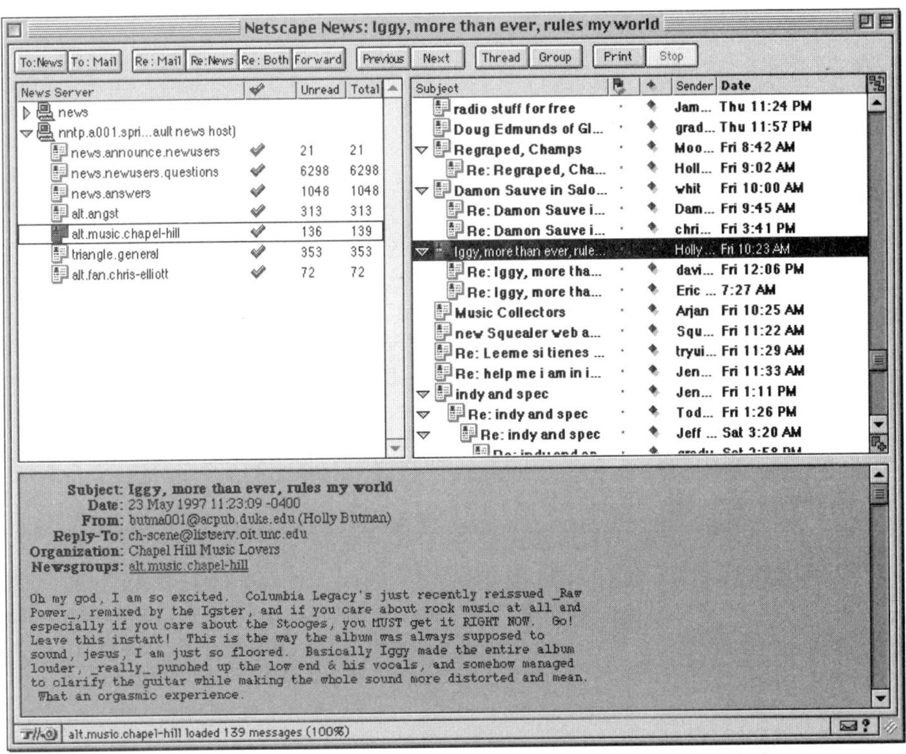

Figure 20-14: The three-part Netscape News window includes a list of subscribed newsgroups on the top left, a list of posts in the selected newsgroup on the top right, and the text of a selected post along the bottom.

On the down side, Netscape News's interface is a bit kludgy, and it's not as powerful as some of the other newsreaders available for Macs. Hardcore news groupies should probably stick to a stand-alone reader like InterNews, NewsWatcher, Nuntius, or Yet Another NewsWatcher.

Netscape Mail Netscape's e-mail program uses a three-part design that's similar to the newsreader. The inbox is at the top left, new messages are kept at the top right, and the text of the messages is displayed across the bottom.

To be honest, if you have Claris Emailer, there's no real reason to use Netscape Mail. Emailer is much more powerful, easier to understand and configure, and has filtering and addressing features not available in Netscape Mail.

Cyberdog

It's no secret that dear old Apple has been going through some tough times lately. The company has been trying to get focused, cut the fat, and concentrate on areas where it can succeed. Sadly, this means that some projects are getting the axe before they get their chance.

Cyberdog is one of these unlucky projects. Apple announced in April 1997 that it was no longer going to support OpenDoc, its proprietary component technology. The plan is to focus on Java-based software, since Java is fast becoming the industry standard. (For more information about OpenDoc, see Chapter 12.)

Cyberdog is based on OpenDoc, so it appears that its days are numbered. It's shipping with Mac OS 8, but the company is not planning any major updates. In fact, Cyberdog's parent company, CI Labs (a collaboration between Apple and IBM), has already shut its doors.

Too bad, because Cyberdog is a pretty nice little program. It uses OpenDoc's component technology to do some pretty wild things. For example, it's possible to embed e-mail mailboxes, FTP sites, AppleTalk zones, and even other Web pages in a Cyberdog page (see Figure 20-15). The browser simply displays the embedded object as a window in the main page.

Cyberdog also rethinks the bookmarks file. Its Notebook file can contain links not only to Web pages, but also to e-mail messages, newsgroups, Telnet sessions, and AppleTalk zones. To add more items, simply drag and drop their Me icon (the small page icon next to the page's title) into the Notebook. To add files to the Notebook, simply drag their Finder icon onto it. You can also import bookmarks from Netscape and e-mail addresses from Emailer or Eudora (another popular e-mail program).

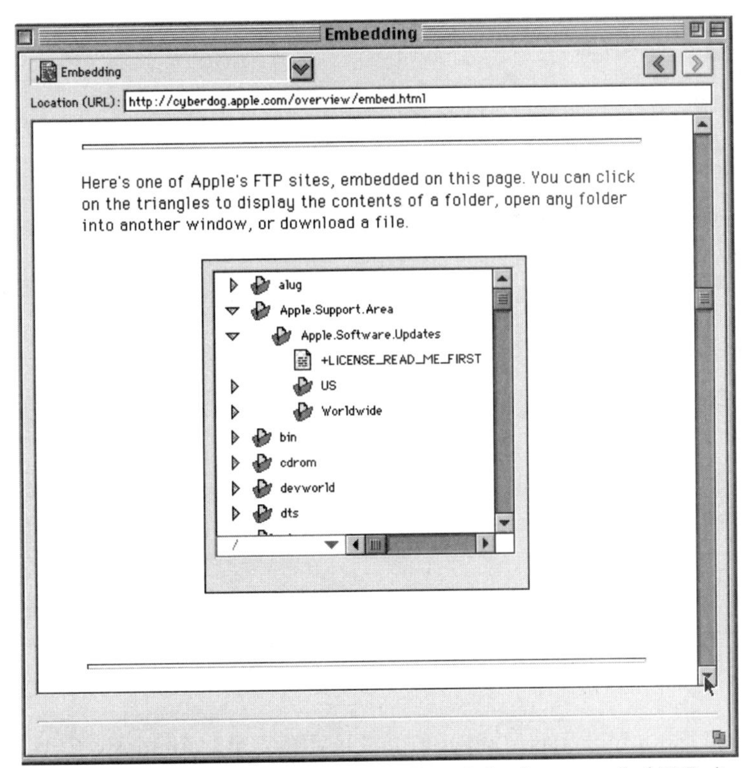

Figure 20-15: Because it's based on OpenDoc, Cyberdog can embed FTP sites, other Web pages, and even AppleTalk zones in its pages.

The program also features something called the Log, which is a history of the last 200 things you did with Cyberdog (see Figure 20-16). It tracks new entries in the Notebook and visits to FTP sites and even reads e-mail. The Log allows you to backtrack to interesting pages or recap your trip through the Net.

Because Cyberdog is based on OpenDoc, it can be enhanced by including other OpenDoc components. Cyberdog ships with DocBuilder, a component builder, so users can conceivably build custom applications with embedded live views of favorite pages or newsgroups.

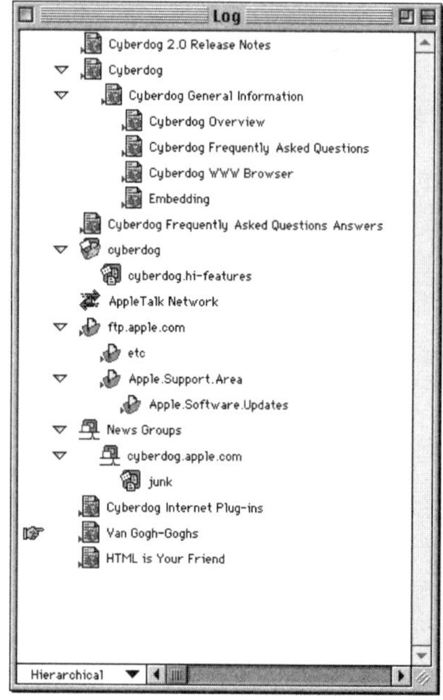

Figure 20-16: Cyberdog's Log tracks recent activities in Cyberdog.

Even though it's based on completely different technology, Cyberdog actually has a lot in common with Netscape Navigator. Like Navigator, Cyberdog is able to do more than just browse pages. It can handle FTP and Gopher transfers, newsgroups, and e-mail; it displays mail and news in a much more attractive way (see Figure 20-17); and it has more powerful sorting tools. Cyberdog also allows you to connect to Telnet sites, something Navigator uses a helper application to do.

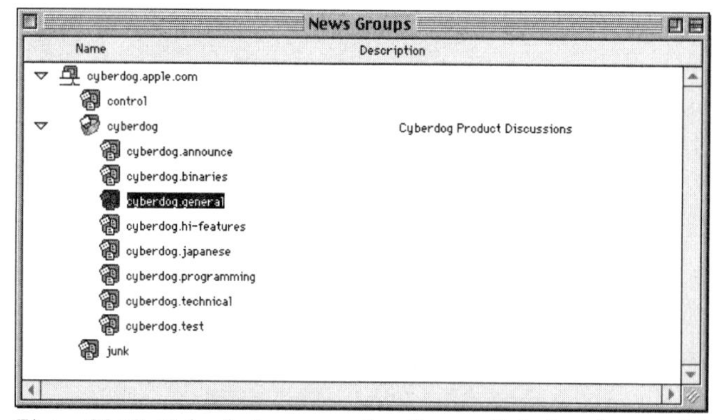

Figure 20-17: Cyberdog's news and mail are well designed, powerful, and nicely integrated with the rest of the program.

Cyberdog can use many Netscape Navigator plug-ins, and it can display QuickTime and QuickTime VR files as well as a wide variety of graphics and sound files. Heck, it even supports unofficial Netscape tags like <BLINK>, <CENTER>, and <FONT>.

Cyberdog is a powerful, flexible, and, at times, amazing application. It's got some kinks, but the real tragedy is that it will never get the chance to shine—too bad; with some tweaks, it could give Netscape a run for its money.

Adobe Acrobat Reader

Transferring files between two computers is the essence of the Internet; unfortunately, it can also be a real pain in the neck. This is especially true for documents created by word processing and page layout programs.

Because no two computers are the same, a file that looks great on one system may look like garbage—or may not even work—when transferred to another system. Even if a file is transferred between two identical computers with all the same fonts and programs, there's no guarantee the document will look the same when it gets to its destination.

As a result, people were forced to make a choice between compatibility and design. If they translated the file into a format like plain ASCII text, it would run on most machines. However, it probably wouldn't look much like the original. If they stuck with the original format, other users may not be able to view the file.

This was the situation until a couple of years ago, when Adobe introduced Acrobat. This cross-platform (Mac, UNIX, and Windows) program creates and reads Portable Document Format (PDF) files, which are platform- and application-independent files. Acrobat can also translate documents created in other programs—PageMaker, QuarkXPress, Microsoft Word—into PDF. The new files include all the fonts, graphics, and other visual items of the original files. This allows people to share complex documents without worrying about maintaining their original look and feel. Totally cool.

Of course, in order to use these files, the recipient computer needs to have the ability to read PDF documents. That's where Acrobat Reader comes in. Reader is a PDF viewer that is distributed freely on the Internet and by user groups. Now it's part of the basic Mac OS install.

Before we get into what Reader can do, let's outline what it is—and what it is not. Reader is not Acrobat. Acrobat is an application that can be used to make new PDF files; Reader is a PDF viewer that can only read existing files. On the bright side, Acrobat sells for about $300, while Reader is totally free.

So if you can't create new things with Reader, what good is it? Well, it's your only option when downloading a lot of user manuals nowadays—many of Apple's online manuals are now in PDF form, an example of which is shown in Figure 20-18.

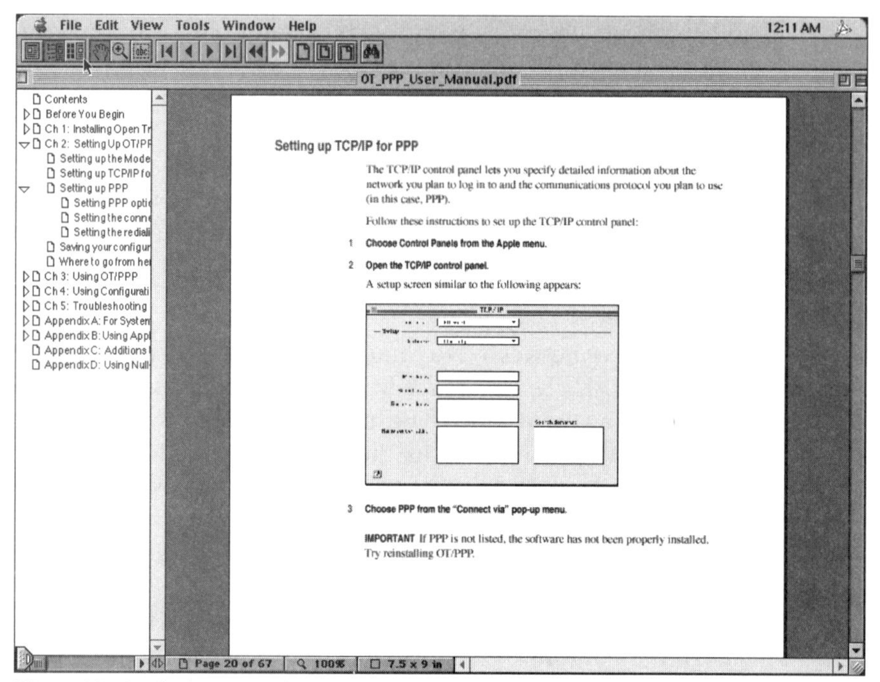

Figure 20-18: The basic Acrobat Reader window. Users can navigate around the document by using the scroll bars or the index on the left.

Besides, Reader is a lot more powerful than it first appears. Because PDF is so flexible, users have a great deal of control over how the document is displayed. Reader allows you to zoom in and out, find text, and display information as either a continuous scroll, one page at a time, or as facing pages.

Adobe has more information about Reader and the full version of Acrobat at its Web site, http://www.adobe.com/prodindex/acrobat/main.html.

DropStuff & StuffIt Expander

DropStuff and StuffIt Expander are really two sides of the same coin. In fact, they both grew out of StuffIt, Aladdin Systems's popular file compression and extraction program. These programs create and read compressed and encoded files and archives. StuffIt Expander can open a variety of compressed file formats, while DropStuff uses a drag-and-drop interface to create new archives.

There is a wide variety of file compression utilities out there, but StuffIt products are the dominant force on the Mac side. They're fast, they're generally bug-free, and StuffIt archives have become so common that almost every Mac user will eventually use one. But, before we jump into a discussion about StuffIt Expander and DropStuff, it's important to understand why files are compressed and encoded.

Why Compress or Encode Files?

There are two main reasons to compress files: time and money. Since compressed files and archives are smaller, they take less time to transmit between computers or through the Internet. They also take up less space on the hard drive, so some users compress rarely used files to make room for new files. Liberal use of DropStuff can help stave off the need for a new hard drive or a faster modem. Figure 20-19 shows the contents of a folder in uncompressed and compressed formats. Notice that when compressed, the folder (Stationary folder.sit) is no larger than on any of the five documents inside the uncompressed folder.

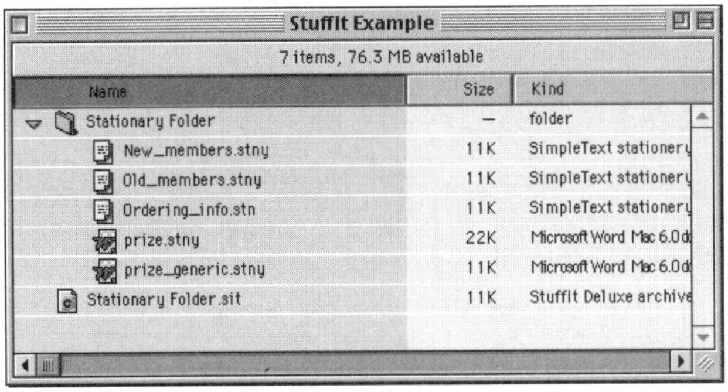

Figure 20-19: By compressing several files in a folder, you can save large amounts of disk space.

There are also two reasons to encode files: data security and cross-platform capability. When files encoded in BinHex or MacBinary (two of the most popular encoding schemes) are transmitted, they suffer fewer problems with lost data, compatibility, and so on. If you were to pass an unencoded file between Macintoshes via non-Mac-OS computers, chances are it will be corrupted. However, even if the only Macs in a chain of 50 computers are the first and last ones, an encoded file will usually go through unscathed.

StuffIt Expander

If you're like most people, you'll receive more information from the Internet than you'll send. Therefore, you'll probably spend quite a bit of time with StuffIt Expander running in the background. Luckily, this utility is extremely simple to use; it runs just fine with no tweaks.

With no changes, Expander can decompress StuffIt and Compact Pro archives (files ending in .sit, .sea, and .cpt) and decode Macbinary (.bin) and BinHex (.hqx) files. It can also handle the larger, multipart BinHex files commonly found in newsgroups (like comp.binaries.mac). You can set the program to delete archives after expanding, join split archives, move the new files to a specific folder, or convert text files to Mac format, as shown in Figure 20-20.

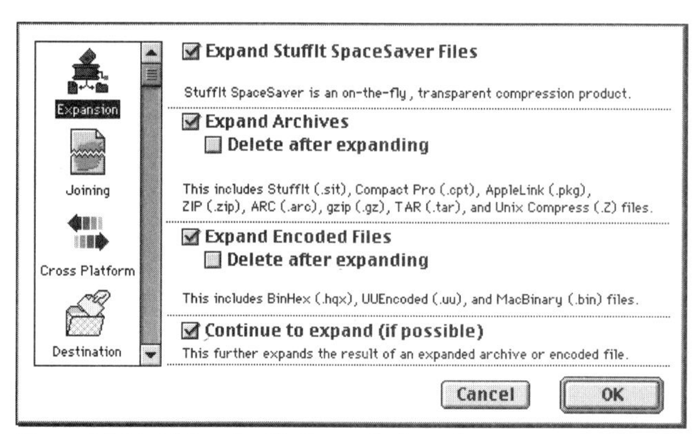

Figure 20-20: Using StuffIt Expander's preferences screen, you can determine how the program deals with compressed and encoded files.

StuffIt Expander can also "watch" a folder and expand any new files it finds (see Figure 20-21). The program periodically checks the contents of a user-specified folder for unexpanded archives or encoded files. If it finds a new archive, it expands it in the background. This is useful for dealing with multifile downloads from Internet sites; while new files are being downloaded, Expander can decompress others.

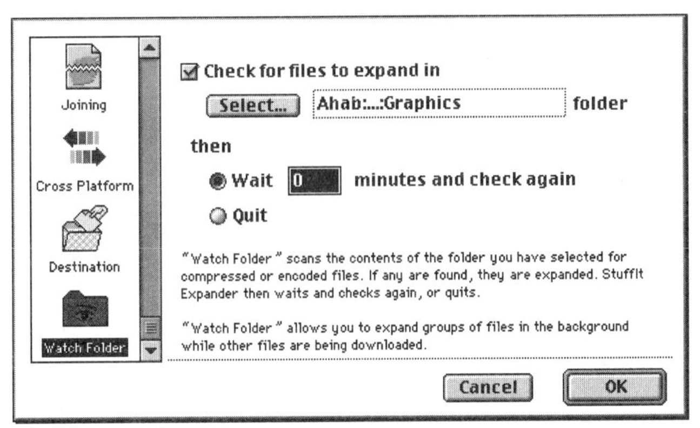

Figure 20-21: StuffIt Expander can "watch" certain specified folders for new archives and encoded files. It then expands the files in the background.

Expander Enhancer

The basic installation of StuffIt Expander works well with Mac-based compression schemes like Compact Pro, but it can't handle non-Macintosh files like PC Zip (.zip) or UNIX Tar archives (.tar).

To deal with those files, you need to install DropStuff, the sister program of Expander. The DropStuff w/EE 4.0 installer adds the Expander Enhancer to your system, which allows you to decompress files like ZIP and ARC archives from PCs, UNIX Tar archives, Z and GZIP compressed files from UNIX, AppleLink packages, and UU-encoded files. Needless to say, if you're receiving a lot of files from PC or UNIX users—or if you're downloading graphics from newsgroups—this enhancement is a welcome one.

DropStuff 4.0

There's a kind of "chicken-and-egg" conundrum at work in the world of StuffIt programs. Expander can open compressed files, but first they have to be stuffed by DropStuff. DropStuff adds to the confusion by including the StuffIt Engine, a.k.a. Expander Enhancer, an extension that adds flexibility to both programs.

Well, even if we don't know which one comes first, we can spend a bit of time getting to know DropStuff. This program was designed to allow people to create StuffIt archives quickly and efficiently through a drag-and-drop interface. To use it, simply drag folders and/or files onto the DropStuff icon. The program creates a new archive and compresses a copy of the files or folders. Simple as that. Figure 20-22 shows the compression options that are available to a user.

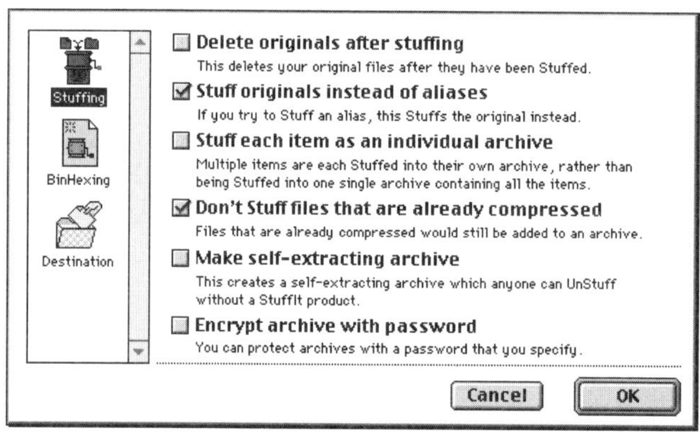

Figure 20-22: DropStuff can compress files, create password-protected and self-extracting archives, or encode files in BinHex.

DropStuff is pretty simple, so there's little reason to worry about settings. However, by using DropStuff's preferences screen, you can affect how the program deals with its archives. For example, if you are sending a file across the Internet, you can use DropStuff to first compress and then BinHex it. Or, if you are sending a file to someone who doesn't have StuffIt Expander, you can use DropStuff to create a self-extracting archive—an archive file that decompresses itself when double-clicked.

Other Useful Online Utilities

As we've seen, the Mac OS 8 makes it possible to go online and begin working mere minutes after installation. By including Netscape Navigator, Cyberdog, Claris Emailer, Adobe Acrobat, and the StuffIt utilities, the engineers at Apple ensured that even the most novice Internaut has the tools and applications needed to use the Net.

Of course, these are not the only Internet and Web applications available. There are thousands of Mac applications written to work on the Net. While many of them are simply alternates to these popular programs—there are literally hundreds of e-mail programs out there—many of them are useful additions. Best of all, most of them are shareware or freeware, so you won't break the bank while stocking up.

A Word (or Several) About Shareware

While the Macintosh platform hasn't traditionally had the same volume of commercial software as Wintel machines, Macs have a long and proud tradition of shareware—software uploaded to public sites and available on a use-before-you-buy basis. Generally, these programs are small, simple applications and utilities that enhance larger commercial products and add functionality to the Mac OS or are simply silly, fun activities.

The deal with shareware is simple: if, after using it for a while, you decide you can't live without it, then send payment to the author. Generally, most shareware is available for a nominal fee; some, called freeware, is available at no cost.

Shareware is a long-standing tradition on the Internet. Many of the most popular programs began life as shareware; some of the best still are. In fact, three of the programs we discussed earlier, Acrobat Reader, Internet Config, and DropStuff are shareware. StuffIt Expander is freeware.

Please remember, if you use shareware, you have to pay for it. These programs are available on the honor system; don't mess up a good thing by not paying.

Here are some other Internet programs to check out:

- **Fetch.** Fetch, an FTP program that was created at Dartmouth College, is a fast, easy-to-learn, and easily configurable FTP application. Many people prefer Fetch to Navigator because the browser occasionally crashes or freezes on some FTP sites.
- **Anarchie.** Anarchie is an Archie and FTP client that's popular with Mac users. Along with basic FTP transfers, Anarchie can do Archie searches. (Archie is a cataloging system designed to keep track of items on FTP servers. It's a great idea, but they're often out-of-date, so it's easier to go to a large FTP site and look for things there.)

These programs and many, many other shareware applications are available at most of the large FTP libraries, including the Info-Mac Archive (ftp://hyperarchive.lcs.mit.edu/) and the University of Michigan Mac archive (ftp://mac.archive.umich.edu/mac/).

- **NewsWatcher**. NewsWatcher is a good, solid newsreader that is better organized than Netscape News, and it allows you to perform complicated searches on newsgroups.
- **Disinfectant.** Disinfectant is an anti-virus program. If you're going to be wandering around the Net downloading files, you're running the risk of catching a computer virus. This free application can keep your hard drive virus free.

Conclusion

Apple invented the first commercial personal computer 20 years ago, and Mac OS 8 continues to improve on the basic principle of its first operating system: make it simple, make it powerful, and most importantly, make it fun! Mac OS 8 implements many improvements as well as several new features to help you harness the power of not only a personal computer, but the Internet and the World Wide Web.

I hope you find that Mac OS 8 meets your expectations.

PART IV

Appendices

APPENDIX A

About the Companion CD-ROM

The Companion CD-ROM included with your copy of The Mac OS 8 book contains valuable software, including e-mail, HTML authoring, text editing, sound editing, and image editing programs, as well as Netscape Navigator plug-ins and art.

To view the CD-ROM

Macintosh PPC Double-click on the "Launch Mac PPC" file.

Macintosh 68K Double-click on the "Launch Mac 68K" file.

You will see a small menu screen offering several button choices: ReadMe, Launch Installer, and Exit. The buttons allow you to view the CD-ROM's ReadMe file, install a program, or exit the viewer, respectively.

Software

Abstract & Graphic Backgrounds, Vol 1.

One hundred license- and royalty-free TIFF photo images by top professional photographer, Paul Smith. Visit http://www.aztech.com for more information.

Andromeda Series 4 Techtures

A demo version of the Andromeda Series 4 Techtures, offering 900 hand-rendered, realistic techtures, maps, and environments to explore and modify. To find out more about Andromeda Software's products, visit http://www.andromeda.com.

A Smaller GIF

A Smaller GIF compresses animated GIFs, saving memory and making downloading easier without affecting image quality. A Smaller GIF provides full viewer functions—play, forward, backward, fast view F/B, pause, random access, and more. Visit http://www.peda.com for more information.

BBEdit Demo

This is the demo version of the high performance text editor for the Macintosh. BBEdit is optimized for the editing, searching, transformation, and manipulation of text. It provides an array of general-purpose features which are useful for many tasks, and includes many features which have been specifically developed in response to the needs of software developers and HTML authors. For more info about the full version of BBEdit, visit http://www.barebones.com/bbedit.html.

clip2gif

clip2gif is a freeware utility for the Macintosh to convert PICT, GIF, TIFF, and JPEG images to any of these formats, written by Yves Piguet. clip2gif's main features include: display of PICT, GIF, TIFF, and JPEG files; GIF output (transparency, interlacing, depth of 1, 2, 4 or 8 bits/pixels, gray shades output); TIFF output (bilevel, grayscale, palette-color or RGB/Packbits compression when useful); and more. For more information, visit http://iawww.epfl.ch/Staff/Yves.Piguet/clip2gif-home/ on the World Wide Web.

Color It!

Color It! is an award-winning, fully featured 32-bit photographic image editing program with sophisticated paint tools. It's easy to learn and easy to use. Work with exisiting images and photographs, scan in new ones, or create original works of art from scratch. Easily manipulate and blend images in ways limited only by your imagination!

Crescendo

Crescendo is a Midi plug-in for Netscape 2.0 browsers which lets users listen to Midi files embedded in Web pages. Web site developers can now add background music to their Web pages. You need Apple Quicktime 2.1 or greater to use this plug-in.

DeBabelizer Toolboox Demo

DeBabelizer Toolbox is an essential tool for anyone working with computer graphics. This award-winning product combines graphics processing, palette optimization, and translation in one program. With easy "Watch Me" scripting and batch features, thousands of images can be processed automatically to specifications. A true production powerhouse, DeBabelizer Toolbox translates between 70+ bit-mapped graphics, animation, and digital video formats, including DOS/Windows, Amiga, Sun, XWindows, Alias, Electric Image, SoftImage formats, and more. DeBabelizer Toolbox supports Photoshop and third-party Acquire, Filter, and Export plug-ins, as well as AppleScript. It includes dozens of image-editing and palette-manipulation tools, including SuperPalette which automatically creates the best palette for a series of images. DeBabelizer Toolbox complements all paint, scan, and image processing programs. Visit http://www.equilibrium.com.

Deniart Sampler

Sample characters from Deniart Systems' Symbol Font Library, including: Egyptian Hieroglyphics, Alchemy Symbols, Mayan Glyphs, American Sign, and Castles & Shields. Check out http://www.deniart.com to find out more about Deniart Systems' products.

Envoy

Envoy is a plug-in for Netscape Navigator 2.0 or 3.0 that enables viewing of envoy documents. Envoy is a rich document format that preserves any document's page layout, fonts, and graphics in a compact format ideal for Web publishing. For more information or Tech Support FAQs, visit http://www.twcorp.com/help/h_help.htm.

Eudora Lite

With nearly three million users, Eudora is the most popular and proven electronic mail software on the Internet. Eudora's easy-to-use features save you time in composing, organizing, and replying to your electronic mail. Visit http://www.eudora.com.

Floral Tapestry

Aztech New Media's Floral Tapestry collection features 100 high-quality license- and royalty-free TIFF photo images of exotic wild flowers. Each image is annotated with a brief description. Visit http://www.aztech for more information.

Fractal Design Detailer Demo

Fractal Design Detailer is an amazing graphics program that lets you paint directly onto the surface of 3D models. It's the closest thing to actually holding an object in your hand and painting it! If you're a 3D artist, Detailer is a one-stop shop for creating texture, bump, and other surface maps for your 3D models. You'll enjoy substantial time savings, increased accuracy, greater control, and real-time results. If you're a 2D artist, Detailer provides the enormous flexibility of 3D with the compositional simplicity of 2D. With Detailer, you can easily create rendered 3D objects which become elements of your image-editing designs. The Detailer demo is a save-disabled version of this award-winning application for Mac OS. It will show you all the capabilities but without the ability to save, print, export, or copy objects to another application.

Fractal Design Expression Demo

Fractal Design Expression combines the stylistic expressiveness of traditional artist's tools with the flexibility, speed, editability, and resolution independence of a vector-based drawing application. If you're a graphic designer or illustrator, Fractal Design Expression will change the way you think about vector-based illustration and the way you work as a computer artist. Expression's power and agility come from its exclusive Skeletal Strokes technology. For the first time ever, artists can use a single vector path to draw sophisticated, multi-element strokes or even complete illustrations. Simply select a drawing tool and a stroke style, and begin drawing.

Fractal Design Painter Demo

With more than 150 unique brushes, Painter's rich set of painting tools and special effects empowers your creativity. Painter 4 mixes raster and vector artwork, offers exciting Web features, and supports collaborative painting across a network. Painter's astounding Natural-Media® features simulate the tools and textures of traditional artists' materials. From crayons to calligraphy, oils to airbrushes, pencils to watercolor, Painter turns your computer into an artist's studio. Whether you are an experienced Painter user or you've never seen its extensive capabilities, you'll see how easily version 4 can transform the way you create!

Gif•glf•giF

Gif·glf·giF is a simple program for producing GIF animations. Use Gif·glf·giF to produce animated software demonstrations that can be placed on the Web. The animations are viewable with a Web browser without add-ons, plug-ins, or helper applications. Visit http://www.peda.com for more information about Gif·glf·giF.

GoMac

A program bar and start menu for the Mac OS. GoMac has a keyboard switcher for convenient program switching and a perpetual calendar available instantly within any program. For more info, visit http://www.proteron.com/gomac on the World Wide Web.

HVS ColorGIF

HVS ColorGIF is a successor to award-winning HVS Color. Now available as filters, HVS allows Web developers to maintain 24-bit image quality at 8 bits or less (256 colors) and download up to 70 percent faster. Visit http://www.digfrontiers.com for more information.

Itsagif

Itsagif makes colorful GIFs that are not limited to 256 colors. Visit http://www.peda.com for more information.

Kai's Power Tools Demo

A demonstration version of MetaTools, Inc.'s Kai's Power Tools 3.0. KPT 3.0 is available as a 32-bit native application extension for the Intel-based Windows 95/NT platforms, as well as for the Apple Macintosh/Power Macintosh platforms. Kai's Power Tools 3.0 is a unique and powerful collection of extensions that expand the power of image-editing applications which support the Adobe plug-in specifications. Visit http://www.metatools.com.

Mailto Converter

Mailto Converter makes it possible to use forms on your Web pages without any access to a CGI-script. It can read a single file, a folder of files, the clipboard, or Netscape and Eudora mailboxes. Files can be dropped onto the application to convert text and save it into files or in the clipboard. With only one click, or just a drag-and-drop action, all your form results can be saved into a single file, ready to import into your favorite database. Mailto Converter supports both the standard BinHex conversion method and ISO Latin-1, used in Western Europe. One of the first programs of its kind for the Mac! Visit http://www.calles.pp.se/nisseb to learn more about this and other Nisseb products.

Mapper

Mapper is the easiest way to create image maps for the World Wide Web in CERN, NCSA, and Client Side formats. It combines an easy-to-use WYSIWYG interface with powerful tools which will be useful even for the most experienced user. Just open the image, place the objects, and save! Mapper can open and save in all formats. Requires: System 6.0.7, QuickTime to open GIF and JPEG files. Visit http://www.calles.pp.se/nisseb.

MetaPhotos

MetaPhotos is a breathtaking collection of high-resolution, royalty-free drum scanned images that make standard stock photography obsolete. This demo version of MetaPhotos comes with 240 art-directed photo poses of 20 different characters and props. To ensure consistent quality, all files have been thoroughly cleaned and color-corrected by the same digital imaging experts. Go to http://www.metatools.com.

PageSpinner

PageSpinner is an HTML Editor for Mac OS. It supports HTML 2.0, HTML 3.2, plus additional Netscape extensions and is useful for both the beginner and the more advanced Web author.

Question Mark

Question Mark is an authoring tool that helps you create quizzes, tests, and surveys to be delivered via the Web. Visit http://www.questionmark.com for more information about this product.

RTFtoHTML

RTFtoHTML is designed to translate existing RTF documents into HTML, the format of the World Wide Web. By converting RTF documents to HTML, RTFtoHTML allows you to publish Microsoft Word, Word Perfect, FrameMaker, Claris Works, and other word processing documents on the WWW. RTFtoHTML can also be used to author new documents specifically for the WWW. To find out more about this product, check out http://www.sunpack.com/RTF.

Sizzler

Sizzler plug-in is a stream-based multimedia softare plug-in for Netscape Navigator that allows Web users to play live, real-time interactive animation and multimedia. Sizzler Converter allows creative Web page designers to convert files to the sizzler format in order to incorporate animation and multimedia to their Web site.

SoundApp

SoundApp will play or convert sound files dropped onto it. Using QuickTime 1.6 or later, SoundApp can also convert audio CD tracks. It requires at least System 7.0, Apple's Sound Manager 3.1 or greater, the Drag Manager (aka Macintosh Drag and Drop), and at least a Macintosh with a 68020 processor or a Power Macintosh.

SoundEffects

SoundEffects is a powerful sound editor for the Mac. Its strength resides in the capability of applying many digital effects to recorded sound, and since the effects are plug-in modules, you can enhance the program at any time by just adding any new modules as they become available. For more information, visit http://members.aol.com/sndeffects/index.html.

SoundMaker

This demonstration version of SoundMaker is save-disabled, but otherwise fully functional. SoundMaker gives you all of the tools you need to create and modify digital sound. You can import sounds at any sampling rate from clip sound disks or audio CDs, or record straight from your Mac's microphone. SoundMaker then lets you modify sounds any way you desire and provides you with multiple tracks so you can work on individual pieces. For more information go to http://www.allegiant.com/soundmaker/prod_desc.html on the World Wide Web.

Talker

Talker is a Netscape plug-in that lets Web pages talk and sing to Macintosh users, using Apple computer's text-to-speech software. (Users can download all the software they need, including Apple's text-to-speech software, from MVP Solutions' Talker Page at http://www.mvpsolutions.com/PlugInSite/Talker.html). This talker page has many links to other sites that tell stories, sing, and speak in other interesting ways to Web surfers who have the Talker plug-in installed on a Macintosh computer.

VivoActive Player

VivoActive software enables production and viewing of streaming video and audio from Web sites over low-bandwidth connections, using existing Web infrastructure (HTTP, TCP/IP). No special server hardware or software or modifications to firewalls is required.

Watermarks & Ghosted Backgrounds Volume 1

The first in Aztech's ArtEffects series of TIFF image collections designed by David Hushion and specifically created for graphic designers. Contains 25 easy-to-use, high-quality, and print-ready image files. These are low resolution versions of the images. High resolution versions are available from Aztech New Media as well. Visit http://www.aztech.com to learn more about Aztech New Media's products.

Wusage

Wusage is a statistics system that helps you determine the true impact of your Web server. By measuring the popularity of your documents, as well as identifying the sites that access your server most often, Wusage provides valuable marketing information. Practically all organizations, whether commercial or educational or nonprofit, need solid numbers to make credible claims about the World Wide Web. Wusage fills that need. Visit http://www.boutell.com/.

Technical Support

Technical support is available for installation-related problems only. The technical support office is open from 8:00 A.M. to 6:00 P.M. Monday through Friday and can be reached via the following methods:

Phone: (919) 544-9404 extension 81

Faxback Answer System: (919) 544-9404 extension 85

E-mail: help@vmedia.com

FAX: (919) 544-9472

World Wide Web: **http://www.vmedia.com/support**

America Online: keyword *Ventana*

Limits of Liability & Disclaimer of Warranty

The authors and publisher of this book have used their best efforts in preparing the CD-ROM and the programs contained in it. These efforts include the development, research, and testing of the theories and programs to determine their effectiveness. The authors and publisher make no warranty of any kind expressed or implied, with regard to these programs or the documentation contained in this book.

The authors and publisher shall not be liable in the event of incidental or consequential damages in connection with, or arising out of, the furnishing, performance, or use of the programs, associated instructions, and/or claims of productivity gains.

Some of the software on this CD-ROM is shareware; there may be additional charges (owed to the software authors/makers) incurred for their registration and continued use. See individual program's README or VREADME.TXT files for more information.

APPENDIX B

Installing or Updating Mac OS 8

If you've recently purchased a new Mac or Mac clone, Mac OS 8 might already be installed. However, if you purchased your computer in the spring or early summer of 1997, it probably came with Mac OS 7.6 or 7.6.1. If this is the case, you might be entitled to a free upgrade to Mac OS 8. Check the Mac OS home page at http://macos.apple.com for more information. Finally, you might have a much older Mac for which you recently purchased Mac OS 8. In all these cases, this appendix is for you because it will cover the steps involved in the following:

- Performing a new installation of Mac OS 8
- Reinstalling Mac OS 8
- Installing selected parts of Mac OS 8

If you've never installed system software or components before, don't worry. After all, it's the Mac OS we're talking about here—it can't be too difficult!

Performing a New Installation of Mac OS 8

The mechanics of installing the Mac OS, whether it's a new installation, a reinstallation, or a selected installation, are all pretty much the same. The big difference is in performing a new installation; you'll need to be careful what you do with your existing system software so you don't accidentally lose anything important. I'll get to that in a minute, but first let's look at the steps involved in installing the software.

The first step to installing the Mac OS successfully is to reboot your Mac and quit any applications that might have been automatically launched on start-up. Most software installation programs, including the Mac OS installer, require that you quit all applications prior to the installation process because the files being installed could become corrupt if another program interferes with them during the installation process.

The next step is to insert the CD-ROM or disks containing the Mac OS 8 installation program to launch the installer. Figure B-1, for example, shows the folder containing all the files necessary to perform an installation, including the installation program and the Mac OS 8 installation document. It doesn't matter which one you launch, however.

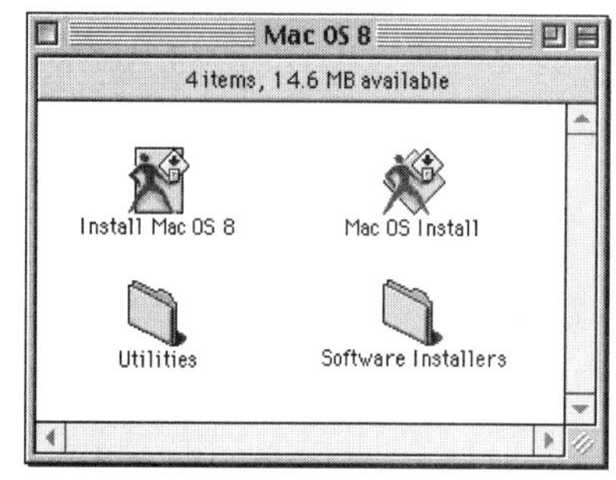

Figure B-1: A typical Mac OS 8 installation folder.

Once the installer has been launched, you will need to perform four main tasks:

1. Choose a disk onto which the OS is to be installed.
2. Read the Important Information document that details known problems and incompatible hardware. This is a very important step.
3. Complete the software license agreement.
4. Choose the software to be installed.

Once you have completed these four main tasks, the installation program will check your hard disk to ensure that it is capable of supporting the installation of the software.

Step 1: Select a Destination Disk

The first step is to select a destination disk, and if you have multiple disks from which to choose, the installation program will automatically evaluate each one to determine if there is room enough for an installation of Mac OS 8. Figure B-2, for example, shows how a drive other than the boot drive has been selected.

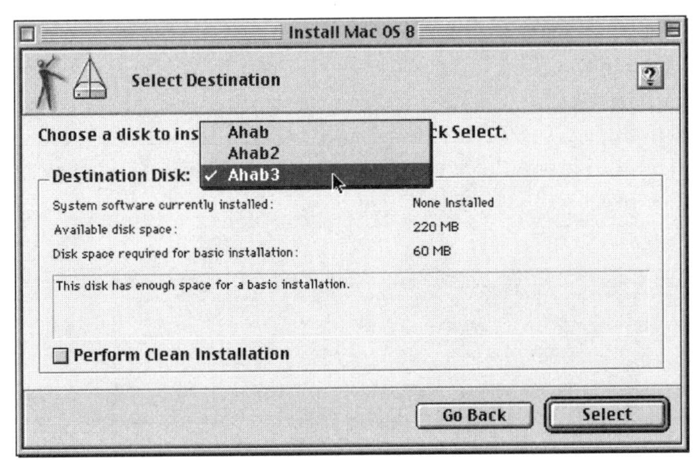

Figure B-2: Select a destination disk for Mac OS 8.

Check the box entitled Perform Clean Installation if you want to create a new System folder into which Mac OS 8 is to be installed. If you've run into problems installing Mac OS 8 before, you should check this box.

Step 2: Read the Installation Notes

Without a doubt, you should read every word of the installation notes to ensure that your hardware fully supports Mac OS 8. There are known problems with every version of the Mac OS in relation to certain hardware platforms, so you should find this out now rather than later when your system has deleted the report that is due at the end of the day!

Step 3: Complete the Software License Agreement

You will not be permitted to install Mac OS 8 unless you agree to the terms of the license agreement. After all, you technically don't own the software; Apple is selling you a license (subject to terms, conditions, and caveats) to use a copy of it on your machine.

Step 4: Choose the Software to Install

The final step is to select what software to install. You can choose from a basic installation of Mac OS 8 and certain applications and utilities, or you can perform a customized installation that includes all the software or just a single program. Figure B-3 shows a custom installation of Mac OS 8 and three components.

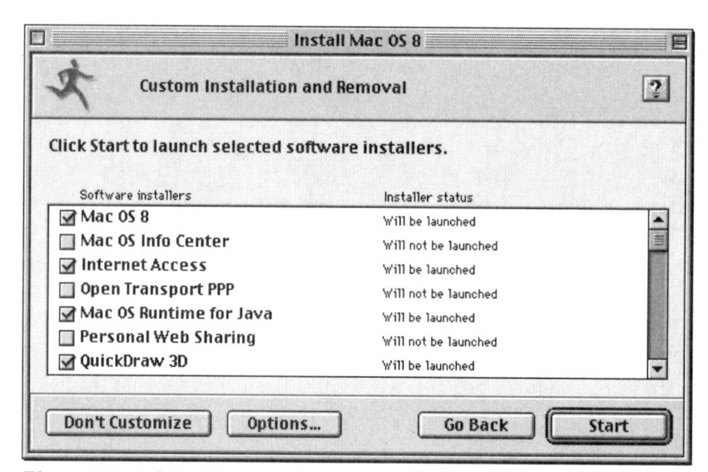

Figure B-3: Select either a basic or customized installation of Mac OS 8.

At any time between steps 1 through 4, you can click the Help icon for context-sensitive help. A window that addresses the issues presented in the current installation screen will be displayed, explaining what each option is and the consequences of each possible selection. Figure B-4 shows what a Help window looks like for the custom installation.

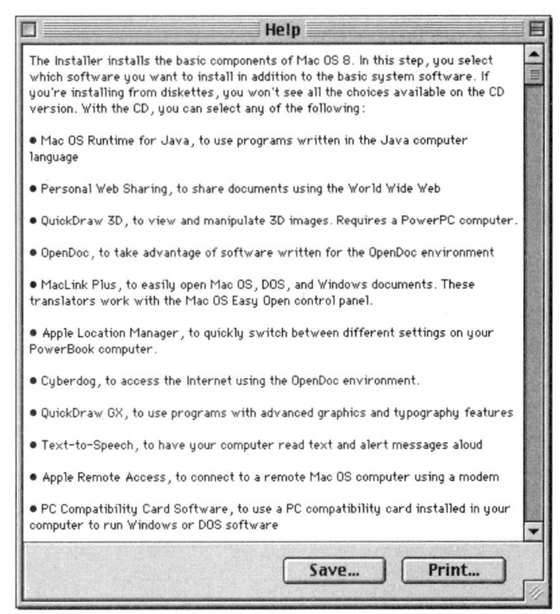

Figure B-4: Take advantage of the Help information for the Mac OS 8 installation process to better understand what you are about to install.

Once you're done selecting the software to be installed, select the Start button to begin the process, which could take just a few minutes up to almost an hour, depending on the software being installed and the speed of your computer.

Reinstalling Mac OS 8

If for some reason you need to reinstall Mac OS 8, go back to steps 1 through 3 paying careful attention to step 1, in which you were asked whether or not you wanted to perform a clean installation. If your system is behaving strangely for any reason and if you have enough disk space available, consider performing a clean installation. If you're convinced you don't have enough disk space, proceed to step 4 and install the software that you think is needed.

Installing Selected Parts of Mac OS 8

You may find that you need to install or reinstall selected parts of Mac OS 8. To do so, follow the steps for installing Mac OS 8 but select only what you want to install. You do not have to install or reinstall the Mac OS just to install a single component, such as Mac OS Runtime for Java, for instance. Just select it, or any other item, from the Install Software screen, as in Figure B-5.

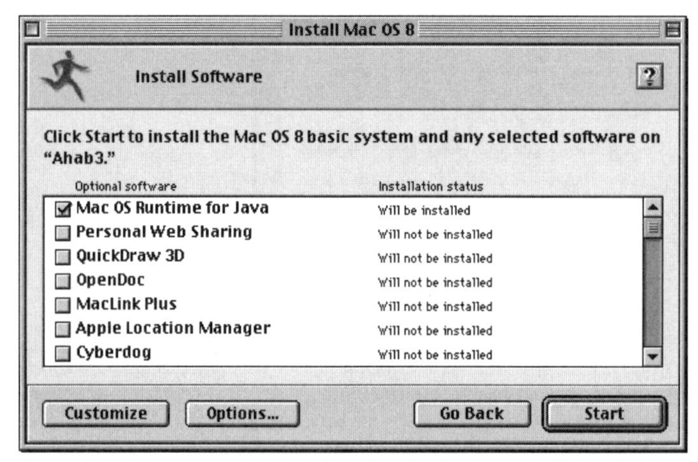

Figure B-5: You may opt to install just a single element of Mac OS 8.

Index

A

B

C

D

E

F

G

H

I

J

K

L

M

Q

R

S

T

U

VENTANA

Macromedia Director 5 Power Toolkit

$49.95, 552 pages, illustrated, part #: 1-56604-289-5

Macromedia Director 5 Power Toolkit views the industry's hottest multimedia authoring environment from the inside out. Features tools, tips and professional tricks for producing power-packed projects for CD-ROM and Internet distribution. Dozens of exercises detail the principles behind successful multimedia presentations and the steps to achieve professional results. The companion CD-ROM includes utilities, sample presentations, animations, scripts and files.

The Comprehensive Guide to Lingo

$49.99, 700 pages, illustrated, part #: 1-56604-463-4

Master the Lingo of Macromedia Director's scripting language for adding interactivity to presentations. Covers beginning scripts to advanced techniques, including creating movies for the Web and problem solving. The companion CD-ROM features demo movies of all scripts in the book, plus numerous examples, a searchable database of problems and solutions, and much more!

Shockwave!

$49.95, 400 pages, illustrated, part #: 1-56604-441-3

Breathe new life into your web pages with Macromedia Shockwave. Ventana's *Shockwave!* teaches you how to enliven and animate your Web sites with online movies. Beginning with step-by-step exercises and examples, and ending with in-depth excursions into the use of Shockwave Lingo extensions, Shockwave! is a must-buy for both novices and experienced Director developers. Plus, tap into current Macromedia resources on the Internet with Ventana's Online Companion. The companion CD-ROM includes the Shockwave plug-in, sample Director movies and tutorials, and much more!

The Director 6 Book

$49.99, 560 pages, part #: 1-56604-658-0

Macintosh, Windows 95/NT
Intermediate to Advanced

Raise your standards—and your stock—as a multimedia specialist by harnessing what's new in Macromedia Director 6. This professional-level guide focuses on key techniques for creating, manipulating and optimizing files. Your projects will look, sound and play back better and more consistently than ever.
Provides:

- Undocumented tricks for Director 6.
- Tips for moving from Director 5 to 6.
- Issues and answers for cross-platform presentations.
- Techniques for integrating Director 6 with JavaScript, CGI and Shockwave audio.

The CD-ROM includes more than 50 sample Director movies with code included, plus Macromedia and gmatter Xtras, shareware and more.

The Lingo Programmer's Reference

$39.99, 500 pages, part #: 1-56604-695-5

Windows 95/NT, Macintosh
Intermediate to Advanced

The Ultimate Resource for Director Professionals!
High-level mastery of Lingo is the only route to real Director expertise. This comprehensive reference goes beyond tutorials and simple listings to provide thorough explanations of every aspect of Lingo, supported by practical examples, professional tips and undocumented tricks. Includes:

- What's new in Director 6, property lists for sprites and other objects, and a JavaScript reference for Lingo programmers.
- In-depth discussions, including types of parameters to pass to properties, commands, functions and type of data returned.
- Encyclopedic listing, extensively cross-referenced for easy access to information.

The CD-ROM features a searchable, hyperlinked version of the book.